MAGILL'S
LITERARY ANNUAL
2018

*Essay-Reviews of 150 Outstanding Books
Published in the United States During 2017*

With an Annotated List of Titles

Volume II
L-Z

Edited by
Jennifer Sawtelle

SALEM PRESS
A Division of EBSCO Information Services, Inc.
Ipswich, Massachusetts

GREY HOUSE PUBLISHING

Cover photo: Việt Thanh Nguyễn, photo by David Levenson/Getty Images

Magill's Literary Annual, 2018, published by Grey House Publishing, Inc., Amenia, NY, under exclusive license from EBSCO Information Services, Inc.

∞ The paper used in these volumes conforms to the American National Standard for Permanence of Paper for Printed Library Materials, Z39.48-1992 (R2009).

Publisher's Cataloging-In-Publication Data
(Prepared by The Donohue Group, Inc.)
Names: Magill, Frank N. (Frank Northen), 1907-1997, editor. | Wilson, John D., editor. | Kellman, Steven G., 1947- editor. | Goodhue, Emily, editor. | Poranski, Colin D., editor. | Akre, Matthew, editor. | Spires, Kendal, editor. | Toth, Gabriela, editor. | Sawtelle, Jennifer, editor.
Title: Magill's literary annual.
Description: <1977->: [Pasadena, Calif.] : Salem Press | <2015->: Ipswich, Massachusetts : Salem Press, a division of EBSCO Information Services, Inc. ; Amenia, NY : Grey House Publishing | Essay-reviews of ... outstanding books published in the United States during the previous year. | "With an annotated list of titles." | Editor: 1977- , F.N. Magill; <2010-2014>, John D. Wilson and Steven G. Kellman; <2015>, Emily Goodhue and Colin D. Poranski; <2016>, Matthew Akre, Kendal Spires, and Gabriela Toth; <2017->, Jennifer Sawtelle. | Includes bibliographical references and index.
Identifiers: ISBN 9781682176801 (2018 edition : set) | ISBN 9781682176825 (2018 edition : vol. 1) | ISBN 9781682176832 (2018 edition : vol. 2) | ISSN: 0163-3058
Subjects: LCSH: Books--Reviews--Periodicals. | United States--Imprints--Book reviews--Periodicals. | Literature, Modern--21st century--History and criticism--Periodicals. | Literature, Modern--20th century--History and criticism--Periodicals.
Classification: LCC PN44 .M333 | DDC 028.1--dc23

FIRST PRINTING
PRINTED IN THE UNITED STATES OF AMERICA

CONTENTS

CONTENTS

COMPLETE ANNOTATED LIST OF CONTENTS

VOLUME I

Paul Auster's first novel in seven years, 4 3 2 1, is a sprawling family saga focusing on the capricious nature of fate, as illustrated through the trials endured by four alternative, parallel versions of the life of a youthful protagonist.

This is a collection of sixteen stories, previously published in literary magazines, focusing on young women living in an uneasy limbo of loveless relationships while yearning for order and normality.

Omar El Akkad's debut novel, American War, *imagines a future in which the United States is embroiled in a bloody civil war over the use of fossil fuels.*

An American Sickness, the first book by Dr. Elisabeth Rosenthal, examines the shortcomings of the modern American health-care system and provides readers a guide for navigating those shortcomings.

An Extraordinary Union is a historical romance set during the American Civil War. Protagonist Ellen Burns is a Union spy with a perfect memory. She poses as a slave in Virginia to acquire sensitive military information, but a romance with a white man threatens to upend her mission.

Ali Soufan offers an overview of Islamic terrorism, focusing on how the death of Osama bin Laden led to the splintering of his al-Qaeda organization and the rise of newer groups such as the Islamic State of Iraq and Syria (ISIS). While the book suggests this cycle of terrorism will continue, it provides valuable insight into the people and processes involved.

In Anything Is Possible, *author Elizabeth Strout loosely links nine short stories with connections to Lucy Barton, the character in her previous novel, My Name Is Lucy Barton. People in Lucy's hometown of Amgash, Illinois, read and reflect on Lucy's memoir while dealing with the everyday pain, loss, and love in their own lives.*

cocaine and opioids. Ohler's groundbreaking book sheds new light on the depravity of the Third Reich.

    The Blood of Emmett Till provides an account of the murder of Emmett Till, a black fourteen-year-old who was killed near Money, Mississippi, after he allegedly insulted a white woman. Timothy B. Tyson examines the case itself but also its immediate background and its ongoing legacy.

    Part memoir, part history, Charles Campisi's Blue on Blue: An Insider's Story of Good Cops Catching Bad Cops *provides a treasure trove of New York City cop lore and constitutes a valuable source of information from an authority on law-enforcement efforts to reduce police corruption and misconduct.*

    In A Book of American Martyrs, *Joyce Carol Oates examines a volatile, divisive issue. She dramatizes the aftereffects of a violent confrontation between a fundamentalist antiabortion activist and a sympathetic doctor dedicated to the pro-choice cause, and humanizes those whose lives are forever changed by events beyond their control.*

    In The Book That Changed America: How Darwin's Theory of Evolution Ignited a Nation, *author Randall Fuller traces the relationship between the reception of Charles Darwin's 1859 book* On the Origin of Species *and the abolitionist movement in the United States. Fuller situates the reception of the text in the intellectual circle of Ralph Waldo Emerson, Henry David Thoreau, and the Alcott family, emphasizing its widespread and deeply felt influence on the development of the American intellectual community.*

    In the desolate landscape of a derelict metropolis, a handful of ragged humans in a battle for survival scavenge for food while dodging bioengineered monsters created by a now-defunct firm known as the Company. Amid the rubble, a young woman finds and nurtures a creature she calls Borne, which looks like a plant, acts like an animal, and strives to become human.

    In The Brain Defense, *Kevin Davis presents an illuminating study of the ways in which modern neuroscience is becoming a contested tool in American jurisprudence. He focuses on the bellwether case of Herbert Weinstein, whose brutal murder of his wife was attributed by his defense to the effects of a brain tumor. Davis evenhand-edly explores the debate over whether brain injuries negate free will and personal responsibility in criminal cases.*

Portia Carmichael is determined to remain single and to open her own business, but when an old family friend arrives, her plans are challenged by an unexpected attraction to Kent Randolph. As the two get to know each other, they face challenges that could undermine their growing relationship.

Nina Riggs wrote The Bright Hour: A Memoir of Living and Dying *as she strug-gled with the repercussions of a cancer diagnosis that would eventually take her life. In this memoir, she shares the everyday moments that people often take for granted as well as the difficulties of living with and through a terminal illness.*

Having previously published a nonfiction book about creatures that feed on blood, zoologist and biology professor Bill Schutt next examines the phenomenon of animals—from insects to humans—that consume their own kind. Filled with interest-ing facts, helpful illustrations, and characteristic humor, Cannibalism: A Perfectly Natural History *provides a wealth of information about a largely understudied and misunderstood topic in the science world.*

Noted scholar Richard Rothstein provides an exhaustively researched look at the official and unofficial governmental policies that led to a long history of highly segregated housing in the United States and argues that because these policies were both official and unconstitutional, the government has a responsibility to make things right today.

The Cooking Gene *excavates the history of African American foodways from the earliest eras of slavery in the American South to the present day. The book fuses the genres of history and autobiography to trace the intertwined stories of food, culture, and bloodlines in the South.*

Drabble explores the varied issues of aging in this character study about several people who are moving into the golden years of their lives.

COMPLETE ANNOTATED LIST OF CONTENTS

Gather the Daughters *is a work of speculative fiction about a group of teenage girls who live on a dystopian island where misogyny reigns. It is American author Jennie Melamed's debut novel.*

Ginny Moon *is the story of an autistic teen who struggles with being understood as her adoptive parents prepare for the birth of a child.*

A fierce indictment of warmakers and peace negotiators entangled in the complex politics of the Middle East, The Girl in Green *spans more than two decades of sectarian conflict. The taut, sometimes farcical narrative demonstrates both the ultimate senselessness of war, as well as the opportunity for personal redemption for individuals swept up in the chaos of battle.*

Glass House *traces the rise and fall of an "all-American" corporate town through the complexities of the conjoined fates of the Anchor Hocking corporation and the town of Lancaster, Ohio. The narrative opens when town and corporation had a local and at least somewhat symbiotic relationship. Author Brian Alexander traces the economic, social, and psychological fallout for Lancaster following the shattering of this paradigm by international investment models.*

Armand Gamache is confronted with a murder in his small town of Three Pines, but murder is the least of his problems as he and his team plot to take down at least one major case of criminal activity in Québec.

The distinguished German philosopher and biographer Rüdiger Safranski presents a comprehensive and compelling biography of Johann Wolfgang von Goethe. A multifaceted literary genius, over a long career Goethe produced novels, poetry, and plays, including his most celebrated masterpiece Faust (1808–32). Safranski argues that Goethe worked to make his life as much a work of art as he did his writings.

Francis Spufford's first novel, Golden Hill, *about power, artifice, and race, vividly conjures the city of New York in the years before the American Revolution.*

Set in the United States during the presidency of Barack Obama, Salman Rushdie's twelfth novel, The Golden House, *follows the fortunes of a real-estate developer from India as he and his sons relocate to Manhattan.*

COMPLETE ANNOTATED LIST OF CONTENTS

Part history, part mystery, the English translation of the complex, multilayered Heretics *follows the fortunes of a Jewish family in Havana, Cuba, where former policeman Mario Conde is asked to help track a lost Rembrandt painting and to search for a young woman gone missing.*

Linda is a teenager living in a nontraditional home in northern Minnesota with people who may or may not be her birth parents. When new neighbors move into a house across the lake, she seeks to belong to a family that looks safe on the outside. As her relationship with the family grows, however, she comes to realize that not all is as it seems.

In Hit Makers: The Science of Popularity in an Age of Distraction, *Derek Thompson explores the multitude of factors that make a work of art, a piece of technology, or a trend popular.*

The result of nearly a quarter century of research by British historian Laurence Rees, The Holocaust: A New History *offers a complete chronological history of the systematic extermination of more than six million people at the hands of Adolf Hitler's Nazi regime.*

Award-winning journalist Alia Malek chronicles her family history through several generations while depicting the history of Syria during the same periods.

Homesick for Another World *is a collection of fourteen stories by Ottessa Moshfegh. Set in various locations across the United States, the collection offers an intimate view of the lives of misfits—both average people and those who defy public convention. From chronic gamblers to the newly divorced or widowed to the elderly and lonely, Moshfegh's characters are at once extraordinary and relatable.*

David Grossman's award-winning novel A Horse Walks into a Bar *presents an aging, bitter Jewish stand-up comedian in what may be his final performance: an unforgettable routine that covers a gamut of topics, from the consideration of what is humorous to the nature of guilt and remembrance.*

House of Names, *the award-winning Irish author Colm Tóibín's 2017 novel, is a reimagining of an ancient Greek myth.*

How Emotions Are Made: The Secret Life of the Brain *is a summation of the groundbreaking research of Dr. Lisa Feldman Barrett, an expert in neuroscience and psychology. It is her first nonacademic book.*

In The Hungry Brain: Outsmarting the Instincts That Make Us Overeat, *Stephan J. Guyenet explains the complex brain processes that cause humans to overeat and, in many cases, develop obesity.*

In I Was Told to Come Alone: My Journey behind the Lines of Jihad, *author Souad Mekhennet discusses her development as a reporter focusing on Islamist extremism, the various major stories she has covered, and the disturbing future that may await a world in which violent jihadism is far from defeated.*

In The Idiot, *Elif Batuman crafts a semi-autobiographical saga about love, language, and the frustrations and musings, exhilarations and self-innovations that are characteristic of coming-of-age transitions.*

An unsettling thriller spanning three decades, Ill Will *concerns two disturbing sets of events separated by thirty years: a mass murder in Nebraska and a series of drowning deaths in Ohio, both possibly the result of satanic rituals. The novel delves into the nature of memory, the definition of sanity, and the issue of trust.*

Imagine Wanting Only This *is a graphic memoir by debut author Kristen Radtke. When Radtke's beloved uncle dies suddenly while she is in college, she becomes obsessed with the presence of ruins both metaphorical and literal. Through explorations of the recent and ancient past and communities touched by the impermanence of the landscapes around them, she attempts to discover the origin of her own obsession with these places.*

COMPLETE ANNOTATED LIST OF CONTENTS

VOLUME II

Amber Patterson has her sights set on rich and handsome Jackson Parrish, but he is married to the seemingly perfect Daphne. Amber's schemes to replace Daphne lead to a surprising twist, and only the best woman will win.

Lisa Ko's debut novel, The Leavers, *is a coming-of-age story that explores identity, immigration, and motherhood.*

An octogenarian walks the streets of New York City, reliving moments from her illustrious past as a poet, advertising copywriter, wife, and mother. She speaks to everyone she meets along the way and is determined to live life on her own terms.

Award-winning short-story writer George Saunders's first novel melds historical fiction with earnest metaphysical inquiry as he considers the post-death fate of Abraham Lincoln's son Willie and the other souls that exist in a limbo between the world of the living and the afterlife.

In July 1965, Ruth Malone, separated from her husband, becomes the prime suspect in the murder of her two children, largely because she is young, attractive, and does not behave according to society's expectations of a mother. Pete Wonicke, a reporter fascinated by both the enigmatic Ruth and the case, works tirelessly to learn the truth, but the intrigue and obstacles mount.

Little Fires Everywhere, *Celeste Ng's second novel, tells the interconnected stories of the Richardson family, living a privileged life in a comfortable suburb, and Mia and Pearl Warren, a single artist and her daughter whose arrival triggers conflicts within the family and the larger community.*

Written by Yale Law School professor James Forman Jr., Locking Up Our Own: Crime and Punishment in Black America *explores how black civic leaders unwittingly contributed to the mass incarceration of black people.*

The Lonely Hearts Hotel, *a love story set in the seedy underworld of early-twentieth-century Montreal, follows the lives of two talented orphans.*

with him in an effort to avoid either of them meeting a similar fate and, ultimately, to avenge the death.

The Signal Flame *is a novel that explores the nature of loss. It is the sequel to American author Andrew Krivák's award-winning book* The Sojourn *(2011).*

Sing, Unburied, Sing *is a novel that follows an African American family living on the Gulf Coast in Mississippi that is haunted by the past. It is American writer Jesmyn Ward's third novel.*

Roddy Doyle's novel Smile, *though darker and more downbeat in tone than much of his previous work, contains familiar elements: blunt and folksy dialogue, well-drawn characters, and forgotten memories of events from the past that, once remembered, resonate in unexpected ways in the lives of those trapped in the present.*

A critically acclaimed experimental novel, Solar Bones *creatively presents the thoughts, memories, and philosophical musings of a small-town civil engineer in western Ireland. Marcus Conway draws strength from the bonds of family and takes comfort in the mathematical certainty of science in the process of navigating an increasingly complicated and chaotic world.*

Jenny Zhang's debut short-story collection, Sour Heart, *explores young womanhood and the Chinese immigrant experience through the eyes of various narrators.*

Ayobami Adebayo's debut novel, Stay with Me, *tells the story of a Nigerian marriage.*

In The Tea Girl of Hummingbird Lane, *Lisa See deploys intimate themes of destiny and chance, motherhood and custom, to explore the enigmatic albeit prevailing boundaries between the historical forces of timeworn tradition and inescapable change.*

Adopting the format of a sermon, academic and ordained Baptist minister Michael Eric Dyson delivers a moving polemic against American racism, urging his audience to examine their beliefs and take steps to change.

reestablishes herself as a woman, intellectual, and mother.

COMPLETE ANNOTATED LIST OF CONTENTS

Poet, author, and filmmaker Sherman Alexie wrote this memoir of his life as a tribute to his mother after her death. The book explores his complicated relationship with his parents, life on an American Indian reservation, and his health problems, along with a number of other personal and broader cultural issues.

The Last Mrs. Parrish

Author: Liv Constantine (pseudonym of Lynne and Valerie Constantine)
Publisher: Harper (New York). 400 pp.
Type of work: Novel
Time: Present day
Locales: Bishops Harbor, Connecticut; New York City

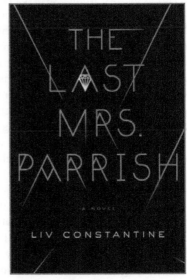

Courtesy of HarperCollins Publishers

Amber Patterson has her sights set on rich and handsome Jackson Parrish, but he is married to the seemingly perfect Daphne. Amber's schemes to replace Daphne lead to a surprising twist, and only the best woman will win.

Principal characters

AMBER PATTERSON, a deceptive gold-digger
DAPHNE PARRISH, a wealthy socialite
JACKSON PARRISH, Daphne's husband, a wealthy real estate mogul
TALLULAH, Daphne and Jackson's quiet older daughter
BELLA, Daphne and Jackson's demanding younger daughter
MEREDITH STANTON, a friend of Daphne

The Last Mrs. Parrish is the debut novel of Liv Constantine, a pen name of sisters Lynne and Valerie Constantine. Lifelong avid readers, the sisters decided to try their hand at writing, resulting in *Circle Dance* (2004), a novel about Greek American sisters. For their next collaboration, they decided to explore the thriller genre and adopted their pseudonym. *The Last Mrs. Parrish* makes skillful use of psychological suspense, pulling readers in with unexpected twists and turns in the fashion of a true page-turner.

Structurally, the novel is split into three parts. The first part, told in third person, introduces Amber Patterson, a young woman whose greatest desire is to marry a wealthy man and live a privileged life. As that has not happened naturally, she has chosen a target—the rich, handsome, and already married Jackson Parrish—and is doing everything she can to achieve her goal. The first thirty-five chapters tell this story from Amber's point of view. The second part, containing thirty chapters, focuses on Daphne Parrish, the wife of Amber's target, and is narrated in the first person. The third part switches between Amber and Daphne's perspectives, after Amber's plan has reached a new phase. This section of the novel covers eight chapters in third person and provides a sense of closure for at least one of the women.

The title of the novel holds dual meaning, which is reflected in the structure of the book. "Last" can be interpreted as meaning either "former" or "final," hinting at the competition between the two women to be either the final or the former Mrs. Parrish.

The alternating points of view reinforce this competition as the plot develops and the statuses of the two women evolve. Yet the successfully executed plot twists keep this relatively simple concept from becoming too predictable.

The skillful character development is one of the most engaging features of the novel. The first part of the book primarily establishes the personalities of Amber and Daphne. Amber's desire for Jackson Parrish and his money, her jealousy of Daphne for merely being his wife, and her insidious plot to get what she wants are deftly illustrated. From the first pages, Amber insinuates herself into Daphne's home by creating a fictional younger sister, Charlene, who has supposedly died of cystic fibrosis, the same disease that killed Daphne's younger sister Julie. Amber uses this false link to build a relationship with Daphne, who has never stopped grieving for Julie. Once she is accepted by the Parrish household, Amber begins her plot to wholly displace Daphne by any means necessary.

Amber's greed is clearly the driving force behind her actions, but Constantine occasionally sneaks in a suggestion that Amber might feel guilty at times for using Daphne as she does. For instance, when Daphne talks about Julie, Amber admits to feeling some measure of sympathy. However, her true nature quickly reappears and the sympathy is channeled into envy. These glimpses into a possible gentler side of the character give hope for redemption, providing just enough depth to keep Amber from being wholly dislikeable. At the same time, however, hints about Amber's past are also thrown in that suggest she may be even more sinister than she appears. These threads provide a connection that is further developed in the second and third parts of the novel.

The second part of the book takes readers into Daphne's life. She has been presented from Amber's point of view in the first portion of the book and seems a bit flat as a result, but it becomes clear that Amber's perceptions are limited. Amber sees Daphne as a sweet, stupid, and selfish woman who does not appreciate the bounty she has been given as Jackson's wife. As the novel progresses and readers are introduced to the real Daphne Parrish through her own narration, it emerges that she is much more complicated than Amber realizes.

During this portion of the novel, Daphne relates the history of her relationship with Jackson. Despite the ideal life that Amber sees, Daphne's marriage is frighteningly dysfunctional, and readers learn that Jackson is in fact a controlling, abusive, and narcissistic sociopath. His abuse goes beyond verbal insults and underestimating his wife's intelligence. He physically and emotionally terrorizes her, separates her from her mother, and tears their daughters down, destroying their self-esteem. Fortunately for Daphne, Jackson's self-centeredness means he is easily distracted when Amber enters the picture. Daphne stays with Jackson out of fear, but she may have more up her sleeve than either her husband or her apparent rival could guess.

The tagline on the cover of the novel claims, "Some women get everything. Some women get everything they deserve," and the third portion of the novel depicts just how Daphne, Amber, and Jackson all get what they deserve. Though this will be satisfying to many readers, it does not necessarily mean justice is served in the traditional sense. Constantine does an excellent job of suggesting that Amber and Jackson, particularly, will get away with their crimes, keeping the overarching tone relatively dark. These closing chapters, however, add a touch of dark humor as a final unexpected and ironic twist emerges for the antagonists.

The page-turning plot and the vivid characterization are the driving forces behind *The Last Mrs. Parrish*, but Constantine proves adept at using literary techniques such as irony and foreshadowing to add another layer of interest to the novel. A number of themes are crucial to the suspenseful plot, but also touch on deeper, problematic social issues. These include the sometimes fine line between generosity and exploitation, the horrors of domestic abuse, and questions of self-identity versus outward representation. The first of these themes is highlighted by Amber's use of Daphne's involvement in a cystic fibrosis foundation as a way to insinuate herself into her life. Amber manipulates others' generosity for her own benefit as she climbs the social ladder. On the other hand,

Liv Constantine is the pseudonym of sisters Lynne and Valerie Constantine. They previously collaborated under their own names on the novel Circle Dance *(2004). Lynne Constantine is also the author of the novel* The Veritas Deception *(2016) as well as a number of short stories.*

Jackson has used his own apparent generosity—he and Daphne first met at a benefit for her foundation—to blind those around him to his true nature.

The human capacity to manipulate and exploit is also apparent in the book's portrayal of domestic abuse, whether emotional, psychological, verbal, or physical. In looking back on her marriage, Daphne sees how Jackson's early efforts to help her and her family were really a means of gaining ultimate control. Once he had established his power over her, his abuses grew more and more serious. In detailing such a serious subject, Constantine often uses emotionally descriptive language that helps flesh out Daphne's character. For example, she narrates, "Everything had begun with such promise. And then, like a windshield chipped by a tiny pebble, the chip turned into deep cracks that spread until there was nothing left to repair." The writing makes Daphne not just a victim, but a human with whom the reader can sympathize.

Daphne is also a prime example of how Constantine explores concepts of identity, especially how identity shifts with point of view. The woman who appears to be the perfect upper-class housewife is trapped in a terrible marriage, but is also more than a stereotypical victim. The other two main characters are also shown to be more than they first appear, a common theme in suspense novels but one that is handled well. Jackson's true personality is hidden behind a public façade, but as the novel progresses, his actions show him for what he really is. Amber's deception is immediately central to her character, but deeper threads from her past emerge to add new layers, and it ultimately becomes clear that she may not be the manipulative genius she appears to be. This web of shifting identity is primarily revealed through the twisting plot, but the overarching three-part structure with changing points of view helps reinforce the broader theme that who someone is depends on who is telling the story.

With its effective blend of gripping plot, strong characters, and thematic complexity, *The Last Mrs. Parrish* was met with primarily positive critical reception. Many reviewers lauded the onslaught of twists that lead to a strongly satisfying conclusion. Also highly praised was the utterly devious Amber as a highly memorable, love-to-hate type of character. The novel's focus on a manipulative sociopath drew frequent comparisons to other works with deviant central figures, such as *The Talented Mr. Ripley* by Patricia Highsmith, *A Kiss before Dying* by Ira Levin, *Gone Girl* by Gillian Flynn, and *The Girl on the Train* by Paula Hawkins. Indeed, some noted that *The Last Mrs. Parrish* was one of the strongest entries in a subgenre of thrillers based around antihero women that has emerged since the publication of *Gone Girl* in 2012.

While some critics noted that the story can at times feel too lengthy, especially in the first section, it was widely agreed that the novel is ultimately a well-crafted piece of entertainment. As Mary Todd Chesnut wrote for her *Library Journal* review, "Lynne and Valerie Constantine . . . have constructed a deliciously duplicitous psychological thriller that will lure readers until the wee hours and beyond." Overall, *The Last Mrs. Parrish* presents an intriguing plot that will keeps readers engaged as they absorb hints that add a depth to the story line. The novel's attention to serious topics will also make readers think about the façades we all create.

Theresa L. Stowell, PhD

Review Sources

Review of *The Last Mrs. Parrish*, by Liv Constantine. *Kirkus Reviews*, vol. 85, no. 16, 15 Aug. 2017. *Literary Reference Center Plus*, search.ebscohost.com/login.as px?direct=true&db=lkh&AN=124595215&site=lrc-plus. Accessed 13 Feb. 2018.

Review of *The Last Mrs. Parrish*, by Liv Constantine. *Publishers Weekly*, 14 Aug. 2017, p. 44. *Literary Reference Center Plus*, search.ebscohost.com/login.aspx?dir ect=true&db=lkh&AN=124625800&site=lrc-plus. Accessed 13 Feb. 2018.

Todd, Mary Chesnut. Review of *The Last Mrs. Parrish*, by Liv Constantine. *Library Journal*, 15 June 2017, p. 75. *Literary Reference Center*, search.ebscohost.com/ login.aspx?direct=true&db=lfh&AN=123997366&site=eds-live. Accessed 13 Feb. 2018.

Verma, Henrietta. Review of *The Last Mrs. Parrish*, by Liv Constantine. *Booklist*, Sept. 2017, p. 52. *Literary Reference Center*, search.ebscohost.com/login.aspx?di rect=true&db=lfh&AN=125075728&site=eds-live. Accessed 13 Feb. 2018.

The Leavers

Author: Lisa Ko (b. 1975)
Publisher: Algonquin Books of Chapel Hill
(Chapel Hill, NC). 352 pp.
Type of work: Novel
Time: 1990s and present day
Locales: New York; Fujian, China

Lisa Ko's debut novel, The Leavers, *is a coming-of-age story that explores identity, immigration, and motherhood.*

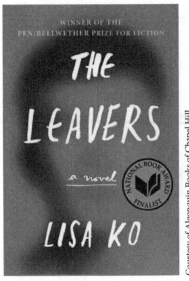

Courtesy of Algonquin Books of Chapel Hill

Principal characters

DEMING GUO, a.k.a. Daniel Wilkinson, the novel's young, Chinese American protagonist
POLLY GUO, a.k.a. Guo Peilan, his mother, who disappears when he is eleven years old
LEON, his mother's fiancé
VIVIAN, Leon's sister
MICHAEL, his childhood best friend, Vivian's son
PETER WILKINSON, his adoptive father
KATHRYN S. "KAY" WILKINSON, his adoptive mother
ROLAND FUENTES, his friend
ANGEL HENNINGS, his friend, a fellow transracial adoptee

Lisa Ko's debut novel, *The Leavers*, follows the story of a young boy named Deming Guo as he navigates the various threads of his identity. Jumping around in time, Ko's narrative begins when Deming is eleven years old. He lives in the Bronx with his mother, Polly, a Chinese immigrant from Fuzhou. The two share a cramped apartment with Leon, Polly's fiancé; Leon's sister, Vivian; and Vivian's young son, Michael. Their lives are precarious and difficult—Polly works at a nail salon and Leon butchers pigs and cows at an industrial slaughterhouse in the Bronx—but ultimately happy. Why then, the day after Polly floats the idea of moving the family to Florida to pursue a waitressing job, does she disappear without a trace? This question and the painful fallout of Polly's disappearance animate Ko's novel about identity, immigration, and motherhood. *The Leavers* is divided into four parts, alternately narrated by Deming and Polly. Ko's novel is populated by doppelgangers; glimpses of identities associated with roads not taken. Months after Polly disappears, Deming becomes Daniel Wilkinson, the adoptee of a well-meaning, wealthy white couple in upstate New York. Twists of fate are swift for Deming and his mother, whose lives, as he comes to learn, are shaped by forces beyond their control.

Courtesy of Bartosz Potocki

Lisa Ko is an award-winning novelist. The Leavers, her debut, won the 2016 PEN/Bellwether Prize for Socially Engaged Fiction and was later short-listed for the National Book Award in 2017.

The Leavers is Ko's first novel. It won the 2016 PEN/Bellwether Prize for Socially Engaged Fiction, given by novelist Barbara Kingsolver for a novel that deals with social justice and the effect of culture and politics on relationships, and was a finalist for the 2017 National Book Award for fiction. Ko began writing the book in 2009, after reading a *New York Times* article about a woman named Xiu Ping Jiang. Jiang, an undocumented Chinese immigrant, was arrested while traveling from New York to Florida to start a new job. She was detained by Immigrations and Customs Enforcement (ICE) for a year and a half. Jiang, who spent much of her imprisonment in solitary confinement, was also forcibly separated from her son, who was detained by ICE, placed in the foster care system, and adopted by another family, in Canada. Ko incorporates aspects of Jiang's story—which is not singular among other stories involving immigration and ICE—in crafting the story of Polly Guo. While Deming is the protagonist of Ko's tale, Polly is its heart. Polly, or Peilan, grows up in Minjiang, a small village outside of Fuzhou, in the province of Fujian, China. Her father is a fisherman; her mother has died. Peilan is expected to marry one of her neighbors when she comes of age but yearns to be free of her poor, rural life. She leaves home to work in a factory in Fuzhou as a teenager but becomes pregnant. Hamstrung by China's birth policies, Polly takes out a fifty-thousand-dollar loan to come to the United States as an undocumented immigrant.

In New York, Polly lives in a tiny apartment in Chinatown with a handful of other women. She gives birth to Deming, taking out more loans to care for him. Polly is surprised by the intense love she feels for her son. Her early struggles to care for Deming while also paying down her astronomic debt are stirring. She brings him to the sweatshop where she works fourteen-hour shifts, setting him in a small open box at her feet. Trying to feed him, she flubs a hem and is sent home without pay. In a moment of desperation, Polly almost abandons Deming at the waterfront in Manhattan. She eventually decides to send him back to her father in Minjiang until she can pay down her debt and afford to care for a child. Ironically, she must take out more loans to facilitate this arrangement. Five years later, Polly is still chipping away at her debt, sending money home when she can, when her father unexpectedly dies. Polly takes out more loans to bring Deming back to New York. She gets a job at a nail salon, taking out yet more loans to afford to "apprentice" there before receiving pay, and eventually meets, falls in love with, and moves in with Leon. Polly's life, like the lives of the immigrant women who inspired her story, is characterized by the gut-wrenching choices she must make to survive. Ko does an admirable job of rendering Polly as a full and complicated person. She is practical, but also charmingly profane. For years afterward, Deming will remember her sharp, barking laugh. Polly also has her own dreams and ambitions; she refuses to be beaten by the systems that seek to oppress her, not just for Deming, but for herself.

When the reader first meets Deming, five years have passed since he returned to the United States from Minjiang, and he has learned to trust and rely on his mother. Still, he is initially horrified at the prospect of moving to Florida. Michael, Vivian's young son, is like a brother to Deming, and he worries about what will happen if Michael and his mother decide to stay in the city. Deming eventually comes around to the idea but never gets to express his change of heart. His mother disappears without a trace the next day. At first, Deming believes she has gone to Florida without him, but as the weeks go by, this conclusion seems less and less likely. He wonders why she has not called, even just to check up on him. Not long after that, Leon disappears, and Vivian, unable to care for two children alone, places Deming with a foster family. With disorienting speed, Deming finds himself in foster care, with a white couple named Peter and Kay Wilkinson. Peter and Kay live in a fictional small college town in upstate New York called Ridgeborough. Both are professors and published authors and welcome Deming into their life of relative affluence. They shower Deming with love, but insist that he formally change his name to Daniel Wilkinson. Daniel, they assure him, is far easier to pronounce than Deming. Ko manages to portray Peter and Kay as both loving and willfully ignorant about Deming's cultural background. Even their attempts to reach out—Deming suffers through Kay's conversations in mangled Mandarin and her Chinese cooking—reek of condescension. Deming comes to understand their motivations. Late in the book, Ko writes, "For a brief, horrible moment, he could see himself the way he realized they saw him—as someone who needed to be saved."

Deming does eventually settle into his new life as Daniel, making friends like Roland Fuentes, the only other student of color at his small school, and even coming to love his foster parents, who eventually adopt him. Deming's passion is playing guitar, but Peter pushes him to pursue a degree in a more employable discipline. Ever the people-pleaser, Deming complies with this request, only to develop a gambling addiction during his first semester of college that derails his life plans. The bulk of the book finds Deming struggling to manage his addiction, appease his loved ones, and follow his dreams, while figuring out, in a spiritual sense, who he really is. Living on Roland's couch in New York City and trying to make it as a musician, Deming receives a message from Michael, now a medical student at Columbia University. The connection opens a portal to Deming's past. Deming, desperate for answers that might help him discover his own life's path, decides to find his mother, who is, surprisingly, alive and well in Fuzhou, and find out why she left him ten years before.

The Leavers takes place across New York City, Ridgeborough, and Fujian, and Ko renders each setting in meticulous detail. From the squalid basement recording studios of Brooklyn and Queens, to the burnt, autumn smells of Minjiang, Ko conjures a sprawling, believable world for her characters to inhabit. This breadth of experience makes Peter and Kay's insular views seem all the more oblivious, but also reveals the enormous gulf that exists between Deming and his adoptive parents. Transracial adoption is an important aspect of *The Leavers*; Ko demonstrates how adoptees can be hurt by their parents' casual racism. One character, Deming's friend Angel Hennings, is also an Asian child with particularly clueless wealthy, white adoptive parents. Angel's mother, Elaine, spends one afternoon pompously explaining a Chinese folktale, while showing no interest in Deming's actual experiences or opinions about Chinese culture.

The Leavers received generally positive reviews from critics. A reviewer for *Kirkus* called it a "stunning tale of love and loyalty," while others praised Ko for creating a compelling, nuanced tale about a topical subject. Gish Jen, who reviewed the book for the *New York Times*, was more reserved in her praise. Jen criticized the structure of Deming's story, which "eventually devolves into a conventional narrative of a young person learning to follow his bliss." She added, recalling the theme of gambling that runs through the novel, "It's hard not to see this book as one that takes risks but then hedges its bets." Although Amy Weiss-Meyer, in her review for the *Atlantic*, characterized *The Leavers* as a political novel, she wrote that Ko largely avoids "the sentimentality and thudding moralism that haunt the genre." This may be so, but as the story moves toward resolution and redemption, it comes perilously close. *The Leavers* is at its most affecting on a small scale. For instance, one day, Polly enjoys rare time off from the salon and rides the subway to the end of the line in Brooklyn. Anonymous and alone, she is free to imagine all of the possible routes her life might have taken and might still take. Saddled with debt, she dares to imagine a future for herself in which she is truly free.

Molly Hagan

Review Sources

Hong, Terry. "*The Leavers* Inspired by a Real Story, Confronts Transracial Adoption." Review of *The Leavers*, by Lisa Ko. *The Christian Science Monitor*, 2 May 2017, www.csmonitor.com/Books/Book-Reviews/2017/0502/The-Leavers-inspired-by-a-real-story-confronts-transracial-adoption. Accessed 19 Nov. 2017.

Jen, Gish. "Migration, a Makeshift Family, and Then a Disappearance." Review of *The Leavers*, by Lisa Ko. *The New York Times*, 16 May 2017, www.nytimes.com/2017/05/16/books/review/the-leavers-by-lisa-ko.html. Accessed 19 Nov. 2017.

Review of *The Leavers*, by Lisa Ko. *Kirkus*, 23 Jan. 2017, www.kirkusreviews.com/book-reviews/lisa-ko/the-leavers/. Accessed 19 Nov. 2017.

Review of *The Leavers*, by Lisa Ko. *Publishers Weekly*, 13 Feb. 2017, www.publishersweekly.com/978-1-61620-688-8. Accessed 19 Nov. 2017.

Weiss-Meyer, Amy. "*The Leavers* Is a Wrenching Tale of Parenthood." Review of *The Leavers*, by Lisa Ko. *The Atlantic*, 14 May 2017, www.theatlantic.com/entertainment/archive/2017/05/lisa-ko-the-leavers-book-review/526179/. Accessed 19 Nov. 2017.

Lillian Boxfish Takes a Walk

Author: Kathleen Rooney
Publisher: St. Martin's Press (New York).
304 pp.
Type of work: Novel
Time: New Year's Eve, 1984
Locale: New York City

Courtesy of Macmillan

An octogenarian walks the streets of New York City, reliving moments from her illustrious past as a poet, advertising copywriter, wife, and mother. She speaks to everyone she meets along the way and is determined to live life on her own terms.

Principal characters

LILLIAN BOXFISH, renowned ad copywriter, poet, and avid walker
MASSIMILIANO GIANLUCA "MAX" CAPUTO, her husband
MASSIMILIANO GIANLUCA CAPUTO JR., a.k.a. Gian Caputo, Johnny, and Gianino, her son
HELEN MCGOLDRICK, her best friend
OLIVE DODD, her archrival at Macy's
CHESTER "CHIP" EVERETT, her boss

Lillian Boxfish, the eighty-something protagonist of Kathleen Rooney's second novel, is a flaneur, an avid walker and wanderer in her much-loved New York City. She is quick-witted, outspoken, and a fashion trendsetter. She strikes up a conversation with almost everyone she meets and lets very little, including the city's current crime wave, deter her from walking to a young friend's New Year's Eve party on the last day of 1984. Boxfish, with her smart banter and hard-earned wisdom, is the best reason to read *Lillian Boxfish Takes a Walk*.

Rooney's protagonist was inspired by real-life adwoman Margaret Fishback, who, like Lillian, was employed by Macy's department store in the 1920s and 1930s, became the world's highest-paid female ad copywriter in the 1930s, and was a published poet and writer of etiquette books. Rooney follows the arc of Fishback's life in terms of her career and family, sometimes referencing historical facts from her research in Fishback's archive, but Lillian's interior life, which comprises much of the novel, is pure fiction. The novel begins on the last day of 1984, with Lillian talking to her son, Gian, on the phone. He attempts to get his mother to move out of the city for her own safety as she prepares for her annual New Year's Eve dinner at her favorite local Italian restaurant, Grimaldi. A half package of mindlessly eaten Oreo cookies, however, ruins her appetite and launches Lillian on a 10.4-mile walk around the city, where she meets and talks with locals along the way. When she is not reminiscing about her past—her job at Macy's, her arrival in the city, her poetry, as well as her marriage and mother-hood—she offers her astute observations on the city she has loved and lived in for more than sixty years. Although Lillian acknowledges some low points, she does not dwell on them as she recounts much of the twentieth century through her own vivid and purposeful life.

Rooney is especially adept at creating Lillian as a full and multifaceted character and someone who has specific goals and lives life on her own terms. Eager to live independently in New York City as her Aunt Sadie did years ago, and despite the reluctance of her parents, a young Lillian finds a copywriting job at Macy's with the help of her new friend and roommate Helen McGoldrick. Lillian is talented and ambitious and is soon promoted to head copywriter in her department. After the *New York World-Telegram* writes a prominent profile on Lillian, celebrating her as the best and highest-paid woman copywriter in the world, Lillian asks her boss, Chester Everett, for a raise:

> "Lillian, I'm sympathetic, but these fellows whose salaries you aim to match have families to support."

> "Nobody asked these fellows with salaries to reproduce themselves," I said. "And were I ever to have a family, you wouldn't let me keep working here. Ladies get the boot the instant they show signs of spawning. Not that that matters to me, since I'd sooner die than join the wife-and-mother brigade."

It is doubtful Lillian will receive the raise, and she is fairly certain she will not get it even before she asks for it, but that does not deter her from making the request or advocating her position by pointing out the double standard. Should she become married and pregnant, she would lose her job for that reason alone, and through this conversation, not only does Rooney communicate the wit and tenacity of her protagonist, but she offers a sympathetic portrayal of single, independent women in the early part of the twentieth century and the difficulties they faced. Later in the novel, Lillian meets Max Caputo, Macy's head rug buyer, and after years of declaring she would neither marry nor have children, she does both. Love is unexpected and even unwanted for Lillian, but when she is faced with it, she embraces it, despite what people say behind her back. Lillian will not let gossip and criticism interfere with what she realizes she wants, and she is confident and independent enough to change her mind after repeatedly insisting it could not be changed. The marriage does not survive, which is evident at the beginning of the novel, but Lillian has no regrets. Rooney has created a protagonist who is fearless in her ability to speak her mind and own up to her mistakes, lest they get in the way of her happiness.

Other defining features of Lillian's character are her deep sense of curiosity and her insistence on living in the present rather than the past. As Lillian roams the city on New Year's Eve, she reminisces about the past, but she also makes it clear that understanding the people and trends of today is important. She is most savvy when she combines the past with the present, such as choosing her New Year's Eve outfit and makeup, which include the Helena Rubenstein Orange Fire lipstick she stockpiled in the 1950s when it was discontinued and combining it with a stylish contemporary outfit of a boxy, green velvet dress with a navy-blue fedora hat. She fosters a unique sense of style, and her dedication to current trends is not limited to lipstick and clothes but includes music and culture as well. Lillian proclaims her admiration for rap music, and she shops at a local bodega to find a hostess gift for the party she will be attending. Her curiosity is most pronounced in her interactions with people. She talks to absolutely everyone. She asks their names and about their lives, offering wit and wisdom where she can. In one instance, she walks by a local hospital and encounters Maritza, who is clearly very pregnant and in pain. Lillian stops, introduces herself, and when she realizes Maritza needs help and comfort, she offers her that, waiting with Maritza until the baby's father, Luis, returns from parking the car. Luis's spoken English is not yet strong, and Maritza is worried that if they are separated, language will be a barrier and he will not be with her when she delivers their child. Lillian stays with Maritza and engages her in conversation until Luis arrives, then wishes them well before continuing her walk. Lillian is clearly delighted by people and her conversations with them, and Rooney captures her timeless energy as well as the interest she has in the present and the future, working against the stereotype of elderly characters who live in the past.

Kathleen Rooney is a founding editor of Rose Metal Press and teaches at DePaul University. She won a Ruth Lilly Fellowship from Poetry *magazine and has published a total of eight books across three genres, including poetry, fiction, and nonfiction.* Lillian Boxfish Takes a Walk *is her second novel.*

Rooney's Lillian is effervescent and sassy, and her quips and engaging character carry the novel. While critics universally admired Rooney's ability to create such a deeply interesting character who sheds light on the past while living a full life in the present, some critics felt the novel was too breezy, meaning it avoided deep-seated conflict. For example, Lillian mentions the "Subway Vigilante" incident from December 1984, in which Bernhard Goetz, a white man, shot four unarmed African American young men on the subway when they asked for money. The men said they were panhandling but Goetz believed he was being robbed and responded by shooting them, injuring them seriously. The incident received much publicity and was thought to be emblematic of the rising crime and vigilantism in New York City in the mid-1980s. Gian raises the incident with his mother on their New Year's Eve phone call to encourage her to leave the city, but she ignores him. Issues like this are raised occasionally in the book, but only in passing. The incidents are a vehicle for Lillian to engage another character, but they are not explored in any depth. Later in the novel, when Lillian encounters three young African American men who demand money, she refuses to see the incident as an attempted robbery and instead talks to the young men as she would talk to anyone else she meets on the street in a witty and light-hearted way. These are moments where the novel strains at credibility. A woman in her eighties is walking around the city at night, and although she is in good health and mobile, it seems unrealistic that she meets so little conflict, with so little consequence. Additionally, Lillian has some difficult moments in her past, such as a serious hospitalization, and though it is addressed, the address is quick and perfunctory. Once the incident is resolved, life goes on as usual and Lillian is back to her old self with no obvious repercussions, which, again, seems unrealistic. Rooney chooses to focus on Lillian's independence rather than dwell on the negative aspects of her life or the difficulties she has faced.

In *Lillian Boxfish Takes a Walk*, Rooney has created a character who is independent, ahead of her time, and deeply curious. She has a rich, fulfilling life—one she shares unreservedly with her fellow New York City residents, where she has lived for the last sixty years. She is inextricable from the city and the city is inextricable from her, making the novel as much a love song to the city, and all its past glory, as it is to Lillian herself. Rooney makes both the city and her protagonist come alive with vivid description, snappy dialogue, and the ability to cover much ground at a swift pace, much like Lillian herself.

Marybeth Rua-Larsen

Review Sources

Arthur, Jason. Review of *Lillian Boxfish Takes a Walk*, by Kathleen Rooney. *The Rumpus*, 15 Mar. 2017, therumpus.net/2017/02/lillian-boxfish-takes-a-walk-by-kathleen-rooney/. Accessed 2 Oct. 2017.

Kephart, Beth. "Chicago Author Kathleen Rooney Takes a Pleasant Stroll in *Lillian Boxfish* Novel." Review of *Lillian Boxfish Takes a Walk*, by Kathleen Rooney. *Chicago Tribune*, 18 Jan. 2017, www.chicagotribune.com/lifestyles/books/sc-lillian-boxfish-takes-a-walk-kathleen-rooney-books-0118-20170117-story.html. Accessed 2 Oct. 2017.

Review of *Lillian Boxfish Takes a Walk*, by Kathleen Rooney. *Kirkus Reviews*, 15 Oct. 2016, www.kirkusreviews.com/book-reviews/kathleen-rooney/lillian-box-fish-takes-a-walk/. Accessed 2 Oct. 2017.

Ryan, Marian. Review of *Lillian Boxfish Takes a Walk*, by Kathleen Rooney. *Star Tribune*, 13 Jan. 2017, m.startribune.com/review-lillian-boxfish-takes-a-walk-by-kathleen-rooney/410580805/. Accessed 2 Oct. 2017.

Zipp, Yvonne. "*Lillian Boxfish Takes a Walk* Celebrates a Remarkable NY Character." Review of *Lillian Boxfish Takes a Walk*, by Kathleen Rooney. *The Christian Science Monitor*, 3 Feb. 2017, www.csmonitor.com/Books/Book-Reviews/2017/0203/Lillian-Boxfish-Takes-a-Walk-celebrates-a-remarkable-NY-character. Accessed 2 Oct. 2017.

Lincoln in the Bardo

Author: George Saunders (b. 1958)
Publisher: Random House (New York). 368 pp.
Type of work: Novel
Time: 1862
Locales: Oak Hill Cemetery; Washington, DC

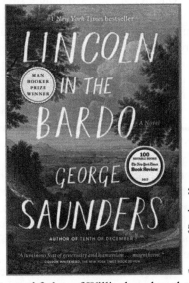

Award-winning short-story writer George Saunders's first novel melds historical fiction with earnest metaphysical inquiry as he considers the post-death fate of Abraham Lincoln's son Willie and the other souls that exist in a limbo between the world of the living and the afterlife.

Courtesy of Random House

Principal characters

ABRAHAM LINCOLN, president of the United States and father of Willie; based on the historical figure of the same name
WILLIE LINCOLN, his son, a spirit in Oak Hill Cemetery; based on the historical figure of the same name
HANS VOLLMAN, a spirit in Oak Hill Cemetery
ROGER BEVINS III, a spirit in Oak Hill Cemetery
THE REVEREND EVERLY THOMAS, a spirit in Oak Hill Cemetery

It is human nature to cling to life. Although some among the dying welcome their death as an end to suffering, there is an instinct as human beings, both physically and mentally, to resist. People use euphemisms for illness, insist that they are doing better than they really are, and fight off the end with every ounce of willpower. Similarly, those who are destined to remain among the living while their loved ones depart for some undefined afterlife often have trouble letting go. The first stage of the Kübler-Ross model of grief is, after all, denial, and those on both sides of the death spectrum—those about to die and those coming to terms with the loss of a close relative or friend—must overcome this tendency to negate the truth to achieve closure.

In his first novel, *Lincoln in the Bardo*, which was short-listed for the 2017 Man Booker Prize, award-winning short-story writer George Saunders considers each side of this divide by drawing on and expanding a historical anecdote involving US president Abraham Lincoln. Saunders had read that Lincoln visited the grave of his eleven-year-old son Willie several times in the days immediately following the boy's death, even going so far as to open his tomb and hold the lifeless body of the child. Whatever the historical accuracy of this anecdote, it sets up a poignant image that stands at the center of Saunders's structurally playful, meditative, and moving novel about the death of Lincoln's son, Willie, and his parents' subsequent grief during the Civil War.

One of Saunders's signature strengths as a short-story writer is his ear for voice. Many of his stories are told in the first person and involve a protagonist using a very specific vernacular to narrate an absurd situation. What draws the reader's attention are the improbable setups of the stories, many of which offer dark commentary on the contemporary world. However, what makes the works stand out as more than mere curios is the precision with which Saunders captures his characters' unique speech patterns and thus their essential humanity.

Because of the limited scope of these works, Saunders inevitably confines himself to a single voice in most of the stories; in *Lincoln*, however, he uses the broader canvas to skillfully introduce a multiplicity of voices that add a richness to the work unavailable in his shorter pieces. The book is narrated in two different formats. In the first format, Saunders assembles a range of historical voices, taken from biographies, letters, diaries, and other real-life source material, and arranges these different perspectives in a collage of short quotations. These passages not only provide the historical background that is required but also comment on the process of making history. If all these contemporary eyewitnesses differ (if only slightly) in their reports, then it must be accepted that there is no such thing as a totally objective, monolithic history.

Having established this subjective stance toward history, Saunders is then free to play with it as much as he pleases, and, in the second format, he fashions a metaphysical tragicomedy out of a broad array of (mostly) fictional voices. These passages, which take place in Washington, DC's Oak Hill Cemetery, are narrated by a series of characters who all exist as spirits, trapped between the living and the dead in some sort of limbo. (The "bardo" of the book's title refers to such a liminal state in the Buddhist religion, although Saunders's theology exists without reference to any specific faith.) In a series of quotations attributed to the various spirits, these passages outline the characters' metaphysical quests. In addition, they give Saunders a chance to try out different narrative voices. Although the main characters all speak in a somewhat similar language, Saunders has fun giving most of the lesser characters more distinctive speech patterns, allowing him to show off his virtuosity.

The principal speakers are a trio of spirits, Hans Vollman, Roger Bevins III, and the Reverend Everly Thomas, who occupy the Oak Hill graveyard, resting in their graves during the day and coming out to talk at night. Although it is clear to the reader that they are dead, the characters do everything they can to deny this fact, referring to their coffins as "sick-boxes" as if they will suddenly recover and return to the living.

The spirits are soon joined by a new resident at the cemetery, Willie Lincoln, and Saunders uses this plot point to show the refusal of the living to let go of life. Willie's father, amid the struggles of the Civil War, comes to visit his son's grave several times and holds him in his arms, refusing to acknowledge his death. In these moving scenes, readers are given access to the elder Lincoln's thoughts: "I remember him. Again. Who he was. I had forgotten somewhat already. But here: his exact proportions, his suit smelling of him still, his forelock between my fingers."

Because his father keeps coming to visit him, Willie refuses to allow himself to move on to the real afterlife, tarrying behind in the liminal state of the graveyard.

George Saunders is the author of eight books of fiction and two of nonfiction. He is the recipient of the Guggenheim and MacArthur fellowships as well as the PEN/Malamud Award for Excellence in Short Fiction. He teaches creative writing at Syracuse University.

Children who stay in this state suffer special torments that the adults do not, such as being continually bound by growing tendrils, and so Vollman, Bevins, and Everly attempt to persuade Willie to move on to the afterlife proper. But as long as his father keeps visiting him, Willie refuses. Therefore, the trio proceed to enter Lincoln's body—a bit of trickery that creates a melding of the dead and the living—to persuade Lincoln to try to convince his son to let go. This refusal to let go on both sides—the living of their dead, and the dead of their lives—ignites the book's central plotline.

By rendering a vividly evoked netherworld in which the not-yet fully dead and the half-dead living can interact and voice their metaphysical concerns, Saunders has created a philosophical staging ground for humanity's various hopes and fears. This is particularly evident in one memorable scene where two spirits, Professor Edmund Bloomer and Lawrence T. DeCroix, appear and are given voice. Readers are told that these spirits are literally "conjoined at the hip from their many years of mutual flattery," and indeed they do go to ridiculous lengths to flatter each other, DeCroix vouching for Bloomer's unpublished scientific studies and Bloomer testifying to the excellence of the other's pickle business. However, while there is an element of comedy to these scenes, they ultimately serve as a poignant reminder of the inability to leave a lasting impact on the world and the sadness that comes from understanding that many go unremembered. "Strange, isn't it?" ponders DeCroix, "to have dedicated one's life to a certain venture, neglecting other aspects of one's life, only to have that venture, in the end, amount to nothing at all, the products of one's labor utterly forgotten?"

Of course, this sense of historical oblivion does not apply to Lincoln, who, in many ways, is the book's central character. His deep grief over his son's death mingles with his apprehension over the Civil War, which, at the time of the narrative, is not going well. Lincoln's meditations form the spiritual heart of the book and the way in which his reflections on personal death meld with that of the vast national slaughter going on around him is skillfully handled throughout. "Did the thing merit it," Lincoln ponders about the Civil War, after visiting his son's body for the last time, "merit the killing. On the surface, it was a technicality (mere Union) but seen deeper, it was something more. How should men live? How could men live?" Just as Lincoln struggles to find meaning in his son's death (or accept its meaninglessness), so he has to justify in his mind the death that he is causing by his decision to pursue the Civil War.

That this death is about more than just the concept of the Union is something that both Lincoln and Saunders understand. In one of the more startling passages, Saunders details the horrors that a young slave girl has suffered. Because she has been rendered mute by her repeated rapes, the woman who looks after her (also a slave), narrates what has happened to her and the visceral horrors of slavery are presented to readers in such a way that they understand the necessity of pursuing the Civil War. Thus, when Lincoln struggles over the need to fight that war, readers are firmly in his corner, even as they understand the difficulty of his situation. Because men must be killed, a whole country is confronted with the imminence of death and Saunders expertly uses this confrontation to ask the reader to consider all its implications as well. While he draws on a highly fanciful scenario, with its very specific conception of a post-death limbo to push forth his inquiry, the questions he raises and ponders are those that affect all human beings regardless of what they expect to find on the other side of death.

Andrew Schenker

Review Sources

Crain, Caleb. "The Sentimental Sadist." Review of *Lincoln in the Bardo*, by George Saunders. *The Atlantic*, Mar. 2017, www.theatlantic.com/magazine/archive/2017/03/the-sentimental-sadist/513824/. Accessed 31 July 2017.

Kakutani, Michiko. "Review: *Lincoln in the Bardo* Shows a President Haunted by Grief." Review of *Lincoln in the Bardo*, by George Saunders. *The New York Times*, 6 Feb. 2017, www.nytimes.com/2017/02/06/books/review-george-saunders-lincoln-in-the-bardo.html. Accessed 31 July 2017.

Kunzru, Hari. "*Lincoln in the Bardo* by George Saunders Review—Extraordinary Story of the Afterlife." Review of *Lincoln in the Bardo*, by George Saunders. *The Guardian*, 8 Mar. 2017, www.theguardian.com/books/2017/mar/08/lincoln-in-the-bardo-george-saunders-review. Accessed 31 July 2017.

Mallon, Thomas. "George Saunders Gets Inside Lincoln's Head." Review of *Lincoln in the Bardo*, by George Saunders. *The New Yorker*, June 2017, www.newyorker.com/magazine/2017/02/13/george-saunders-gets-inside-lincolns-head. Accessed 31 July 2017.

Sheehan, Jason. "Letting Go Is the Hardest Thing for *Lincoln in the Bardo*." Review of *Lincoln in the Bardo*, by George Saunders. *NPR*, 18 Feb. 2017. www.npr.org/2017/02/18/514376361/letting-go-is-the-hardest-thing-for-lincoln-in-the-bardo. Accessed 31 July 2017.

Little Deaths

Author: Emma Flint
Publisher: Hachette Books (New York). 320 pp.
Type of work: Novel
Time: 1965–70
Locale: Queens, New York City, New York

In July 1965, Ruth Malone, separated from her husband, becomes the prime suspect in the murder of her two children, largely because she is young, attractive, and does not behave according to society's expectations of a mother. Pete Wonicke, a reporter fascinated by both the enigmatic Ruth and the case, works tirelessly to learn the truth, but the intrigue and obstacles mount.

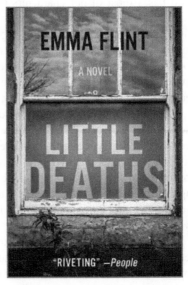

Courtesy of Hachette

Principal characters

RUTH MALONE, single mother accused of murdering her children; based on real-life murder suspect Alice Crimmins

PETE WONICKE, rookie reporter who becomes obsessed with Ruth and the case against her

FRANK MALONE, Ruth's estranged husband, father of Frankie and Cindy Malone

CHARLIE DEVLIN, lead detective in Ruth's case who is convinced of her guilt

GINA EISSEN, Ruth's neighbor and only friend

Emma Flint's debut novel, *Little Deaths*, is not a typical crime novel with stock characters and predictable plotlines, where the only real questions are "who did it?" and "why?" Flint delves deeply into the psyche of protagonist Ruth Malone, who has been accused of murdering her children, with special attention paid to the stereotypes and misogyny surrounding women in the 1960s. Ruth is inundated with scandal and criticism because she does not behave as young wives and mothers are expected to behave, and Flint deftly portrays Ruth as complex and enigmatic, as someone who hides her emotions because of her fear of judgment. While Flint portrays some minor roles more stereotypically, she takes great care to develop main characters Ruth and reporter Pete Wonicke with distinctive details and depth. This depth of character, the commentary on the consequences of rigid expectations placed on women, and Flint's ability to build tension to the very end, make *Little Deaths* a thought-provoking and satisfying crime novel.

In the acknowledgements section of the novel, Flint credits real-life figure Alice Crimmins (b. 1939) as the inspiration for Ruth Malone. During the summer of 1965, Crimmins was accused of and put on trial for murdering her two young children in their Kew Gardens Hills neighborhood in the New York City borough of Queens. Flint bases most of her characters on real-life counterparts in Crimmins's life, but she fictionalizes the story and creates her own ending. In the real case, Crimmins was tried, convicted, and released on appeal, and then retried and reconvicted, spending much of the late 1960s and 1970s in a courtroom or jail before her eventual parole in 1977. Crimmins served less than three years, total, in prison but was continuously embroiled in legal battles, since her convictions were based on circumstantial evidence that stretched the bounds of credulity.

The Crimmins case remains unsolved, but in Flint's version, the true culprit is identified at the very end. Crimmins received an overwhelming amount of negative press during the search for her children and the trials, and through Ruth Malone, Flint explores a mother and wife who is atypical, choosing not to grieve publicly and to continue working as a cocktail waitress, dressing provocatively, drinking, and engaging in sexual encounters with men. Ruth Malone, like Alice Crimmins, is convicted in the court of public opinion based on her personality and personal choices rather than evidence she committed the crime.

In her portrayal of Ruth, Flint juxtaposes a woman's outward appearances and actions against her inner thoughts and demons. To the police who question her, Ruth appears cool and emotionless, caring more about perfect makeup and a flattering outfit than her missing children. Using a third person omniscient narrator, Flint reveals Ruth's complexities. When Ruth is waiting for the police to arrive after reporting her children missing, for example, she chooses to change into more attractive clothes because "she knew that there would be men, strangers, looking at her, asking questions. Their eyes all over her like hands. She had to be ready for them. She had to look right." Despite her obvious sex appeal and ability to control men sexually, Ruth is insecure, and she uses makeup and clothes to mask that insecurity and present a flawless image. She also believes that by presenting this flawless image, she will be taken more seriously. Ruth is not so much calculating as wanting to meet expectations, expectations she could never meet for her mother, who is cold and rigid in her definitions of right and wrong.

At the same time, however, the reader sees that Ruth is inwardly inconsolable. In the immediate aftermath of the children's disappearance, she clutches her daughter's favorite rabbit doll and worries about her fate, even commenting to the police that her daughter must be missing the toy. Despite such statements showing her vulnerabilities, the police see a woman who is quiet and calm rather than tearful or hysterical, which are the expressions of motherly grief they know and understand. The police see the apparently emotionless Ruth's coiffed hair, carefully applied eyeliner, and tight-fitting clothes and they assume she is guilty from the start. On one hand, Ruth has enough confidence in herself not to change who she is, not to give the police and the public the expected histrionics of a grieving mother; she has her pride. On the other hand, she drinks and is promiscuous to escape the overwhelming pain at the loss of her children, a pain she chooses to suffer alone, a pain only reporter Pete Wonicke makes an effort to find. In her portrayal of Ruth, Flint creates a complicated and sometimes maddening woman who does not realize she is making her life harder and putting her freedom in

jeopardy because she refuses to play the part people expect rather than be who she is.
Many of Flint's secondary characters fit archetypes, such as lead detective Charlie
Devlin, who targets Ruth from the start and invents evidence and witnesses to ensure
her conviction, and Ruth's sometime boyfriend Lou Gallagher, a gangster who pays
for Ruth's lawyer and hires thugs to do his dirty work. However, Pete Wonicke, the
other central character, is another multifaceted personality with real depth. For the
most part, Flint alternates the third person omniscient point of view between Ruth and
Pete, and the back-and-forth shift in perspec-
tive both drives the plot forward and offers   Little Deaths *is Emma Flint's debut novel*
a more sympathetic perspective on Ruth. In   *and was long-listed for the Crime Writ-*
the beginning, Pete is simply eager for an in-   *ers Association Gold Dagger Award, the*
teresting story and to get the story first by   *Baileys Women's Prize for Fiction, and*
outmaneuvering his news colleagues. As the   *the Desmond Elliot Prize.*
novel progresses and Pete hunts down Ruth's
old boyfriends, jobs, and friends, his intrigue and desire for her grows; ultimately, he
falls in love with Ruth and wants to help prove her innocence. Ruth becomes an obsession for Pete, to the point that he is more interested in proving Ruth's innocence than
doing his job. He further isolates himself from family and colleagues, and by the time
he realizes he has lost perspective, he is fired from his job, which simply allows him
more time to work on Ruth's case. He even takes a part-time job in a bookstore and
lives off his savings to help Ruth. At the end of the novel, years later, Ruth is still first
and foremost in his mind. Flint presents a complex portrait of a man who loses touch
with reality yet remains steadfast in his devotion to his morals and the truth.

In addition to the penetrating characterizations, the key element that elevates the
novel into a literary work rather than a quick mystery read is the book's social commentary, which takes a feminist slant. Ruth is young and beautiful, but she is also
unapologetic for living an unconventional lifestyle. She is living separately from her
husband and is in the midst of a divorce by her own choice. She works as a cocktail
waitress and takes numerous lovers, including married men, exerting as much power
and autonomy as she can in an unaccepting society. These themes are introduced naturally and realistically, without preaching; Ruth is portrayed as a victim but also as a
flawed and complex human being. Her marriage to Frank was partly to escape her
small town and live life on her own terms and partly because she thought Frank was
kind and dependable, but she became bored with that dependability and sought more
excitement. Her questionable choices, such as cheating, are not justified, but Flint
provides understandable circumstances, both personal and cultural, that can be seen as
trapping Ruth in her position.

Flint is also successful in rendering the 1960s setting, which only emphasizes the
feminist critique of a society quick to judge an independent and sexually active young
woman. As in the real-life Crimmins case, the public is almost immediately convinced
of Ruth's guilt not because there is any real evidence to prove it, but because they
disapprove of her lifestyle and choices. The brutal court of public opinion is egged
on by the press, eager to print all the lurid details as the case progresses. The lack of
hard evidence at the crime scenes in the era before DNA testing results in a trial that

focuses on Ruth's character, including such irrelevant details as the police finding her home dusty and untidy when they searched it. Flint layers detail upon detail, building sympathy not only for women who choose not to conform but also for single working mothers who struggle against the system. With its real-life inspiration, Ruth's public vilification for not meeting the stereotypes of mothers and wives paints a vivid portrait of the obstacles women faced in the 1960s, while providing additional insight by revealing Ruth's inner mindset; Crimmins's can only be guessed at.

Critics praised *Little Deaths* upon its release, making particular note of its strong central characterizations and astute social commentary. While some critics suggested that many of the secondary characters come too close to stock stereotypes, most believed Ruth is so well drawn that her portrayal alone makes the novel worth reading. Other reviewers offered mild criticism about lack of momentum in the middle of the book. As the police build their case and construct evidence to convict a woman they are certain is guilty, the middle of the novel does become a bit monotonous. However, both the beginning of the novel, especially the search for the children, and the trial at the end are riveting. The resolution, while it may prove a stretch in believability for some, is fascinating and not wholly predictable, and Flint succeeds in saving major revelations for the very end. Even with some quibbles in plot and characterization, most critics agreed that the novel is a noteworthy entry into the crowded field of crime fiction.

There are several other literary, film, and theatrical adaptations of the Crimmins case, most notably including Mary Higgins Clark's *Where Are the Children?* (1975), which launched her novel-writing career and became a best seller. These adaptations had varying degrees of critical and financial success, but none of them focused on the complexity of the protagonist or the societal factors widely seen as resulting in conviction of the accused mother, making Flint's fictionalization of the story compelling, provocative, and worthy of more discussion.

Marybeth Rua-Larsen

Review Sources

Corrigan, Maureen. "Still Unsolved, a Child-Murder Case Inspires a Gripping New Novel." Review of *Little Deaths*, by Emma Flint. *The Washington Post*, 15 Jan. 2017, www.washingtonpost.com/entertainment/books/still-unsolved-a-child-murder-case-inspires-a-gripping-new-novel/2017/01/15/ac841886-d775-11e6-9a36-1d296534b31e_story.html. Accessed 3 Oct. 2017.

Flood, Alison. "*Little Deaths* by Emma Flint Review—Murderer or Good-Time Girl?" Review of *Little Deaths*, by Emma Flint. *The Guardian*, 19 Dec. 2016, www.theguardian.com/books/2016/dec/19/little-deaths-emma-flint-review-alice-crimmins. Accessed 3 Oct. 2017.

LaRosa, Paul. Review of *Little Deaths*, by Emma Flint. *New York Journal of Books*, 16 Jan. 2017, www.nyjournalofbooks.com/book-review/little-deaths-novel. Accessed 3 Oct. 2017.

Orford, Margie. "*Little Deaths* by Emma Flint Review—the Presumed Guilt of a Flawed Woman." Review of *Little Deaths*, by Emma Flint. *The Guardian*, 7 Dec. 2016, www.theguardian.com/books/2016/dec/27/little-deaths-emma-flint-review. Accessed 3 Oct. 2017.

Vancheri, Barbara. "Emma Flint's Novel Fictionalizes Notorious Queens Murders." Review of *Little Deaths*, by Emma Flint. *Newsday*, 14 Feb. 2017, www.newsday.com/entertainment/books/little-deaths-emma-flint-s-novel-fictionalizes-a-notorious-1965-queens-murder-case-1.13105589. Accessed 3 Oct. 2017.

Little Fires Everywhere

Author: Celeste Ng (b. 1980)
Publisher: Penguin Press (New York). 352 pp.
Type of work: Novel
Time: Late 1990s
Locale: Shaker Heights, Ohio

Little Fires Everywhere, Celeste Ng's second novel, tells the interconnected stories of the Richardson family, living a privileged life in a comfortable suburb, and Mia and Pearl Warren, a single artist and her daughter whose arrival triggers conflicts within the family and the larger community.

Courtesy of Penguin Press

Principal characters

ELENA RICHARDSON, a Shaker Heights native and reporter for the local paper whose life revolves around her husband, Bill, her four children, and her home
TRIP RICHARDSON, her firstborn son
LEXIE RICHARDSON, her oldest daughter
MOODY RICHARDSON, her second son
IZZY RICHARDSON, her youngest child
MIA WARREN, an artist and single mother who leads a nomadic life
PEARL WARREN, Mia's teenage daughter
MARK MCCULLOUGH, a Shaker Heights resident who, along with his wife, wants to adopt an abandoned Chinese baby
LINDA MCCULLOUGH, Mark's wife and an old friend of Elena
BEBE CHOW, a young, single waitress who abandons her baby at a firehouse but later tries to regain custody

Celeste Ng's *Little Fires Everywhere* begins with the house fire of the title—a fire that has clearly been set, with multiple points of origin—and traces its way back through a chain of events that triggered not only the fire, but other conflicts and controversy in Shaker Heights, a "model" suburb near Cleveland, Ohio. A buzz of publicity accompanied this best-selling sophomore effort by a critically admired writer whose first book, *Everything I Never Told You*, was Amazon's best book of the year in 2014. With a 1990s setting and a headline-worthy subplot involving interracial adoption, *Little Fires Everywhere* takes on still-current issues of race, class, and conformity. Ng tells a complex tale through multiple points of view, making each character sympathetic even when their aims run counter to each other. She provides a rich and detailed portrait of a quiet suburb (made all the more authentic by the fact that Ng grew up in

Shaker Heights herself) and the tensions beneath its perfect surface without resorting to caricature. *Kirkus Reviews* called it an "incandescent portrait of suburbia and family, creativity, and consumerism."

The story begins with the Richardson family house in flames; matriarch Elena Richardson watches from the lawn in her bathrobe as the older children arrive from sleepovers and basketball practice and the youngest is conspicuously absent. All the Richardson children are sure that their "mental," typically wilder sister Izzy set the fire, though none of them can think of any real motive for such an act. Quietly noted by the narrator—and by Elena and younger son Moody—is the departure, earlier that morning, of their tenant, Mia Warren, and her daughter, Pearl. Mother and daughter drive off with no goodbyes, leaving the keys in the mailbox. The two events have no obvious connection, but attentive readers will understand that the stage has been set.

Initially, *Little Fires Everywhere* seems to be the story of a young woman from an unconventional, bohemian background who is seduced by the suburban, middle-class comforts of the Richardsons and their *Brady Bunch*–like perfection. When Pearl, age fifteen, and her mother move into a rental house owned by Elena, they become more than tenants. Pearl has always had trouble making friends, yet she falls in with the Richardsons and soon becomes a part of their lives. She envies their easy confidence, the security that comes from knowing all their needs will be met. Pearl, who has never lived anywhere long enough to put down roots, is fascinated by the overstuffed sofas, heavy chairs, and curio cabinet stuffed with souvenirs of family vacations, as if the furniture alone is enough reason for the family to stay put. Mia and Pearl move often, travel light, and leave unnecessary items behind.

Even as Pearl is drawn into the safe and comfortable Richardson fold, the Richardsons are intrigued by their tenants' unconventional lives. Lexie decides Pearl is a candidate for a fashion makeover. Moody, infatuated, forms a deep bond of friendship with her. Even Trip, a popular athlete with no shortage of girls who like him, finds something irresistible in Pearl's difference from other girls her age. Izzy, the youngest and most unsettled Richardson child, bonds not with Pearl but with her mother, Mia. Mia becomes almost a surrogate mother to Izzy—an adult woman with a spark of youthful rebellion, a grown-up who proves that there are ways to be in the world without a nine-to-five job, a house in the suburbs, 2.5 children, and a three-car garage. Izzy reminds Mia of her younger self: fierce, single-minded, and subversive.

As for Elena, she is both fascinated and vaguely threatened by Mia's precarious artistic life, her freedom to live without rules and a safety net. After some not-so-subtle questioning about whether Mia is able to live by selling her photographs, she learns that Mia works at the takeout counter of a local restaurant, the Lucky Palace, to cover expenses. In what seems a magnanimous gesture, she insists upon hiring Mia to do housekeeping work at the Richardsons' three times a week for three hundred dollars a month. Ng captures the subtle nuances of the women's arrangement: Elena feels charitable by "helping out" an artist, so she has the financial stability to spend more time on her art, but at the same time, she can keep Mia close, like a "dangerous beast" that bears watching. Mia, meanwhile, is uncomfortable with the arrangement, but as the Richardsons' tenant, she is in a delicate position. Mia's primary reason for agreeing to

Courtesy of Kevin Day Photography

Celeste Ng, who received a Pushcart Prize in 2011, authored the best-selling novels Everything I Never Told You *(2014) and* Little Fires Everywhere *(2017).*

clean for the Richardsons is motherly protectiveness; since Pearl has taken to spending all her time there, Mia will now be in a position to watch over her daughter.

From the point of view of a Shaker Heights native like Elena, it might seem as though Mia is an outsider who comes to stir up trouble in what was a peaceful town, but that was never her intent. After a health scare with Pearl, Mia wanted to give her daughter a more stable, permanent life. Mia is drawn into conflict simply because she befriends Bebe Chow, a waitress at the Lucky Palace, and listened to Bebe's story of how, as a desperately poor new mother, she left her infant at a fire station and now has no idea where her child is. When Mia, working at the Richardson house, hears Lexie talking about their neighbors' newly adopted Asian baby, she puts the facts together and informs Bebe, then supports her in her fight to regain custody, urging her to make her story public. Like the *Jerry Springer Show*, which the Richardson children and Pearl watch with a fascinated mix of laughter and horror, the custody battle that pits the poor, immigrant single mother against the white, upper-middle-class couple has all the elements of a tabloid sensation. A prominent Asian attorney volunteers to represent Bebe, while the team representing the adoptive family, the McCulloughs, includes Elena's husband, Bill.

While interracial adoption has been and remains highly controversial, in *Little Fires Everywhere*, it is not the central conflict. Instead, the custody battle serves as a catalyst for the larger community, for the Richardson family, and for Mia in particular. When Mia learns that her coworker abandoned her baby during a time of postnatal exhaustion and extreme poverty, she immediately and instinctively supports Bebe's desire to get her daughter back; the thought of a mother being separated from her child is unbearable to her. Mia's strong emotion, readers learn, is born from her own experience and ties in to a secret about Pearl's birth that Mia has hidden from everyone, even Pearl. In a series of flashbacks, readers learn about Mia's childhood and adolescence, her artistic drive, and the defining incident that led to her nomadic life as a single parent.

Little Fires Everywhere uses an omniscient narrator to provide a wide-lens vision of events, beginning with a panoramic view but then zooming in to focus closely on one character at a time. In an interview, Ng told the *Guardian* that she chose the omniscient voice because, in a novel about privilege, it felt appropriate to give everyone a chance to tell their story. The original hardcover dust jacket of *Little Fires Everywhere* shows a neighborhood seen from the air, houses so small they look like Monopoly houses.

This bird's-eye view exemplifies the effective style of Ng's novel, which is marked by an authorial viewpoint wide enough to encompass a whole community yet also able to focus deeply on individual characters and relationships. The most important relationships in *Little Fires Everywhere* are those of mothers and daughters, whether chosen (as Izzy marks Mia as the mother she should have had) or natural.

Although critics largely praised Ng's sophomore effort overall, a few reviewers thought *Little Fires Everywhere* could have done more to push against stereotyping and to give all the characters complex, richly developed personalities. Nicole Lee, reviewing the novel for the *Washington Post*, for example, argued that Ng's choice to make white characters the central figures of the plot only serves to reinforce marginalization of Asians. Most reviews of the novel, however, acknowledged Ng's deft prose and even-handed treatment of controversial topics. Sarah Crown, writing for the *Guardian*, lauded the subtle handling of political issues in *Little Fires Everywhere*, giving as an example a scene in which Lexie naively states, "I mean, we're lucky. No one sees race here." In her review for the *New York Times*, Eleanor Henderson applauded Ng's ambitious style and scope, her "powerful and persuasive" narrative voice, and her skilled handling of multiple points of view. *Kirkus Reviews* chose the novel for its list of best books in 2017, calling Ng a "sensitive, insightful writer with a striking ability to illuminate life in America."

Kathryn Kulpa

Review Sources

Crown, Sarah. "*Little Fires Everywhere* by Celeste Ng—Hidden Passions." Review of *Little Fires Everywhere*, by Celeste Ng. *The Guardian*, 18 Nov. 2017, www. theguardian.com/books/2017/nov/18/little-fires-everywhere-celeste-ng-review. Accessed 17 Jan. 2018.

Henderson, Eleanor. "In a Quiet Ohio Town, Who Started the Fire, and Why?" Review of *Little Fires Everywhere*, by Celeste Ng. *The New York Times*, 25 Sept. 2017, www.nytimes.com/2017/09/25/books/review/little-fires-everywhere-ce-leste-ng.html. Accessed 17 Jan. 2018.

Lee, Nicole. "Celeste Ng Grapples with Both Sides of the Debate over Interracial Adoptions." Review of *Little Fires Everywhere*, by Celeste Ng. *The Washington Post*, 18 Sept. 2017, www.washingtonpost.com/entertainment/books/celeste-ng-grapples-with-both-sides-of-the-debate-over-interracial-adoptions/2017/09/18/58 57bdc4-9a36-11e7-b569-3360011663b4_story.html. Accessed 17 Jan. 2018.

Review of *Little Fires Everywhere*, by Celeste Ng. *Kirkus*, 20 June 2017, www. kirkusreviews.com/book-reviews/celeste-ng/little-fires-everywhere. Accessed 17 Jan. 2018.

Review of *Little Fires Everywhere*, by Celeste Ng. *Publishers Weekly*, 17 July 2017, www.publishersweekly.com/978-0-7352-2429-2. Accessed 17 Jan. 2018.

Locking Up Our Own
Crime and Punishment in Black America

Author: James Forman Jr. (b. 1967)
Publisher: Farrar, Straus and Giroux (New York). 320 pp.
Type of work: Literary history
Time: Predominantly 1970s–present day
Locale: Washington, DC

Written by Yale Law School professor James Forman Jr., Locking Up Our Own: Crime and Punishment in Black America *explores how black civic leaders unwittingly contributed to the mass incarceration of black people.*

Principal personages
JAMES FORMAN JR., the author, a former public defender and an educator
MARION BARRY, the mayor of Washington, DC, from 1979 to 1991 and from 1995 to 1999
ERIC HOLDER, US attorney for the District of Columbia, later attorney general under President Barack Obama

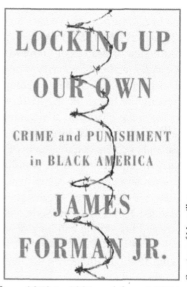

Courtesy of Macmillan

James Forman Jr.'s book *Locking Up Our Own: Crime and Punishment in Black America* explores the roots of America's mass incarceration crisis. Early on, Forman points to the widely cited figure that as of 1995, America accounted for just 5 percent of the world's population yet held about 25 percent of the world's prisoners. By 2016, the US incarcerated more than 2.2 million of its citizens. The vast majority of these incarcerated people are black people and people of color. It was not always this way. In his book, Forman asks: how did America get here? It is a complicated question, rooted in the country's history of racial oppression, but in his debut book, Forman uses the lens of the majority-black city where he lived in the 1990s, Washington, DC, to explore how well-intentioned black civic leaders and politicians unwittingly contributed to the current plight. As Jennifer Senior, who reviewed the book for the *New York Times*, pointed out, this is "exceptionally delicate," but Forman treats his subject with care, using his experiences as a public defender and an educator for at-risk youth to make his case. He argues that mass incarceration came about by increments—"the result of a series of small decisions, made over time, by a disparate group of actors," he writes. He identifies individual moments—the War on Drugs and a rise in violent crime in the 1970s and 1980s, among them—and seeks, with compassion and the historical context of pervading ideas about justice and equality, to understand why black leaders often advocated harshly punitive responses.

Forman is the son of the late James Forman Sr., known for being the executive director of the Students Nonviolent Coordinating Committee (SNCC) during the 1960s civil rights movement, and Constancia Romilly, the daughter of British journalist Jessica Mitford and herself the SNCC chapter coordinator for Atlanta. Forman earned his law degree from Yale and, in the early 1990s, clerked for Supreme Court justice Sandra Day O'Connor. As he relates in the book, he told O'Connor that in his larger career, he wanted to confront racial injustice. She suggested he take a job with the Department of Justice or the National Association for the Advancement of Colored People Legal Defense Fund. She was surprised when he told her that he wanted to be a public defender, working with poor people charged with crimes in Washington, DC. As Forman saw it, the criminal justice system was the "unfinished work of the civil rights movement" in which his parents had fought so forcefully. His work as a public defender reinforced this view, as did his later work at the Maya Angelou Public Charter School, an alternative school that he cofounded for DC students who were in the juvenile justice system or had dropped out of other schools.

Forman's book presents a historical analysis peppered with stories from his own experience. In one such story, a woman named Sandra Dozier asks Forman to help her get her job back. She lost a good job with FedEx, she tells him, because several years before, a police officer searched her car at a traffic stop and found a small amount of marijuana. Dozier was briefly arrested, but no charges were filed against her. Still, the mark on her otherwise clean record had cost her the job, and to Forman's chagrin, there was nothing he could do about it. Forman uses the story to introduce his chapter on stop-and-search, a practice in which police officers pull drivers over for minor infractions—such as a broken tail light or, in Dozier's case, suspicion that her windows were tinted too dark—only to ask to search the car for more serious violations. Dozier, like most people, Forman writes, agreed to the search, if only because she did not realize she could refuse. Did police officers always operate in this way? The practice, Forman writes, began with the intention of getting guns off the street. In 1995, violent crime was a serious problem in Washington, DC, and Eric Holder, then the US attorney for the District of Columbia, was prepared to combat it with all the resources at his disposal. In the long term, he argued, the city would have to address the "social conditions that breed crime"—namely, poverty and a lack of social services. But in the short term, Holder had a more drastic idea, which he called Operation Ceasefire.

The mission of Operation Ceasefire was straightforward: "Stop cars, search cars, seize guns." Holder's idea was inspired by a similar program aimed at pedestrians in New York later known as stop-and-frisk. Holder realized, he said at the time, that his plan would result in the targeting of young black men—in fact, Operation Ceasefire applied to only a few neighborhoods, all of them poor and black, effectively giving white drivers a "free pass" to possess drugs and guns in their cars with impunity—but he felt, again at the time, that this was a small price to pay for what he saw as an issue of life and death. In a speech lobbying for Operation Ceasefire, Holder invoked the legacy of Dr. Martin Luther King Jr. "Did Martin Luther King successfully fight the likes of Bull Connor so that we could ultimately lose the struggle for civil rights to misguided or malicious members of our own race?" It is remarkable, in a world where civil rights

James Forman Jr. is a former public defender and charter school cofounder. He has taught at Georgetown Law and Yale Law School, with a focus on race, class, and criminal justice. His first book, Locking Up Our Own, *was long-listed for the National Book Award for nonfiction.*

activists work tirelessly to end the practice of racial profiling, that Holder—who would, as US attorney general under President Obama, lead the charge against racial profiling in Arizona—supported a program like Operation Ceasefire. But Holder was not alone. The story of Operation Ceasefire is emblematic of the other stories in Forman's book. "When an urgent problem required a short-term solution," Forman argues, "law enforcement was regarded as the only answer."

In this regard, *Locking Up Our Own* explores an important paradox. According to Forman, the black community has historically suffered both "over- *and* under-policing [emphasis his]." Middle-class and wealthy black residents in DC in the 1980s were outraged when drug dealers set up open-air markets in their neighborhoods. Such brazen illegal activity would never be tolerated in a white neighborhood, they argued. Did they not deserve the same protection from harm? Poor black neighborhoods, on the other hand, were thus subjected to policies like Operation Ceasefire. But did everyone who lived in those neighborhoods deserve to be treated like a criminal? As Paul Butler, who reviewed the book for the *Atlantic*, wrote, "Black people have long been vigilant, often to no avail, about two kinds of equality enshrined in our nation's ideals: equal protection of the law, and equal justice under the law." Class is an important part of this equation. The wealthy policymakers in DC tended to air on the side of the former over the latter. Butler, a former prosecutor, praised Forman for avoiding the "'gotcha' spirit" that pollutes similar critiques. His book is not an indictment of black leaders, but a historical document that illustrates how punitive solutions, or at least punitive solutions alone, can tear communities apart.

There was some understanding of this at the time. Forman cites enthusiasm among some DC policymakers for the idea of a "Marshall Plan for urban America," a reference to an all-encompassing effort to rebuild cities in Europe after World War II. These policymakers recognized an urgent need to address the same social conditions that Holder had identified as a root cause of crime. But too often these projects, efforts to address poverty, unemployment, and housing for poor people, fell by the wayside in favor of quick fixes that always seemed to involve more police, more prison, and for those targeted, more violence. Even today, projects that seek to keep people out of the criminal justice system are woefully inadequate in terms of scope. Forman identifies a troubling national attitude when he ruefully observes, while trying to enroll a teenage client in a carpentry program as an alternative to prison, "there were never waiting lists for prison—just for alternatives to prison." Forman concludes with a chapter about the political misdirection of focusing decarceration efforts on nonviolent drug offenders. He makes a powerful plea to Americans to rethink crime, punishment, and rehabilitation: "What if we strove for compassion, for mercy, for forgiveness? And what if we did this for everybody, including people who have harmed others?"

Locking Up Our Own has received well-deserved critical acclaim. It earned starred reviews from *Kirkus Reviews* and *Publishers Weekly*, and was named among the *New*

York Times' top ten books of 2017 and among its top five for nonfiction. The National Book Foundation also long-listed it for the 2017 National Book Award for nonfiction. Those interested in issues of social justice, and US race and class relations in particular, will likewise find Forman's approach innovative and insightful.

Molly Hagan

Review Sources

Butler, Paul. "When Black America Was Pro-Police." Review of *Locking Up Our Own: Crime and Punishment in Black America*, by James Forman Jr. *The Atlantic*, June 2017, www.theatlantic.com/magazine/archive/2017/06/when-black-america-was-pro-police/524481. Accessed 23 Feb. 2018.

Review of *Locking Up Our Own: Crime and Punishment in Black America*, by James Forman Jr. *Kirkus Reviews*, 1 Mar. 2017, p. 21. *Literary Reference Center Plus*, search.ebscohost.com/login.aspx?direct=true&db=lkh&AN=121450760&site=lrc-plus. Accessed 23 Feb. 2018.

Review of *Locking Up Our Own: Crime and Punishment in Black America*, by James Forman Jr. *Publishers Weekly*, 9 Jan. 2017, p. 54. *Literary Reference Center Plus*, search.ebscohost.com/login.aspx?direct=true&db=lkh&AN=120625778&site=lrc-plus. Accessed 23 Feb. 2018.

Muhammad, Khalil Gibran. "Power and Punishment: Two New Books about Race and Crime." Review of *Locking Up Our Own: Crime and Punishment in Black America*, by James Forman Jr., and *A Colony in a Nation*, by Chris Hayes. *The New York Times*, 14 Apr. 2017, www.nytimes.com/2017/04/14/books/review/locking-up-our-own-james-forman-jr-colony-in-nation-chris-hayes.html. Accessed 23 Feb. 2018.

Senior, Jennifer. "*Locking Up Our Own*, What Led to Mass Incarceration of Black Men." Review of *Locking Up Our Own: Crime and Punishment in Black America*, by James Forman Jr. *The New York Times*, 11 Apr. 2017, www.nytimes.com/2017/04/11/books/review-locking-up-our-own-james-forman-jr.html. Accessed 23 Feb. 2018.

The Lonely Hearts Hotel

Author: Heather O'Neill (b. 1973)
Publisher: Riverhead Books (New York).
  400 pp.
Type of work: Novel
Time: 1914 through the 1940s
Locales: Montreal, Canada; New York, New
  York

The Lonely Hearts Hotel, *a love story set
in the seedy underworld of early-twentieth-
century Montreal, follows the lives of two
talented orphans.*

Courtesy of Riverhead Books

Principal characters
ROSE, an orphan with a talent for comedy
  and performance, Pierrot's soulmate
PIERROT, another orphan and a piano
  prodigy, Rose's soulmate
SISTER ELOÏSE, a predatory nun who abuses Pierrot
MCMAHON, an underworld boss with whom Rose becomes involved

Heather O'Neill has a unique relationship with Montreal. The Canadian author was
abandoned by her mother at a young age and subsequently spent her formative years
living with her father in an especially rough neighborhood in that Québec city. There,
she was afforded a view of Montreal that many never get to see—how the urban poor
live and the desperate actions they must take to survive. Such experiences not only
shaped O'Neill's perspective as a writer but also provided her with the gritty setting
and character types that would eventually populate her best-selling fiction. Her debut
novel, *Lullabies for Little Criminals* (2006), for example, follows a twelve-year-old
and her father as they move through the Montreal underworld. Along the way, they
encounter myriad characters whom other authors might avoid—everyone from pimps
to junkies to abused and abandoned children. O'Neill's second novel, *The Girl Who
Was Saturday Night* (2014), follows two children growing up with their folk-singing,
Québec separatist father in a dangerous neighborhood near the city's Boulevard Saint-
Laurent. Like its predecessor, it also features a colorful cast of impoverished misfits.

  The Lonely Hearts Hotel is O'Neill's third novel and a continuation of the author's
desire to portray an unseen side of Montreal. A work of historical fiction, *The Lonely
Hearts Hotel* tells the fate of two soulmates, Rose and Pierrot. Early in the novel,
O'Neill sets up the inevitability of their coupling by demonstrating just how much the
characters' lives align. Both Rose and Pierrot are the product of teenaged motherhood
and subsequently end up at the same Catholic orphanage in 1914. They meet there as
young children, and their chemistry is so powerful that the mother superior insists that

they be separated. It proves impossible to keep Rose and Pierrot apart, however. The two are unlike all the other orphans in that they are gifted; Rose is a superb comedian, Pierrot a piano prodigy. When the two spontaneously give an extraordinary performance at the orphanage's annual Christmas pageant, a rich patron in the audience insists on having them perform in her parlor. They eventually bring their act around the city together, a process that results in them strengthening their craft as well as their emotional bond. By the time they are thirteen years old, they are in love and determined to one day marry one another and start their own circus called "The Snowflake Icicle Extravaganza."

What makes *The Lonely Hearts Hotel* so unique is O'Neill's deft blend of whimsy with darkness. The novel's prose can be described as playful and knowing; there is a cheekiness to the third-person omniscient narration. This produces a decidedly buoyant tone that is maintained throughout the narrative, despite most of the events that comprise Rose and Pierrot's story lines being deeply disturbing. For example, starting at the age of eleven, Pierrot is repeatedly sexually abused by a young nun named Sister Eloïse. When she learns about Pierrot's feelings for Rose, Sister Eloïse beats the fifteen-year-old with a broom handle until she is unconscious. Although the acts of sexual abuse and violence are inherently horrifying, O'Neill describes them in the same quirky, matter-of-fact way that she does happier plot points. In addition to preventing the story from being dragged down by dreariness, this stylistic choice provides it with a fairy-tale quality. Consequently, O'Neill effectively ensures that all the horrible things that Rose and Pierrot experience feel as though they are part of a larger cosmic plan.

O'Neill's characters are exceptionally well crafted. As an author, she fights the innate pressure to make her protagonists wholly altruistic and likeable. Instead, Rose and Pierrot can be described as deeply flawed, star-crossed lovers. When Pierrot's story begins, he is a bon vivant—a happy-go-lucky kid who always smiles. His sunny personality starts to dim once he becomes the victim of Sister Eloïse, who convinces him he is nothing more than a lowly pervert. Such darkness and pain are furthered when he is sent away from the orphanage to live with a wealthy older gentleman named Irving and subsequently loses contact with Rose for many years. When Irving dies, Pierrot begins using heroin to fight off his feelings of self-loathing.

Rose arguably is an even more unusual character. Unapologetically precocious, she always acts on her impulses—even when such impulses are dangerous or unladylike. What makes Rose an especially rare hero in the landscape of contemporary fiction is the fact that from the time she is an adolescent, she respects her own sexual desires instead of feeling ashamed. It is this tendency that causes her to seduce her boss, McMahon, a gangster for whom she is working as a governess. Later, she works as a porn actor. Rose's fearlessness and self-acceptance ultimately enable her to bring her childhood dream of creating a traveling circus into fruition. She is *The Lonely Hearts Hotel*'s true standout character, so well written that her charisma practically leaps off the page.

O'Neill's decision to structure the novel across dozens of short chapters infuses the narrative with a quick pace. There are seventy-one chapters, which span the characters' lives from the time they are born until they are in their thirties. The brevity of each chapter, combined with O'Neill's willingness to leap forward in time, ensures that the story never drags. The chapters toggle back and forth between Rose and Pierrot's story lines, moving the story forward and making the two characters' fates feel deeply intertwined even when they cannot find one another. In one chapter, Pierrot steals a bedazzled apple from a shop because he is feeling bad about himself. In the next chapter, O'Neill reveals that, somewhere across the city, Rose is using an apple to seduce McMahon for the first time. The apple becomes a connective metaphor, a moment in which both characters consciously take actions that fundamentally change the way they see themselves.

Courtesy of Julia C. Vona

Heather O'Neill is a Canadian novelist, essayist, and short-story writer. Her 2006 debut novel, Lullabies for Little Criminals, *became an international best seller.* The Lonely Hearts Hotel *is her third novel.*

The Lonely Hearts Hotel rarely feels like a work of historical fiction. This is not because O'Neill fails to present 1930s Montreal believably, but rather because she chooses for it to be little more than the setting in which her characters' story takes place. Meanwhile, the characters' personalities, dreams, and decisions all feel timeless, universal. Still, the historical setting does affect the narrative's trajectory in several important ways. The conservative values of the early twentieth century, for example, amplify the guilt Pierrot feels about being a sexual assault victim. Living prior to the modern feminist movement, Rose and other women have few options for employment. The biggest role that history plays in *The Lonely Hearts Hotel* is in how the Great Depression affects the quality of life in Montreal. The orphanage overflows with children, crime rises, and drugs such as heroin become rampant. These three effects ultimately compromise Rose and Pierrot's happy ending.

Reviews of *The Lonely Hearts Hotel* have been overwhelmingly positive. Many critics have noted that with this novel, O'Neill further proves herself to be one of the most important fiction writers to come out of Canada in recent years. The acclaim that the novel has earned is largely due to its well-crafted, hypnotic prose. Jack Kirchhoff exalted the quality of O'Neill's writing in his review for the *Globe and Mail*, describing it as "matter-of-fact, street-tough, intensely alive and often wryly funny." No matter what someone's literary taste may be, after reading *The Lonely Hearts Hotel*, they will be impressed by O'Neill's literary talent. It is thanks to this talent that O'Neill can repeatedly plumb the darkest depths of humanity and keep the narrative funny and compelling enough for readers to stay engaged until the end. In her *Washington Post* review, Eugenia Zukerman praised O'Neill's gift for storytelling, describing the novel as "utterly compelling, creating a world where desperation and love coexist."

Still, not all the reviews have been without complaints. In her review for the *Guardian,* literary critic Molly McCloskey argued that many of the novel's plot points feel excessive. McCloskey wrote, "For almost 200 pages, Rose and Pierrot are separated, yearning for each other. There is some wonderful writing along the way, but the innumerable near misses and thwarted meetings pile up to the point of feeling gratuitous." At times, O'Neill's decision to keep Rose and Pierrot apart for so long does feel tired and unrealistic. That the two never stop being in love with one another while living in a compact, accessible city and do not bump into each other requires some suspension of disbelief on the reader's part. It also makes the antagonistic forces of Sister Eloïse, McMahon, and Pierrot's heroin addiction feel like heavy-handed plot devices.

In the end, however, the strengths of *The Lonely Hearts Hotel* vastly outweigh the shortcomings. With O'Neill's well-wrought prose, unpredictable storytelling, and captivating characters, the novel is often difficult to put down. It is a beautiful, original love story—one that walks the fine line of historical fiction and fairy tale in an unforgettable way.

Emily Turner

Review Sources

Kirchhoff, Jack. "Heather O'Neill's *The Lonely Hearts Hotel,* Reviewed: She's Getting Better and Better." Review of *The Lonely Hearts Hotel,* by Heather O'Neill. *The Globe and Mail,* 10 Feb. 2017, www.theglobeandmail.com/arts/books-and-media/book-reviews/heather-oneills-the-lonely-hearts-hotel-reviewed-shes-getting-better-and-better/article33979429. Accessed 5 Jan. 2018.

Review of *The Lonely Hearts Hotel,* by Heather O'Neill. *Kirkus,* 22 Nov. 2016, www.kirkusreviews.com/book-reviews/heather-oneill/the-lonely-hearts-hotel. Accessed 5 Jan. 2018.

Review of *The Lonely Hearts Hotel,* by Heather O'Neill. *Publishers Weekly,* 6 Mar. 2017, www.publishersweekly.com/978-0-7352-1373-9. Accessed 5 Jan. 2018.

McCloskey, Molly. "*The Lonely Hearts Hotel* by Heather O'Neill—Descent into a Fairytale Underworld." Review of *The Lonely Hearts Hotel,* by Heather O'Neill. *The Guardian,* 30 Mar. 2017, www.theguardian.com/books/2017/mar/30/lonely-hearts-hotel-review-by-heather-oneill-review. Accessed 5 Jan. 2018.

Zukerman, Eugenia. "A Story of Two Abandoned Orphans Who Become Dazzling Entertainers." Review of *The Lonely Hearts Hotel,* by Heather O'Neill. *The Washington Post,* 14 Feb. 2017, www.washingtonpost.com/entertainment/books/a-story-of-two-abandoned-orphans-who-become-dazzling-entertainers/2017/02/13/c0916c14-e271-11e6-a453-19ec4b3d09ba_story.html. Accessed 5 Jan. 2018.

The Long Drop

Author: Denise Mina (b. 1966)
Publisher: Little, Brown (New York). 240 pp.
Type of work: Novel
Time: 1957–58
Locale: Glasgow, Scotland

Known for her evocative mystery-suspense novels set in Glasgow, Scotland, and featuring female protagonists, author Denise Mina embarks on a fictionalized account of a true crime in her newest novel. The Long Drop *is a tense account of the murderous work of a serial killer who operated in Scotland in the late 1950s, shifting between his bizarre night spent drinking with a relative of several victims and his trial.*

Courtesy of Little, Brown Company

Principal characters

PETER MANUEL, a career criminal with a long record of housebreaking and rape who has moved on to serial murder; based on the historical figure of the same name

WILLIAM "BILL" WATT, a wealthy businessman who owns a chain of bakery shops and whose family members have been murdered; based on the historical figure of the same name

LAURENCE DOWDALL, Watt's lawyer; based on the historical figure of the same name

DANDY MCKAY, a notorious gangster; based on the historical figure of the same name

MAURICE DICKOV, mob accountant and co-owner of the Gordon Club, a popular pub; based on the historical figure of the same name

SCOUT O'NEIL, a figure on the fringe of Glasgow's underworld; based on the historical figure of the same name

ROBERT MCNEILL, a detective inspector from Glasgow who investigates the murders; based on the historical figure of the same name

WILLIAM MUNCIE, a chief inspector who has pursued Manuel for years; based on the historical figure of the same name

WILLIAM GRIEVE, Manuel's defense attorney; based on the historical figure of the same name

Denise Mina's novel *The Long Drop* illustrates the proverb that truth is stranger than fiction. Based on a true story—the skeleton of the plot was hung on facts gleaned from newspaper accounts of the time and documented court records—the novel animates the twisted character of serial killer Peter Manuel and creatively fleshes in unknown or unrecorded details in Manuel's strange relationship with William "Bill" Watt, a relative of three of the multiple victims Manuel was charged with murdering. Though Mina has had great experience writing in the crime genre, including two series that focus on detective Alex Morrow and investigative reporter Paddy Meehan, this book serves as a bit of a departure in that it is her first to revolve around a real-life crime.

The story is set in the late 1950s, beginning shortly after the first of a series of brutal murders that occurred in Glasgow, Scotland. The third-person, present-tense narration shifts back and forth between late 1957, the time of Manuel and Watt's first encounter, and mid-1958, when Manuel went on trial for his life. *The Long Drop* opens with the meeting at a restaurant between successful businessman Watt and lowlife criminal Manuel, arranged by slick defense attorney Laurence Dowdall. The reason for the meeting is soon explained. Three female members of the Watt family—Bill's wife, Marion; his sister-in-law Margaret Brown; and his seventeen-year-old daughter Vivienne—were all shot dead in their own beds several months earlier. Watt was absent from home at the time of the murders—a ninety-mile drive away on an annual fly-fishing holiday. Despite that seemingly exculpatory detail, the police examine Watt's background and movements anyway, since it is a long-established fact that many murders are committed by relatives or acquaintances of the victims. As they investigate, the police uncover several disturbing pieces of information. They learn, for example that Watt has had several extramarital affairs and is currently in a longtime relationship with a mistress, Phamie. Furthermore, the police keep encountering witnesses who swear they saw Watt on the road on the morning the murders were committed. A ferry operator claims Watt was a passenger while a motorist attests that he passed Watt parked alongside the road to Glasgow.

Because of doubts surrounding Watt's innocence, he spends some time in prison before Dowdall is able to bail him out. Freed, Watt is desperate to clear his name, and via Dowdall, offers money in exchange for information about the murders. The proposition draws forth a sketchy individual, Scout O'Neil, who claims to have sold a Webley revolver to Peter Manuel, possibly the same weapon used in the Watt family murders. Manuel himself contacts the attorney, claiming to have inside information about the murders. Manuel knows, for example, exactly how the Watt house was broken into. He also knows Vivienne was knocked out before being shot to death. Most convincingly, Manuel, who is able to draw an accurate sketch of a Webley revolver, knows the killer smoked several cigarettes, ate a sandwich, and drank gin from a bottle in the Watt house after committing the murders.

When the police do not act on the verbal information received, Watt is determined to take matters into his own hands. He asks Dowdall to contact Manuel. Watt's plan is to treat the small-time crook to a night on the town and get him drunk enough to tell him if he indeed bought the revolver in question, and if so, where to find the handgun. Watt knows he will need a witness at the crucial juncture when Manuel talks about the Webley and plans to recruit his brother, John, for the job.

After meeting, the two new acquaintances spend an epic night drinking to excess at Watt's expense at a succession of watering holes located along the grubby, grimy underbelly of Glasgow, a city whose dark presence, described in detail by Mina, adds a noir atmosphere to the proceedings. During the course of their long evening and morning together, the two men trade personal confidences and bond, in a way. Watt confesses he hopes to join the ancient Trades Hall and Merchants House, two prestigious business organizations that he has thus far been denied entry into despite the success of his thriving bakery shops. Manuel in turn admits he has written a number of stories that he hopes to have published someday. As they sop up liquor, they are approached by Shifty Thomson, a cohort of mob boss Dandy McKay, and ordered to meet McKay at the nearby Gordon Club.

First, however, they meet with Watt's brother, and the three men drive to John's house for breakfast. After eating, Manuel waits for John's wife, Nettie, to leave the room—out of sight, she eavesdrops on their conversation—then launches into a story about the Watt murders, which he claims were the result of a mistake. A burglary, intended to feature the killing of residents to convince a lone survivor to tell where loot was hidden, was planned for the house next door to Watt's. Manuel, who obtained a gun for the job, was invited to participate in the burglary, but the robbers broke into the wrong house and killed everyone inside. When the Watt brothers ask Manuel what happened to the gun he used, he claims he threw it into the River Clyde.

Afterward, Watt and Manuel resume their drinking at a strip club, where they think they will not be found by McKay's thugs. However, Shifty and Scout appear and force them into a car, which is driven to the Gordon Club, where they are taken to the office of club owner Maurice Dickov. From there, Mina creatively utilizes the fact that this book, though grounded in events that transpired in real life, is still a work of fiction to explore lingering questions about Watt's character and his possible role in the murders. In providing a reimagination of the often sensationalized murder trial of Manuel, she gives the reader further insight into his psyche and how his very nature, still not fully understood, plagued the establishment of facts in the case.

Scottish author Denise Mina has written several crime/mystery series, as well as stage and radio plays, short stories, and graphic novels. She won the John Creasy Dagger for best first crime novel for Garnethill *(1998) and earned several top honors for* The End of the Wasp Season *(2011), a Detective Inspector Alex Morrow novel.*

The Long Drop is a suspenseful and intriguing thriller, despite the fact that a reader familiar with the background of the true crime knows in advance the outcome of the story. Interest is maintained by the slow reveal of the complex personalities of the main players and through the linking of events that lead to the inevitable conclusion. Additionally, in adding her own reimagined twist to the story, Mina imbibes the events with an even greater sense of ambiguity and provokes the reader to focus on more than just the black-and-white concept of guilt or innocence. American-born Manuel, who became Scotland's worst serial killer, admitted at trial to a succession of murders, yet he pleaded not guilty. Though he knew he had to die to protect his parents' lives from mob retribution, Manuel, who dismissed his lawyer and handled his own case, mounted a spirited, if incompetent and ultimately futile, defense. He was convicted for seven murders, suspected in at least two more, and was ultimately hanged for his crimes, the third-to-last person to be executed in Scotland prior to the 1965 suspension of the death penalty in Great Britain. The title refers to the hanging technique used in his execution, a scientific method from the late nineteenth century based on the condemned individual's height and weight that determined how much rope slack was required to snap the person's neck while preventing decapitation.

Story tension is generated through the back-and-forth structure of the narration, which advances the plot on two fronts: revelations about the crime and the development of the relationship between Watt and Manuel during their long night of drinking, which are balanced against small details that come to light at the trial that sometimes confirm and at other times contradict previous evidence. The author skillfully manipulates the reader's emotions by withholding or doling out important bits of information and manages to succeed at a difficult task: making unlikable personages—murderer Manuel and even mobster McKay—seem multilayered and alternatively sympathetic for brief periods of time. Critics, who largely praised the book, also noted that even though this novel does not feature the strong female protagonists characteristic of her previous work, Mina still provides a voice for women through the presence of characters who represent the oppression women suffered in chaotic and patriarchal 1950s Glasgow.

Jack Ewing

Review Sources

Corrigan, Maureen. "Denise Mina Looks Inside the Mind of a Psychopath in Her Chilling Novel *The Long Drop*." Review of *The Long Drop*, by Denise Mina. *The Washington Post*, 24 May 2017, www.washingtonpost.com/entertainment/ books/denise-mina-looks-inside-the-mind-of-a-psychopath-in-her-chilling-novel-the-long-drop/2017/05/24/149ba558-3a75-11e7-a058-ddbb23c75d82_story.html. Accessed 19 Sept. 2017.

Harper, Glenn. "Macho-Centric: Denise Mina Takes on Classic Noir." Review of *The Long Drop*, by Denise Mina. *Los Angeles Review of Books,* 1 June 2017, lareviewofbooks.org/article/macho-centric-denise-mina-takes-on-classic-noir. Accessed 19 Sept. 2017.

Kelly, Stuart. Review of *The Long Drop*, by Denise Mina. *The Scotsman*, 8 Mar. 2017, www.scotsman.com/lifestyle/culture/books/book-review-the-long-drop-by-denise-mina-1-4386280. Accessed 19 Sept. 2017.

Review of *The Long Drop*, by Denise Mina. *Publishers Weekly*, 13 Mar. 2017, www.publishersweekly.com/978-0-316-38057-7. Accessed 19 Sept. 2017.

Ross, Peter. "*The Long Drop* by Denise Mina Review—Meet Scotland's Worst Serial Killer." Review of *The Long Drop*, by Denise Mina. *The Guardian*, 1 Mar. 2017, www.theguardian.com/books/2017/mar/01/the-long-drop-by-denise-mina-review. Accessed 19 Sept. 2017.

The Lost City of the Monkey God
A True Story

Author: Douglas Preston (b. 1956)
Publisher: Grand Central (New York). 304
pp. Illustrated.
Type of work: Archaeology, history
Time: The sixteenth century to the present
Locales: Honduras, the United States

In The Lost City of the Monkey God: A True
Story, *Douglas Preston recounts a ground-breaking archaeological expedition in search
of a lost city in the rainforests of Honduras.*

Principal personages
DOUGLAS PRESTON, the author, a prolific
   writer and journalist
STEVE ELKINS, the leader of the expedition
BRUCE HEINICKE, a Honduras-based fixer
ANDREW "WOODY" WOOD, the expedition's logistics chief
CHRIS FISHER, the expedition's lead archaeologist
DAVE YODER, a photographer for National Geographic and a member of the expedition team
JUAN ORLANDO HERNÁNDEZ, the president of Honduras at the time of the expedition

Courtesy of Grand Central Publishing

Among the many legends that have captured the imaginations of the public over the centuries, some of the most compelling have centered on lost cities—hidden relics of ancient civilizations that, if discovered, could yield both physical treasures and even more valuable clues about the history of humankind. One such city, often known as the Lost City of the Monkey God, was thought to exist somewhere in the rainforests of Honduras. The legends of the city, long known to the indigenous peoples of the region and first reported by Europeans in the sixteenth century, spread throughout Central America and beyond over the subsequent centuries, fueling intense speculation about the nature of the city and its exact location. That speculation in turn prompted efforts to locate the city and uncover its secrets, culminating in the 2015 discovery of the remains of a large settlement in the La Mosquitia region of Honduras. In *The Lost City of the Monkey God: A True Story*, Douglas Preston chronicles that expedition, an effort funded by a team of American filmmakers and carried out under the supervision of multiple archaeologists and with the cooperation of the Honduran government. Preston is a journalist who has written extensively for publications such as the *New Yorker* and *National Geographic*, both of which originally published portions of what would become *The Lost City of the Monkey God*. He had been aware of plans for a potential expedition since the mid-1990s and accompanied the expedition team on its first journey into Mosquitia. Over the course of the book, he not only recounts his experiences traveling into the rainforest and his impressions of the structures and artifacts the team found there but also details the aftermath of the visit, which offered insights into both the history of the region and its relevance to twenty-first-century society.

Early in *The Lost City of the Monkey God*, Preston provides a thorough introduction to the legendary city and, more broadly, the Mosquitia region in eastern Honduras. Preston explains that in a 1526 letter to the king of Spain, the conquistador Hernán Cortés reported that a large, wealthy, and densely populated province was located in a mountainous region of Central America, between eight and ten days on foot from his location near the town of Trujillo. That letter, Preston reports, has been widely identified by historians as the likely source for many of the legends about a large city or other settlement that was never invaded by Europeans, located deep in the jungle of what is now Honduras. The legends took on additional significance in the 1830s, when explorer John Lloyd Stephens rediscovered the ruins of a Mayan city in northwestern Honduras. The site, which featured pyramids, statues, and other structures, demonstrated the capabilities of the historical indigenous cultures of the region, and its discovery fueled speculation about the locations of similar cities. Rumors of lost cities in Mosquitia, in eastern Honduras, continued to spread, and a series of expeditions were mounted in the region. Some explorers succeeded in uncovering structures and artifacts that were not Mayan in origin, suggesting that a different culture had flourished in the area. However, the archaeological sites located during that period were not generally considered to have been the lost city of legend, which had become known as the Lost City of the Monkey God or the White City. Preston provides an intriguing historical overview of the various expeditions, which notably included one conducted by Theodore Morde and Laurence C. Brown, a journalist and geologist, respectively, who traveled to Honduras in 1940 with the stated purpose of searching for the city. Upon their return, they claimed to have located the city, although they never revealed its location. However, Preston reveals that while researching the lost city, he learned from Morde's unpublished journals that the pair in fact did not locate or even search for the city during their time in Honduras; rather, they spent their expedition attempting to mine gold.

By the 1990s, Preston explains, the legends of an ancient city within Mosquitia had made their way to Steve Elkins, a cinematographer who was fascinated by such stories. Having made one attempt to locate the city on foot, Elkins realized that searching the rainforest without an adequate knowledge of the target's location was inadequate. To narrow down his search, he both researched the many past efforts to locate the city and sought out experts in interpreting satellite imagery, who observed that structures that appeared human-made were present in the jungle. As the available satellite imagery was not able to provide particularly detailed images, Elkins eventually turned his attention to the technology known as lidar, or light detection and ranging, which can use lasers to create higher-resolution imagery of terrain from above. Lidar had been previously used to map the Maya archaeological site of Caracol. Preston, who first became aware of Elkins's search in 1996, was eventually invited to join the expedition team. He wrote that in 2012, he and other team members gathered in Honduras while a plane carrying a lidar device conducted a survey of several promising areas within Mosquitia. The resulting images revealed what appeared to be human-made structures within the target areas. The team decided to focus on an area dubbed Target One, or T1, a valley area almost completely surrounded by mountains.

In February 2015, a team assembled in Honduras and traveled to T1 by helicopter, which enabled them to avoid a long and dangerous journey through the jungle. In addition to Elkins and Preston, who was tasked with documenting the expedition for *National Geographic*, the team included lead archaeologist Chris Fisher, logistics chief and jungle survival expert Andrew "Woody" Wood, *National Geographic* photographer Dave Yoder, and several additional researchers and crewmembers responsible for documenting the project. The expedition was carried out with the support of the Honduran government under the leadership of president Juan Orlando Hernández, who hoped that any discovery would be beneficial to the country's economy and morale. In vivid and engaging prose, Preston chronicles his eight days in T1, a period that saw the discovery not only of the large human-made mounds and other structures suggested by the lidar imagery but also of an undisturbed cache of sculptures, grinding stones, and other artifacts. In addition to the archaeological finds revealed during the trip, Preston devotes significant attention to the surrounding environment and it inhabitants, which included a troop of spider monkeys that had never before seen humans, a venomous fer-de-lance snake, and many, many bugs.

Although the 2015 expedition is the focal point of much of *The Lost City of the Monkey God*, Preston devotes only five of the book's twenty-seven chapters to it. For readers particularly intrigued by Preston's discussions of the valley's environment, the team's discovery of structures and artifacts, or simply the logistical details of jungle survival, the remainder of the book, which deals largely with the events after his return from T1, may be less compelling. However, it is within that latter section that many of Preston's most significant observations lie. Following their return from the city, which the Honduran government named *La Ciudad del Jaguar* (the City of the Jaguar), Preston and several other members of the team, including Fisher and Yoder, learned that they had contracted the disease leishmaniasis. Spread by parasites and typically transmitted by sand flies, the disease is common in tropical regions and, as global temperatures increase, is beginning to become a greater threat in areas such as North America. In addition to recounting his treatment for the disease at the National Institutes of Health, Preston links that discussion to the ways in which infectious diseases devastated Central America following the arrival of European conquerors and posits that it was disease that caused the City of the Jaguar to be abandoned. His focus on infectious disease is perhaps unsurprising, as previous books such as Jared Diamond's *Guns, Germs, and Steel* and Charles Mann's *1491* have covered the devastating impact of European diseases in the so-called New World and their effects on the large civilizations of Central and South America in depth. However, Preston effectively provides crucial historical and environmental context as well as a pointed warning of the dangers presented by the spread of tropical diseases into previously unaffected regions.

Overall, *The Lost City of the Monkey God* is a fast-paced, intriguing, and vividly written account of an archaeological effort that could make significant contributions to the understanding of pre-Columbian history. Preston's narrative is full of colorful characters. Some are past explorers, such as the fraudulent Morde. Others are individuals who assisted Elkins with his mission, such as the jungle expert Wood, who memorably beheaded a large fer-de-lance during the team's first night in T1, and the fixer Bruce Heinicke, who shared stories about looting, drug smuggling, and gunfights with Preston as they waited for the lidar survey to be completed in 2012. Throughout his amply researched work, Preston provides historical context that gives readers with only a passing familiarity with ancient Central American cultures a greater understanding of the major cultures of the region. He likewise explains technology such as lidar in an accessible and easy-to-understand manner and also provides a primer on the political and economic history of Honduras, which he notes has been greatly shaped by the direct interference of the banana industry. Al-

Courtesy of Mark Adams

Douglas Preston is the author of numerous novels, many cowritten with fellow novelist Lincoln Child, as well as several works of nonfiction. His writing has been published in magazines such as Smithsonian, *the* New Yorker, *and* National Geographic.

though his work is highly informative, Preston cannot answer many of the reader's potential questions about the culture that once occupied the City of the Jaguar and the other Mosquitia settlements, as the answers have yet to be determined. However, he makes it clear that the 2015 expedition and subsequent work in the area are merely starting points for what will likely be many years of extensive—and academically fruitful—archaeological research.

Reviews of *The Lost City of the Monkey God* were largely positive, with critics highlighting Preston's engaging and entertaining chronicle of his experiences and explanations of the history and science essential to understanding it. Writing for the *New York Times*, Brendan I. Koerner described the work as "a warm and geeky paean to the revelatory power of archaeology," praising Preston for constructing a thoughtful and nuanced narrative that avoids delving into jungle-adventure clichés. Reviewers likewise appreciated the book's detailed discussions of the history of the region, the numerous early expeditions in search of the lost city, and the technological advances that made the city's ancient structures possible to detect from a distance. In a review for the *Chicago Tribune*, Carson Vaughan praised Preston's accessible tone and manner of writing about such potentially dense topics, noting that the author "dives headfirst into historical context without losing the momentum of the adventure." Although generally impressed with Preston's work, some critics identified areas to which Preston could have devoted more attention. Koerner, for instance, observed that the book reveals little about the perspectives of the residents of Honduras or their opinions about the archaeological exploration of Mosquitia. However, the majority of critics focused primarily on Preston's compelling prose and enlightening approach to the expedition, its historical context, and its personal and professional aftermath.

Joy Crelin

Review Sources

Holahan, David. "Douglas Preston's 'Lost City' Is a Real Find." Review of *The Lost City of the Monkey God*, by Douglas Preston. *USA Today*, 2 Jan. 2017, www.usatoday.com/story/life/books/2017/01/02/the-lost-city-of-the-monkey-god-douglas-preston/95890866/. Accessed 31 Oct. 2017.

Koerner, Brendan I. "A Novelist Scours the Honduran Jungle for Pre-Columbian Ruins. The Jungle Scours Him Back." Review of *The Lost City of the Monkey God*, by Douglas Preston. *The New York Times*, 18 Jan. 2017, www.nytimes.com/2017/01/18/books/review/lost-city-of-monkey-god-douglas-preston.html. Accessed 31 Oct. 2017.

Review of *The Lost City of the Monkey God*, by Douglas Preston. *Kirkus*, 20 Oct. 2016, www.kirkusreviews.com/book-reviews/douglas-preston/the-lost-city-of-the-monkey-god/. Accessed 31 Oct. 2017.

Review of *The Lost City of the Monkey God*, by Douglas Preston. *Publishers Weekly*, 16 Jan. 2017, www.publishersweekly.com/9781455540006. Accessed 31 Oct. 2017.

Vaughan, Carson. "Douglas Preston Hunts for the 'The Lost City of the Monkey God.'" Review of *The Lost City of the Monkey God*, by Douglas Preston. *Chicago Tribune*, 25 Jan. 2017, www.chicagotribune.com/lifestyles/books/sc-lost-city-of-the-monkey-god-douglas-preston-books-0124-20170123-story.html. Accessed 31 Oct. 2017.

Magpie Murders

Author: Anthony Horowitz (b. 1955)
First published: 2016, in the United Kingdom
Publisher: HarperCollins (New York). 496 pp.
Type of work: Novel
Time: 1955 and the present
Locales: Saxby-on-Avon and London, England

Anthony Horowitz's novel Magpie Murders *is a murder mystery wrapped in a murder mystery.*

Principal characters
SUSAN RYELAND, a book editor in London
ALAN CONWAY, a best-selling mystery novelist
ATTICUS PÜND, the 1950s detective who serves as the protagonist of Conway's popular murder mystery series

Anthony Horowitz's novel *Magpie Murders* is really two novels combined into one. The first, also called *Magpie Murders*, is an old-fashioned whodunit in the mold of prolific and beloved detective novelist Agatha Christie (1890–1976). It begins in bucolic Saxby-on-Avon, a fictional village in the English countryside, in 1955. A funeral is underway for local busybody Mary Blakiston, who worked as a housekeeper for Sir Magnus Pye, the village's wealthy landowner. She met her death, tragically, after tripping while vacuuming and tumbling down the stone stairs at Pye Hall. A rumor spreads that her adult son, Robert, threatened his mother the night before her death—could this accident really have been murder? Joy Sanderling, Robert's fiancée, does not think so, and in desperation, she takes the train to London to seek the services of the book's hero, an eccentric half-Greek, half-German detective and Holocaust survivor named Atticus Pünd. At first, Pünd refuses to take her case, preoccupied as he is with a terminal diagnosis of brain cancer, but a day later, when Pye himself is gruesomely murdered, Pünd, and his dim-witted secretary, James Fraser, travel to Saxby-on-Avon to investigate.

Horowitz successfully unspools this tale for approximately two hundred pages, stopping abruptly before its dramatic conclusion, before beginning his next mystery. In this tale, the protagonist is Susan Ryeland, a delightfully flawed middle-aged woman. As the editor for best-selling mystery novelist Alan Conway, Ryeland had sat down to read *Magpie Murders*, Conway's ninth volume in the Atticus Pünd series, with wine and some cigarettes; she is just as frustrated as the reader with its lack of conclusion.

Her quest to acquire the missing final chapters, however, puts her at the center of her own real-life murder mystery, one that bears striking similarities to the story in the book.

A novelist and television writer, Horowitz has a perfect pedigree to go toe-to-toe with Christie, one of the most successful mystery writers of all time. His first book, published in 1979, was a children's mystery titled *The Sinister Secret of Frederick K. Bower*. Years later, he wrote a series of enormously popular young-adult spy novels featuring a boy named Alex Rider. However, he has spent most of his career writing old-fashioned mysteries. In 1997, he began writing for a new British detective drama series titled *Midsomer Murders*, about a pair of detectives investigating murders in an English village. Filming for the twentieth season of the show, adapted from a series of novels by Caroline Graham, began in 2017. Horowitz also created another British detective series that premiered in 2002 titled *Foyle's War*, about a detective solving crimes on the coast of England during World War II. The series ended, after eight seasons, in 2015. Additionally, Horowitz has adapted a number of Christie's novels and stories for television for the series *Agatha Christie's Poirot*. He has also been commissioned by the estates of Ian Fleming and Sir Arthur Conan Doyle to write books featuring the classic characters James Bond and Sherlock Holmes; his 2011 novel featuring Holmes, titled *The House of Silk*, was an international best seller.

Magpie Murders is both an homage to and a deconstruction of Christie's work. The title, for instance, comes from a children's nursery rhyme, a favorite Christie flourish. Each line of the rhyme, about counting magpies and their connection to good or bad luck, provides a chapter heading that correlates to an important clue. And Pünd, with his unusual accent and gilded walking stick, is as peculiar and unassuming as Christie's old spinster, Miss Marple, or her Belgian dandy, Hercule Poirot. With a wink and a nod, Horowitz also uses the tropes of a classic whodunit—a cast of eccentric suspects, a smattering of red herrings, a gathering of parties for the big reveal—to great effect. In the first half of *Magpie Murders*, he introduces the readers to these concepts in action. The omniscient narrator of Conway's novel pulls back the curtains of a seemingly sleepy Saxby-on-Avon, revealing simmering resentments and possible motives for murder while leaping from the perspective of one character to another.

Blakiston had a few enemies, the reader discovers, but the pot really starts to boil after Pye is found decapitated by his own antique sword. No one in the town seemed to have liked the greedy old man. (Each one, at some point, finds time to express this to Pünd: "The fact is that half the village will have been glad to see him dead and if you're looking for suspects, well, they might as well form a line," the local doctor says upon meeting him.) While the vicar is furious that Pye had planned to raze the town's dell, Pye's twin sister, Clarissa, humiliated that her brother cut her out of the family estate so long ago, is likely seeking her revenge. At least, that is what people are saying; rumor has it, Mary Blakiston saw Clarissa steal poison from the doctor. As for Lady Pye, she has a young lover in London and a stage career to return to. Would things just be easier without her controlling and abusive husband around? Clues lead to context—Robert Blakiston's estranged father is that man in the hat lurking around the church—and a broadening of the world. When the reader first sees Saxby-on-Avon, it appears

Anthony Horowitz is the best-selling novelist of the young-adult spy series featuring Alex Rider and a screenwriter for the television mystery series Midsomer Murders *and* Foyle's War. *Additionally, he has written books featuring James Bond and Sherlock Holmes.*

idyllic, even boring. By the time Pünd comes to investigate, however, it is anything but.

Horowitz feeds his second story, featuring Susan Ryeland, through the same plot mechanisms. Susan is an editor at a middling press in London. She loves mystery stories, she concedes, because they are so much more interesting than her own life. When a real-life death occurs and is seen as a suicide, she begins to perceive discrepancies appearing and feels compelled to investigate. Those discrepancies—a suicide note is handwritten, but the envelope is typed—become clues that lead to context. By the end of this tale, Susan sees her own life, and the people in it, in a very different light. Horowitz adds additional layers here as well. Conway, Susan finds, never much liked writing the Pünd novels. An artist trapped, albeit by wild success, doing hack work, he often put people from his own life into his books to amuse himself. His hedge-fund manager neighbor John White becomes Johnny Whitehead, a small-time crook and antiques dealer in Saxby-on-Avon. His young lover, James Taylor, becomes Pünd's sidekick James Fraser. His sister, Claire, who once asked to be paid for her work on the Pünd books, becomes the vengeful twin, Clarissa Pye. He also plays with names; all the characters in *Magpie Murders* are named after birds, and some of the place names are references to Christie novels, as Susan dutifully notes. Conway loves codes as well, and Susan must work to discover any clues regarding the case that he might have left behind in his writing.

This second story is told differently than the first. Susan is the narrator, and unlike the unknowable Pünd, who only reveals what he is thinking at the tale's dramatic conclusion, she expresses her confusion and incredulity at every turn. She muses about the detective know-how she has picked up from books but similarly asks herself if such things are possible in real life. A real investigator is furious with her, telling her that this is not how real life works. Why would someone leave a trail of clues if they knew they were going to be murdered? Here Horowitz, or Susan, rather, takes a moment to appreciate why people crave murder mysteries. "We are surrounded by tensions and ambiguities, which we spend half our life trying to resolve, and we'll probably be on our own deathbed when we reach that moment when everything makes sense. Just about every whodunnit provides that pleasure. It is the reason for their existence." This aside is one of the many instances in which Horowitz, like Conway, is playing a game. In a similar vein, he also cheekily references his own *Midsomer Murders* television show a handful of times in the book.

Horowitz sets a number of expectations under the guise of describing a successful whodunit. In the book's first pages, immediately emphasizing the book's overall cryptic tone, he boldly promises—through Susan's explanation of how her involvement with Conway's story essentially upended her life—a conclusion that the reader never saw coming, and on this, almost frustratingly, he makes good. *Magpie Murders* is a well-told story about the pleasures of a story well told. The book and its author received positive reviews to this effect when it was published in the United States in 2017. "Much like his character Alan, he is both prolific and a bona fide student of the golden age of detective fiction—and his knowledge shines through in this book, which is catnip for classic mystery lovers," Sarah Begley wrote of Horowitz in her review of *Magpie Murders* for *Time* magazine. "As a Christie disciple, he is near equal to his master." His attention to detail makes the overall structure of a mystery within a mystery even more effective, with his setup of Conway's novel even including a title page, author biography, Atticus Pünd series list, and promotional blurbs to provide a sense of authenticity to draw the reader into the story further. Additionally, a reviewer for *Publishers Weekly* praised Horowitz's facility with "wicked twists," while a reviewer for *Kirkus*, who gave the book a starred review, described it as "the most fiendishly clever puzzle—make that two puzzles—of the year."

Molly Hagan

Review Sources

Begley, Sarah. "Review: Anthony Horowitz's *Magpie Murders* Is Catnip for Classic Mystery Lovers." Review of *Magpie Murders*, by Anthony Horowitz. *Time*, 15 June 2017, time.com/4819586/magpie-murders-anthony-horowitz-review. Accessed 27 Feb. 2018.

Finch, Charles. "From the Creator of *Foyle's War*, a Delightful Homage to Agatha Christie." Review of *Magpie Murders*, by Anthony Horowitz. *The Washington Post*, 2 June 2017, www.washingtonpost.com/entertainment/books/from-the-creator-of-foyles-war-a-delightful-homage-to-agatha-christie/2017/05/31/04ff40e8-30d7-11e7-9534-00e4656c22aa_story.html?utm_term=.602ccdbeb42e. Accessed 27 Feb. 2018.

Flood, Alison. "*Magpie Murders* by Anthony Horowitz Review—Fiendish Whodunnit." Review of *Magpie Murders*, by Anthony Horowitz. *The Guardian*, 10 Dec. 2017, www.theguardian.com/books/2017/dec/10/magpie-murder-anthony-horowitz-review. Accessed 27 Feb. 2018.

Review of *Magpie Murders*, by Anthony Horowitz. *Kirkus*, 7 Mar. 2017, www.kirkusreviews.com/book-reviews/anthony-horowitz/magpie-murders. Accessed 27 Feb. 2018.

Review of *Magpie Murders*, by Anthony Horowitz. *Publishers Weekly*, 6 Feb. 2017, www.publishersweekly.com/978-0-06-264522-7. Accessed 27 Feb. 2018.

A Man for All Markets
From Las Vegas to Wall Street, How I Beat the Dealer and the Market

Author: Edward O. Thorp (b. 1932)
Publisher: Random House (New York). Illustrated. 416 pp.
Type of work: Memoir
Time: 1932–2016
Locale: United States

In A Man for All Markets: From Las Vegas to Wall Street, How I Beat the Dealer and the Market, *Edward O. Thorp recounts a life of intellectual curiosity and his resulting discoveries in the arenas of gambling and investing.*

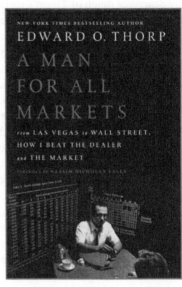

Courtesy of Random House

Principal personages
EDWARD O. THORP, the author, a mathematics professor, blackjack expert, and investor
JACK CHASSON, a high school teacher and mentor
VIVIAN SINETAR THORP, Thorp's wife
EMMANUEL KIMMEL, a financial backer for Thorp's blackjack experiments
EDDIE HAND, a financial backer for Thorp's blackjack experiments
CLAUDE SHANNON, a professor at the Massachusetts Institute of Technology and the coinventor of the first wearable computer
JAY REGAN, a stockbroker and cofounder of Convertible Hedge Associates, Thorp's first investment firm

Few individuals have pursuits as varied—and yet in some ways highly specific in nature—as Edward O. Thorp. Trained as a mathematician, he spent two decades as a professor of mathematics while simultaneously conducting research into beating two entities widely considered unbeatable: the casino dealer and the stock market. Thorp's publication of his methods for gaining an advantage at the game of blackjack made him a celebrity in gambling circles in the 1960s, while his subsequent work in the field of investing made him not only quite wealthy but also a respected expert on hedge funds and quantitative investment techniques. In his 2017 book *A Man for All Markets: From Las Vegas to Wall Street, How I Beat the Dealer and the Market*, Thorp recounts his notable breakthroughs in detail and chronicles the events of his childhood and young adulthood that shaped him as a researcher and human being. A compelling mix of memoir and financial guide, *A Man for All Markets* presents readers with a little-known life story while allowing Thorp to dispense some of the wisdom gained over his long and eventful career.

Following a brief preface and a foreword by researcher Nassim Nicholas Taleb, *A Man for All Markets* begins with a chapter titled "Loving to Learn." Indeed, that title aptly describes much of Thorp's early life, which featured a great deal of independent learning and amateur research spurred on by Thorp's highly inquisitive nature. Born during the Great Depression, Thorp spent his early years in Chicago, Illinois, before moving to Lomita, California, with his parents and younger brother. Although he did not speak until he was about three years old, Thorp began to demonstrate an affinity for mathematics shortly thereafter, learning to count to large numbers and perform mental arithmetic before ever attending school. He likewise became an avid reader and chess player at an early age. After enrolling in Narbonne High School, the graduates of which were generally not expected to go to college, Thorp flourished academically thanks in part to the mentorship of teacher Jack Chasson and also developed into an amateur scientist outside of school, conducting experiments with radios, homemade explosives, and military surplus weather balloons in his spare time. Having earned a scholarship by placing first in a Southern California physics exam, Thorp enrolled in the University of California, Berkeley, after high school, initially planning to study chemistry. He later switched his focus to physics. After a year, he transferred to the University of California, Los Angeles (UCLA), where he met his wife, Vivian. Thorp remained at the university for graduate school, earning his PhD in mathematics in 1958. After teaching at UCLA for a year, he moved to Massachusetts to take an instructor position at the Massachusetts Institute of Technology (MIT).

The remainder of the book's chapters could be divided into three sections based on their focus, the first of which deals with Thorp's research into the games of blackjack and roulette. His interest in such games, developed early in life, was at last able to be put to use following his move to MIT, where he had access to a variety of resources that proved crucial to his research. Thorp was particularly interested in determining whether it was possible for players to predict the outcomes of the games of blackjack and roulette in a casino setting and thus to gain an edge over the casino in which they are gambling. Beginning with blackjack, he assessed through mathematical means the edge held by the player or the dealer throughout the game as the cards left in the deck changed. Based on his findings, he developed card-counting strategies that he went on to test in Nevada casinos, bankrolled by wealthy businessmen Emmanuel Kimmel and Eddie Hand. He later published these strategies in works such as the 1962 book *Beat the Dealer*. He went on to collaborate with MIT professor Claude Shannon to determine whether it was possible to predict where a ball would land on a roulette wheel.

After becoming too recognizable among casino owners—he writes that his notoriety led one casino to go as far as to drug him to prevent him from winning—Thorp shifted focus to the world of investing and in 1969 founded Convertible Hedge Associates alongside stockbroker Jay Regan. The company, an early hedge fund specializing in quantitative investing practices, was later renamed Princeton Newport Partners (PNP) after its offices in Princeton, New Jersey, and Newport Beach, California. Thorp devotes several chapters to recounting the development of PNP and the techniques that made him successful as an investor, which included the identification of unique arbitrage opportunities that other investors did not notice. Drawing from his background in mathematics, Thorp used mathematical formulas to determine whether to invest in securities such as options, which are contracts that give the buyer the right to buy or sell shares of a stock at a specific price. He discusses the results of such methods in detail, demonstrating the level of research and preparation that made him a success at both the casino and in the market.

The final chapters of *A Man for All Markets* expand upon the lessons Thorp learned during his decades as an investor. The author provides advice and informative overviews related to financial topics such as hedging, compound interest, index funds, and the causes and characteristics of financial crises. In the book's final chapter, "Thoughts," Thorp particularly emphasizes the importance of education, which he notes "made all the difference" for him. He particularly advocates for increased study of probability, statistics, and finance in schools, arguing that knowledge of such subjects is essential to making informed choices later in life. Solidifying his book's status as an educational work, Thorp follows the text of his memoir with a series of appendices of financial information, including tables presenting the impact of inflation, historical returns for a variety of asset classes, and the yearly financial performance of PNP.

Edward O. Thorp is the author of several books, including Beat the Dealer *(1962) and* Beat the Market *(1967). A former professor of mathematics and finance at institutions such as New Mexico State University and the University of California, Irvine, he also founded several investment firms.*

Over the course of *A Man for All Markets*, Thorp details a life and career that evolved significantly throughout the twentieth and early twenty-first centuries, taking new technologies, techniques, and other developments into account. Of particular interest is Thorp's long-standing relationship with technology, the use of which enabled him to complete his best-known projects. Thorp notes that while researching the game of blackjack, he found that it would take hundreds of years to perform the necessary calculations by hand. As an MIT employee, however, he had access to the IBM 740 computer then shared by MIT and many other Boston-area universities. Using that early computer, Thorp was able to complete his calculations in a tiny fraction of the time. He again turned to technology while collaborating with Shannon on their roulette research, which culminated in the creation of a small device—later considered the first wearable computer—that the two researchers used to track the movement of a roulette wheel and predict where the ball would stop. Thorp's approach to investing similarly mixed mathematics with computer technology: in the early days of PNP, he programmed a Hewlett-Packard 9830A computer to calculate fair prices for various options based on a mathematical formula.

Also of particular significance to readers interested in the state of the finance industry in the early twenty-first century is Thorp's discussion of the Bernie Madoff Ponzi scheme that was revealed in 2008. Carried out by one of finance's best-known figures, the scheme involved the fabrication of positive investment returns based in part on trades that never actually took place. Thorp writes that while the scheme came as a surprise to many in the industry, he had in fact detected that fraud was taking place within Madoff's firm as early as 1991 and recounts his experience auditing the portfolio of a consulting company that had invested funds with Madoff. Thorp's early recognition of Madoff's fraudulent activity is impressive and, along with his academically notable childhood and accomplishments in multiple fields, makes him appear almost omniscient at times. However, Thorp also does not shy away from recounting some of the more challenging moments in his career in finance, most notably the government investigation that ultimately led to the dissolution of PNP in the late 1980s. The investigation, which concerned stock manipulation and fraud allegedly taking place in the firm's Princeton office, was tied to a larger investigation focused on financier Michael Milken, who was later found guilty of several securities violations. Thorp, who worked in PNP's Newport Beach office, was not implicated in the suspected criminal activity but does not avoid discussing the investigation, his opinions on its true motivations, and his decision to close the firm. Readers familiar with Thorp and those connected to him may notice, however, that he does not touch on his son Jeffrey's later investigation for trading violations, choosing instead to discuss only PNP and high-profile cases such as the Milken investigation and the Madoff fraud.

Upon its publication, *A Man for All Markets* received largely positive reviews, with critics such as the reviewer for *Kirkus* deeming it both "instructive" and a pleasure to read. Critics particularly praised Thorp's handling of the portions of the book dealing with his early life as well as his detailed discussions of his processes for developing card-counting, roulette-predicting, and investing methods. *A Man for All Markets* likewise received its share of criticism, with some reviewers, including the critic for *Publishers Weekly*, noting that some of Thorp's digressions in the later sections of the book were less successful than the earlier, more memoir-like sections dealing with his early life and career. In an otherwise positive review for the *Financial Analysts Journal*, Mark S. Rzepczynski also noted that the book could have delved more deeply into Thorp's methods of identifying profitable opportunities for investment. Despite such comments, critics on the whole appreciated *A Man for All Markets*, deeming it an enjoyable and enlightening glimpse into the life and career of a little-known yet highly accomplished figure.

Joy Crelin

Review Sources

Malkiel, Burton G. "The Math Whiz and the Money." Review of *A Man for All Markets: From Las Vegas to Wall Street, How I Beat the Dealer and the Market*, by Edward O. Thorp. *The Wall Street Journal*, 29 Jan. 2017, www.wsj.com/articles/the-math-whiz-and-the-money-1485733245. Accessed 30 Sept. 2017.

Review of *A Man for All Markets: From Las Vegas to Wall Street, How I Beat the Dealer and the Market*, by Edward O. Thorp. *Kirkus*, 20 Nov. 2016, www.kirkus-reviews.com/book-reviews/edward-o-thorp/a-man-for-all-markets/. Accessed 30 Sept. 2017.

Review of *A Man for All Markets: From Las Vegas to Wall Street, How I Beat the Dealer and the Market*, by Edward O. Thorp. *Publishers Weekly*, 31 Oct. 2016, www.publishersweekly.com/978-1-40-006796-1. Accessed 30 Sept. 2017.

Rzepczynski, Mark S. Review of *A Man for All Markets: From Las Vegas to Wall Street, How I Beat the Dealer and the Market*, by Edward O. Thorp. *Financial Analysts Journal*, 2017, www.cfapubs.org/doi/full/10.2469/br.v12.n1.11. Accessed 30 Sept. 2017.

Manhattan Beach

Author: Jennifer Egan (b. 1962)
Publisher: Scribner (New York). 448 pp.
Type of work: Novel
Time: Early 1930s to mid-1940s
Locale: New York City

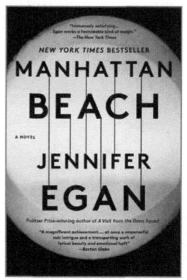

Manhattan Beach *is a heavily plotted, historical novel with a spunky heroine, a shipwrecked father, a gangster lover, and lots of well-researched period detail.*

Principal characters

ANNA KERRIGAN, a young woman who becomes one of the military's first female divers

EDDIE KERRIGAN, her father

DEXTER STYLES, a nightclub owner and ex-gangster

LYDIA KERRIGAN, her disabled sister

AGNES KERRIGAN, her mother

BRIANNE KERRIGAN, her aunt and Eddie's sister

HARRIET STYLES, Dexter's wife

MR. Q., Dexter's boss

Courtesy of Scribner

Reviewers who admired Jennifer Egan's book, *A Visit from the Goon Squad* (2010), which won a Pulitzer Prize in 2011 for its experimental manipulation of point of view and narrative form, have expressed puzzlement in their admiration for her 2017 novel, *Manhattan Beach*. This book, which some reviewers have termed an "old-fashioned page-turner," is a traditional historical novel that combines crime noir styling with social realism, women's rights, and lost-at-sea adventure.

The novel is set in Brooklyn, New York, in the years that bridge the Great Depression and World War II. In the prologue, the heroine, Anna Kerrigan, is eleven-years old when her father Eddie takes her to visit a post-Prohibition gangster named Dexter Styles. Styles lives in a large home on Manhattan Beach and Eddie has been working for him as a bagman, carrying payoff money from a corrupt union boss to government officials. Eddie, who hopes to get a higher-paying job with Styles, needs the additional income to purchase a wheelchair for Anna's sister Lydia, an invalid who cannot walk or speak.

The reader is thus introduced to the three major characters whose lives continually intertwine throughout this novel, and to Anna's fascination with the sea, which serves as a background metaphor for the action. As Anna watches the sea from Styles's Manhattan Beach home, she wonders what hidden treasures lie beneath the water—from sunken ships to the charm bracelet that fell from her wrist into a storm drain, to the dead bodies that her father tells her about, because for him, the ocean is "a wasteland."

In the first four chapters of the novel, the reader is introduced to a young Anna and her family. The story then leaps forward in time and situates Anna as a nineteen-year-old woman working for the war effort in a pedestrian job at a Brooklyn navy yard. The reader learns that her father, Eddie, deserted the family when Anna was thirteen and she cannot picture him clearly any more. But her life changes one day when she sees a man at the navy yard being dressed in a heavy canvas suit, and she is spellbound, for she had never heard of a deep-sea diver. She feels there is something familiar about the suit, as if it appeared to her from a dream or a myth, and she tries to picture the diver at the bottom of the bay. She experiences a "seismic rearrangement" in herself, knowing she has always wanted to be a diver and to walk along the bottom of the sea.

The book fluctuates between plotlines that focus on Anna fighting prejudice against women who work and learning to dive; on Dexter Styles trying to manage a legitimate post-bootlegger life; and eventually on Eddie getting shipwrecked and struggling to survive. Egan develops several backstories throughout the novel, as well, such as that of a young Eddie becoming a protégé of a gambler who gives him his pocket watch. The watch plays an important role much later in the novel when Anna becomes a diver. Throughout, Egan has created a world in this thickly plotted, fully detailed novel where all that is hidden is ultimately uncovered, and secrets and mysteries inform the characters' motivations.

As the novel moves through time, Anna visits a nightclub where she recognizes Dexter Styles, who now owns several clubs and gambling spots in wartime New York. After this encounter, Anna begins to think her father has not run away, but has been killed by a gang. Although Anna conceals her identity from Styles, she asks him to take her and her sister Lydia to the beach, since Lydia has never seen the ocean. Lydia speaks only in a senseless babble and cannot sit up on her own, but when Styles takes them to Manhattan Beach, where his house is located, the ocean creates a change in Lydia that seems miraculous. As she confronts the sea, her lips move "like a mythical creature whose imprecations could summon storms and winged gods." But the change in Lydia is only temporary and she begins to grow weak, dying shortly thereafter.

Anna and Styles soon become passionate lovers and Anna tells Styles that Eddie Kerrigan is her father. Styles tells her that her father has been killed by gangsters and that his body is in the ocean not far from shore. This revelation leads Anna, with Styles's help, to make a dive in search for her father. When Anna finds only her father's watch and gets in trouble underwater, Styles, who has never dived before, puts on a suit and dives down to help her. But Styles's dive has more importance than demonstrating his heroism; it has a metaphysical significance, for he is impressed by "the primeval dark of nightmares," knowing how the water covers secrets such as drowned children and sunken ships. The reader observes his character change as he indicates that his proximity to the sea had made everything else in his life insignificant.

The last quarter of the novel shifts to Eddie, who has been serving in the merchant marine and has, in 1943, just passed his third mate's examination and signed up on the ship *Elizabeth Seaman* in San Francisco. The *Elizabeth Seaman* is torpedoed by an enemy submarine and the men escape on lifeboats, only to be struck by a storm. The final chapters focus on the shipwreck and the reader gets detailed descriptions of the characters' survival efforts.

As the novel closes, the action returns to the changing relationship of Styles and Anna and its ensuing complications. Anna continues to make bold choices in her life, and characters the reader encountered earlier in the novel return to play significant and surprising roles.

Egan acknowledges she researched dozens of sources, such as books, interviews, oral history accounts, and more in writing this book, and indeed, there are multiple historical and technical details about diving, shipyards, the war effort, movie stars, war news, and so forth. Much of the book's styl-

Jennifer Egan won the Pulitzer Prize in Fiction in 2011 for her book A Visit from the Goon Squad.

ing also pays homage to pulp novels, noir, and World War II movies, with the resulting dialogue sounding at times somewhat stilted, though accurately reflecting nuances of the period. Film stars of the 1930s through the 1950s such as Tyrone Power, Victor Mature, Betty Grable, and Veronica Lake, are woven into the narrative and radio serials such as *The Guiding Light* (1937–56), *Young Doctor Malone* (1939–60), and *Against the Storm* (1939–52), are used to further enhance the historical realism of the novel's setting. Egan carefully describes the paraphernalia of diving—putting on the "dress" or two-hundred-pound suit that makes walking almost impossible. The historical details are specific and ground the story firmly in the period; for example, the narrator notes that after a dance the orchestra concluded with "Tangerine," from "that not very good picture starring Dorothy Lamour." Egan confidently imparts these details into the book and says in the Acknowledgments that if nothing more came of the years she spent working on the novel than the pleasure of researching it, she would consider herself lucky.

Readers, too, will benefit from the scrupulous details of novel. As Dwight Garner, writing for the *New York Times*, noted: "You learn things while reading this novel. Egan's fiction buzzes with factual crosscurrents, casually deployed."

Meghan O'Rourke, in her *Guardian* review, calls the novel "cinematic" in scope, and indeed, one might suspect that with its missing father and noir romance plot lines, its plucky female protagonist proving herself worthy to chauvinistic bosses, its shipwreck and lost-at-sea story, it is ready-made for a Hollywood movie, albeit an old-fashioned Hollywood movie. The metaphysical mystery of the sea that seems to possess both Styles and Anna provides additional atmosphere and richness to their characters' stories.

Charles E. May

Review Sources

Charles, Ron. "In *Manhattan Beach*, Jennifer Egan's Heroine Dives Deep for Family Secrets." Review of *Manhattan Beach*, by Jennifer Egan, *The Washington Post*, 26 Sept. 2017, www.washingtonpost.com/entertainment/books/jennifer-egans-new-heroine-dives-deep-for-family-secrets/2017/09/26/467e3b12-a230-11e7-b14f-f41773cd5a14_story.html. Accessed 1 Dec. 2017.

Franklin, Ruth. "Jennifer Egan's Surprising Swerve into Historical Fiction." Review of *Manhattan Beach*, by Jennifer Egan. *The Atlantic*, Nov. 2017, www.theatlantic.com/magazine/archive/2017/11/jennifer-egan-manhattan-beach/540612/. Accessed 1 Dec. 2017.

Garner, Dwight. "Jennifer Egan Updates the Old-Fashioned Page-Turner in *Manhattan Beach*." Review of *Manhattan Beach*, by Jennifer Egan. *The New York Times*, 27 Sept. 2017, www.nytimes.com/2017/09/27/books/review-manhattan-beach-jennifer-egan.html. Accessed 1 Dec. 2017.

O'Rourke, Meghan. "Manhattan Beach by Jennifer Egan Review—Remarkable Cinematic Scope." Review of *Manhattan Beach*, by Jennifer Egan. *The Guardian*, 29 Sept. 2017, www.theguardian.com/books/2017/sep/29/manhattan-beach-jennifer-egan-review. Accessed 1 Dec. 2017.

Prose, Francine. On the Wilder Shores of Brooklyn." Review of *Manhattan Beach*, by Jennifer Egan. *The New York Review of Books*, 12 Oct. 2017, www.nybooks.com/articles/2017/10/12/jennifer-egan-manhattan-beach-wilder-shores-brooklyn/. Accessed 1 Dec. 2017.

Towles, Amor. In Manhattan Beach, Jennifer Egan Sets a Crime Story on the Waterfront." Review of *Manhattan Beach*, by Jennifer Egan. *The New York Times*, 3 Oct. 2017, www.nytimes.com/2017/10/03/books/review/jennifer-egan-manhattan-beach.html. Accessed 1 Dec. 2017.

Marlena

Author: Julie Buntin (b. 1987)
Publisher: Henry Holt (New York). 288 pp.
Type of work: Novel
Time: ca. 2000–present day
Locales: Silver Creek, Michigan; New York
City

Julie Buntin's debut novel tells the story of teenager Cat, who has recently relocated with her mother to a small, rural town in northern Michigan, and her friendship with her troubled new neighbor Marlena. Framed by adult Cat's story line in present-day New York City, the book's rich atmosphere encapsulates the intense bond often experienced between teenage girls.

Principal characters

CAT, an intelligent, rebellious teenage girl
MARLENA, her neighbor and best friend
JIMMY, her older brother
MOM, her newly divorced mother
RYDER, Marlena's longtime boyfriend
GREG, a friend of Ryder and Marlena
TIDBIT, Greg's sometimes girlfriend
BOLT, a predatory friend of Marlena's father
SAL, Marlena's younger brother.

Calling a book "haunting" can border on cliché, but occasionally a work is so true to its characters, its setting, and the sense of an irrevocably lost period in one's life that it does indeed conjure spirits of sorts. *Marlena*, the debut novel from Julie Buntin, accomplishes this in just under three hundred pages. Within the first twenty, the narrator, Cat, tells the reader that her friend and kindred spirit Marlena died the November after she turned eighteen; she was found in the woods, where she slipped and drowned in six inches of running stream. The rest of the novel is structured as Cat narrating the time in which she came to know Marlena, punctuated by chapters of Cat's current life almost twenty years later. Knowing that the sometimes enchanting, sometimes infuriating girl who has captured Cat's attention is already doomed as the story progresses creates a tension for the reader: one cannot help but be drawn into her world, while also feeling her short life quickly coming to its end.

Set in the poverty-stricken town of Silver Creek in rural northern Michigan, the main narrative of *Marlena*—the girls' friendship—takes place over a short period of time. Cat and Marlena know each other for barely a year, but that is what makes their bond all the more profound and mysterious. When Cat, her brother Jimmy, and their mother show up at the modular home that their mother bought with the divorce settlement she received, Cat is in a state of despair. The year before, Cat had attended an exclusive private school on scholarship; now she has been taken to a small town where she knows no one, away from her beloved father, and forced to attend public school.

When her new neighbor Marlena shows up by their van the day they move in, Cat is intrigued but still too despondent to see the potential of a friend. The meeting is described as unremarkable, but as Cat reminds the reader, that is how so many stories begin. Buntin skillfully sets the scene as a beginning loaded with life-changing significance for both of the main characters. Cat says later of the meeting, from her position as an adult living in New York, "Whenever I hear the word *danger*, I see Marlena and me starting into the mouth of that U-Haul in the winter hour between twilight and dark. Two girls full of plans, fifteen and seventeen years old in the middle of nowhere. Stop, I want to tell us. Stay right where you are, together. *Don't move*. But we will. We always do. The clock's already running."

Before long, Cat has been taken under Marlena's wing. Within a few weeks, she narrates, they are best friends, with a quickly deepening bond forged from mutual intelligence and rebelliousness. Buntin depicts the development of the relationship through scenes that could easily appear trite, but are elevated by nuanced description and realistic emotion. A school-skipping scene along the lines of those in countless teen-rebel books and films avoids cliché through the power of Buntin's writing. Cat, who is loath to attend the local public high school, decides on her first day to see how long she can sit in the hallway before anyone notices she is gone. Soon Marlena walks into school, sees Cat, and invites her to spend the day with her and her friends, who are all skipping. Vivid details scatter across Cat's narration: a pill Marlena pops while they are smoking marijuana behind the school, a glimpse of a complex system of instruments inside a closet at the hotel where everyone goes to hang out with Marlena's boyfriend Ryder, a distinct chemical smell hanging in the air as they sit around watching television.

A sinister subtext also prevents the story from drifting into sentimentality. While Cat is quickly becoming attached to Marlena, she is also being submerged in the world of rural opioid use and meth production and dealing. Despite the fact that she herself never takes either drug, she sees the toll it takes on those around her, and the adult Cat questions herself repeatedly through her narrative, wondering how she could have saved Marlena from her impending demise. Meanwhile, Cat is falling into her own addiction to alcohol. The depictions of both typical teenage experimentation and the pervasive creep of drug dependency in rural America are stark yet balanced, favoring realism over judgment.

The present-day counter-narrative propels the story. Cat, now a thirtysomething woman living in Brooklyn and working as a librarian, receives a phone call from Marlena's younger brother Sal, who wants to meet with her to hear about his long-dead sibling. Still struggling with substance abuse issues, which she tries to keep hidden from her husband, Liam, Cat is thrown into a spiral by the call. Buntin's adept

Courtesy of Nina Subin

Michigan native Julie Buntin teaches fiction writing at Marymount Manhattan College and is the director of writing programs at publisher and writing school Catapult. Her work has appeared in various outlets, including the Atlantic, Slate, O, the Oprah Magazine, *and* Cosmopolitan. Marlena *is her first novel.*

positioning of Cat's adult self next to her younger self, with Marlena completing the trio, invites the reader to see the similarities between all three, as well as the differences. The structure provides a steady reminder that one of the girls does make it out of their bleak circumstances, and allows for an emotional climax. There is darkness everywhere, but there is also hope, particularly when the focus on adult Cat reveals the ways in which Marlena has stayed alive in Cat's current life and memories. Of course, this remembrance is difficult and painful, and Cat is haunted by her friend's death. It is as if the intensity of their bond was never severed but transformed, and now it is on Cat to carry the load of both their demons.

The fully formed characters of Marlena and Cat lie at the heart of *Marlena*. Buntin expertly enters the world of teenage girls and carefully, thoughtfully explores the moments that allow the two girls to become reflections of each other. Critics agreed that the deep characterization is one of the qualities that make the book a resounding success and suggest Buntin to be a premier new talent. Deborah Shapiro captured this sentiment in her review for the *New York Times*, noting the wide appeal of reading about "the kind of coming-of-age friendship that goes beyond camaraderie, into a deeper bond that forges identity; it's friendship as a creative act, a collaborative work of imagination, and what happens when that collaboration—terribly, inevitably—falls apart." The friendship is believable because it is real—as real as a fictional world can be, at least. As Cat and Marlena spend countless nights at each other's houses, evenings on the swings at the nearby playground, and days at the lake or riding around together in any car they can get their hands on, plotting their future and dissecting their present, the small moments coalesce to create a behemoth of a relationship whose energy is so electrified, it seems too hot to last.

The realism of the relationship is likely due to the fact that Cat's friendship with Marlena was inspired by Buntin's own high school friendship with a girl who later died of liver failure following addiction. Before *Marlena* was published, in July 2014, Buntin wrote an essay for the *Atlantic* titled "She's Still Dying on Facebook," in which she recounts her experience watching her own magnetic "Marlena" figure descend into drug addiction and eventually death. Combined with the fact that Buntin is herself from northern Michigan, where she grew up in a resort town that emptied out for half of the year, it is not surprising that she is able to create such a tangible world. Her mastery as a writer is apparent in more than just the characterization; the landscape, too, is alive with Buntin's prose. The story essentially flows from winter to fall, and the subtle changes to the seasons carry along the narrative. The reader knows that Marlena only has until November, creating a tension when the snow cracks with thaw, the leaves "blaze red and orange," or the lake has become warm enough for swimming.

Marlena received critical acclaim upon its release in the spring of 2017, with rave reviews coming from *Vogue*, the *Atlantic*, the *New York Times*, *Kirkus Reviews*, and other prestigious outlets. Some compared Buntin's work with other chronicles of close-knit teenage female friendships, including Emma Cline's novel *The Girls* (2016) and Elena Ferrante's Neapolitan novels, but all agreed that Buntin's take is unique in its perspective and timely in its subject matter. At a time when the opioid epidemic rages across the United States, particularly in rural communities, Buntin offers a glimpse into the lives and communities affected, and does so with compassion and elegance. Her ability to bounce between Brooklyn and small-town America shows her depth of understanding and keen observation of the world around her.

At the novel's conclusion, Cat meditates on the final time the two girls were with each other, what they said, and what they did. Cat says, "Marlena—look. I didn't forget. I wrote it down." These simple words create a startling intimacy between Cat, Marlena, and the reader, as if Cat was using the reader as medium all along to contact her missing friend, her missing piece. The effect is both exhilarating and chilling, as one is left to mourn the girl who filled the past pages with life. Cat's story reads almost as a confession—of the secrets of adolescents, the secrets of the woods, the secrets of friendship.

Melynda Fuller

Review Sources
Gilbert, Sophie. "My Brilliant (Doomed) Friend." Review of *Marlena*, by Julie Buntin. *The Atlantic*, 13 Apr. 2017, www.theatlantic.com/entertainment/archive/2017/04/marlena-the-girls-the-strays-literary-friendship/522786/. Accessed 2 Oct. 2017.
Review of *Marlena*, by Julie Buntin. *Kirkus Reviews*, 2 Feb. 2017, www.kirkusreviews.com/book-reviews/julie-buntin/marlena/. Accessed 2 Oct. 2017.
Morrison, Cassandra. "Julie Buntin's *Marlena* Is a Gritty Coming-of-Age Story about a Troubled Friendship." Review of *Marlena*, by Julie Buntin. *The Washington Post*, 25 Apr. 2017, www.washingtonpost.com/entertainment/books/julie-buntins-marlena-is-a-gritty-coming-of-age-story-about-a-troubled-friendship/2017/04/25/cc3e4b0c-2940-11e7-a616-d7c8a68c1a66_story.html. Accessed 2 Oct. 2017.
Parsons, Kimberly King. Review of *Marlena*, by Julie Buntin. *Bookforum*, 13 June 2017, www.bookforum.com/review/18054. Accessed 2 Oct. 2017.
Shapiro, Deborah. "A Debut Calls a Ferrante-Style Female Friendship to the Fore." Review of *Marlena*, by Julie Buntin. *The New York Times*, 18 Apr. 2017, www.nytimes.com/2017/04/18/books/review/marlena-julie-buntin.html. Accessed 2 Aug. 2017.

Martin Luther
Renegade and Prophet

Author: Lyndal Roper (b. 1956)
Publisher: Random House (New York). 576 pp.
Type of work: Biography
Time: First half of the sixteenth century
Locale: Germany

Historian Lyndal Roper combines histori-cal research with psychological analysis to create a portrait of Martin Luther, whose ef-forts to reform the Roman Catholic Church eventually led to an irreconcilable split that became the Protestant Reformation.

Courtesy of Random House

Principal personages

MARTIN LUTHER, Augustinian monk and leader of a reform movement
HANS LUDER, his father
JOHANN VON STAUPITZ, his mentor in the Augustinian community
PHILIPP MELANCHTHON, his protégé and an early supporter of the Reformation
GEORG SPALATIN, a supporter of his in the political arena
JOHANNES ECK, a lifelong antagonist of his ideas
KATHARINA VON BORA, a Catholic nun, later his wife
ANDREAS KARLSTADT, an early follower
JUSTUS JONAS, a disciple
JOHANNES AGRICOLA, a disciple

Published in the year of the five hundredth anniversary of Martin Luther's (alleged) posting of his famous ninety-five theses challenging church practice on the door of All Saints' Church in Wittenberg, Germany, Lyndal Roper's *Martin Luther: Rene-gade and Prophet* offers yet another portrait of perhaps the most important figure in Christian church history since the crucifixion of Jesus Christ in the early first century CE. Luther's life has been the focus of numerous biographies, the first of which ap-peared within years after his death. Many of the early ones were written as apologies or defenses of Luther's radical views on matters of theology and church policy. That he needed defending early is no surprise; his strenuous efforts to reform the Roman Catholic Church led to the permanent division within Christianity. Small wonder that he was persecuted, even threatened with death, by the Catholic hierarchy and many of the secular rulers whose cozy relationship with the church was one of the causes of Luther's discontent.

While some of the early biographies played fast and loose with the facts of Luther's life—the famous incident of his nailing his theses to the church door may not, in fact, have actually taken place; Luther himself only acknowledged having mailed them to the archbishop of Mainz and the bishop of Brandenburg, in accordance with church protocol—over the years details about his family history, his life in the Augustinian monastery and at the new University of Wittenberg, his early efforts to reform the Catholic Church and his eventual permanent break from it, his work to evangelize both clergy and laity in accepting the reforms he proposed, and his struggles to create a new church that would survive his death became well known. By the twentieth century, biographies of Luther often presented these same facts, differentiating themselves by the various interpretations that attempt to explain the man and his theology. Roper's *Martin Luther* is such a book, distinguished by her combination of exceptional scholarly research and engaging writing style; yet it is also more than that, focusing on Luther as a man as well as a church figure, probing his childhood and how it informed his character as an adult. Roper clarifies some complex matters of theology and politics while bringing into focus the life of a flawed yet principled man, an "awkward hero" who was determined to serve God as best he could.

Roper admits that her study bears similarities to the psychobiographies of Erik Erikson (*Young Man Luther*, 1958) and Erich Fromm (*The Fear of Freedom*, 1941), but her training as a historian leads her to view Luther in the context of his times. Her aim is "to understand Luther himself," to "explore his inner landscapes" and especially his "contradictions." The links between Roper's study and those of Erikson and Fromm are evident in her discussions of Luther's relationship with his father, Hans Luder, a mining magnate in central Germany, and of his dealings with his followers, particularly close disciples such as Philipp Melanchthon, Justus Jonas, and Johannes Agricola. Roper explains how the psychological dynamics of the father-son relationship shaped Luther's thinking about theology and influenced his behavior toward those who made the bold step of abandoning the Catholic Church to preach the new theology that Luther was promulgating.

In addition to her understanding of the importance of psychology in shaping personality, Roper's wide knowledge of German history and culture allows her to provide readers a sense of how Luther came to understand his place in the clerical and political world of sixteenth-century Germany. Luther's decision to become a monk may have been in some sense an act of unconscious rebellion against a domineering father and an attempt to replace him with a new father figure, the Augustinian friar Johann von Staupitz, who became his mentor and who had a hand in establishing the University of Wittenberg in 1502. Nevertheless, Luther's life as an Augustinian provided him ample opportunity to strike out on his own intellectually, particularly after he earned his doctorate and joined the faculty at Wittenberg. As Roper astutely points out, in the relatively unsettled intellectual environment at Wittenberg, Luther was free to contemplate current church practices and develop reasoned arguments for reform. Perhaps, Roper speculates, in a more established university, tradition and regimen might have prevented him from even undertaking such a task.

It is fairly common knowledge that the young Luther was distressed by the practice of selling indulgences. The Catholic Church had long taught that good works could earn indulgences, which were essentially a form of remission for one's sins. By the late Middle Ages, it had become customary to include contributions to the church among good works eligible for earning indulgences—only one step from exchanging money for promises of heavenly bliss. Luther's reading of scripture convinced him not only that the practice of granting indulgences was wrong, but also that the theology behind it was flawed. God's grace—and grace alone—was the source of salvation; one could not purchase one's way into heaven, either with good deeds or with money. Adopting this radical, even heretical, view was dangerous, as it was a given that the church hierarchy would react when this belief was promulgated. Still, Roper insists, the move toward revolution was not inevitable; it was Luther's intransigence, met by intolerance for dissent on the part of church hierarchy, that set the Augustinian monk on a collision course with the pope and his supporters.

While Luther's public dissent began in 1517, it took nearly four years for the Catholic Church to finally excommunicate him. By that time, the movement he had launched was too widespread to die, and he was too firmly entrenched in reformist theology to submit to Rome. Luther was constantly having to answer charges by theologians such as Johannes Eck, who was loyal to Rome and particularly incensed by Luther's attacks. Additionally, quite a number of loyalist theologians saw no problem in stooping to satire and invective to attack him. Luther responded by publishing numerous important tracts that laid out his positions. Roper's analyses of many of these tracts demonstrate how skillful Luther was in attacking weaknesses in traditional Catholic doctrine and practice while promoting a new theology based on scripture and the writings of the early church fathers. "For Luther," Roper writes with certitude, "the Word of God is absolutely clear and plain in its meaning, and 'conscience' is the individual's internal knowledge of that objective meaning of God's Word." Such a belief, if accepted, would have made the hierarchy that had evolved in the Roman Catholic Church superfluous, and perhaps inimical. Hence, when the pope issued the final bull of excommunication in January 1521, it had become impossible to ignore Luther or dismiss his ideas; the movement that came to be known as the Protestant Reformation was well under way.

Like all revolutions, the one Luther led against the Catholic Church did not go smoothly. Roper is particularly good at describing the political environment in which the Reformation arose, as German princes sided either with the pope or with the evangelical radicals. Tensions between these same princes and Rome, or between them and the Holy Roman emperor, of whom they were titularly subjects, played as great a role in determining the fate of the new Protestant congregations. At the same time, the movement did not remain unified for long, and Roper is careful to examine Luther's reaction to some of the more radical elements within his own following. Men such as onetime supporter Andreas Karlstadt and Swiss reformer Huldrych Zwingli quickly became thorns in Luther's side, much as he had become a thorn in the side of the pope and the leaders of the Holy Roman Empire. Dozens of sects arose, some later becoming established Protestant denominations. Many leaders of these factions fought as bitterly over matters of doctrine and practice as Luther and his original followers had against the central authority of the Catholic Church, the pope, and the various church councils whose word on theology and spiritual practice was, until the sixteenth century, final among Catholics. Although Roper traces the origins and resolution of several early controversies that arose as a result of Luther's proclamations on the need for church reform, the one that is woven throughout her narrative is the ongoing battle Luther had with the sacramentalists, those theologians who argued that the presence of Christ in the Eucharist is merely symbolic and that Mass is simply a memorial of the Last Supper.

It may be difficult for twenty-first-century readers, especially those educated in principally secular societies, to imagine how blood could be spilled over disputes concerning the character of Christ's presence in the Eucharist. The answer, of course, lies in the historical milieu in which such theological questions arose; simply put, in the sixteenth century, religion mattered—really mattered, not only to priests and theologians such as Luther (and women such as his eventual wife, the former nun Katharina von Bora), but also to the laity, from regal princes to menial workers. The zeal with which reformers pursued their agendas, and the equally zealous efforts of clergy and laity aligned with the Roman Catholic Church, led in some instances to violence, even death. Roper does not shy away from assigning blame to both sides in tracing the course of hostilities, which continued long after Luther's death and which bred mutual hostilities between Rome and Protestantism that continued through the centuries.

© John Cairns

Lyndal Roper is Regius Professor of Modern History at Oxford University. She is the author of several important historical studies, including Witch Craze: Terror and Fantasy in Baroque Germany *(2004) and* The Witch in the Western Imagination *(2012).*

As an explanation of the origins of the Protestant Reformation, Roper's *Martin Luther* is both insightful and judicious. As a portrait of the man at the center of this movement, it is equally insightful and notably sympathetic. Yet Roper is careful not to paint Luther as a heroic figure without flaws. He may have been the catalyst for much-needed reform in Christianity, but his vilification of the pope prompted a centuries-long animosity between Protestants and Rome, his intolerance for some of the ideas of his fellow reformers made him difficult to deal with, and his sermons and tracts reveal a virulent strain of anti-Semitism that appalled even his contemporaries on occasion. Yet it is undeniable that he remains a towering figure in the history of Christianity, and Roper's portrait does justice to his stature.

Laurence W. Mazzeno

Review Sources

Dirda, Michael. "How Well Do We Know Our Heroes? A New Book Shows the Darker Side of Martin Luther." Review of *Martin Luther: Renegade and Prophet*, by Lyndal Roper. *The Washington Post*, 19 Apr. 2017, www.washingtonpost. com/entertainment/books/how-well-do-we-know-our-heroes-a-new-book-shows-the-darker-side-of-martin-luther/2017/04/18/123b2b78-206a-11e7-ad74-3a742a6e93a7_story.html. Accessed 2 Oct. 2017.

Fulton, Elaine. "Luther: The Flawed Reformer." Review of *Martin Luther: Renegade and Prophet*, by Lyndal Roper, and *Martin Luther: Visionary Reformer*, by Scott H. Hendrix. *History Today*, Jan. 2017, www.historytoday.com/reviews/luther-flawed-reformer. Accessed 2 Oct. 2017.

Pettegree, Andrew. "A New Biography of Martin Luther Reveals the Life beyond the Theses." Review of *Martin Luther: Renegade and Prophet*, by Lyndal Roper. *The New York Times*, 14 Apr. 2017, www.nytimes.com/2017/04/14/books/review/martin-luther-renegade-and-prophet-lyndal-roper.html. Accessed 2 Oct. 2017.

Thomson, Ian. Review of *Martin Luther: Renegade and Prophet*, by Lyndal Roper. *The Guardian*, 26 June 2016, www.theguardian.com/books/2016/jun/26/martin-luther-renegade-prophet-lyndal-roper-review. Accessed 2 Oct. 2017.

Walsham, Alexandra. "*Martin Luther* by Lyndal Roper Review: The Reformer as Prophet of Sexual Liberation." Review of *Martin Luther: Renegade and Prophet*, by Lyndal Roper. *The Guardian*, 7 Sept. 2016, www.theguardian.com/books/2016/sep/07/martin-luther-lyndal-roper-review. Accessed 2 Oct. 2017.

The Men in My Life
A Memoir of Love and Art in 1950s Manhattan

Author: Patricia Bosworth (b. 1933)
Publisher: Harper (New York). Illustrated.
    400 pp.
Type of work: Memoir
Time: The 1930s through the 1960s
Locales: California, Switzerland, and New
    York

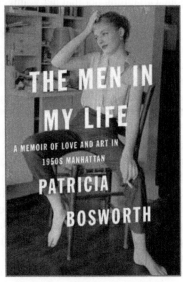

Courtesy of HarperCollins Publishers

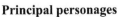

In The Men in My Life: A Memoir of Love *and Art in 1950s Manhattan, Patricia Bosworth chronicles her experiences as a young woman in the 1950s, a period shaped in large part by the suicides of her brother and father.*

Principal personages

PATRICIA BOSWORTH, the author, an actor,
    journalist, and biographer
BARTLEY CRUM, her father, a lawyer known for his work for celebrities and leftist
    causes
ANNA GERTRUDE CRUM, her mother, a novelist
BART CRUM, her younger brother
JASON BEAN, her first husband, an artist
MEL ARRIGHI, her second husband, a novelist, playwright, and screenwriter

Few people have had a life as eventful as that of Patricia Bosworth. A model and actor who later transitioned into a career in journalism and became a critically acclaimed biographer, she grew up in a family with both Hollywood and political connections. She began working as an actor during a formative period in American theater, during which some of the twentieth century's most acclaimed actors, directors, and playwrights were gathering and working in New York. Her later work as a biographer built on the connections formed during that period, as she published volumes on actors Marlon Brando and Jane Fonda, whom she had studied alongside at New York's famed Actors Studio; photographer Diane Arbus, for whom she modeled as a teenager; and actor Montgomery Clift, who had been her father's client. Focusing primarily on the 1950s and early 1960s, Bosworth's 2017 memoir *The Men in My Life: A Memoir of Love and Art in 1950s Manhattan* chronicles a tumultuous period in her life, one that brought professional success but also difficult personal experiences. Chief among those experiences were the suicides of her brother and father, which bookended the 1950s and shaped both the structure of the author's life and her memoir.

   Bosworth, who was born Patricia Crum in 1933, begins *The Men in My Life* with a prologue recounting what, for her, became the defining event of the early 1950s. On

December 13, 1953, while she was attending Sarah Lawrence College, she received a phone call telling her that her younger brother, Bart, had killed himself while at college in Oregon. She immediately returned to her parents' brownstone in New York City to be with her mother, Anna Gertrude Crum. Her father, Bartley Crum, was in California for business and urged his wife and daughter to travel to California for the funeral. Deeply in denial and insisting that her son must have been murdered, Gertrude refused to attend the funeral, and Bosworth remained in New York to keep her mother company. It would be more than thirty years before she first visited her brother's grave. However, she remained deeply connected to Bart during the intervening years, carrying out imagined conversations with her brother at key points in her life. Such conversations are featured throughout her memoir and were, she writes, "as real to [her] as the traffic outside [her] window, the rain pelting against [her] cheeks."

Patricia Bosworth previously authored the memoir Anything Your Little Heart Desires *(1997) as well as biographies of Montgomery Clift, Jane Fonda, and others. A former model and actor, she is a journalist and contributing editor for* Vanity Fair.

Following the prologue, the bulk of *The Men in My Life* is divided into four parts. The first, "Waking Up," deals with Bosworth's childhood and teen years, a period in which the seeds of both her future professional aspirations and her brother's tragic death were planted. Her immediate family is the focus of much of her attention during the book's early chapters, as she describes her close relationship with Bart and delves into the careers of her novelist mother and lawyer father. As she explains, the family's life changed significantly in the late 1940s as anti-Communist sentiments among US lawmakers led to the investigation of various major Hollywood figures for suspected Communist sympathies. A lawyer who defended the so-called Hollywood Ten, Bartley Crum became the subject of extensive surveillance by the Federal Bureau of Investigation (FBI) and lost many major corporate clients, although he remained a respected figure in leftist circles. In the late 1940s, the family moved from California to New York, where Bosworth's father briefly operated the left-wing *New York Star* newspaper. He twice tried to kill himself in early 1950, and his abuse of alcohol and prescription drugs continued throughout the decade.

Having provided key background information about her family, Bosworth goes on to chronicle her tumultuous teen years, which were marked by attempts to assert her independence from her parents. As teenagers, she and her brother were both sent away to boarding schools, Bosworth to the International School of Geneva in Switzerland and Bart to Deerfield Academy in Massachusetts. Both were sent home after less than a year, Bosworth for breaking curfews to meet up with various boyfriends. Bart, on the other hand, was dismissed from Deerfield Academy after the suicide of a close friend, whom Bosworth later determined likely killed himself after the two boys had a sexual encounter. Driven into a deep depression by his friend's suicide and likely his own struggles with his sexual orientation, Bart pulled away from his sister, and their previously close relationship became distant. While attending Sarah Lawrence College, Bosworth eloped with aspiring artist Jason Bean to the dismay of her parents and brother. Bean proved to be physically and emotionally abusive during the marriage, which lasted less than two years, and she devotes several chapters to their relationship and her eventual decision to divorce Bean, a controversial act at the time. Representing the beginning of a new stage in Bosworth's life, the divorce also marks the beginning of the memoir's second segment, "Focusing."

After documenting her last meetings with Bart, Bosworth devotes chapter 10 to the aftermath of his death and her attempts to determine why her brother had ended his life. She explains that in an attempt to process her grief, she sought to hide her emotions and instead concentrate on her career as a model and actor, which serves as the focus of much of the remainder of the book. In addition to documenting the progression of her career, she recounts her experience joining the Actors Studio, the prestigious training school known as the birthplace of method acting. She also discusses her romantic life in depth, detailing various, often unhealthy, relationships but also recounting her early meetings with the man who would become her second husband, the writer Mel Arrighi. In the third and fourth parts of *The Men in My Life*, "Making Choices" and "Changing," she continues to document her work and relationships while also exploring her unexpected pregnancy and difficult decision to have an abortion, a physically and emotionally traumatic process for her. Further trauma came in December 1959, when her father took a fatal overdose of pills shortly before the sixth anniversary of Bart's death. In the years following her father's suicide, she made several major life changes, transitioning into what would become a successful career in journalism and marrying Arrighi, to whom she would remain married until his own death in 1986. *The Men in My Life* concludes with an afterword in which she recounts her first visit to her brother's grave, providing her memoir with a bittersweet sense of closure.

As a whole, *The Men in My Life* provides an engaging and affecting look at a period that was highly significant not only for Bosworth herself but also for the United States as a nation. Many of the writers and other creative professionals she encountered during that period, including Tennessee Williams, Gore Vidal, and Elia Kazan, remained highly influential for decades after their initial meetings with her, and many of the events she experienced were both major societal moments and intensely personal ones. The anti-Communist sentiments of the Red Scare, for example, were prevalent in American culture and media during the 1950s but had a particularly significant effect on the Crum household, and the assassination of US president John F. Kennedy, discussed in chapter 26, was a national tragedy that also prompted Bosworth to rekindle her relationship with Arrighi after a breakup. Overall, Bosworth paints a compelling portrait of an era and a place, populating her world with the countless intriguing figures she encountered during her time as a model and actor. Some readers may tire of her frequent brief mentions of such celebrities, but they truly establish the memoir's overarching sense of time and place. Also helpful are the various photographs included in the book, which enable the reader to connect faces with names and further place the book within its historical context.

As much of Bosworth's memoir makes clear, the book's title is an appropriate one. Indeed, although her world, and consequently the book itself, was populated with numerous influential women—including her mother, future biography subjects Arbus and Fonda, theater peers Elaine Stritch and Ellen Burstyn, and film stars Marilyn Monroe and Audrey Hepburn—the theatrical and wider worlds she occupied during the 1950s and 1960s were clearly dominated by men, and men, both cruel and kind, feature heavily in her accounts. Through anecdotes, she calls attention to the toxic masculinity that was present in environments such as the Actors Studio, details her efforts to avoid the so-called casting couch, and explores the prevailing attitudes toward domestic violence. However, as Bosworth herself explains in the author's note, the memoir's title truly references not the men who featured in her romantic and professional lives but the two who most shaped her life and experiences during the period: Bartley and Bart Crum. The loss of those two men is felt throughout the book, even before the loss is truly complete; Bosworth describes Bart as having pulled away from her years before his suicide, and her father's descent into alcoholism and drug addiction likewise made the process of losing him a lengthy one. Although Bosworth worked to suppress her emotions in her day-to-day life, her grief is palpable throughout *The Men in My Life* as she explores memories that remain painful more than half a century later.

Upon its publication in 2017, *The Men in My Life* met with a largely positive response from critics, who praised Bosworth's entertaining and moving chronicle of her early life. In addition to lauding the memoir's engaging portrait of 1950s New York, critics particularly appreciated her approach to social issues such as misogyny and homophobia, which fuel a number of the events she depicts. In her review for the *Los Angeles Times*, M. G. Lord called attention to Bosworth's approach to writing about the illegal abortion she underwent in 1958, arguing that the author's brave depiction of the trauma she experienced is among her greatest achievements. Although *The Men in My Life* primarily received positive reviews, *New York Times* critic Dwight Garner found that the memoir lacked a "warming narrative fire" and that the dialogue Bosworth records tends to make its speakers sound "lobotomized." Despite such critiques, Garner praised Bosworth's manner of writing about her romantic life as well as her thoughtful presentation of her grief and dread. Reviewers widely observed that the book covered some of the same ground as Bosworth's 1997 memoir *Anything Your Little Heart Desires*, which focuses on her father and the Hollywood Ten, but they generally found *The Men in My Life* to be the more emotionally engaging work in which, as an anonymous reviewer wrote for *Publishers Weekly*, she "comes into her own as a memoirist."

Joy Crelin

Review Sources

Garner, Dwight. "Review: A Biographer Whose Past Was as Dramatic as Her Subjects'." Review of *The Men in My Life*, by Patricia Bosworth. *The New York Times*, 24 Jan. 2017, www.nytimes.com/2017/01/24/books/review-patricia-bosworth-men-in-my-life.html. Accessed 31 Oct. 2017.

Lord, M. G. "In the 1950s, Patricia Bosworth Acted with the Best, Married the Worst, and Lost Those She Loved." Review of *The Men in My Life*, by Patricia Bosworth. *Los Angeles Times*, 26 Jan. 2017, www.latimes.com/books/jacketcopy/la-ca-jc-patricia-bosworth-20170119-story.html. Accessed 31 Oct. 2017.

Review of *The Men in My Life*, by Patricia Bosworth. *Kirkus*, 5 Oct. 2016, www.kirkusreviews.com/book-reviews/patricia-bosworth/the-men-in-my-life. Accessed 31 Oct. 2017.

Review of *The Men in My Life*, by Patricia Bosworth. *Publishers Weekly*, 24 Oct. 2016, www.publishersweekly.com/978-0-06-228790-8. Accessed 31 Oct. 2017.

The Ministry of Utmost Happiness

Author: Arundhati Roy (b. 1961)
Publisher: Knopf (New York). 464 pp.
Type of work: Novel
Time: 1950s–2010s
Locale: India

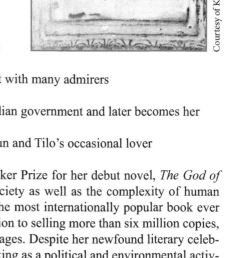

Courtesy of Knopf

The Ministry of Utmost Happiness examines India's changing sociopolitical landscape during the second half of the twentieth century. It is award-wining Indian writer Arundhati Roy's second novel.

Principal characters

ANJUM, a Muslim transgender woman who makes a home for herself in a Delhi graveyard

SADDAM, a jack-of-all-trades who comes to live in her guesthouse

TILO, an architecture student turned activist with many admirers

NAGA, Tilo's husband

BIPLAB, Tilo's friend who works for the Indian government and later becomes her landlord

MUSA, a Kashmiri freedom fighter on the run and Tilo's occasional lover

In 1997, Arundhati Roy won the Man Booker Prize for her debut novel, *The God of Small Things.* An exploration of Indian society as well as the complexity of human desire, *The God of Small Things* became the most internationally popular book ever written by a non-expatriate Indian. In addition to selling more than six million copies, it was translated into more than forty languages. Despite her newfound literary celebrity, Roy spent the years that followed working as a political and environmental activist. She focused her writing efforts on nonfiction essays and books about the negative effects of India's modernization and how the government was allowing the nation's farmers, its poorest citizens, and its natural life to suffer for the sake of new industry.

The Ministry of Utmost Happiness is the follow-up to *The God of Small Things* that Roy's fans have been waiting twenty years to read. Long-listed for the 2017 Man Booker Prize, it is a unique work that combines both the author's talent for fiction as well as her passion for political activism. These two forces are brought together through the novel's primary protagonists, Anjum, a Muslim transgender woman living in Delhi, and Tilo, a former architecture student who becomes involved in the Kashmiri separatist movement. Spanning several decades, *The Ministry of Utmost Happiness* provides a firsthand look at the changing sociopolitical landscape of India and the forces driving such change.

In many ways, the character of Anjum serves as a metaphor for modern India. Anjum is a Hijra, a Hindi-Urdu group name for transgender and intersex people. Born with intersex genitalia, Anjum realized early on that she identified as female despite her parents raising her as a boy named Aftab. Roy utilizes the feeling of chaos within the body of young Anjum to draw a parallel to the feeling of chaos that exists across the different communities that comprise India. While Anjum knows she is female, her adolescent body argues otherwise. At the age of fourteen, her voice deepens and she begins to grow tall and muscular. Meanwhile across the country, Hindus and Muslims are fighting about the identity of India. Anjum bears witness to the depth of this societal conflict when traveling one day to Gujarat. She gets caught in a riot where thousands of Hindu pilgrims are massacred. The response was to target its Muslim citizens, retaliating especially against Muslim women and children. The event proves to be so traumatic that she moves into a Delhi graveyard and for years is despondent. Over time, she builds a little house for herself there, which she calls Jannat, meaning "paradise," and starts renting out rooms. By welcoming people in need to Jannat and accepting them without judgment, Anjum creates the titular ministry of utmost happiness. Ultimately, it is a vividly wrought setting that at once feels immensely realistic and ripped from a fairy tale.

Courtesy of Mayank Austen Soofi

Arundhati Roy is an Indian writer and activist who resides in New Delhi. Her first book, The God of Small Things, *won the Man Booker Prize for fiction in 1997. The book has been translated into dozens of languages.*

In many ways, the character of Tilo appears to be modeled after Roy herself. Like the author, the character is a former architecture student with a Christian parent and a Hindu parent. Furthermore, Tilo is an activist. Roy initially introduces Tilo to the narrative from the perspective of a man named Biplab. He is one of three men whom Tilo befriends while studying architecture, each of whom have feelings for her. Of the three men, Tilo marries Naga even though she does not seem to be in love with him. Her love is reserved for Musa, the third and most complex of these men. Much of Tilo's story line revolves around her decision to travel to Kashmir to visit Musa, who is working in the Muslim separatist movement. Here, Tilo acts as a stand-in for readers; while she initially has her reservations about Musa's involvement in an extremist group, this doubt quickly fades after she witnesses the terror that the Indian government inflicts on the Kashmiri people. It affects her so much that she joins the cause. After enduring numerous disturbing scenes of violence against the Kashmiris, which Roy depicts with brutal honesty, readers are also likely to support Musa.

Roy's writing often has an undercurrent of magic realism. Her prose is rich with striking imagery. What makes Roy an especially interesting writer, however, is the fact that her vivid, poetic style is most often employed to describe ugliness. Whether it is pollution, poverty, or violence, the author spares no detail and uses the kind of language and literary tools most others would reserve for life's most beautiful moments. The way she describes dogs searching for severed limbs to eat in a hospital, for example, is haunting and impossible to forget. Roy's writing is also succinct and straightforward. By matter-of-factly recounting scenes where people are being beaten to death, she effectively demonstrates how often such events take place. This style creates a disturbing, resonant effect, which in turn enables Roy to bring international attention to serious issues that continue to persist.

To read *The Ministry of Utmost Happiness* is to be transported to India. Every page of the novel is packed with contextual detail, and the result is a highly immersive experience. As her characters move through their story lines, Roy ensures that readers of all backgrounds understand the significance of everything they say and do. To this end, she describes the different dishes they cook and eat, the kinds of birds that sit in the trees above them, and whether a rain shower is a "minor" or "major" like a typhoon. Often, she will include Hindi or Urdu lines of dialogue with translations below. Arguably one of the most interesting ways that Roy enables readers to better understand India is the way that important historical events are integral parts of her characters' lives. The violence that Tilo experiences in Kashmir is based on experiences that Roy or her friends witnessed firsthand. The Hindu massacre that Anjum gets caught in before moving to the graveyard is based on the real-life 2002 Gujarat riots that largely targeted Muslim women. Roy also describes many of her characters' memories of where they were during the assassination of Indira Gandhi by her Sikh bodyguards in 1984 and its aftermath. Whether Roy focuses on these historical anecdotes as important plot points or shares them casually in passing, they enrichen the narrative and provide a fuller picture of the complex forces that have shaped her nation.

Roy renders the characters who populate *The Ministry of Utmost Happiness* not only by revealing how they look, but also by ensuring that readers understand the characters' familiar backgrounds. It quickly becomes clear that in India, religion, class, and region determine not only how someone is treated but the way in which they see the world and subsequently act. For example, when describing Mrs. Gupta, the Hindu wife of one of Anjum's clients, Roy focuses on the fact that she is a Gopi, or female worshipper of Lord Krishna, who believes that she is living through the seventh and last cycle of rebirth. Because she believes that she will not have to pay for her sins in the next life, Mrs. Gupta is a free spirit willing to engage in less conventionally accepted activities. Roy's decision to add such nuanced, culturally specific details about her characters enhances their realness.

The Ministry of Utmost Happiness is a compelling read that belongs in the canon with Salman Rushdie's *Midnight Children* (1980), another book that balances history with magical realism. Roy succeeds in blending historical events with her proclivity for whimsy and dramatic irony to create a beautiful, heartbreaking narrative. Despite, or perhaps because of, their myriad backgrounds, the characters are all relatable and enjoyable to spend time with. More than anything, however, what makes *The Ministry of Utmost Happiness* such a significant book is its desire to draw attention to pervasive issues that continue to affect many poor, disenfranchised Indian citizens. The way in which Roy depicts these issues with extraordinary, haunting details infuses the narrative with a feeling of urgency.

Still, the novel is not without its criticisms. In her review for *The New York Times*, Michiko Kakutani praises the underlying intent of *The Ministry of Utmost Happiness* but argues that it has too many moving parts, describing it as an "ambitious but highly discursive novel that eventually builds to a moving conclusion but bogs down, badly, in the middle and is sometimes so lacking in centripetal force that it threatens to fly apart into pieces." It is true that, at times, the novel is overwhelmed by the number of story lines, characters, and perspective shifts. As such, it does not follow the classic structure of a traditional drama, which in turn dilutes the feelings of suspense. However, as a nontraditional work of fiction, *The Ministry of Utmost Happiness* arguably succeeds thanks to its experimental storytelling style as well as its appropriate conclusion.

Other critics have complained about the amount of violence throughout the novel. Writing for the *New Yorker*, Joan Acocella argues that the number of disturbing scenes are overwhelming and make the entire novel feel imbalanced in its cynicism. She writes, "You feel the need for some large-scale salvation, some great cleansing, which, when it comes, of course can't really do the job." While it cannot be denied that much of *The Ministry of Utmost Happiness* is a look at the ugliness of humanity, Roy never waivers in her portrayal of these real, violent events or her commitment to make the rest of the world accountable for them. And while the novel lacks a traditional happy ending, it does provide a glimmer of hope, which feels appropriate to the story. Ultimately, *The Ministry of Utmost Happiness* is the story that Roy has been waiting twenty years to tell.

Emily Turner

Review Sources

Acocella, Joan. "Civil Wars." Review of *The Ministry of Utmost Happiness*, by Arundhati Roy. *The New Yorker*, 5 June 2017, pp. 98–101. *Literary Reference Center Plus*, search.ebscohost.com/login.aspx?direct=true&db=lkh&AN=123247 288&site=lrc-plus. Accessed 20 Feb. 2018.

Kakutani, Michiko. "Arundhati Roy's Long-Awaited Novel Is an Ambitious Look at Turmoil in India." Review of *The Ministry of Utmost Happiness*, by Arundhati Roy. *The New York Times*, 5 June 2017, www.nytimes.com/2017/06/05/books/review-arundhati-roy-ministry-of-utmost-happiness.html. Accessed 20 Feb. 2018.

Review of *The Ministry of Utmost Happiness*, by Arundhati Roy. *Kirkus Reviews*, 15 Apr. 2017, pp. 23–24. *Literary Reference Center Plus*, search.ebscohost.com/login.aspx?direct=true&db=lkh&AN=122748641&site=lrc-plus. Accessed 20 Feb. 2018.

Walter, Natasha. "The Ministry of Utmost Happiness by Arundhati Roy Review—A Bright Mosaic." Review of *The Ministry of Utmost Happiness*, by Arundhati Roy. *The Guardian*, 2 June 2017, www.theguardian.com/books/2017/jun/02/ministry-utmost-happiness-arundhati-roy-review. Accessed 20 Feb. 2018.

Mississippi Blood

Author: Greg Iles (b. 1960)
Publisher: William Morrow (New York). 704 pp.
Type of work: Novel
Time: Present day
Locales: Natchez, Mississippi; Pollock, Louisiana; New Orleans, Louisiana

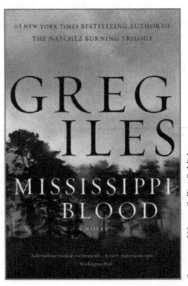

Mississippi Blood *is the sixth book in Greg Iles's Penn Cage series and the final novel in a trilogy that began with* Natchez Burning *(2014). Mayor Penn Cage, a former prosecutor, seeks to defend his father, Dr. Tom Cage, for the supposed murder of Viola Turner, the elder Cage's former nurse. The revelations that come out in this final installment have devastating repercussions for Cage and his city.*

Courtesy of HarperCollins Publishers

Principal characters

PENN CAGE, the white mayor of the small town of Natchez, Mississippi; a former prosecutor who is investigating the murder case against his father

TOM CAGE, his father, a respected white doctor and Korean War veteran accused of murdering Viola Turner by euthanasia

VIOLA TURNER, an African American nurse and his father's former lover, who was killed

CHESTER "SNAKE" KNOX, his nemesis and the leader of the Double Eagles white supremacist group

LINCOLN TURNER, his resentful, vindictive half brother; Viola's son

QUENTIN AVERY, the African American lawyer handling his father's defense

WILL DEVINE, a member of the Double Eagles whose pickup truck was seen near where Viola Turner died

DELORES "DEE" ST. DENIS, an African American woman whom he interviews and protects

PEGGY CAGE, his mother

ANNIE CAGE, his eleven-year-old daughter

TIM WEATHERS, his bodyguard, assigned to protect him due to the volatile nature of his father's murder trial

SERENITY "TEE" BUTLER, a famous black writer and former army corporal who has come to Natchez to cover the Viola Turner case

WALT GARRITY, a friend of the Cage family; a former Texas Ranger and a fellow veteran

Following the events of *The Bone Tree* (2015), the second book in Iles's trilogy, *Mississippi Blood* opens with widower Penn Cage still reeling from the death of his fiancée, newspaper publisher Caitlin Masters, at the hand of the Double Eagles, a splinter faction of the Ku Klux Klan. The Double Eagles may also be implicated in the death of Viola Turner, the woman whom Penn's father, Tom Cage, is charged with murdering. Tom reportedly entered into an assisted-suicide pact with Viola should either of them become terminally ill, though assisted suicide or mercy killings remain illegal under Mississippi law.

Penn is traveling back from meeting his father in prison when he and his family are intercepted by a pair of bikers from a white supremacist gang known as the VK, or Varangian Kindred. One biker is shot and killed by Tim, the bodyguard protecting Penn and his daughter. Penn manages to shoot the other biker, who delivers a message to him before dying. The biker warns Cage that defense lawyer Quentin Avery plans on blaming Viola's death on Snake Knox, a white supremacist who leads the Double Eagles. Should that happen, the biker warns, Cage's daughter will be killed.

When Penn delivers the message to his father in prison, Tom confesses that he did kill Viola, then dying of cancer, but refuses to say why. He also urges his son to investigate a Double Eagle member named Will Devine. Penn asks a young black reporter, Keisha Harvin, what she knows about him. He seeks Devine out, but Devine refuses to speak to him. Keisha is soon viciously attacked by a white woman who is loyal to the Double Eagles, in revenge for the deaths of the two VK bikers.

The assault on Keisha brings Serenity Butler, a famed black writer and former teacher of Keisha's, to Natchez. Serenity and Penn begin investigating the case further together, coming across a light-skinned black woman named Delores "Dee" St. Denis, whose first husband was lynched for supposedly marrying a white woman. Serenity and Penn travel to New Orleans to meet with Dee, who identifies the men who murdered her husband and sexually assaulted her, providing evidence that might help the Cages.

Tom Cage's trial begins, and it does not seem to be going well, with a great deal of evidence being laid forth against him. However, Quentin still believes that they will win, saying that he believes that the Double Eagles are connected to Viola's death but not how he knows this. Quentin's wife, Doris, confides in Penn that she is afraid that Quentin is going to throw the trial.

During the trial, Lincoln Turner, Viola's son, is called to the stand and gives unflattering testimony that is damaging to Cage's character. The case is further hampered by the damning testimony of Major Matthew Powers, who recounts how, during the Korean War, Tom had euthanized several injured soldiers who sought to die rather than be captured by the Chinese. Penn, increasingly infuriated by the way Quentin is handling the case, demands that Quentin step down and he be allowed to take over. However, Tom refuses to allow it and insists that Quentin stay on.

What emerges during Penn and Serenity's independent investigation and the trial proceedings is a tangled web of lies and secrets, brutal assaults and murders, retributions, mercy killings, and morally dubious acts of self-defense. The plot heats up when a former Double Eagle agrees to take the stand in Tom's defense and dies suddenly while offering his testimony. Soon after, VK gang members shootout the Cage family home and attempt to abduct Annie Cage.

Eventually, Tom Cage takes the witness stand and admits to the pact, but says that when the time came, he could not go through with it and that he bluffed Viola. He at last draws the connection between Viola and the Double Eagles and makes an explosive assertion about why Viola was killed. It then seems that Tom may well be acquitted, but at the last minute, he inexplicably opts to change his plea to guilty. With the guilty verdict, Tom is stripped of his medical license and sentenced to three years in prison for the crime of manslaughter.

Novelist and rock musician Greg Iles is the author of more than a dozen best-selling thrillers.

The action does not end there, however. Readers learn that Tom has been covering for someone else and why, and the final pieces of how Viola Turner really died emerge at last. In the end, Penn teams up with an unlikely ally for a furious, deadly battle against the Double Eagles, and an unexpected denouement will leave readers astonished.

When it was published on March 21, 2017, *Mississippi Blood* received near-universal acclaim from critics, who hailed it as a bold ending to the trilogy that Iles had begun with *Natchez Burning* and compared it to the work of John Grisham, John D. MacDonald, and even William Faulkner. Writing for the *Pittsburgh Post-Gazette*, Margie Romero noted that the release of the third book is "a major accomplishment for the novelist: three king-size books that are page-turning entertainments with an edge of history and a deep understanding of race relations in the American South." Bill Sheehan for the *Washington Post* wrote, "*Mississippi Blood* is the capstone to what could legitimately be called a magnum opus. Iles has emerged from an excruciating ordeal to create a superb entertainment that is a work of power, distinction and high seriousness."

Although nearly all the reviews for *Mississippi Blood* were laudatory, some critics felt that Iles's book left too many narrative threads hanging. Jackie K. Cooper, writing for the *Huffington Post*, said, "This is supposed to be the final chapter in this story but there are enough questions left unanswered to fill another book at least. If you are going to write a trilogy then have that third and last book contain all the answers to the questions you have been raising." The critic for *Kirkus Reviews* was more generous, calling it a "a clean conclusion—though with the slightest hint of an out, in case Iles decides to stretch the trilogy into another book or two." And fans will be happy to learn that Iles has intimated that although the trilogy is meant to stand alone, he plans to write a seventh installment of the Penn Cage series.

In 2011, Greg Iles was in a near-fatal car accident that left him in a coma for eight days and forced the partial amputation of his right leg. Prior to the accident, he had begun writing the first draft of *Natchez Burning*. At the time, it was intended to be another entry in his ongoing Penn Cage series; three previous Cage novels had been published between 1999 and 2009. Over the course of his three-year recovery, Iles revisited *Natchez Burning* with a new sense of purpose and the goal of telling a sprawling epic saga that not only served as a legal thriller but also a history of the complex and volatile race relations in the Deep South. Many consider the completed trilogy to be Greg Iles's magnum opus. "When I began the trilogy, I had two legs, I felt young, and my kids were beginning high school," he told Gregory Cowles in a March 2017 interview for the *New York Times*. "Now I have one leg, I feel old, and my kids are in college or graduating." In this sense, *Mississippi Blood* can be seen as the concluding chapter in a triumphant personal and professional comeback for Greg Iles.

Jeremy Brown

Review Sources

Cooper, Jackie K. "As Great as It Is, *Mississippi Blood* Leaves Too Many Unanswered Questions." Review of *Mississippi Blood*, by Greg Iles. *The Huffington Post*, 20 Mar. 2017, www.huffingtonpost.com/entry/as-great-as-it-is-mississippi-blood-leaves-too-many_us_58d028fbe4b0e0d348b34663. Accessed 19 Feb. 2018.

Foster, C. F. "*Mississippi Blood* Wraps Up Long Southern Story." Review of *Mississippi Blood*, by Greg Iles. *The Florida Times-Union* [Jacksonville, FL], 26 Mar. 2017, www.jacksonville.com/entertainment/literature/2017-03-26/book-review-mississippi-blood-wraps-long-southern-story Accessed 19 Feb. 2018.

Review of *Mississippi Blood*, by Greg Iles. *Kirkus Reviews*, 26 Dec. 2016, www.kirkusreviews.com/book-reviews/greg-iles/mississippi-blood/. Accessed 19 Feb. 2018.

Romero, Margie. "*Mississippi Blood*: The Satisfying Conclusion of Trilogy That Began with *Natchez Burning*." Review of *Mississippi Blood*, by Greg Iles. *The Pittsburgh Post-Gazette* (PA), 26 Mar. 2017, www.post-gazette.com/ae/books/2017/03/26/Mississippi-Blood-Greg-Iles-conclusion-to-Natchez-Burning-and-Bone-Tree-book-review/stories/201703140009. Accessed 19 Feb. 2018.

Sheehan, Bill. "Greg Isles Concludes His Spectacular Natchez Burning Trilogy." Review of *Mississippi Blood*, by Greg Iles. *The Washington Post*, 22 Mar. 2017, www.washingtonpost.com/entertainment/books/greg-iles-concludes-his-spectacular-natchez-burning-trilogy/2017/03/22/4110f4fe-0f22-11e7-9d5a-a83e627dc120_story.html. Accessed 19 Feb. 2018.

The Mountain

Author: Paul Yoon (b. 1980)
Publisher: Simon & Schuster (New York).
256 pp.
Type of work: Short fiction

The Mountain *is made up of six stylized stories about people in a variety of times and
places, from post–World War II France to
late-twentieth-century China, displaced from
their homes and distanced from reality.*

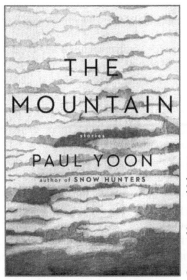

Courtesy of Simon and Schuster

Paul Yoon's *Once the Shore* (2009), a collection of tightly controlled, lyrical short stories centered on a small island just south of
the Korean Peninsula in the years following
World War II, was enthusiastically received
by critics. Yoon's novel, *The Snow Hunter*, like his stories, is tightly poetic and lyrical,
and received very good reviews in 2013. His second collection, *The Mountain*, written with the support of a fellowship from the New York Public Library, is somewhat
less focused and more meandering than his first two books. Charles Larson noted in
his review in *Counterpunch* that the stories "ramble along" as the characters wander
through unfamiliar territories and usually end without any real sense of closure. However, most reviewers have praised Yoon's continuing ability to capture a large amount
of conflict and human emotion using concise, austere prose.

The opening story, "The Willow and the Moon," begins with the first-person narrator recounting in choppy, short sentences how his mother, a French pianist, met his
father in New York City before World War I and then worked in a sanatorium in the
Hudson Valley when he was a child. The narrator was friends with Theo, the son of the
British resident doctor, but Theo's family leaves the sanatorium and the narrator never
sees him again. When the narrator grows up and the World War II begins, his mother
becomes addicted to morphine and his father deserts the family. The story begins in
earnest when the narrator is twenty-nine and joins the Red Cross in England during the
war. Caught in London during the Blitz, he writes nightly letters to Theo that cannot
be mailed. He thinks that Theo had something "deep and bright" in his life that was
never in his own life.

Years later he returns to the sanatorium and lives there alone. One day a young
woman named Elsa, the daughter of a former patient, stops with her small son on her
way to Montreal. The narrator and Elsa sit together with her son and watch a rowboat
become untethered and drift away as if being pulled by a string. Less a story than a
rhapsodic memory, with a narrator who seems lonely and detached, unconnected to
anything but the past, nothing really happens in this account except the passage of

time. This opening story introduces the reader to the kind of lonely aimlessness that characterizes most of these stylized pieces.

"Still a Fire," which takes place in 1947 and 1948, has two parts—one dealing with Mikel and the other with Karine. Mikel is twenty-four and has worked for the past two years for companies hired to sift through the rubble of the city of Calais in France after World War II. He and his neighbor Artur, a Romanian, must often scrounge for food; Artur's brother Emil paints shacks in various colors from whatever cast-off paint he can find. Mikel seems to be absolutely alone; when the two brothers rest their heads against one another, "the sudden physical intimacy tears something in him." This image is echoed by a memory of his parents with bowed heads as though they were conversing in their dreams.

Mikel and Artur are offered work locating unexploded land mines, for which there is a market. An explosion kills Artur and tears off Mikel's hand, and he is cared for by Karine, a volunteer for the Red Cross, who gives him morphine, which she also uses regularly. Mikel later finds out that the explosion blew parts of Artur's body into him, which makes him feel he has become a coffin for Artur. The tone of this story, comprised of short sentences with no introspection, focusing only on immediate sensations, puts characters like Mikel at some distance from reality and the self. Mikel's portion of the story simply ends with him walking away and never reappearing. Characters in Yoon's stories often simply walk away and disappear.

Paul Yoon's debut collection of short stories, Once the Shore, *was chosen by the* New York Times *for its 100 Notable Books of 2009. His novel,* Snow Hunters, *won the New York Public Library's 2014 Young Lions Fiction Award. His stories have appeared in* The Best American Short Stories *and* The O. Henry Prize Stories.

The Karine portion of the story begins after Mikel leaves, with Karine in a half-conscious state that seems distant from physical reality. Artur's brother Emil finds her in the car where Mikel has left her and takes her to a shanty where she goes through withdrawal. In an encounter at a landfill, she fights off a crazed Emil by brutally smashing in his face. Karine then travels toward Bordeaux, hopping train cars and catching rides. Because of the staccato way her journey is described, she seems distant from reality, almost in a daze, although it seems she has kicked the morphine habit. She later meets Luc, an-eleven-year old who has lost a thumb. Karine and Luc are left waiting, but for whom we do not know. She watches the boy's chest rise and fall and hears the bending branches of the tree under which they sit and "then the sound of a small, bright thing overhead, crossing." The story seems to shift from the real, physical world to a world of Karine's projections or imagination—or perhaps the poetic world of Paul Yoon.

"Galicia" is the story of Antje and her husband, Mathis, who are living in San Sebastián, Spain. He manages the hotel where she works. When she loses her week-old son because of a heart problem, she walks out of the hospital and just keeps walking until she can go on no longer. Yoon describes her emotional transformation as "a shift inside her. A restructuring. As though there was something new inside, somewhere beneath her ribs. Or something old she never knew was there." This is another story of someone distanced from contact with reality, made up of short repetitive sentences with little sense of connection between them—just one thing after another. Mathis goes to a conference, leaving Antje alone. When she goes to the train station to meet him on his return, a man asks where she is going, and she says, without thinking, Galicia, where there has been an explosion. The man says he is going there too and offers her his hand, which she accepts, without comprehending what is happening. Again, the central character of this story moves passively through the world without conscious intention or purpose. After Antje has several encounters with strangers, the man disappears. Like the other stories, "Galicia" ends in mid-wait, as Antje makes her return to San Sebastián and whatever awaits her there.

"The Mountain" is about twenty-six-year-old woman named Faye, who has lived in the South Korean port city of Incheon for ten years. It begins with her sitting on a bench at a bus stop when a man, Tad, mysteriously asks her to "come back home," offering her work in Shanghai, China. She takes a ferry with others and gets a job in a plant on an assembly line putting cameras together. She meets another woman in the complex named Yonha, with whom she attends a party. They go on a truck to another party in the country, and she encounters Tad again. However, like many other characters in this collection, Tad disappears. And like others, Faye seems passively detached from reality.

She remembers a painting of a mountain that her father found in the trash, which they gave to her mother for her birthday, although she cannot remember her mother looking at it or why her father lied about where it came from or why she joined him in the lie. Tad returns, and they ride into the mountains and go into a mansion, where she sees statues of horses, one of which seems to come alive and approach them. "It was as though they had stumbled upon somewhere even farther than where they were," Yoon writes. When Faye talks to the groundskeeper, the groundskeeper alludes to Faye harboring a major secret and wanting to know why she was keeping it from Tad. The parting line emphasizes the stylized, literary world of these stories: "From across the distance, morning came into the mountains."

The final story, "Milner Field," begins: "Before my father died, he told me a story." The father was a doctor in a town in New York, just north of the city, having emigrated from South Korea in 1976. Once in a while he would tell the narrator a story from his life, unexpectedly, as though he were finishing a private thought. The narrator says it was like they were speaking, "like he wanted me to be a part of whatever memory he had tunneled into." The father tells a story about Takashi Inoue, a childhood neighbor who accidently killed his fifteen-year-old sister and was sent away, never to see his family again. The family spent the rest of their lives "vanishing into themselves."

The story then shifts to the narrator's daughter, Philippa, who, at age twenty-two, loses a leg from the knee down and must wear a prosthesis. She becomes a geologist, and the narrator, who is separated from his wife, moves to London to be with her. In the last part of the story, he vacations with Philippa at an estate called Milner Field. While he waits for her, he sees a horse that looks up in his direction and then goes away into the field. Then, in town, he meets Maya, a Japanese woman who works in a shop, but she disappears, followed by some horses as she drives away. The story ends with the narrator and Philippa in a moment of sharing some secret as they go to dinner together.

Thus ends Paul Yoon's new collection of stories, which creates a highly stylized world that, like all great literature, says more in what is not written than in what is.

Charles E. May

Review Sources

Athitakis, Mark. Review of *The Mountain*, by Paul Yoon. *Star Tribune* [Minneapolis], 11 Aug. 2017, www.startribune.com/review-the-mountain-by-paul-yoon/439735343/. Accessed 26 Dec. 2017.

Larson, Charles R. Review of *The Mountain*, by Paul Yoon. *Counterpunch*, 22 Sept. 2017, www.counterpunch.org/2017/09/22/review-paul-yoons-the-mountain. Accessed 26 Dec. 2017.

Masad, Ilana. "Paul Yoon's 'The Mountain' Is Quiet, Restrained and Howling beneath the Surface." *Los Angeles Times*, 18 Aug. 2017, www.latimes.com/books/jacketcopy/la-ca-jc-paul-yoon-20170818-story.html. Accessed 26 Dec. 2017.

Review of *The Mountain*, by Paul Yoon. *Kirkus Reviews*, 6 June 2017, www.kirkus-reviews.com/book-reviews/paul-yoon/the-mountain-yoon. Accessed 26 Dec. 2017.

Review of *The Mountain*, by Paul Yoon. *Publishers Weekly*, 19 June 2017, www.publishersweekly.com/978-1-5011-5408-9. Accessed 26 Dec. 2017.

Strauss, Leah. Review of *The Mountain*, by Paul Yoon. *Booklist*, July 2017, www.booklistonline.com/The-Mountain-Paul-Yoon/pid=8903263. Accessed 26 Dec. 2017.

My Life, My Love, My Legacy

Author: Coretta Scott King (1927–2006)
   As told to Rev. Dr. Barbara Reynolds
Publisher: Henry Holt (New York). 368 pp.
Type of work: Memoir
Time: 1927–2006
Locale: United States

Coretta Scott King, widow of civil rights leader Dr. Martin Luther King Jr., shares the story of her life as a wife, single mother, civil rights leader, and peace activist with Rev. Dr. Barbara Reynolds.

Principal personages

CORETTA SCOTT KING, civil rights leader
   and peace activist
MARTIN LUTHER KING JR., her husband and
   leader of the 1950s and 1960s civil rights movement
YOLANDA, her oldest daughter
MARTIN LUTHER KING III, her oldest son
DEXTER, her youngest son
BERNICE, her youngest daughter
HOSEA WILLIAMS, friend of Dr. King and coleader of the Southern Christian Leadership Conference (SCLC)
RALPH ABERNATHY, friend of Dr. King and cofounder of the SCLC

One of the photographs appearing in Coretta Scott King's memoir *My Life, My Love, My Legacy* is of Jacqueline Kennedy offering condolences to King on April 9, 1968, the day of Dr. Martin Luther King Jr.'s funeral. As the widows of iconic leaders who were assassinated, the women, both dressed in black, warmly clasp gloved hands in mutual understanding. Approximately two months after this image was captured, the two women would console another widow whose well-known husband was also killed by a gunman—Ethel Kennedy, wife of presidential candidate Robert F. Kennedy.

The 1960s was a bloody decade. White supremacists and African Americans clashed—often with fatal results—in the American South; thousands of soldiers and civilians died as the Vietnam War raged overseas; and students on college campuses engaged in spirited and sometimes violent protests against the social and political establishments. And Martin Luther King Jr.'s wife, Coretta Scott King, was a key figure in this turbulent time in American history. In *My Life, My Love, My Legacy*, she emerges from the shadow of her iconic husband to share the story of her life before, during, and after the 1950s and 1960s, when the civil rights movement was at its peak. She writes, "There is a Mrs. King. There is also Coretta. . . . I'm proud to have been a wife, a single parent, and a leader. But I am more than a label. I am also Coretta. . . . In reading this memoir, I hope somehow you see *Coretta*."

King begins her recollections, which were collected and taped over years of meetings with her friend and mentee Rev. Dr. Barbara Reynolds, with stories from her childhood during the late 1920s and 1930s. African Americans in the segregated South were denied basic rights, including the right to vote, attend schools with white children, and use the same restrooms and water fountains as their white neighbors. The threat of violence was always present. One Thanksgiving night, when King was fifteen, white racists burned down the house her father built with his own hands. She credits her parents with instilling in her the resilience and faith she would later draw upon as a civil rights activist.

King sought to escape the racism of the South by attending Antioch College, a socially and politically progressive school in Yellow Springs, Ohio. An elementary education major, she applied to be a student teacher in the Yellow Springs public school system. Her academic supervisor discouraged her and advised that she complete her student teaching requirements in a segregated school located nine miles away. Outraged, she appealed to the president of the college—and was disappointed that he did not lend his support. However, the school eventually awarded her a scholarship from the Antioch Interracial Scholarship Fund to help her pay for the next step in her education.

King found Boston, Massachusetts, and the New England Conservatory of Music more welcoming. Boston was not devoid of racism, but the stimulating intellectual environment nurtured the talent and interests of all students. For the first time in her life, King enjoyed friendships with both whites and African Americans and could develop her gift as a singer without the fear of being prejudged because of her skin color. In a chapter titled "I Have Something to Offer," she declares, "Overall, I was extremely happy." For the first time, she began to see herself as a talented, independent woman who was capable of forging her own path.

But her life veered sharply away from her chosen career when a friend suggested she date Martin Luther King Jr. From the first, he made it plain that he was looking for a suitable wife. As their courtship progressed, her dream of promoting racial equality by traveling the world as a concert singer was derailed by her budding relationship with the charismatic Boston University PhD candidate. She loved him but was reticent about sharing a future with him. She admits that before they married and moved back to Atlanta, she was "not thrilled about leaving Boston" because she worried that her "will would be compressed and subjugated." When they talked about returning to the South, she comments ominously, "I heard the shackles forming around my legs."

That she uses an image reminiscent of slavery is telling. Not only does she acknowledge misgivings about relinquishing her professional career, she also voices apprehension about becoming a pastor's wife in the segregated South. In addition, she might also have felt constrained by her husband's view of a "woman's place." When she expressed a desire to continue her musical career after they married, he bluntly told her that "a man should be able to take care of his wife, and she should not work." His comment may surprise twenty-first century readers, but such chauvinism was a prevalent mindset among men in the 1950s. Later in the chapter, she paints a more moderate picture of Dr. King's attitude toward women. When he agreed to remove the traditional promise to "obey" from their wedding vows, she claims it was because "his view of women was more progressive than that of most men of his generation." Yet, many years after his death, she was asked if she would ever marry again. She explains, "I waited on Martin hand and foot. He'd step out of his pajamas and leave them right in the middle of the floor, and I'd pick them up. I'd bring his food to him in bed if he felt like staying in bed. Can you imagine me doing all that now, at my age?" Except for a few instances such as these, she does not offer many domestic glimpses in the book. When she does, she vacillates between sharing candid observations about her family life and preserving the public image of her husband.

Once the King family moved to Montgomery, Alabama, King embraced her role as a wife, mother, and pastor's spouse. But she was not prepared for the threatening phone calls, burning crosses, and bombings her family and other black citizens endured. The violence committed against her family only reinforced her "warrior spirit," as well as her faith in God. The challenging years that saw the Rosa Parks protest, Montgomery bus boycott, lunch counter sit-ins, mass demonstrations, Dr. King's imprisonment in the Birmingham jail, the Selma campaign, the Freedom Rides, the Washington rally where Dr. King famously delivered his "I Have a Dream" speech, and other watershed events of the civil rights era honed King's skills in activism and deepened her commitment to nonviolent change.

In reflecting upon her marriage to Dr. King, she acknowledges that she was "married not only to him but to the movement." Her responsibilities as the spouse of one of the movement's most prominent leaders took her to other parts of the country, where she would raise money through speaking engagements and concerts. Although Dr. King was appreciative of her efforts, he sometimes expressed disapproval concerning her activities. She quotes a revealing exchange where he said to her, "You see, I am called [by God], and you aren't." She recalls responding, "I have always felt that I have a call on my life, too. I've been called by God, too, to do something. You may not understand it, but I have a sense of calling, too." The traditional "calling" of women in the prefeminist era was that of wife and mother. Although King admirably fulfilled these roles, it is apparent from the conversation she relates that she chafed under the expectation that wives should submit to the wishes of their husbands.

Coretta Scott King was an American civil rights and peace activist, an international human rights champion, and a writer.

Unfortunately, tragedy led King to forge her own identity as a leader. When Dr. King was assassinated, she lost the man she loved and became a single mother to their children. She also inherited her husband's mantle as an activist. It was a turning point that enabled her to use her hard-won knowledge and experience to work for justice, peace, and reconciliation. In a chapter titled "My Fifth Child," she details the challenges that she faced when she decided to build the King Center in Atlanta, Georgia. Her conception for the center was not limited to a brick-and-mortar building, but instead she envisioned it as "an extension of Martin's personality," a place that "would advocate not just for civil rights but for human rights" and "agitate for national political empowerment and promote social and economic justice around the world."

King's goal was laudable, but she ran into opposition from the start. The reverends Hosea Williams and Ralph Abernathy accused her of attracting donations away from the Southern Christian Leadership Conference (SCLC), which her husband had co-founded. Her faith in God and her "warrior spirit" empowered her to stand her ground. She attributed their resentment to a deep-rooted bias against women: "Remember, this was the early 1970s, and these were primarily Baptist preachers with a strong sense of male superiority. Most thought that women should stay in the shadows." She was not deterred by their criticism, however, and dealt with the "labor pangs" that ensued, including raising the necessary donations, finding the right executive director, revital-izing the surrounding neighborhood, and instituting educational programs focusing on Dr. King's philosophy of nonviolence. Her dream was realized when, in the early 1980s, construction was completed and the site became a mecca for people of all ethnicities, faiths, social backgrounds, and political persuasions who wanted to learn about Dr. King's legacy.

King passed away in 2006, so it is natural to wonder why her book was published eleven years after her death. In an afterword titled "The Making of Her Memoir," Reynolds states that in 1997, King asked her to help her write her autobiography. But nothing came of their plans because, Reynolds speculates, King may have been reluc-tant to allow publication while she was still alive. In a 2017 radio interview, Reynolds offered a different reason for the book's delay. She suggested it took more time than she expected to craft her research materials to better reflect King's voice. Finally, a third possibility exists. A contentious legal battle developed between her children, Bernice, Dexter, and Martin Luther King III (Yolanda had already passed away), dis-puting the rights to King's writings, photographs, and personal property. By 2009, the book deal was in jeopardy. Eventually, however, the King children agreed to allow Reynolds to submit the manuscript for publication.

Overall, the book certainly reveals the content of King's character, including her courage, determination, commitment to her Christian faith, and dedication to non-violence as an instrument for social and political change. How much of the narrative reflects Reynolds's own interpretation is open to question. Nonetheless, King's first-hand account of key events in American history is powerful, informative, and worth reading—especially for those who want an inside look at the civil rights movement and its aftermath.

Pegge Bochynski

Review Sources

Cook, Mattie. Review of *My Life, My Love, My Legacy*, by Coretta Scott King. *Library Journal*, 15 Dec. 2016, p. 103. *Literary Reference Center Plus*, search. ebscohost.com/login.aspx?direct=true&db=lkh&AN=120470053&site=lrc-plus. Accessed 28 Nov. 2017.

Jones, Charisse. "Coretta Scott King's Memoir Will Inspire." Review of *My Life, My Love, My Legacy*, by Coretta Scott King. *USA Today*, 16 Jan. 2017, www. usatoday.com/story/life/books/2017/01/16/my-life-my-love-my-legacy-coretta-scott-king-book-review/96412826/. Accessed 28 Nov. 2017.

Mondor, Colleen. Review of *My Life, My Love, My Legacy*, by Coretta Scott King. *Booklist*, 15 Dec. 2016, pp. 12–13. *Literary Reference Center Plus*, search. ebscohost.com/login.aspx?direct=true&db=lkh&AN=120219037&site=lrc-plus. Accessed 28 Nov. 2017.

Review of *My Life, My Love, My Legacy*, by Coretta Scott King. *Kirkus Reviews*, 15 Nov. 2016, p. 1. *Literary Reference Center Plus*, search.ebscohost.com/login.aspx ?direct=true&db=lkh&AN=119454277&site=lrc-plus. Accessed 28 Nov. 2017.

Review of *My Life, My Love, My Legacy*, by Coretta Scott King. *Publishers Weekly*, 28 Nov. 2016, p. 63. *Literary Reference Center Plus*, search.ebscohost.com/login. aspx?direct=true&db=lkh&AN=119714841&site=lrc-plus. Accessed 28 Nov. 2017.

Williams, Patricia J. "Mrs. King and Coretta: A Posthumous Memoir Explores Public and Private Selves." Review of *My Life, My Love, My Legacy*, by Coretta Scott King. *The New York Times*, 11 Jan. 2017, www.nytimes.com/2017/01/11/books/ review/coretta-scott-king-memoir-my-life-my-love-my-legacy.html. Accessed 28 Nov. 2017.

The New Odyssey
The Story of the Twenty-First Century Refugee Crisis

Author: Patrick Kingsley (b. 1989)
First published: *The New Odyssey: The Story of Europe's Refugee Crisis*, 2016, in Great Britain
Publisher: Liveright (New York). 368 pp.
Type of work: Literary history, current affairs
Time: 2012–16
Locales: Europe, Africa, and the Middle East

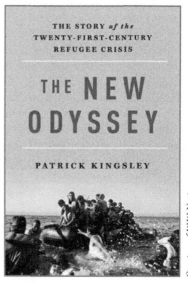

THE STORY *of the* TWENTY-FIRST-CENTURY REFUGEE CRISIS

THE **NEW**

ODYSSEY

PATRICK KINGSLEY

Courtesy of W.W. Norton

Award-winning journalist Patrick Kingsley follows the present-day odyssey of Syrian refugee Hashem al-Souki while reporting on the larger refugee crisis in Europe in The New Odyssey: The Story of the Twenty-First Century Refugee Crisis.

Principal personages

HASHEM AL-SOUKI, a Syrian refugee, a former civil servant
HAJJ, a human smuggler in Libya
ERIC KEMPSON, a humanitarian volunteer on the Greek island Lesvos
HANS BREUER, a Jewish shepherd and a humanitarian volunteer in Austria

London-born journalist Patrick Kingsley began his career as the UK *Guardian* foreign correspondent in Cairo, Egypt, in 2013, two years after the Arab Spring first roiled Tahrir Square. In February 2015, the newspaper named him their first migration correspondent after record numbers of migrants arrived on the proverbial doorstep of Europe seeking entry. That year, some 170,000 migrants, mostly from Syria, Eritrea, and sub-Saharan Africa, arrived in Italy via Libya—almost three times the previous record. A new European gateway, Greece, became the sought-for entry point for an estimated 850,000 refugees (including Afghans and Iraqis as well). Kingsley notes that between 2014 and 2016, some 1.4 million people from Africa and the Middle East had sought refuge in Europe, constituting the world's largest mass migration since World War II.

Kingsley's second, well-received book, *The New Odyssey*, draws largely from his reporting between 2014 to 2016. In it, he follows men, women, and children as they embark on dangerous journeys by truck across the Sahara Desert, on foot across the Balkans in southeastern Europe, and by inflatable rubber dinghy or fishing trawler across the Mediterranean and Aegean Seas. These routes, navigated by well-connected smugglers, cell phones, and GPS devices, are both modern and strikingly ancient, reminiscent of the mythic Odyssey of the title. This dichotomy is best expressed in one anecdote about a precise, detailed set of instructions that Kingsley found on the social media website Facebook, instructing prospective travelers how best to travel on foot from Athens to Hungary. Kingsley notes the cruel irony of his own freedom of movement as compared to that of his subjects: in the week it took him to cross nine or ten borders, he told a reporter for National Public Radio (NPR), more than 1,200 refugees died trying to cross just one. The crude horror of their plight appears as out of another, long ago time.

Kingsley was named foreign affairs correspondent of the year 2015 at the British Journalism Awards for his four-part series chronicling the individual odyssey of a Syrian refugee named Hashem al-Souki. That piece provides the backbone of *The New Odyssey*. Al-Souki, a forty-year-old civil servant, lived near Damascus with his wife, a teacher named Hayam, and their three sons when the war began in 2011. In mid-April 2012, on his eldest son's birthday, al-Souki was arrested. He spent six months in a prison where he was beaten and tortured. After his release, the family moved several times, trying to escape the constant bombing. He applied for a passport in 2013, but in doing so, al-Souki was arrested again. Mercifully, he was released days later. In June, he succeeded and the family endured a dangerous journey to Egypt. Once they arrived, however, a military coup engendered an abrupt policy change; al-Souki and his family were then in danger of arrest. Kingsley first encountered the family in September 2014, after they attempted to cross the Mediterranean Sea in a rubber boat in the hope of reaching Europe. They were arrested in that attempt, but perversely the setback ended up saving their lives. The boat they attempted to board later sank, killing as many as five hundred passengers.

When al-Souki decided to try the crossing again, this time alone, in 2015, Kingsley offered to chronicle his experience, seeking to answer why someone would choose to attempt such a dangerous journey a second time. As Kingsley discovered, most migrants (he prefers "migrant" to "refugee," for reasons explained in the book) will risk regular drownings and extortion and torture at the hands of smugglers to attempt crossings many times over. Kingsley emphasizes this point, and in this way, the book is a plea to European countries and the United States, which continue to adopt isolationist policies and ignore the suffering of those trying to reach their borders. The people will not stop coming, Kingsley writes. There is no way to stop them, only ways to organize their arrival. A case in point: in 2014, Italy ended a crucial naval mission called Operation Mare Nostrum that had rescued over 100,000

Courtesy of Tom Kingsley

Award-winning journalist Patrick Kingsley was the first migration correspondent at the UK Guardian. *He serves as the* New York Times *bureau chief in Turkey. His first book,* How to Be Danish: A Journey to the Cultural Heart of Denmark, *was published in 2012.*

migrants on the Mediterranean that year alone. The decision was strategic: perhaps other countries would be forced to step in and finally pick up some of the slack. No such aid was offered, however. A British politician, echoing a popular line of thinking, argued that continuing a rescue mission would entice and thus endanger more migrants. In early 2015, more migrants attempted the crossing anyway, and eighteen hundred (up from ninety-six the previous year) drowned in the process.

Perhaps unsurprisingly, Kingsley sharply criticizes Europe's response to the crisis. Why, he asks, must a country like Lebanon absorb 1 million refugees into its population of 4.5 million, while the European Union has offered to accept only 120,000 refugees into a population of 500 million over the course of two years? The United States is not exempt from his ire either. After two perpetrators of the 2015 terrorist attacks in Paris, France, were labeled Syrian refugees, thirty-one US governors proposed to halt resettlement programs for Syrian refugees in their states. With the exception of the overburdened Germany and Sweden, Europe's response, Kingsley writes in one damning passage, "constitutes an abdication of decency." One Syrian man tells Kingsley, waiting to cross the Mediterranean outside of Cairo:

> Even if there was a [European] decision to drown the migrant boats, there will still be people going by boat because the individual considers himself dead already. Right now, Syrians consider themselves dead. Maybe not physically, but psychologically and socially [a Syrian] is a destroyed human being, he's reached the point of death.

And not merely Syrians, Kingsley notes. He briefly describes the crushing lot of Eritreans, who hail from a small coastal country in northeast Africa and, in their midteens, are conscripted into military service for life. Others fleeing war and insurgency in Afghanistan and Iraq provide a strong endorsement for the words of the Somali British poet Warsan Shire, whom Kingsley quotes in one of the book's epigraphs: "no one puts their children in a boat / unless the water is safer than the land."

After arriving safely in Italy, al-Souki's journey was far from over. He hoped to make it undetected all the way to his brother-in-law in Sweden, the country where, he believed, he had the best chance of applying for asylum and being reunited legally with his wife and children, who remain in Egypt. If al-Souki were stopped in Italy, France, or Germany, it could be years before he saw his family again because of the bureaucratic asylum process there. In other words, the stakes of his seemingly mundane train journey were quite high. Kingsley, who accompanied him on this leg of the trip, describes each fumbled disguise and nervous cigarette in Alfred Hitchcockian detail. In his interview with NPR, Kingsley referred to his protagonist as an Everyman, but al-Souki comes across as a textured individual. His story may constitute the bulk of Kingsley's book, but other personages—from refugees to smugglers to a few Europeans quixotically trying to shepherd the arriving migrants to safety themselves—are subject to Kingsley's same probing, empathetic gaze. One volunteer, Hans Breuer, a shepherd by profession, drives refugees from Hungary to Austria using an old network of unmarked trails, in part because his parents were Holocaust survivors. He is not the only one with fresh memories of fleeing atrocity. A number of the refugees Kingsley meets are refugees several times over. Nasser, another Damascene, tells the author that his parents fled Palestine in 1948. He was born in Kuwait, but his family fled again when Iraq invaded in 1991. When Kingsley meets him, of course, he, his pregnant wife, and their toddler son are on the move again.

The stories give the impression of a perpetually shifting landscape. At one point, Kingsley tagged along with a group as it crossed the border between Greece and Macedonia. No markers denoted their passage, only a field of sweet corn and then a vineyard. "In moments like these, you realise the absurdity of dividing the earth into fairly arbitrary parcels of turf," he writes. "It's a facile point to make, but sometimes even the facile feels profound when you're wandering through Europe with people whose future depends on repeatedly flouting these invisible divisions, and whose own homeland is currently in the process of being divvied up into a new set of arbitrary parcels." Reading with this in mind, it is not hard to empathize with Yama Nayab, an Afghan surgeon, who says wearily, "Wherever I find a safe place, a country that accepts me and gives me a chance, I will start my life there."

Molly Hagan

Review Sources

Jasanoff, Maya. "*The New Odyssey* and *Cast Away* Review—Stories from Europe's Refugee Crisis." Review of *The New Odyssey: The Story of the Twenty-First Century Refugee Crisis*, by Patrick Kingsley, and *Cast Away*, by Charlotte McDonald-Gibson. *The Guardian*, 21 May 2016, www.theguardian.com/books/2016/may/21/the-new-odyssey-patrick-kingsley-cast-away-charlotte-mcdonald-gibson-europes-refugee-crisis-review. Accessed 3 Dec. 2017.

Review of *The New Odyssey: The Story of the Twenty-First Century Refugee Crisis*, by Patrick Kingsley. *Kirkus*, 5 Oct. 2016, www.kirkusreviews.com/book-reviews/patrick-kingsley/the-new-odyssey. Accessed 3 Dec. 2017.

Review of *The New Odyssey: The Story of the Twenty-First Century Refugee Crisis*, by Patrick Kingsley. *Publishers Weekly*, 19 Sept. 2016, www.publishersweekly.com/978-1-63149-255-6. Accessed 3 Dec. 2017.

Norton, James. "*The New Odyssey* Follows the Men, Women, Children Streaming to Europe." Review of *The New Odyssey: The Story of the Twenty-First Century Refugee Crisis*, by Patrick Kingsley. *The Christian Science Monitor*, 10 Jan. 2017, www.csmonitor.com/Books/Book-Reviews/2017/0110/The-New-Odyssey-follows-the-men-women-children-streaming-to-Europe. Accessed 3 Dec. 2017.

The Ninth Hour

Author: Alice McDermott (b. 1953)
Publisher: Farrar, Straus and Giroux (New
  York). 256 pp.
Type of work: Novel
Time: Early twentieth century
Locale: Brooklyn, New York

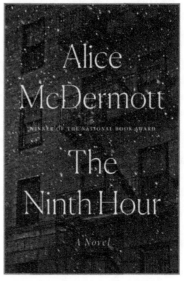

Courtesy of Macmillan

*In her eighth novel, Alice McDermott fol-
lows the lives of poor Irish Catholic immigrant families living in Brooklyn, New York,
in the early twentieth century and the group
of nuns who assist them.*

Principal characters
  Sally, the protagonist, an Irish American
who was born after the death of her father,
Jim
  Annie, her mother
  Sister St. Saviour, a nun who finds work for Annie in the convent laundry
  Sister Jeanne, a young, gentle nun who befriends Annie
  Sister Illuminata, the convent laundress
  Sister Lucy, a nun who is a severe but effective nurse
  Patrick Tierney, Sally's husband
  Michael Tierney, Patrick's father
  Mrs. Costello, a patient at the convent
  Red Whelan, a man paid to take the place of Patrick's grandfather in the Civil War

In the prologue to *The Ninth Hour* (2017), an Irish immigrant named Jim, who has
been fired from his job as a subway trainman in Brooklyn, New York, turns on the
gas in his apartment and kills himself, leaving his pregnant wife, Annie, without any
means of support. Sister St. Saviour, a Catholic nun of the Little Nursing Sisters of the
Sick Poor is in the neighborhood when the escaping gas starts a fire in the apartment.
In the fire's aftermath, she befriends Jim's widow, Annie, and provides her with a place
to stay and a job at the convent. The novel follows the life of Annie's daughter, Sally,
from her birth to her old age.

A family novel that spans three generations, *The Ninth Hour* is narrated in part by
the future children of Sally and her husband, Patrick Tierney. Though unidentified,
their voices occasionally interject to describe events that foreshadow their own births
such as their parents being pushed along in strollers by their grandparents. This chorus
layers a ghostly voice to the anecdotes and stories revealed in McDermott's narrative.
Patrick Reardon, in his *Chicago Tribune* review, suggests that *The Ninth Hour* is about
the ghosts that haunt families. And indeed, the reader meets several spirits that haunt

the family throughout this book—first, the ghost of Jim, and later Red Whelan, a man who took Patrick Tierney's grandfather's place in the Civil War. Critically wounded, Whelan spent his life secluded in an attic room and cared for by Patrick's great-aunt Rose. When Patrick's grandfather dies, Patrick's mother tells her husband, Michael, that she will not be plagued by his ghost, adding that if he is going to haunt anyone it would be Patrick.

The other important familial characters in the novel are three nuns of the Little Nursing Sisters of the Sick Poor who take in Annie and her child, Sally. Sister Illuminata, the convent washerwoman, is a wizard in the laundry room, with a laboratory of ingredients she mixes to purify clothes as she follows an unyielding routine of rigorous washing. The laundry room embodies a central theme in the novel that underlies much of its action: the basic Christian story of the church's attempt to transform the physical into the spiritual and cleansing of mortal sins. Young, gentle Sister Jeanne becomes a friend to Annie, while Sister Lucy is a no-nonsense person and a fine nurse. Sister Jeanne believes that fairness demands that wounds should heal and insults be recompensed. Sister Lucy, on the other hand, would have preferred a contemplative life alone with God.

The title *The Ninth Hour* is derived from the Catholic Church's designation for mid-afternoon prayers that occur at 3 p.m., or the ninth hour, the time of the death of Jesus Christ. The time of prayer is a central detail to the characters' lives in the convent. However, as is typical of the juxtaposition of the physical and the spiritual in this novel, McDermott also uses the ninth hour to denote the time of Jim's suicide, as well as a sexual rendezvous Annie has later in the novel.

Partially due to its setting, the novel includes many descriptions of the bodily fluids of the sick and dying. Sister Illuminata says that "down here" in the laundry room she and her helpers, who include Annie and her daughter Sally, are like priests who do their best to "transform what is ugly, soiled, stained" and send it back up into the world like "a resurrected soul." In her *New York Times* review, Mary Gordon singles out McDermott's hyper-realistic depiction of illness and disease as an important achievement of the novel, for, she suggests, the plight of the body situates the life of a nun where it ideally belongs. Most basically, the theme of the book is the central theme of Christianity: finding a way to deal with the "feral smell" of physicality and its inevitable implication, death. Sister Illuminata says that because of original sin, all things human tend to filth and squalor, all things mortal tend toward pain and suffering. The life of a nursing Sister, she says, is "A life immaculate and pure," an antidote to suffering and pain.

Having spent most of her childhood observing the work of the nuns, Sally decides she wishes to emulate them. A central scene in the novel details her train trip to Chicago to begin her novitiate to become a nun in the church. A dirty woman, who is running away from her husband, sits beside Sally and using coarse language, horrifies Sally with intimate descriptions of her and her husband. Sally is further appalled by a woman who mistreats her small son, dragging him about the train car and shouting at him. Finally, she is conned out of her money by a young girl who tells her a phony sob story. Sally knows that her vocation is being tested. She thinks she smells fire and brimstone, a fit odor for this "hellish train" that seems so far from the "pretty joy" she had felt earlier about the consecrated life she felt called to. When she arrives in Chicago she tells the two nuns who meet her at the train station that she has thought better of joining them and immediately buys a return ticket home.

There are stories within stories in this novel. For example, when Michael Tierney and his son Patrick leave the funeral of the elder Patrick Tierney, Michael tells his son the story of Red Whelan coming home after the war missing an arm and a leg and being taken to the attic room where he would spend the rest of his life. Aunt Rose, just a child at the time, went on to care for him until he died. The final blow to the family, who bear the guilt of Whelan's dismemberment, is that

Alice McDermott won the National Book Award in Fiction for her novel Charming Billy *in 1998.*

Courtesy of Epic Photography Jamie Schoenberger

he outlives the elder Patrick. After his death, Aunt Rose writes to tell the family that her brother was an unhappy man, weighed down all his life by the "burden of gratitude."

Sister Jeanne tells the story of Jeanne Jugan, in France in the last century, who took in old women and cared for them. Jeanne Jugan goes to the priest and asks if the women can form a religious community of their own, and thus the Little Sisters of the Sick Poor is born. But the priest visits Rome and tells the church officials that he was the one who started the order, the one who first found a blind widow on the street and told Jeanne Jugan to take care of her. Sister Jeanne says that the point to remember "is that truth finds the light. Lies, big or small, never stay hidden."

Sister Illuminata tells of a time when she saw a couple engaged in sex and thinking "there is a hunger," a long-forgotten lesson she recalls when Sally returns from Chicago and discovers Annie's affair with Mr. Costello. Sister Illuminata tells Sally they can pray for her mother's soul and perhaps do additional works of mercy in the name of her mother—a penance to gain indulgence for her soul. Sally chooses to sit with Mrs. Costello, who has lost her leg to an infection. Sally knows her mother lives in mortal sin and that if she died nothing would prevent her mother from falling into Satan's arms except the indulgence she is earning for her by caring for Mrs. Costello.

Mrs. Costello's troubles come to seem endless, and finally Sally decides to abandon her, feeling she has once again failed in her good intentions. Sally then devises a terrible plot against Mrs. Costello to help her mother, and when Mrs. Costello dies soon after, Sister Jeanne tells Sally that she did not harm the woman, insisting, "God is fair. He knows the truth." But Sally, having seen Mrs. Costello die, thinks she cannot live knowing that "feral smell of death" is what her life is aiming her toward.

The final chapter sums everything up, with Sally's nameless descendants listening to family stories told by their father. The ultimate resolution, however, is spiritual rather than historical, and belongs to the gentle Sister Jeanne, who asks the children if they have ever worn an itchy old coat and know what it is like to remove the coat and feel the air in the house "as cool and as sweet as silk . . . That's how you'll feel when you get to heaven, see?" she says. She whispers, "God has hidden these things from the wise and prudent" and "revealed them only to the little ones."

Charles E. May

Review Sources

Begley, Sarah. "Review: Grace and Gumption in Alice McDermott's *The Ninth Hour*. Review of *The Ninth Hour*, by Alice McDermott. *Time*, 21 Sept. 2017, time.com/4951196/alice-mcdermott-the-ninth-hour. Accessed 29 Nov. 2017.

Gordon, Mary. "In Alice McDermott's Novel, A Cloistered Life Blows Open." Review of *The Ninth Hour*, by Alice McDermott. *The New York Times*, 2 Oct. 2017, www.nytimes.com/2017/10/02/books/review/the-ninth-hour-alice-mcdermott. html. Accessed 29 Nov. 2017.

King, Lily. "Alice McDermott's New Novel Begins with Suicide and Culminates in Murder." Review of *The Ninth Hour*, by Alice McDermott. *The Washington Post*, 14 Sept. 2017, www.washingtonpost.com/entertainment/books/alice-mcdermotts-new-novel-begins-with-suicide-and-culminates-in-murder/2017/09/14/dde9b18a-94ce-11e7-aace-04b862b2b3f3_story.html. Accessed 29 Nov. 2017.

Review of *The Ninth Hour*, by Alice McDermott. *Kirkus Reviews*, 19 Sept. 2017, www.kirkusreviews.com/book-reviews/alice-mcdermott/the-ninth-hour. Accessed 29 Nov. 2017.

Review of *The Ninth Hour*, by Alice McDermott. *Publishers Weekly*, Sept. 2017, www.publishersweekly.com/978-0-374-28014-7. Accessed 29 Nov. 2017.

Reardon, Patrick T. Review of *The Ninth Hour*, by Alice McDermott. *Chicago Tribune*, 11 Oct. 2017, www.chicagotribune.com/lifestyles/books/ct-books-ninth-hour-alice-mcdermott-1015-story.html. Accessed 29 Nov. 2017.

Yacovissi, Jennifer Bort. "*The Ninth Hour*: A Novel." Review of *The Ninth Hour*, by Alice McDermott, *Washington Independent Review of Books*, 5 Oct. 2017, www.washingtonindependentreviewofbooks.com/index.php/bookreview/the-ninth-hour-a-novel. Accessed 29 Nov. 2017.

No One Cares About Crazy People
The Chaos and Heartbreak of Mental Health in America

Author: Ron Powers (b. 1941)
Publisher: Hatchette Books (New York).
384 pp.
Type of work: Current affairs, history, memoir

Pulitzer Prize–winning journalist and author Ron Powers writes movingly of a family tragedy and a national crisis in his book No One Cares About Crazy People.

Principal personages
RON POWERS, the author
HONOREE, his wife
DEAN, his oldest son, who was diagnosed with schizophrenia
KEVIN, his youngest son, who was diagnosed with schizophrenia

"Extraordinary and courageous . . .
No doubt if everyone were to read this book, the world would change."
—*New York Times Book Review*

No
One
Cares
About
Crazy People

My Family and the Heartbreak
of Mental Illness in America

RON POWERS
NEW YORK TIMES BESTSELLING AUTHOR

Courtesy of Hachette

Ron Powers's book *No One Cares About Crazy People: The Chaos and Heartbreak of Mental Health in America* takes its title from a 2010 email exchange between the aides of then Wisconsin gubernatorial candidate Scott Walker. At the time, Walker was concerned that reports of mismanagement at a Milwaukee mental health facility, including allegations of death by starvation and sexual assault, would upset his campaign. An aide reassured him, writing, "No One Cares About Crazy People." The remark, which Powers relays in the first pages of his book, is breathtakingly callous. As his narrative unfolds, alternating between the sorry history of mental health treatment in Great Britain and the United States and Powers's sons' struggles with schizophrenia, the phrase changes shape. A throwaway remark becomes the emblem of a national philosophy in which some people are worthy of empathy and care while others are not. *No One Cares About Crazy People* is a history book and a memoir written with the intensity and anger of a parent who has lost a child.

The historical and scientific chapters of Powers's book begin with a brief overview of schizophrenia. Powers works hard not to overstep his authority in describing the disease, which is incurable and poorly understood. It is likely, for instance, that schizophrenia is not one particular illness but a category of illnesses that affect people in different ways. It is also likely that schizophrenia arises from genetic malfunctions, which can then be triggered by environmental stress. In some people, schizophrenia causes hallucinations, including disembodied voices, and delusions of grandeur. Others with schizophrenia are extremely withdrawn, or experience memory loss or a general erosion of cognitive ability. Schizophrenia most often manifests in one's twenties, just as one's brain finishes developing. In this chapter, Powers also introduces a related concept called anosognosia, a condition in which people suffering from schizophrenia or other disorders come to believe that they are not ill and refuse treatment.

Powers's historical overview begins in London in the Middle Ages. London pioneered the view of the mentally ill as disposable people. A hospital called St. Mary of Bethlehem—later shortened to Bethlem and colloquially known as Bedlam—began admitting "lunaticks" in 1403. Bedlam was the first mental institution, though it functioned more like a torture chamber, with inmates chained to walls, routinely beaten, and exposed to extreme cold. (It was widely believed that the insane did not feel heat, cold, or pain.) Powers's history follows Bedlam's influence to the United States, where reformers such as Dorothea Dix sought more humane treatment for the mentally ill. The narrative then goes on to explore evolution and how Charles Darwin's ideas were perverted to support eugenics, the pseudoscience that in turn supported the Nazis' theory of an Aryan master race. Why talk about eugenics in a book about schizophrenia? It goes back to the idea of the disposable person. In the view of eugenicists, the mentally ill are merely nature's mistakes.

Powers briefly touches on recent barbarities such as lobotomies, but he also explores how distrust of psychiatry—popularized by a man named Thomas Szasz, and also by Scientology founder L. Ron Hubbard—and a policy known as deinstitutionalization inform current American attitudes toward mental health care and the mentally ill. Szasz famously denied the existence of mental illness at all, blaming psychiatry for telling people that they were mentally ill when they just thought differently. He denounced psychiatric treatment as an infringement on one's civil liberties—a crucial point in regard to current laws about involuntary treatment. Deinstitutionalization, meanwhile, was spurred by the invention of so-called wonder drugs, pills that appeared to "cure" madness, leading to a large-scale emptying of mental institutions in the 1960s. Today, Powers reports, there are only forty-five thousand inpatient psychiatric beds available to any of the ten million Americans living with mental illness. Powers explains how deinstitutionalization led to mass homelessness, and how the mentally ill are also more likely to be incarcerated. He draws a powerful comparison between conditions in Bedlam and in modern-day American prisons, writing about places such as Rikers Island, a jail complex located outside of New York City, where roughly 40 percent of imprisoned people are mentally ill and receive little to no care. "Too many of the mentally ill in our country live under conditions of atrocity," Powers writes.

Powers won the 1973 Pulitzer Prize for criticism for his work as a television critic for the *Chicago Sun-Times*. In 1985, he won an Emmy Award for his media commentary on *CBS News Sunday Morning*. His best-known book, the New York Times best seller *Flags of Our Fathers* (2001), cowritten with historical author James Bradley, tells the stories of the six men who appear in the iconic World War II photograph raising a flag at Iwo Jima. Powers has also written a handful of historical nonfiction books, including two books about Mark Twain, *Dangerous Water: A Biography of the Boy Who Became Mark Twain* (1999) and *Mark Twain: A Life* (2005). Another book, *Tom and Huck Don't Live Here Anymore: Childhood and Murder in the Heart of America* (2001), was inspired by Twain's hometown of Hannibal, Missouri, where Powers was also born and raised. That book explores the character of the community during Twain's boyhood, during Powers's own boyhood in the 1940s and 1950s, and during the 1990s, when two teenage boys murdered a stranger. The book also touches on Powers's relationship to his abusive father.

Powers uses a similar structure—contrasting larger societal problems with his own painful history—in *No One Cares About Crazy People*. Powers and his wife, a scientist, raised their two sons in bucolic Middlebury, Vermont. Their older son, Dean, was a sensitive child who grew up with a love for words and literature; their younger son, Kevin, was a musical prodigy. Powers writes about watching Kevin, as a toddler, lifted onstage to pretend to play guitar with a well-known folk band. Kevin went on to form his own bands, and to study at the prestigious Interlochen Center for the Arts and then, briefly, the Berklee College of Music. He began to show signs of schizophrenia at seventeen; he took his own life shortly before his twenty-first birthday. Dean, as a young adult, was a wanderer; he worked as a mechanic, a political organizer, and a journalist. He was subject to unusual mood swings, and sometime after his brother's death, he suffered a psychotic break, walking around his family's neighborhood and knocking on doors to announce that he was the Messiah. He, too, was diagnosed with schizophrenia.

Ron Powers is a Pulitzer Prize–winning nonfiction author, novelist, and journalist.

Powers paints a thorough picture of his sons' lives before their diagnoses. He describes magical summers at the Bread Loaf Writers' Conference, a retreat that convinced the family to move to Middlebury from New York City. He also writes about a car accident that nearly ruined Dean's life at seventeen; Dean's girlfriend spent weeks in a coma, and Dean nearly went to prison. (Powers devotes a significant chunk of his narrative to the fallout, revealing a hint of the still-raw feud with the girlfriend's parents.) As the boys get older, Powers sifts through family email chains and remembered phone conversations in an attempt to identify missed clues, as when Dean once casually suggested that a football game was rigged "by the government." Powers is frustrated with himself for not being alive to the possibility of mental illness in his children. He warns other parents not to make the same mistake.

The real horror of his sons' experience, Powers writes, was not the illness itself, but the ways in which laws prevented them from receiving care. When Kevin chose to stop taking his medication, there was nothing Powers or his wife could do. A person cannot be involuntarily committed unless they present a danger to themselves or others—as, perhaps, the law should be, but the protection tends to force people with mental illness to bounce from crash to crash, receiving only emergency care instead of sustained treatment. This course of action is not only emotionally taxing but also, some scientists believe, detrimental to the health of the patient. Evidence suggests that illness left untreated can wreak irreparable damage on the brain. Powers offers no solution to parents except diligence. Among his biggest regrets, he writes, was his and his wife's willingness to accept Kevin's initial diagnosis of bipolar disorder. "When symptoms occur in a loved one, assume the worst until a professional convinces you otherwise," he writes. "Act quickly, and keep acting. If necessary, act to the limit of your means. Tough advice. Tough world."

Powers's book, readers may be surprised to find, offers some hope for improvement in people's understanding of mental illness and how best to serve the mentally ill. (That hope, essentially, lies in people caring about the mentally ill at all; as evidenced by Walker's aide, apathy allows cruel systems to flourish.) Powers's story is heartbreaking, but he manages to find some moments of humor in his narrative. His writing voice is idiosyncratic and gently self-deprecating. He paints himself as the family bloviator, enthralled by the incredible and genuine talents of his wife and children. In the introduction, Powers expresses trepidation about delving into his family's trauma, and it is clear from his writing that doing so is very painful for him. His writing is remarkably immediate and almost entirely without authorly sheen. Powers speaks directly to readers, begging them to care. His sincerity won over most critics, including Pulitzer Prize–winning journalist Ron Suskind, who wrote of the book for the *New York Times*, "No doubt if everyone were to read this book, the world would change. . . . It's impossible to read [Powers's] book without being overcome by empathy for his family, respect for his two beleaguered boys and, by the end, faith in the resilience of the human heart."

Molly Hagan

Review Sources

Review of *No One Cares About Crazy People: The Chaos and Heartbreak of Mental Health in America*, by Ron Powers. *Kirkus Reviews*, 3 Jan. 2017, www.kirkus-reviews.com/book-reviews/ron-powers-2/no-one-cares-about-crazy-people/. Accessed 19 Sept. 2017.

Review of *No One Cares About Crazy People: The Chaos and Heartbreak of Mental Health in America*, by Ron Powers. *Publishers Weekly*, 31 Oct. 2016, www.pub-lishersweekly.com/978-0-316-34117-2. Accessed 19 Sept. 2017.

Peters, Sharon. "Tough New Book Claims 'No One Cares About Crazy People.'" Review of *No One Cares About Crazy People: The Chaos and Heartbreak of Mental Health in America*, by Ron Powers. *USA Today*, 27 Mar. 2017, www.usatoday.com/story/life/books/2017/03/27/no-one-cares-about-crazy-people-the-chaos-and-heartbreak-of-mental-health-in-america-ron-powers-book-review/99190032/. Accessed 19 Sept. 2017.

Suskind, Ron. "One Family's Story of Mental Illness and What Came After." Review of *No One Cares About Crazy People: The Chaos and Heartbreak of Mental Health in America*, by Ron Powers. *The New York Times*, 4 Apr. 2017, www.nytimes.com/2017/04/04/books/review/no-one-cares-about-crazy-people-ron-powers.html. Accessed 19 Sept. 2017.

No Room for Small Dreams
Courage, Imagination, and the Making of Modern Israel

Author: Shimon Peres (1923–2016)
Publisher: Custom House (New York). 240 pp.
Type of work: Memoir
Time: 1923 to 2016
Locale: Israel

Just before his death, Shimon Peres, who was a significant figure in the founding of the modern state of Israel and served the Israeli government in various capacities throughout his life, finished his memoir. It details his political career and his thoughts on war, peace, entrepreneurship, and the future of the Middle East.

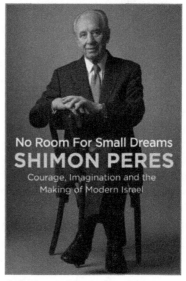

Principal personages

SHIMON PERES, eighth prime minister of Israel and ninth president of Israel
DAVID BEN-GURION, first prime minister of Israel, friend and mentor to Peres
MORDECHAI GUR, chief of staff of the Israel Defense Forces during the 1976 Entebbe raid
YITZHAK RABIN, fifth prime minister of Israel
AL SCHWIMMER, pioneer in the development of Israel's aviation industry
MOSHE DAYAN, Israeli defense minister during the Six-Day War and the Yom Kippur War
SONIA GELLER PERES, Peres's wife

Shimon Peres was born in 1923 in the small village of Vishneva, Poland, near the Russian border. Vishneva was a small, primitive settlement of a few houses, none of which had electricity or running water. Peres's maternal grandfather, Rabbi Zvi Meltzer, served as the community's chief rabbi, and had a profound influence on the life and thought of his young grandson. Throughout his memoir Peres writes of his commitment to the basic values and vision of Judaism, but little of his personal religious beliefs (and indeed, very little about any aspect of his personal life). However, he says that under his grandfather's tutelage, he became "strictly religious" as a young boy, more so than his parents, to the point that when his father turned on a new radio on the Sabbath—an act of "work" which violated the rules of Sabbath observance—young Shimon threw the radio to the floor in a fit of righteous rage.

In 1932, Peres's father, Yitzhak, decided to immigrate to what was then called Palestine, a strip of land in the eastern Mediterranean revered by Jews as their ancestral homeland, but under British control since the end of World War I. The rest of the family joined their father in Palestine two years later. Peres never saw his beloved grandfather again. A few years after the family left Vishneva, Nazi soldiers forced the members of the local synagogue into the building and then set fire to it, killing everyone inside. Like many Jewish young people of his generation, Peres was convinced by the unfolding of the Holocaust in Europe that a permanent homeland for Jews in Palestine—which they called Eretz Israel, the Land of Israel—was the only alternative to ethnic annihilation.

In 1938, while he was still in high school, Peres was sent to the Ben-Shemen Youth Village, southeast of the city of Tel Aviv, a combined farming community and school. There he met Sonia Gelman, the daughter of a carpentry teacher at the school. They were married in 1945. Although he lived only a short time at Ben-Shemen, the place had a deep impact on him; he wrote, "It was—and remains—the most wonderful place I have ever known." While there, Peres joined a Jewish youth movement known as HaNoar HaOved, or Working Youth. On a trip to Haifa on behalf of this group, Peres met David Ben-Gurion, a leader of the movement aiming to establish a permanent Jewish state. Ben-Gurion became a mentor to Peres and did much to shape his life and career.

Shimon Peres served in various elected or appointed positions in Israel throughout his life, including as prime minister and president. He wrote several books, including two previous memoirs. Peres died on September 28, 2016, only a few weeks after completing this book.

Peres spent the majority of his adult life in one or another position of service to the government of Israel, serving in some more than once, including being prime minister from 1984 to 1986 and again from 1995 to 1996. His last formal position in the government was to serve as the ninth president of Israel from 2007 to 2014. This memoir is devoted almost entirely to his public and professional life, with very little attention to his family or any other aspect of his personal life.

Peres divides his life into two parts. The first part was devoted to fighting to secure the establishment and survival of the state of Israel, and the second half was devoted to the search for peace with Israel's Arab neighbors. Since he firmly believed that the military power to defend Israel was essential to the survival of the Jewish people, Peres is unapologetic about his role as one of the major procurers of weapons during the 1948 War of Independence and in the following years. Ironically, Czechoslovakia, which had been occupied by the Nazis during World War II, was one of the first nations to deal with Israel. Czechoslovakia at the time was a part of the Eastern European bloc of nations heavily dominated by the Soviet Union, and yet Czechoslovakia sold weapons to Israel while the Soviets were arming Israel's potential enemies in the Arab world.

Likewise, Peres expresses no regrets about his role in securing nuclear technology for Israel. In 1957, he began negotiating with officials in France to purchase equipment to build a nuclear reactor for power generation. At one point, negotiations with the French government under Prime Minister Maurice Bourgès-Maurnoury were almost complete when Peres learned that the French Parliament was about to take a no-confidence vote on the prime minister. He rushed to Paris but was unable to meet at length with Bourgès-Maurnoury until the day after his government had fallen. However, Bourgès-Maurnoury signed the agreement, affixing the previous day's date to the documents, when he had still been in power. He offered no explanation and Peres asked no questions, but remembered that action with gratitude: "In that moment, what he had done for Israel—what he had done for me—was the most generous display of friendship I had ever known." A nuclear reactor was eventually built at Dimona in the Negev desert in the southern part of Israel (and after Peres's death, the facility was renamed for him in commemoration of his role in getting it established).

Did this nuclear power capability eventually lead to the development of a nuclear bomb? During his presidential administration, US president John F. Kennedy asked Peres directly, "What are your intentions as they relate to nuclear weapons, Mr. Peres?" In reply, Peres said, "Mr. President, I can tell you most clearly that we shall not be the first to introduce nuclear weapons the region." Kennedy did not press the matter further. Although military experts around the world believe it is virtually certain that Israel does have such a weapon, Peres writes that the official policy in Israel since the very beginning has been "nuclear ambiguity"—that Israel will neither confirm nor deny having a nuclear weapon. If potential enemies do not know whether Israel has a nuclear bomb, they must assume it might indeed have one, and this uncertainty provides a measure of deterrence.

Consistent with the twin themes of war and peace, Peres discusses times of conflict and the long, troubled efforts toward peace. "Before Israel was a state," he writes, "and in all the years since it became one, we have had to grow up alongside terrorism, to defend ourselves against it, and to seek its solution." In 1976, when Peres was defense minister under Prime Minister Yitzhak Rabin, terrorists identified with the Popular Front for the Liberation of Palestine hijacked an Air France flight from Israel to Paris, eventually taking the plane and over one hundred Israeli hostages to Entebbe airport in Uganda. The Israeli government debated its options, and considered breaking its long-standing policy of refusing to negotiate with terrorists. Rabin argued forcefully for a rescue mission, even though the Israeli military had never carried out such an operation on foreign soil. Eventually, Mordechai Gur, the chief of the general staff of the Israel Defense Forces, put together a plan that seemed workable. On July 4, 1976, a raid successfully rescued most of the hostages—only four were lost, and casualties among the Israeli forces were light.

While Operation Entebbe was a cause for rejoicing, one of Peres's greatest disappointments was the failure of the efforts in the 1990s to achieve a lasting peace with the Palestinian Arabs living within the borders of Israel and in Jordan. Serving as foreign minister during Rabin's second stint as prime minister, Peres began to seek direct negotiations with the Palestinians. Over many months, Israeli diplomats negotiated with the Palestine Liberation Organization, headed by Yasser Arafat. Eventually, the United States became involved in trying to encourage the process, and in a ceremony in Washington with President Bill Clinton in September 1993, Arafat and Rabin signed what became known as the Oslo Accords. Peres, Arafat, and Rabin received the Nobel Prize for Peace in 1994 for this breakthrough. The Palestinian Authority was created to administer the Palestinian territories, and Arafat was elected its first president. But the hopes for peace were derailed by continued violence by radical groups like Hamas and Islamic Jihad; the Palestinian Authority seemed powerless to block these attacks. Eventually, many Israelis gave up hopes of peace. In the fall of 1995, Rabin and Peres staged a rally for peace, and were astonished to see more than one hundred thousand people turn out, giving hope that support for the peace initiative might be renewed. But as he left the rally, Rabin was assassinated by an extremist Israeli who opposed the peace process. The momentum toward peace was broken, and further progress was derailed.

In the latter part of the book, Peres deals with his promotion of entrepreneurship in Israel, both as a means of economic development, and in hopes that breakthroughs by entrepreneurs might be shared throughout the region, to combat poverty and ultimately, perhaps, contribute to peace. Whatever topic he discusses, Peres's optimism shines through, although he admits to disappointments and setbacks. He believes that peace in the Middle East is inevitable simply because there is no long-term alternative.

Readers should remember that authors of memoirs will usually try to present themselves in the best light possible. While Peres does tell of failures and disappointments he faced in his career, some reviewers have raised questions about things left out of this book, such as Israel's artillery attacks on Lebanon while Peres was prime minister in 1996. Still, reviewers have generally given the book high marks, although it has not received widespread attention in the United States.

Mark S. Joy, PhD

Review Sources

Kershner, Isabel. "Shimon Peres, in Memoir, Takes on Israel Past and Future." Review of *No Room for Small Dreams: Courage, Imagination, and the Making of Modern Israel*, by Shimon Peres. *The New York Times*, 7 Sept. 2017, www.nytimes.com/2017/09/07/world/middleeast/shimon-peres-imemoir-israel.html. Accessed 20 Feb. 2017.

Review of *No Room for Small Dreams: Courage, Imagination, and the Making of Modern Israel*, by Shimon Peres. *Publishers Weekly*, 4 Sept. 2017, www.publishersweekly.com/978-0-06256144-2. Accessed 20 Feb. 2017.

Seidman, Dov, and Lov Seidman. "Shimon Peres' Lessons for an Eight-Year-Old Boy." Review of *No Room for Small Dreams: Courage, Imagination, and the Making of Modern Israel*, by Shimon Peres. *Forbes*, 14 Sept. 2017, www.forbes.com/sites/dovseidman/2017/09/14/shimon-peres-7-lessons-for-an-8-year-old-boy/#2803b2a525df. Accessed 20 Feb. 2017.

Wertheimer, Gila. Review of *No Room for Small Dreams: Courage, Imagination, and the Making of Modern Israel*, by Shimon Peres. *Jewish Book Council*, 2017, www.jewishbookcouncil.org/book/no-room-for-small-dreams-courage-imagination-and-the-making-of-modern-israel. Accessed 20 Feb. 2017.

Nomadland
Surviving America in the Twenty-First Century

Author: Jessica Bruder (b. 1979)
Publisher: W. W. Norton (New York). Illustrated. 320 pp.
Type of work: Current affairs, sociology
Time: 2010–the present
Locales: California, Nevada, Arizona, North Dakota

Jessica Bruder's Nomadland: Surviving America in the Twenty-First Century *is an immersive investigation of a fresh iteration of an age-old phenomenon: the migration of people in search of better living and working conditions. The modern American version of this periodic mass movement, known as workamping, incorporates a large number of senior citizens constantly on the move.*

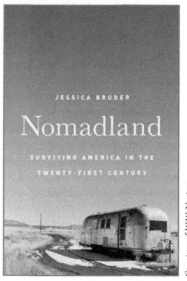

Courtesy of W.W. Norton

Principal personages

LINDA MAY, a woman in her sixties who represents a typical member of the workamping movement

SILVIANNE DELMARS, Linda's occasional companion and coworker, also in her sixties

BOB WELLS, a self-sufficiency author, creator of a website for nomads, and regular workamper

MICHAEL REYNOLDS, a New Mexico–based architect and designer of the Earthship, a passive solar house built from recycled materials

JESSICA BRUDER, an author in her thirties who reported on and participated in the workamper movement

According to Jessica Bruder, author of *Nomadland*, there is a troubling social movement afoot in early twenty-first-century America. Thousands, perhaps millions, of elderly citizens have joined the endless vortex of motorists, restless drifters, and vagabonds swirling across the highways and byways of the continent. (The exact number is not known, as the census cannot locate and count them.) These people, uprooted by circumstance—divorce, bankruptcy, job downsizing, underwater mortgages, bad investments, or bad luck that followed in the wake of the financial crisis of 2008—subsist on often meager Social Security payments and travel not for pleasure, but out of necessity. Individuals who should, by rights, be enjoying the golden years of retirement are instead rejoining the workforce as temporary, seasonal laborers. Called workampers, they travel from place to place to take on low-paid, pensionless, benefit-free, physically demanding, and sometimes hazardous jobs. They stay employed at one location just long enough to earn the cash needed to keep moving in their makeshift homes on wheels. Vehicles owned by "vandwellers" are a motley collection outfitted with sleeping quarters, water tanks and toilets, cooking space, and other homey touches. These rusting vans, beat-up motorhomes, cramped campers, recreational vehicles (RVs) past their prime, augmented pickup trucks, and dilapidated school buses are jury-rigged to stay running, to keep in perpetual motion between "stealth" parking hiatuses. To stop permanently would be to admit defeat, to accept the cruel fact that the American Dream of hard work invariably leading to prosperity and comfortable old age is, for many, a nightmare.

A majority of older workers, readers learn, are women: of some 4.2 million elderly individuals living beneath the poverty line in America in 2015, 2.7 million were female. As women earn on average eighty cents for every dollar earned by a man doing the same work, they are not able to save as much money over the course of their careers and contribute smaller amounts to Social Security. Yet women generally live longer than men, so many must continue working in their later years simply to survive.

Emblematic of the gray-haired mobile masses is Linda May, who held a variety of jobs during her prime working years, including trucker, cocktail waitstaff, contractor, insurance executive, and health-care worker. Returning to work between periods of refuge spent with the family of her adult daughter, Linda has a vague plan for the future. She hopes to save enough to buy a plot of land someplace where building codes are friendly. Her idea is to erect an Earthship—renegade architect Michael Reynolds's vision of a self-sustaining passive solar home constructed from discarded waste materials—where she can live out her final years unencumbered.

Author Jessica Bruder met with Linda multiple times over several years of reporting, producing a number of articles that served as the foundation for *Nomadland*. Eventually, in the process of immersing herself in her subject, Bruder bought and outfitted a secondhand van to be better accepted by the community of vandwellers. She also applied for and worked for a time alongside seniors at typical seasonal jobs.

When first encountered, Linda May, sixty-four, is driving a salvaged Jeep Grand Cherokee Laredo, hauling her residence: a tiny 1970s-vintage trailer appropriately nicknamed "the Squeeze Inn." She is on her way into California's San Bernardino National Forest for another four-month stint as a campground host, a job similar to that of a forest ranger. For slightly more than minimum hourly wages and a place to park her mobile home, she and a similarly aged friend, Silvianne Delmars, will shush noisy drunks, clean up broken glass and scattered litter, drown campfires left carelessly smoldering, and empty and disinfect outhouses. The job comes with few guarantees. Hours are erratic. There is plenty of overtime, incorporating chores outside the job description, but it is usually unpaid. Working conditions are often dismal—for example, no shade or cool water is provided during periods of high summer temperatures. Complaints about shoddy treatment of temporary workers are shuffled between the US Forest Service, which manages these public lands, and concessionaires such as California Land Management, which hire workers to staff a multitude of campgrounds. These complaints are typically ignored in the end.

Work in national parks is just one of many temporary job opportunities available coast-to-coast and border-to-border across the United States to the mobile traveling crowd. Job openings and other items of interest to vandwellers are posted on such websites as CheapRVLiving,com, the brainchild of workamper guru Bob Wells, who has lived and worked on the road since 1995. Other sites, like Workers on Wheels and Workamper News, list a wide range of employment possibilities, many suitable for older workers. Applicants can choose among fruit harvesting, tour hosting, ticket-taking, running concession stands or amusement park rides, or other more exotic work.

A major leg of the senior seasonal employment circuit leads to Amazon, the world's largest internet retailer. In 2008, Amazon began CamperForce, a program to recruit temporary workers during the peak retailing season, the four months prior to Christmas. These workers must travel to out-of-the way locations to staff the company's enormous, approximately million-square-foot warehouses, known as fulfillment centers. The company has openings annually at warehouses in Nevada, Kentucky, California, Tennessee, New Jersey, and Texas. The work is mind-numbingly repetitive and physically demanding: employees typically walk fifteen miles per shift stocking shelves, scanning products, or selecting merchandise to fill customer orders. Nonetheless, Amazon annually attracts thousands of seasonal workers, including many seniors, who appreciate the wages—upward of $11.50 per hour, plus overtime—and the fact that the company usually provides space for parking their mobile dwellings. Amazon, in turn, enjoys the work ethic seniors bring to the job:

A photojournalist who specializes in examining American subcultures and economic issues, Jessica Bruder has written for such publications as Harper's Magazine, *the* New York Times, *and the* Christian Science Monitor. *She has taught at the Columbia School of Journalism since 2008. Her first full-length work was* Burning Book *(2007), a study of the annual Burning Man gathering.*

they are dependable, seldom complain, are not around long enough to unionize, and pack up and leave for other destinations right after the Christmas rush. The company also benefits from senior workers in the form of federal tax credits, which helps increase profitability. Linda May worked at the Amazon warehouse in Fernley, Nevada, in 2013; that location has since closed.

During winter months, Linda May and thousands of other workampers head for small-town Quartzsite, Arizona, to unwind. With numerous RV parks to choose from and spacious federal lands in the area to camp on, Quartzsite, with its temperate weather, is especially welcoming to work-weary seniors. For those still in the market for employment, the sudden influx of people creates a plethora of part-time jobs at local businesses. A highlight of the gathering is the Rubber Tramp Rendezvous, a ten-day period featuring a variety of seminars on subjects of interest—auto repair, carpentry, solar energy, stealth parking techniques, and more—to those who have gone mobile. The Rubber Tramp Rendezvous coincides with another area event, a sports, vacation, and RV show known as the "Big Tent," where recruiters—Amazon, Forest Service concessionaires, harvest laborers, Iowa-based Adventureland amusement park, and others—also collect to offer attendees a variety of future work opportunities.

One such job is the annual sugar beet harvest. In the course of her investigation into the travails of elderly workers, Bruder applied for and was accepted via a temporary agency as a worker for American Crystal Sugar, a leading producer of manufactured sugar operating out of the Red River Valley in America's Upper Midwest. The author worked twelve-hour shifts in a safety vest and hard hat at a massive refrigeration facility near the Canadian border in North Dakota, shoveling the sugary vegetables into hoppers, sampling products, knocking caked mud off machinery, and dodging falling beets the size and weight of bowling balls. Bruder also applied through CamperForce and worked briefly at Amazon's largest warehouse, which is located in Haslet, Texas, near Fort Worth. The only person under fifty years of age, she toiled in Inventory Control Quality Assurance, scanning available merchandise against inventory records, and fending off Kivas, robotic drive units that delivered stacks of merchandise to workstations.

Nomadland has practical use for those of advanced age who are not financially solvent enough to comfortably enjoy their waning years. The book contains a wealth of ideas—including helpful lists of relevant websites—for supplementing meager incomes, especially for those with no fixed abode. However, the information provided may have a limited shelf life. Despite the spirit of camaraderie and helpfulness that prevails among vandwellers and workampers as depicted in *Nomadland*, the near future looks bleak for seasonal mobile workers, especially of the elderly variety.

For example, during the twenty-first century, many US cities have passed laws that complicate the lives of vandwellers and workampers. There are laws that ban sleeping in cars and that restrict camping in national forests; in effect, these laws target low-income workers. Of particular concern is increased enforcement of the Real ID Act of 2005, antiterrorism legislation that increased scrutiny of the addresses used for driver's licenses. Driver's licenses are essential for workampers, but lacking permanent residences, they frequently establish residency through mail-forwarding services via the use of addresses of friends or family or by borrowing the addresses on properties with "for sale" signs. Such antimobility efforts, Bruder maintains, only serve to increase the chasm of economic inequality between the top 1 percent and the rest of the nation, perpetuating what has become a uniquely American caste system.

Jack Ewing

Review Sources

Baker, Peter C. "Have Recreational Vehicles Killed the American Dream?" Review of *Nomadland: Surviving America in the Twenty-First Century*, by Jessica Bruder. *Pacific Standard*, 13 Oct. 2017, psmag.com/magazine/have-recreational-vehicles-killed-the-american-dream. Accessed 17 Nov. 2017.

Kipp, Priscilla. "*Nomadland*: Hop in My Van, Halen." Review of *Nomadland: Surviving America in the Twenty-First Century*, by Jessica Bruder. *Book Page*, 19 Sept. 2017, bookpage.com/reviews/21868-jessica-bruder-nomadland. Accessed 17 Nov. 2017.

Malanga, Steven. "Undone, by Choice." Review of *Nomadland: Surviving America in the Twenty-First Century*, by Jessica Bruder. *City Journal*, 22 Sept. 2017, www.city-journal.org/html/undone-choice-15454.html. Accessed 17 Nov. 2017.

Sehgal, Parul. "On the Road with the Casualties of the Great Recession." Review of
Nomadland: Surviving America in the Twenty-First Century, by Jessica Bruder.
The New York Times, 19 Sept. 2017, www.nytimes.com/2017/09/19/books/
review-nomadland-jessica-bruder.html. Accessed 17 Nov. 2017.

Norse Mythology

Author: Neil Gaiman (b. 1960)
Publisher: W.W. Norton (New York). 304 pp.
Type of work: Literary history, religion, short fiction
Locale: Mythic ancient Scandinavia

In Norse Mythology, *acclaimed speculative fiction author Neil Gaiman presents some of the most compelling stories of the ancient Norse gods in lively modern prose. His tales of Odin, Thor, and Loki capture both the imaginative adventurousness of the originals and their ultimately tragic vision of life. Gaiman's slim volume opens up a lost world to modern readers.*

Courtesy of W.W. Norton

Principal characters

ODIN, the one-eyed leader of the gods
THOR, his son, the strongest of the gods, associated with thunder
LOKI, Odin's blood brother, a trickster who lays traps for the other gods
FREYA, a goddess famed for her beauty
BALDER, a son of Odin, notable for his beauty, wisdom, and good temper

There is a sort of logical and poetic inevitability in Neil Gaiman producing *Norse Mythology*, a retelling of some of the classic stories from the ancient Scandinavian Eddas. A renowned author of fantasy literature, Gaiman became famous as the creator and writer of the immensely popular and influential *Sandman* (1989–96) series of comic books, which interweave mythology, horror, and more conventional elements of comic-book heroics to create a remarkably sophisticated and satisfying story of the capture, escape, and return of Dream, also called Morpheus. *The Sandman* was aimed at an adult audience, and hardbound editions of the graphic novels made it on to the New York Times Best Seller List.

Following the end of the *Sandman* series, Gaiman continued to write comic books and novels, some aimed at adults and others at younger readers, many of which evince his continued interest in mythology. In his novel *American Gods* (2001), incarnations of the Norse gods Odin and Loki engage in a struggle with the godlike avatars of modern technological forces in contemporary America. In an article for the *Telegraph*, published online on January 28, 2017, Gaiman wrote that interest in Norse mythology stems from his childhood interest in Marvel Comics' Mighty Thor, a superhero drawn by the legendary Jack Kirby and scripted by Kirby, Stan Lee, and Larry Lieber. These classic comics, featuring an extravagant science-fictional background for Thor and his fellow Norse gods, stimulated Gaiman to seek out more information on their mythological underpinnings.

He found what he wanted in Roger Lancelyn Green's *Myths of the Norsemen* (1960), which introduced him to the ancient world of the Norse gods—one very different from the Marvel Universe, in which Thor's home of Asgard was a snowbound Viking feasting hall and, instead of aliens and supervillains, the hammer-wielding hero battled frost giants. Especially compelling to the young Gaiman was the tragic fate awaiting the denizens of Asgard: Ragnarok, the twilight of the gods, when they and their enemies the frost giants would perish in a confrontation that would end the world. The indeterminate doom of the Norse gods—was Ragnarok in the past or still to come?—gave their stories an enduring immediacy. For Gaiman, they could not be so easily dismissed as the myths of the Greeks and Romans. For all their obscure roots in the forgotten mists of ancient Germany and Scandinavia, these tales of gods defying an inexorable fate possessed, for him, a fascinating timelessness. As Gaiman matured into a writer, the influence of these stories never left him. His experiment in producing his own version of the Norse myths is very much a labor of love.

Gaiman acknowledges that only a fraction of the stories that the Norse told themselves about their gods and goddesses survive. Those that remain were written down after Christianity had supplanted paganism in Scandinavia. In writing his book, Gaiman worked with English translations of two extant sources. The first is the *Prose Edda*, composed by the thirteenth-century Icelandic scholar Snorri Sturluson, who intended his work to serve as a guide to help his Christian readers understand the content and metrical style of ancient Norse poetry. The second is the *Poetic Edda*, an anonymous collection of Norse poems recounting the deeds of gods and heroes. Between them, these two works preserve most of what is known about Norse mythology. Gaiman's versions of the stories of the Norse gods move freely between both Eddas, taking details and narrative elements from each and recombining them to enhance the dramatic force of the myths.

This does not mean that he gives himself license to fully revise his source material. Gaiman does not invent new stories, or imaginatively speculate on elements of the original myths that the *Prose Edda* and *Poetic Edda* left unexplored or unanswered. Though he makes no claims to serious scholarship, Gaiman strives to provide an authentic rendering of his sources, true to the intentions of the people who originally told these stories, with no attempt to change or modernize them to appease contemporary sensibilities. The protagonists of the Norse myths adhere to mores widely at variance with twenty-first-century norms, often committing acts that today would be considered appalling. Gaiman accepts this; he is interested in recapturing and understanding the vision of a past world, not in transforming that vision into something more currently acceptable. In doing so, he preserves the intriguing and sometimes necessarily unsettling otherness of Norse mythology. Herein lies the book's power: those willing to make the journey are transported into the mental universe of a culture that saw life differently than people do today.

In the only real concession to make the stories appeal to a contemporary public, Gaiman retells them in lively, colloquial language that renders even the alien perspectives of the Norse gods more relatable. His prose is anything but stuffy or pretentious. In his pages, Odin, Thor, Loki, and the other gods, goddesses, and giants of myth speak in accessible, ordinary conversational English. Their behavior may be distinctly old-fashioned, but the language used to describe this behavior is not. Gaiman's tone gives the stories a freshness and approachability that would be lost with a more mannered style. The result is an anthology that pleases the modern ear while maintaining the integrity of the ancient stories.

Gaiman also helps his readers by providing a larger shape and structure to the body of legends with which he works. He begins with stories about the creation of the world and finishes with the climactic battle of Ragnarok, which brings with it the end of the Norse gods, though it sows the seeds of another cycle of life. Within this framework, Gaiman weaves together a series of stories that trace high points in the careers of Thor and other key figures, giving the book the feel and trajectory of a novel. In doing so, he does not iron out the complexities of his material. In the old stories, the characterizations of the gods could be quite inconsistent, and Gaiman's narrative subtly reflects this mythological reality. Nevertheless, this recounting of ancient legends provides readers with a satisfying sense of completeness. Gaiman's skill as a storyteller triumphs over the difficulties inherent in his sources.

The result of Gaiman's literary abilities and his manifest affection for his subject matter is a concise but compelling collection of stories. Gaiman writes with the exuberant energy of an enthusiast daring the reader not to share in his joy. It is difficult to resist his gusto as he moves smoothly from one story to another, combining the charms of a fairy tale with his disarmingly modern narration. Gods, goddesses, giants, and monsters of all sorts, from dragons to giant serpents, meet, mingle, and battle each other in this loving tribute to the imagination of the ancient Norse.

Typical of the tales in *Norse Mythology* is "The Master Builder," the fifth story in the collection (not including a summary of the main characters). With Thor away hunting trolls, marauding frost giants are a very real threat, and the inhabitants of Asgard feel vulnerable. What they need, Odin decides, is a high, stout wall around their home. One day a stranger arrives with his stallion, Svadilfari, and offers to build a wall around Asgard in three seasons if the gods give him the sun, the moon, and the hand of the lovely goddess Freya in marriage. At Loki's urging, the gods accept the stranger's offer on the condition that he complete the wall in one season. They assume that this will make his task impossible, but that his efforts will give them the foundation of a wall that they can then finish themselves at their leisure. Much to their dismay, the stranger and Svadilfari are able to drag immense loads of stone to Asgard, and the wall rapidly nears completion. As it becomes apparent that they might have to pay the stranger's price, the gods angrily turn on Loki, threatening him with the direst consequences if he does not foil the industrious stranger. By this point, the

Neil Gaiman is an award-winning author of many comic books and novels, including the best-selling comic-book series The Sandman *(1989–96) and the novels* American Gods *(2001),* Coraline *(2002),* The Graveyard Book *(2008), and* The Ocean at the End of the Lane *(2013). A number of his works have been adapted as films or television series.*

stranger only needs one more load of stone to be done with the wall. As he whistles for Svadilfari to help him drag the stone to Asgard, the stallion is distracted by the appearance of a beautiful chestnut mare. The mare leads the stallion away, preventing the stranger from winning his wager. He angrily denounces the gods as cheats and ominously begins to grow in size, revealing that he is in fact a mountain giant in disguise. Fortunately for the gods, Thor returns at this moment with his deadly hammer and kills the threatening giant. Much to the gods' amusement, Loki later shows up with a magical foal that affectionately treats him as its mother. "The Master Builder" exemplifies the heady mixture of fantasy, violence, and sometimes ribald humor that pervades the adventures of the Norse gods.

Gaiman's *Norse Mythology* is a book that will delight a wide range of readers. It should appeal to connoisseurs of fine writing as well as aficionados of good stories. Simply and elegantly written, it would also serve brilliantly as a mythology textbook for high school and university students. In a review for the *Library Journal*, Stephanie Klose deemed the book "a spectacularly entertaining and elucidating collection of stories with wide crossover appeal" that is "essential for all collections," while *Booklist* reviewer Ray Olson concluded that "Gaiman's retelling of these ever-striking and strange stories should be every reader's first book of Norse mythology." As the tale of "The Master Builder" indicates, there are occasionally earthy passages that might be unsuitable for younger children. Still, if judiciously edited for bedtime readings, there are wonderful things in this volume for grade schoolers as well. Gaiman's work has the makings of a popular classic. It seems destined to become a standard introduction to the Norse myths for a generation.

Daniel P. Murphy

Review Sources

Klose, Stephanie. Review of *Norse Mythology*, by Neil Gaiman. *Library Journal*, 15 Feb. 2017, p. 92. *Academic Search Complete*, search.ebscohost.com/login.aspx?direct=true&db=a9h&AN=121212855&site=ehost-live. Accessed 6 Feb. 2018.

Review of *Norse Mythology*, by Neil Gaiman. *Kirkus Reviews*, 1 Dec. 2016, pp. 84–85. *Academic Search Complete*, search.ebscohost.com/login.aspx?direct=true&db=a9h&AN=122748286&site=ehost-live. Accessed 6 Feb. 2018.

Review of *Norse Mythology*, by Neil Gaiman. *Publishers Weekly*, 12 Dec. 2016, p. 119. *Academic Search Complete*, search.ebscohost.com/login.aspx?direct=true&db=a9h&AN=120250453&site=ehost-live. Accessed 6 Feb. 2018.

Olson, Ray. Review of *Norse Mythology*, by Neil Gaiman. *Booklist*, 15 Dec. 2016, p. 6. *Academic Search Complete*, search.ebscohost.com/login.aspx?direct=true&db=a9h&AN=120218928&site=ehost-live. Accessed 6 Feb. 2018.

Shippey, Tom. "Neil Gaiman on the Old Norse Myths." Review of *Norse Mythology*, by Neil Gaiman. *The Wall Street Journal*, 3 Feb. 2017, www.wsj.com/articles/neil-gaiman-on-the-old-norse-myths-1486150476. Accessed 6 Feb. 2018.

Yuknavitch, Lidia. "The Story of Thor, in the Voice of Neil Gaiman." Review of *Norse Mythology*, by Neil Gaiman, read by Gaiman. *The New York Times*, 15 May 2017, www.nytimes.com/2017/05/15/books/review/norse-mythology-neil-gaiman-audio.html. Accessed 6 Feb. 2018.

The Novel of the Century
The Extraordinary Adventure of *Les Misérables*

Author: David Bellos (b. 1945)
Publisher: Farrar, Straus and Giroux (New York). Illustrated. 336 pp.
Type of work: History, literary biography, literary history
Time: Nineteenth century
Locales: France, Belgium, Jersey, Guernsey

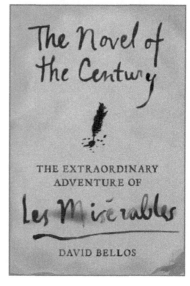

In The Novel of the Century, *author David Bellos explores, in enormous detail, the writing, reception, content, and meanings of Victor Hugo's enduringly popular novel Les Misérables.*

Principal personages
VICTOR HUGO, novelist
ADÈLE FOUCHER HUGO, his wife
CHARLES HUGO, their son
NAPOLEON III, president and then emperor of France

Courtesy of Macmillan

David Bellos's book *The Novel of the Century: The Extraordinary Adventure of* Les Misérables, which focuses on Victor Hugo's lengthy masterpiece *Les Misérables* (1862), might easily have been titled *The Novel of Two Centuries*. Hugo's book, after all, not only was enormously popular in its own day but remains enduringly influential today, roughly 150 years after it was first published. (This is why it is somewhat astonishing to learn from Bellos that a complete—and completely accurate—English translation of the work appeared for the first time only in 2008.) Of course, much of the novel's present fame derives from the exceptionally popular musical adaptation it inspired, which ran for decades on stages all over the world and was revived on Broadway in 2014. A 2012 film of the musical was itself well received, and the list of other adaptations of the novel—not just for film, but for television, radio, and manga as well—is long and ever-growing. But none of these adaptations could have occurred if Hugo had not spent years writing the original, which was an instant best seller as soon as it appeared.

Bellos, a professor of French at Princeton University, has penned a consistently fascinating account of practically every aspect of the novel's origins, circumstances, writing, publication, and reception. Some readers, in fact, may think that Bellos's book, like the novel he extols, is a bit too long. Readers learn about the details of French coins, the significance of various colors, the ins and outs of dyeing cloth in the nineteenth century, and, inevitably, a great deal about the ups and downs of French political developments. But anyone truly interested in biography, history, literature, and their various interconnections will find Bellos's work immensely satisfying. He tells readers everything they might ever have wanted to know about *Les Misérables* as well as both the culture and the man that produced it. He also offers readers much more information than they might ever have considered relevant to the book, giving them great insight into Hugo's life and times. The book provides a thorough sense of French history in the nineteenth century, and some readers may even wish that it had been made twice as long by tracing in detail the intriguing story of the novel's popularity in the many decades since then. Simply explaining the impact of the London musical would take a lengthy book in itself. Perhaps Bellos has, or should have, a sequel in mind.

In any case, the book Bellos has written will more than satisfy anyone deeply interested in the original novel. *The Novel of the Century* is full of facts but never seems dryly academic; Bellos writes with a nice, light wit and makes his story broadly accessible. He tells how he himself first came, almost by accident, to read and fall in love with the book, and he recounts the devotion it inspired in him and continues to inspire in an astonishing number of readers, despite its extraordinary length of roughly fifteen hundred pages. (He notes that it consists of exactly 365 relatively short chapters and thus can easily be read in a year, if it is not in fact consumed voraciously over several days, as was the case during his own first encounter with it.) Bellos comments that "what makes *Les Misérables* such an amazing work of art is that despite its length, its complexity and its vast scope, every detail and every dimension—even if not made explicit—was designed, calculated and decided by the author." Everything fits, even though the novel took years and years to write. After finishing Bellos's book, many readers will be willing to agree to the bold claim he makes in the beginning: that "among all the gifts France has given to Hollywood, Broadway and the common reader wherever she may be, *Les Misérables* stands out as the greatest by far."

Bellos opens by providing maps that clearly indicate all the places mentioned in the text. He outlines the novel's plots and characters, discusses the traits and significance of the main persons Huge depicts, compares and contrasts the book with similar novels of its era (especially those of Charles Dickens), and asserts that the text's main theme is the idea "that moral progress is possible for all, in every social sphere." It is, Bellos contends, "a work of reconciliation—between the classes, but also between the conflicting currents that turn our own lives into storms. It is not a reassuring tale of the triumph of good over evil, but a demonstration of how hard it is to be good."

Bellos provides plenty of information about Hugo's life, drawing on a wide range of primary sources. He has clearly done his homework, as he can explain the tiniest details mentioned in the novel. His aim is not to be pedantic but, instead, to give modern readers access to the kind of knowledge the book's first readers could (and did) take for granted. Hugo lived a fascinating life, rising to great fame, wealth, and status at a remarkably young age before being eventually exiled from his beloved France by Napoleon III, the country's newly elevated emperor, whom Hugo managed to offend. Hugo vowed never to return to France while Napoleon III was still in power, and he was a man of his word. Therefore, much of *Les Misérables* was written outside the territorial limits of France, even though it is obsessively concerned with all things French. Hugo saw his novel as a work relevant to everyone, everywhere, and the

Courtesy of Natalie Bellos

David Bellos is a professor of French at Princeton University. He has translated more than twenty books from French into English and has written eight books of his own, including The Novel of the Century. *His book* Georges Perec: A Life in Words *(1993) won the 1994 Prix Goncourt for biography.*

exceptionally positive worldwide reception it received immediately proved him right.

Bellos discusses such matters as the incident that inspired Hugo write such a novel, the socioeconomic conditions that made the novel so timely and enduringly relevant, the various works by other writers that influenced Hugo's thought, and the political contexts of the work. In an especially intriguing statement, Bellos asserts that *Les Misérables* "offers no criticism of capitalism or of the conditions of industrial labour. Quite the contrary: far from being one of the causes of poverty, 'wage-slavery' is presented in the novel as a providential cure." Bellos argues that the novel implies no narrow political ideology or specific economic program, and that attempts to read it as a piece of propaganda for one cause or another are misguided. Later adaptations of the book, he claims, have often not been especially faithful to Hugo's original intentions. The book does show how people fall into, and stay stuck within, the so-called poverty trap, but Hugo, according to Bellos, was more concerned with spiritual and moral transformation than with mere economic fixes.

Bellos relates practically every detail of the novel to something in Hugo's life, although he also notes that the author often drew on reports from friends and family members about aspects of life with which he was himself unfamiliar. As readers make their way through Bellos's text, they come away with a renewed appreciation of how such a long and complicated book came to be composed, bit by bit, chapter by chapter. Hugo started the novel on November 17, 1845, but it was not published until 1862. By then, much had changed in the author's own life—for one, Hugo, though still immensely famous in France, was living as a political exile—and, in the final stages of writing the novel, he thoroughly revised it. When *Les Misérables* was eventually published in Paris, after a clever publicity campaign organized by Hugo's wife, it was an instant best seller. Bookstores could not keep enough copies in stock to satisfy the huge demand. The novel was quickly translated into many different languages, and it is almost shocking to learn how mangled was the first translation published in Great Britain. The translation published in the United States was, by contrast, thoroughly professional.

Bellos spends so much time and so many pages setting the novel in its numerous historical contexts that some readers may wish that he had devoted more attention to the book's techniques as a work of art. These, surely, are a major key to its success. Bellos does discuss the kinds of French Hugo used, the massive impact of Latin on his ways of thinking and expressing himself, and the novel's use of slang. A particularly interesting section explores (and illustrates) Hugo's use of classical rhetorical devices, thus giving readers some insight into the details of the novel's style. Fuller explication of this sort would have been welcome, but it seems clear that for Bellos, and for most readers, the truly appealing aspects of the novel involve its characterization and themes.

All the main characters are discussed in detail, especially Jean Valjean, whose name, Bellos shows, was chosen to sound as generic as possible, thus making him a kind of "everyman" figure. (If Hugo had written in English, Bellos notes, he might easily have called his hero "John Doe.") Bellos persuasively argues that Valjean's story is almost a reverse version of the Faust legend: instead of making a pact with the devil, Valjean encounters a virtuous man whose morality and spirituality inspire him to reform his own life. The struggle of a single person to become ethically and spiritually better and better is, Bellos shows, deeply embedded in most of the world's great religions and other moral systems. This, he believes, also helps account for the enduring impact of *Les Misérables*. Bellos maintains that later adaptations often simplify the morality of the story. His own book, in contrast, complicates, deepens, and enriches one's understanding of Hugo's novel in practically every way imaginable. Those who have already read *Les Misérables* for themselves will probably want to read it again, as soon as possible, after finishing Bellos's volume; those who have never read the novel will, thanks to Bellos, probably want to acquire it as quickly as they can.

Robert C. Evans, PhD

Review Sources

Armstrong, Judith. "*The Novel of the Century* Review: David Bellos Reveals the Story of *Les Miserables*." Review of *The Novel of the Century: The Extraordinary Adventure of* Les Misérables, by David Bellos. *The Sydney Morning Herald*, 21 Apr. 2017, www.smh.com.au/entertainment/books/the-novel-of-the-century-review-david-bellos-reveals-the-story-of-les-Misérables-20170414-gvky9p.html. Accessed 2 Oct. 2017.

Graham, Liza. "*Novel of the Century* Is a Lively Companion to *Les Misérables*." Review of *The Novel of the Century: The Extraordinary Adventure of* Les Misérables, by David Bellos. *NPR*, 28 Mar. 2017, www.npr.org/2017/03/28/520994034/novel-of-the-century-is-a-lively-companion-to-les-mis-rables. Accessed 2 Oct. 2017.

Grey, Tobias. "The Legacy of *Les Misérables*: Charting the Life of a Classic." Review of *The Novel of the Century: The Extraordinary Adventure of* Les Misérables, by David Bellos. *The New York Times*, 31 Mar. 2017, www.nytimes.com/2017/03/31/books/review/novel-of-the-century-les-miserables-david-bellos.html. Accessed 2 Oct. 2017.

Scurr, Ruth. "*The Novel of the Century* by David Bellos Review: The Story of *Les Misérables*." Review of *The Novel of the Century: The Extraordinary Adventure of* Les Misérables, by David Bellos. *The Guardian*, 18 Jan. 2017, www.theguardian.com/books/2017/jan/18/the-novel-of-the-century-review-the-story-of-les-miserables-victor-hugo. Accessed 2 Oct. 2017.

Otis Redding
An Unfinished Life

Author: Jonathan Gould (b. 1951)
Publisher: Crown Archetype (New York).
544 pp.
Type of work: Biography
Time: Primarily 1941–67
Locale: United States

Otis Redding: An Unfinished Life *is a detailed chronicle of the life and untimely death of a man considered to be one of the greatest singers of all time and an icon of soul and rhythm and blues. Author Jonathan Gould, himself a former musician, draws on newly available sources in cooperation with Redding's family to deliver what may be the most comprehensive portrait of Redding yet in print.*

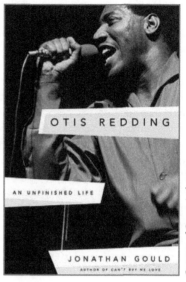

Courtesy of Crown Archetype

Principal personages

OTIS REDDING, legendary soul singer killed in a 1967 plane crash
ZELMA REDDING, his wife
PHIL WALDEN, his longtime manager
STEVE CROPPER, his collaborator and guitarist of Booker T. and the MGs
JIM STEWART, Stax Records cofounder and music producer
JERRY WEXLER, Atlantic Records executive and music producer
AHMET ERTEGUN, Atlantic Records cofounder

Jonathan Gould's biography *Otis Redding: An Unfinished Life* opens in 1967 at the Monterey Pop Festival, a massive musical gathering where such rock icons as the Jefferson Airplane, the Who, and Jimi Hendrix took to the stage and thrilled audiences over the course of three days. Also on the bill, in sharp contrast to the rock acts on display, was Otis Redding, a soul singer out of Memphis, Tennessee. Gould recounts how anticipation of the audience's reception to Redding was of considerable concern, particularly to Atlantic Records executive and producer Jerry Wexler. Wexler had been key in orchestrating the relationship between Atlantic Records and Redding's label, Stax, and had worked hard to convince Redding's manager that the festival would be a great place to bring his client's music to a new audience. However, Gould notes, Redding was one of only three black artists on the bill (the other two being Jimi Hendrix and Lou Rawls), and his style of music, which Wexler considered to be more polished and slick, was sharply opposed to the raucous, freewheeling sound of the other rock groups.

However, as Gould goes on to describe, Wexler need not have worried. Redding's high-energy performance, which included a powerful cover of the Rolling Stones' "Satisfaction," dazzled the crowd and left them cheering for more. The ensuing extended ovation was proof of the massive pop crossover appeal of an artist who had already reached the heights of the soul music market. Sadly, Redding would die just months after this landmark performance, before a new chapter of his career could fully unfold. Yet the film footage of his Monterey performance, along with his posthumous megahit "(Sittin' On) The Dock of the Bay," helped seal Redding's legendary status.

From Monterey in 1967, Gould turns the clock back to the nineteenth century to examine the environment that gave rise to Redding. A prime focus is how the songs of writers such as Stephen Foster and George and Ira Gershwin, as well as the minstrel shows of the Deep South, helped to shape the sound of gospel and soul music. The book offers a deep and thorough examination of the racial tensions and cultural upheavals that formed the foundations of not only African American music but also the broader world into which Redding was born on September 9, 1941.

Redding's father worked at the local air force base near Macon, Georgia, so the Redding family was eligible to move to a federal housing project in the city when Otis was young. However, their updated living situation did little to protect the Reddings from the Jim Crow laws that were so prevalent in the American South at that time. In a city like Macon, the Reddings were restricted or excluded from amenities such as swimming pools, theaters, and parks. Still, Gould notes, Redding remained a bright, happy, and optimistic child. Even when his parents' marriage began to show signs of strain, he remained upbeat.

When Otis Sr., Redding's father, contracted tuberculosis, it impacted his ability to work and, as a means of keeping busy, he became a deacon at the Vineville Baptist Church. It was at this church that Redding began his musical pursuits in earnest, performing with the choir. Soon, he had formed a musical quartet called the Junior Spiritual Crusaders and began performing in local churches. In addition to gospel music and crossover singers such as Sam Cooke, he was inspired by the early rock and roll of Little Richard and local performers.

There are relatively few sources for personal details of Redding's early life—he gave few interviews and did not receive much media attention until after his death. Gould's account benefits greatly from his meticulous research, but most noticeably from his interviews with the singer's surviving family members. Their quotes help fill out a picture of Redding's personality beyond his universally beloved stage presence. As the book progresses, Gould also weaves the known facts of Redding's life story with key historical moments, especially in the struggle for civil rights. For example, he recounts the story of Emmet Till, the fourteen-year-old boy who was beaten and murdered in 1955 for supposedly insulting a white woman in Mississippi. He notes that both Till and Redding turned fourteen in the same year.

As he moves into documentation of Redding's music career, Gould continues to place events in their proper historical context, illustrating how, for all of his prodigious talent, Redding was often at the mercy of things that were beyond his control. Gould is also unflinching in his effort to pull back the curtain on even the most seemingly positive relationships. For example, he quotes Phil Walden, a white music booker who was the same age as Redding and would eventually become his manager, in saying that he and Redding "really hit it off instantly." However, Gould goes on to suggest, that connection may have been more one-sided than Walden realized, driven by deep racial experience. While the two may have indeed genuinely liked each other from the start, the stark reality is that black Southerners often gave white people the impression that they liked them in order to ingratiate themselves. In an era where a black man could be beaten or hanged for giving the wrong impression, being cordial and outgoing was not just good manners, it was a survival skill.

The book continues to mix biography and social history as it chronicles Redding's travels to Los Angeles in the early 1960s. There, the emerging singer encountered a city that was, in many ways, even more segregated than Macon, thanks largely to the efforts of police chief William J. Parker, a staunch white supremacist. Still, in spite of rampant racism, Redding's talent landed him in a recording studio, where he cut his first recordings and received a $100 advance from music publisher Al Kavelin. Otis took that advance and used it to buy a bus ticket back to Macon in order to be with his girlfriend, Zelma, and their newborn son.

In 1962, Redding found himself in the studio of Stax Records in Memphis, Tennessee. With a distinctive sound owing much to the house band Booker T. and the MG's, the label would eventually be credited with the creation of the southern soul and Memphis soul sounds, with artists including Wilson Pickett, Sam & Dave, and the Staple Singers. Yet in 1962, Stax was just getting started, and was about to find its biggest star. Redding was there almost by accident, as he had been tasked with driving singer and guitarist Johnny Jenkins, who had no driver's license, to a recording session. When the Stax musicians were unimpressed with Jenkins's performance, they decided to abandon the session. However, it was noted that the session was already paid for and, with time left on the clock, it was decided to let Redding have a turn at the microphone. Gould, in the interest of being thorough, notes that, years later, Jenkins claimed credit for suggesting that Redding be allowed to sing. Regardless, whoever was responsible, Redding had been given an opportunity.

Gould recalls how Otis first tried a song called "Hey Hey Baby," which Stax studio chief Jim Stewart dismissed as sounding too much like Little Richard. Shifting gears, Atlantic Records representative Joe Galkin suggested Redding try a ballad he had called "These Arms of Mine." As Gould recounts, MGs musician Steve Cropper sat at the piano and was told by Redding, "Just play me those church things." Cropper began a gospel progression and Redding launched into the song. Here, Gould offers an attempt to separate the mythology that has formed around Redding from the facts. He notes that in Cropper's account, the performance was hair-raising and immediately convinced everyone present of the need to record the young singer. However, Gould also presents Stewart's less enthusiastic memory to temper the story. "No one was particularly impressed," Stewart said. "It was different, but I don't think anyone jumped up and down."

Whatever the feeling when it was first presented at Stax, the fact remains that "These Arms of Mine" was the song that opened the doors for Redding. In many ways, it launched the label as well, as Redding became Stax's first major star. Yet, rather than using this moment to launch into a didactic recitation of the highs and lows of Redding's subsequent (and brief) career, Gould tries to give readers the fullest picture of Redding possible by continuing to illustrate the times and events that occurred around him. At times, he shifts the focus away from Redding entirely, devoting passages of the book to other black artists of the era such as James Brown, Sam Cooke, and Little Richard. However, far from being random digressions, these all serve to help tell the story of Redding by showing the perils, pitfalls, and promise of being a young black singer in the early 1960s.

Author Jonathan Gould was a professional musician for years, playing in bands and working in recording studios. His first book, Can't Buy Me Love: The Beatles, Britain, and America *(2007), was a well-received examination of the social context of the Beatles.*

Gould does not spend an inordinate amount of time on Redding's tragic death in a plane crash at just twenty-six years old. He devotes only one chapter to the incident and does not dwell on the particulars of what happened. He moves quickly through the crash, its aftermath and investigation, and Redding's funeral, and then steers the narrative to the posthumous release of "(Sittin' On) The Dock of the Bay." Coming after his Monterey exposure and heralding a significant change in style, the song became Redding's biggest hit and a pop classic. According to Gould, the song and its new sound indicate Redding's maturation as an artist, drawing inspiration from innovative contemporary works such as the Beatles' *Sgt. Pepper's Lonely Hearts Club Band* (1967). Gould further offers insight into the decision to release the record, noting that Stewart was not a fan and did not believe it to be enough of an R & B song to merit release. However, Wexler felt the record's somber, reflective tone made it the perfect song to release in the wake of Redding's death.

Otis Redding: An Unfinished Life was released to almost universal acclaim. Many critics noted that it successfully met the challenge of depicting a figure whose brief life was poorly documented at the time and in many ways does not lend itself to dramatization. In the *New York Review of Books*, Geoffrey O'Brien wrote, "Gould has written an absorbing and ambitious book about a life cut short, a life devoid of the melodrama and self-destruction that enliven the biographies of so many of Otis Redding's contemporaries." The book also received particular praise for its placing Redding's rise in an historical context.

At once a detailed biography of one of the pioneers of '60s soul and an unflinching look at a tumultuous and divisive time in America's history, *Otis Redding: An Unfinished Life* manages to go beyond the usual musical biography to offer a comprehensive portrait of both a man and the times that shaped him.

Jeremy Brown

Review Sources
Johnston, Maura K. "Otis Redding's Revolution." Review of *Otis Redding: An Unfinished Life*, by Jonathan Gould. *The Boston Globe*, 19 May 2017, www.bostonglobe.com/arts/books/2017/05/18/otis-redding-revolution/FbUTTgZz-kVNmSeawSJ2g8N/story.html. Accessed 6 Feb. 2018.
Kreps, Daniel. "Epic New Otis Redding Biography Sheds Light on the Singer's Life and Times." Review of *Otis Redding: An Unfinished Life*, by Jonathan Gould. *Rolling Stone*, 2 Aug. 2017, www.rollingstone.com/music/news/new-otis-redding-biography-an-unfinished-life-our-review-w495427. Accessed 6 Feb. 2018
Light, Alan. "Soul of the '60s: Otis Redding's Short Life and Long Reach." Review of *Otis Redding: An Unfinished Life*, by Jonathan Gould. *The New York Times*, 2 June 2017, www.nytimes.com/2017/06/02/books/review/otis-redding-an-unfinished-life-jonathan-gould.html. Accessed 6 Feb. 2018.
O'Brien, Geoffrey, "Five Magnificent Years." Review of *Otis Redding: An Unfinished Life*, by Jonathan Gould. *The New York Review of Books*, 28 Sept. 2017, www.nybooks.com/articles/2017/09/28/otis-redding-five-magnificent-years/. Accessed 6 Feb. 2018.
Review of *Otis Redding: An Unfinished Life*, by Jonathan Gould. *Kirkus Reviews*, 21 Mar. 2017, www.kirkusreviews.com/book-reviews/jonathan-gould/otis-redding/. Accessed 6 Feb. 2018.

Pachinko

Author: Min Jin Lee (b. 1968)
Publisher: Grand Central (New York). 496 pp.
Type of work: Novel
Time: 1910–89
Locales: Korea and Japan

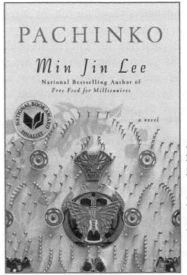

Courtesy of Grand Central Publishing

Min Jin Lee's multigenerational epic takes its name from a popular Japanese gambling game of chance. Through oppression, war, and more intimate forms of heartache, Lee explores how fate and luck shape people's lives.

Principal characters

SUNJA, the novel's central character; she leaves Korea as a teenager and settles in Japan after becoming pregnant out of wedlock
KOH HANSU, her older lover and father of Noa
ISAK BAEK, her husband, a pastor and father of Mozasu
NOA, her oldest son, an intelligent and meticulous youth who struggles with his identity even as he grows older
MOZASU, her youngest son, a bright boy who later becomes the millionaire owner of several pachinko parlors

Spanning nearly one hundred years, Min Jin Lee's novel *Pachinko* tells the story of multiple generations of one Korean family living in Japan. Sunja is the daughter of a kind, deformed boardinghouse owner named Hoonie and his wife, Yangjin; she is raised in coastal Yeongdo, Korea. It is the early 1910s, and Japan has just annexed Korea, but more directly important to the family's life is the premature death of the beloved Hoonie and the daily work that must be done to house and feed the local fishermen during the lean times of economic depression. Sunja's life requires hard labor—a woman's fate is to suffer, Yangjin says, in what becomes one of the book's most common refrains—but she is happy. She washes the fishermen's clothes on the beach and haggles for produce at the village market.

When Sunja is sixteen, she captures the attention of a wealthy businessman named Koh Hansu. Hansu slowly wins the girl's trust, and one day, while gathering wild mushrooms in the forest, he takes advantage of her. Their trysts become routine, and though it barely registers to the innocent Sunja that she is having sex, she soon becomes pregnant. When she tells Hansu, he is overjoyed, though he explains to her that he is already married with children in Japan. Sunja is devastated and, now, deeply shamed; having a child out of wedlock will mark her for life—but fate and luck intervene. One boarder, a sickly young pastor named Isak Baek, seizes on Sunja's cause. Yangjin and her daughter saved his life, he argues. In return for their benevolence, he offers to marry Sunja and raise her child as his own.

Sunja and Yangjin readily accept Isak's offer, and Sunja follows her new, and luckily for her, deeply kind, husband to Osaka, Japan, to live with his older brother Yoseb and his wife, Kyunghee, in 1933. One problem has been solved for Sunja, but another arises. As Koreans living in Japan, Sunja and her new family face a difficult path. The young girl is shocked by the poverty of the Korean ghetto where her in-laws live, unable to find Japanese landlords who will rent or sell to them elsewhere in the city. This stigma and oppression, one of the novel's central themes, will reverberate through the generations of Sunja's family.

Courtesy of Elena Seibert

Min Jin Lee spent several years working as a lawyer before beginning to write short fiction. Her first novel, Free Food for Millionaires, *was published in 2007.* Pachinko, *her second novel, was a finalist for the National Book Award for fiction in 2017.*

In her acknowledgements, Lee writes that she was first inspired to write a book about Koreans in Japan in 1989. The ethnic Korean community in Japan are called Zainichi, a term that literally means "foreign resident staying in Japan." Perversely, the term even applies to fourth- and fifth-generation Koreans born in Japan. These people, as Lee touches on late in the book, are still required to reapply for alien status every three years. After moving from the United States to Tokyo with her husband in 2007, Lee rewrote the entire novel based on the stories she heard interviewing Koreans in Japan.

After Sunja arrives in Japan, she gives birth to a son, Noa, and another son, this time by Isak, named Mozasu. Then, in a cruel twist of fate, Isak is sent to prison and held captive for approximately two long years as World War II begins. Sunja and Kyunghee make ends meet by selling homemade kimchi and candy at the market, but the old-fashioned Yoseb is resentful of the women's contribution. Their success breeds unrest among the family, again striking the theme of female hardship. It is not enough for women to suffer poverty; at every turn, they suffer humiliation, shame, and fear rooted in their gender as well. As the war wears on, fate intervenes again. The wealthy businessman Hansu reappears with a warning: the Americans are planning to bomb Osaka and Sunja and her family must leave the city. In the first of many such instances, Sunja is resentful of Hansu's intervention, but she wisely follows his advice. He arranges for her to stay with a Japanese farmer in the countryside. Here, the family safely waits out the rest of the war. Hansu is a gangster, amassing untold sums of money on the black market, but he is also, for the ever-struggling Sunja, a godlike figure, swooping in to save her when she needs it most. Years down the line, his constant meddling will come at a steep price, but in the moment, particularly in his aid for Sunja during the war, Lee illustrates the poverty of ideals when it comes to matters of survival. When Noa realizes who Hansu is, he laments the man's "dirty money," and blames his mother; idealistic and ultimately narrow-minded, Noa may have preferred dying in Osaka without Hansu's help. Thus, Sunja feels her guilt compounded, blaming herself for her weakness in wanting to protect her own children.

Lee's novel, which ends in 1989, is full of such moral quandaries. Isak, the kind pastor, has no use for money but realizes how foolish this position sounds when he must care for his wife and children. It is difficult to lead an ethically pure life when fate can be so unexpectedly cruel. But fate, as Lee shows, can be kind as well. Sunja's younger son, Mozasu is a poor student but becomes an extraordinarily wealthy pachinko parlor owner. Pachinko, a popular game in Japan, is a lot like pinball, with metal balls rolling past precisely set pins, but it is also a form of gambling, like a slot machine. The game is perfectly legal; the gambling aspect, however, lends the business an unseemly connotation. At the same time, pachinko parlors, unlike most other professions in postwar Japan, tended not to discriminate against Koreans. As a pachinko parlor owner, Mozasu could seek his fortune. He also understands the game on a metaphorical level. Later in the book, Lee writes, "Mozasu believed that life was like this game where the player could adjust the dials yet also expect the uncertainty of factors he couldn't control. He understood why his customers wanted to play something that looked fixed but which also left room for randomness and hope."

The central figure of Lee's novel is Sunja, though the author alternates between the points of view of a host of captivating characters, ranging from Sunja's estranged son Noa to a woman named Ayame, the wife of one of Mozasu's close friends. Ayame's story has little to do with Sunja or even Mozasu, but like all the others, it adds texture to the expansive world of *Pachinko*. Given the novel's length, Lee's style is surprisingly spare and semidetached. A sample sentence from the early pages, "Yangjin was fifteen and mild and tender as a newborn calf, the matchmaker said," offers a good indication of Lee's narrative voice. In this way, each character earns their complete narrative attention. There are no minor characters in *Pachinko*; the novel is a tapestry of full and complex lives, with each character well developed despite the book's impressive breadth. In its style and scope, *Pachinko* resembles a nineteenth-century novel. It would not be hyperbolic to say that it has more in common with George Eliot's *Middlemarch* (1871–72) than other contemporary novels about the immigrant experience. This is perhaps because *Pachinko* is not merely about assimilation or identity; it is about all the trials and triumphs that make an entire life. Throughout the novel, characters take the odds they are given and try their best to keep playing.

Lee herself was born in South Korea and moved to the Queens borough of New York City when she was seven years old. Her first novel, *Free Food for Millionaires* (2007), explores the lives of Korean immigrants living in New York City in the 1990s. In the book, a young woman named Casey Han struggles to find her path. Her parents, Korean immigrants, are horrified when she passes up an opportunity to study law at Columbia University. Like *Pachinko*, the novel follows the lives of other characters, including members of Casey's parents' generation, to offer a fuller, more complex picture of the world. At over six hundred pages, it shares the epic scale of *Pachinko* as well. The novel was well received, but, thanks to Lee's own painstaking research process, her follow-up work was not published until about a decade later. However, critics have largely deemed *Pachinko* worth the wait. The novel was a finalist for the National Book Award for fiction and was named by the *New York Times* as one of the ten best books of 2017. Lee is highly capable of writing on a large scale, Krys Lee suggested in her *New York Times* review. "Like most memorable novels, however, *Pachinko* resists summary," she wrote. "In this sprawling book, history itself is a character. *Pachinko* is about outsiders, minorities and the politically disenfranchised. But it is so much more besides."

Molly Hagan

Review Sources

Aw, Tash. "*Pachinko* by Min Jin Lee Review—Rich Story of the Immigrant Experience." Review of *Pachinko*, by Min Jin Lee. *The Guardian*, 15 Mar. 2017, www.theguardian.com/books/2017/mar/15/pachinko-min-jin-lee-review. Accessed 8 Dec. 2017.

Lee, Krys. "Home but Not Home: Four Generations of an Ethnic Korean Family in Japan." Review of *Pachinko*, by Min Jin Lee. *The New York Times*, 2 Feb. 2017, www.nytimes.com/2017/02/02/books/review/pachinko-min-jin-lee.html. Accessed 8 Dec. 2017.

Review of *Pachinko*, by Min Jin Lee. *Kirkus*, 26 Sept. 2016, www.kirkusreviews.com/book-reviews/min-jin-lee/pachinko/. Accessed 8 Dec. 2017.

Review of *Pachinko*, by Min Jin Lee. *Publishers Weekly*, 21 Nov. 2016, www.publishersweekly.com/978-1-4555-6393-7. Accessed 8 Dec. 2017.

Zimmerman, Jean. "Culture Clash, Survival and Hope in *Pachinko*." Review of *Pachinko*, by Min Jin Lee. *NPR*, 7 Feb. 2017, www.npr.org/2017/02/07/512910187/culture-clash-survival-and-hope-in-pachinko. Accessed 8 Dec. 2017.

The Patriots

Author: Sana Krasikov (b. 1979)
Publisher: Spiegel & Grau (New York). 560 pp.
Type of work: Novel
Time: 1933–2008
Locales: New York City; Moscow, Magnitogorsk, and Kuibyshev (Samara) in the Soviet Union (later, the Russian Federation)

Beginning with the story of an American Jewish woman who migrates to the Soviet Union during the Great Depression in search of a truly just society, The Patriots *traces the experiences of her family across multiple generations.*

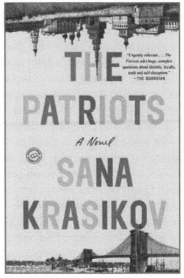

Courtesy of Spiegel & Grau

Principal characters

FLORENCE FEIN, a young Jewish woman from New York City's Brooklyn borough who immigrates to the Soviet Union

LEON BRINK, a Jewish American expatriate whom she marries in the Soviet Union

JULIAN BRINK, their son; his name is sometimes given in its Hebrew form, Yulik

LENNY BRINK, Julian's son

ESSIE FRANK, a young woman who emigrates from the United States to the Soviet Union at the same time as Florence

CAPTAIN HENRY ROBBINS, a US Air Force pilot held captive in a Soviet prison camp

SIDNEY FEIN, Florence's younger brother

SERGEY SOKOLOV, a Soviet engineer who helps inspire Florence to go to the Soviet Union

While many novels deal with the experiences of immigrants coming to the United States, Sana Krasikov's *The Patriots* turns this theme on its head. In the midst of the Great Depression, Florence Fein, a young Jewish woman from New York City, comes to doubt the possibility of true social and economic justice under the American capitalist system and decides to immigrate to the Soviet Union. The move is to have a profound impact on her life, and the novel uses multiple styles to convey the complexity of the situation that she, and eventually her family, faces. There are aspects of romance, historical drama, comedy, and political thriller, all connected by deeply researched facts that bring the varied settings to life.

Above all, *The Patriots* is a family saga. While Florence is arguably the central character and certainly the one who sets the story in motion, this is a multigenerational novel that covers not only her experiences, but also those of her son, Julian Brink, and of Julian's son, Lenny Brink. While Florence's story starts in the early 1930s in the United States and carries on for decades in the Soviet Union, another plot focuses on Julian and Lenny as adults in Moscow in 2008. Flashbacks and memories, as well as passages of historical context, fill in the gaps. Throughout, Krasikov explores the question of how totalitarian rule shapes individuals and institutions.

The novel begins with a brief prologue in which a young Julian is reunited with his mother after spending years in orphanages while his parents were imprisoned by the Soviet state. The narrative then jumps back to 1933, as Florence departs for the Soviet Union on a ship. She is partly motivated by belief in the promise of an egalitarian socialist society, and partly by a desire to continue a relationship with a Soviet engineer she met while he was stationed in the United States. When she arrives in the Soviet Union, however, she quickly finds that it does not offer the society she sought. Yet she stubbornly refuses to give up on her faith in the regime and settles in permanently to begin a family even as government crackdowns threaten.

Alternating chapters present the viewpoint of an adult Julian, who fills in his own backstory and grapples with his mother's legacy. When changing international relations led to a loosening of Soviet restrictions on Jewish citizens leaving the country in the 1970s, he took the opportunity to immigrate to the United States, where he connected with his uncle Sidney. Julian has connections to business endeavors in the post-Soviet Russian Federation through his involvement in the international oil business. Though he characterizes the economic might of Big Oil as contributing more to improved international relations than diplomacy ever did, Julian comes face to face with the industry's (and capitalist Russia's) deep corruption on a 2008 business trip to Moscow. He is also on the trip in hopes of reaching his son, Lenny, who was born in Soviet Russia but raised and educated in the United States. Intrigued by curiosity about his roots but more so by lucrative business opportunities, Lenny has moved back to Russia to seek his fortune and has become entangled in questionable affairs.

Krasikov explores many powerful themes through the stories of Florence, Julian, and the rest of their family and friends. One is the basic issue of identity—how does one choose to identify oneself? Florence turns her back on capitalist America, but in the Soviet Union, her facility in English and her American background sometimes work in her favor. When Julian is born during World War II, Florence decides to list his nationality on his birth certificate as American, believing it is safer to be identified as an American than having his Jewish ethnicity officially recorded. After Julian leaves the Soviet Union to settle in the United States, he never looks back in ideological terms, although business and family ties lead him to physically return to Russia on several occasions.

Loyalty is also a recurring them in the book. Going to the Soviet Union when the Great Depression made it appear that capitalism was failing, Florence embraces the dream of a socialist utopia with the zeal of a convert, even when confronted by many Soviets who have come to doubt these very dreams. When her husband, Leon, is arrested for allegedly trying to promote a Zionist plot, he is never seen again. For months, Florence takes Julian every week to the prison where she believes Leon is being held, remaining blindly optimistic that he is alive even when everyone else understands his sentence was a euphemism for execution. Even her own imprisonment for supposedly distributing anti-Soviet propaganda does not destroy Florence's commitment to the socialist vision, although she finds it wise to keep such loyalty to herself in prison, where zealous followers of the party line are deeply resented by their fellow prisoners. Reflecting on his mother's stubborn loyalty, Julian initially concludes that it comes down to a simple refusal to see the truth. He likens her condition to the medical term "agnosia," in which stroke patients suffer the inability to recognize something for what it is. Only as he digs into records of Florence's past does Julian gain a more nuanced understanding of his mother's actions.

Krasikov skillfully depicts how the changing winds of doctrine in a totalitarian system can dictates one's fate. Those who were model Soviet citizens or even heroes one day could become enemies of the state overnight. During World War II, Leon and

© Alexis Calice

Sana Krasikov was born in the Soviet Union and immigrated to the United States as a child. Her first book, the short-story collection One More Year *(2008), brought her much critical acclaim and won the Sami Rohr Prize for Jewish Literature.* The Patriots *is her first novel.*

some of his intellectual Jewish compatriots were put to work for the Jewish Anti-Fascist Committee, writing propaganda to attract international support for the fight against Nazi fascism. But after the war, the very work the state encouraged them to do is seen as evidence of subversive intentions, leading to Leon's arrest. In a world where the oppressor today might become the victim tomorrow, Florence finds that she can gain leverage on her interrogators by threatening to inform on them about a slip of the tongue that suggested they admired Nazi Gestapo interrogation tactics. With skill or luck, one can turn the paranoia of the system against itself to some degree. Julian learns how his mother survived in this way, and he uses similar methods in an effort to help Lenny.

The historical context of international events that impact Florence and her family is carefully considered throughout the novel. Krasikov shows that while World War II brought great suffering to the Soviet Union, the "Great Patriotic War" also brought to some a renewed commitment to the Soviet cause. Because of suspicions about her background, Florence had been dismissed from a good job and reduced to doing menial work; the war gave her a new chance to contribute to society. She and her family are relocated for security reasons to Kuibyshev, a town on the Volga River far to the south and east of Moscow. There, she and Leon find work translating articles and reports on the war into English for publication abroad, to arouse support and raise money for the Soviet war effort. Of course, this relatively positive situation does not last, as the complex interrelation between broad sociopolitical currents and individual lives changes as the war goes on.

Other broad social developments are also reflected in the characters' lives. For example, Julian witnesses how orphans, previously resented by many as a drain on the nation's resources, are seen more sympathetically after the war, as it is assumed their parents died heroically serving their country. Later in the book, the Cold War and the Korean War impact Florence's situation. Working in a brutal gulag in Siberia after she is imprisoned, she had not even heard that there was a war going on in Korea. But when an American pilot is shot down over North Korea and sent to a Soviet prison camp, she is recruited to translate for him and encourage him to cooperate as the Soviets attempt to reverse engineer advanced American aircraft.

Importantly, the novel's core narrative, while fiction, aligns with real, documented history and individual experiences that are perhaps little known to most Westerners. Americans like Florence did indeed go to the Soviet Union hoping to help build a "socialist paradise," only to be caught up in the realities of World War II and the Cold War. Many became disillusioned with the brutality and corruption they saw first-hand during Stalin's rule, but the character of Florence illustrates how self-illusion can endure. When the Soviets made it virtually impossible for such expatriates to return to the United States (and the US government made no efforts to aid them), these people truly became men and women without a country. Krasikov both compares and contrasts this precarious position with twenty-first century venture capitalists like Lenny, caught up in the thrill of great potential but eventually faced with the realities of repressive politics and corruption.

The Patriots received generally high praise from critics, with more than one reviewer invoking positive comparisons to Boris Pasternak's sweeping, Nobel Prize–winning epic *Dr. Zhivago* (1957). Many also noted that the book carries an air of authenticity; Krasikov's Jewish family relocated to the United States from the Soviet Union, and the experiences of some of her characters echo those of her relatives. A few more mixed reviews questioned whether the story really demands the extended treatment of over five hundred pages and noted moments of awkward prose. The structure of alternating chapters focused on Florence or Julian, presented nonchronologically, may also make following the story line difficult for some readers. (Each chapter does begin with a dated icon—typically an image of a visa stamp or some other kind of travel document—that helps keep track of the chronology.)

Despite these minor issues, Krasikov's characters are skillfully drawn, and the dialogue and settings—whether grimy industrial cities or Siberian wilderness—ring true. Crucially, the portrayal of Florence as a flawed character is highly compelling. As Viv Groskop wrote in a review for the *Spectator*, readers "become as torn as [Julian] is over whether she should be viewed as heroine, victim, or villain." Perhaps everyone, at one time or another, has played all three roles, which makes Florence a character with whom readers can identify, even if they find her difficult to admire.

Mark S. Joy, PhD

Review Sources

Aslanyan, Anna. "*The Patriots* by Sana Krasikov—Kin and Country." Review of *The Patriots*, by Sana Krasikov. *Financial Times*, 24 Mar. 2017, www.ft.com/content/cf73b8ba-0d62-11e7-a88c-50ba212dce4d. Accessed 5 Dec. 2017.

Groskop, Viv. "Is *The Patriots* the 21st Century's *Doctor Zhivago*?" Review of *The Patriots*, by Sana Krasikov. *The Spectator*, 25 Mar. 2017, www.spectator.co.uk/2017/03/is-the-patriots-the-21st-centurys-doctor-zhivago/. Accessed 5 Dec. 2017.

Rich, Nathaniel. "*The Patriots* Charts a Family's Reverse Journey from Brooklyn to the Gulag." Review of *The Patriots*, by Sana Krasikov. *The New York Times*, 24 Jan. 2017, www.nytimes.com/2017/01/24/books/review/patriots-sana-krasikov.html. Accessed 5 Dec. 2017.

Taplin, Phoebe. "*The Patriots* by Sana Krasikov Review—Stuck in the USSR." Review of *The Patriots*, by Sana Krasikov. *The Guardian*, 24 Mar. 2017, www.theguardian.com/books/2017/mar/24/the-patriots-by-sana-krasikov-review. Accessed 5 Dec. 2017.

Wolfson, Delia. Review of *The Patriots*, by Sana Krasikov. *Jewish Book Council*, 2017, www.jewishbookcouncil.org/book/the-patriots. Accessed 5 Dec. 2017.

Persons Unknown

Author: Susie Steiner
Publisher: Random House (New York). 320 pp.
Type of work: Novel
Time: Present day
Locales: London and Cambridgeshire, England

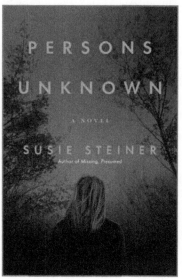

Courtesy of Random House

Manon Bradshaw is back investigating another murder, but this one has ties that are too close to home, endangering the most important relationships in her life.

Principal characters

MANON BRADSHAW, a successful police investigator

FLY DENT, her twelve-year-old adoptive son

DAVY WALKER, her colleague and friend

HARRIET HARPER, her colleague and friend

ELLIE BRADSHAW, her sister

SOLOMON, a.k.a. Solly, her nephew, Ellie's son

JON-OLIVER ROSS, wealthy investment banker and murder victim; Ellie's former boyfriend

SASKIA, a.k.a. Angel, a prostitute with ties to Jon-Oliver

BERNADETTE FIELDING, a.k.a. Birdie, a woman who takes Saskia in

Persons Unknown is the second book in author and former journalist Susie Steiner's detective series revolving around Manon Bradshaw. The first book in the series, *Missing, Presumed*, which was just Steiner's second novel, introduced Manon as a successful and dedicated—if somewhat awkward—police investigator who is re-evaluating her life. Though she has always enjoyed her job, she begins to notice that her personal life is lacking. She becomes embroiled in a missing persons case involving a graduate student, and as the case draws to a close, Manon must face not only the demons of the victim but also those in her own life. Though it is not essential to have read *Missing, Presumed* to follow *Persons Unknown*, readers will find that the previous novel does set up some background information that will enhance this second book.

While the first installment left off with Manon adopting the orphan Fly Dent and moving in with her sister Ellie in London, *Persons Unknown* starts with a description of some of the changes in her life since then. Perhaps most importantly, she is now five months pregnant but still single, having decided to use a sperm donor. She has also left London and her time-consuming job there for a quieter life back in her hometown in Cambridgeshire, bringing Fly, Ellie, and Ellie's young son Solly, with her. She rejoins her former police department, though in a position focused on cold cases rather than active investigations. Unfortunately for Manon, the move and the slower pace of work do not prove as fulfilling as she hoped, and she also finds herself worrying about Fly, who is unhappy being one of the few black children in town.

The mystery plot soon kicks into gear when Jon-Oliver Ross, a wealthy banker who turns out to be Ellie's former boyfriend and Solomon's father, is discovered stabbed to death. Manon's former close colleagues Harriet and Davy are tasked with the investigation, which leads in directions that come ever closer to Manon's personal life. Specifically, Fly is implicated as a suspect in the case due to his appearance on security camera footage, and the justice system seems content to assume he is guilty. Angry and torn between her emotional reaction and her professional instinct, Manon launches her own investigation, as she knows she is the only person who will find justice for the innocent.

It eventually becomes clear that there is more to the case than first appears. The reader is introduced to the kindly, lonely older woman Birdie, who has taken in a mysterious young woman she first knows only as Angel. Angel turns out to be Saskia, a prostitute who worked for a shady international crime organization and counted Ross as a customer. As the mystery spirals deeper, Steiner successfully introduces new twists and turns that keep the plot engaging for even dedicated mystery readers. Throughout, the bonds of family and justice are strained to the brink of collapse, yet with enough realistic humor to round things out.

The novel is organized in two ways. There are larger sections correlating to the time frame of the murder investigation; for example, the first part is titled "Day 1, December 14." The ensuing subsections or chapters are then titled by the name of the character whose point of view predominates. Most are fairly short chapters labeled "Manon" or "Davy" and told by a limited omniscient narrator. By contrast, those focused on Saskia and Birdie are in first-person narration. The single chapter centered on Gary Stanton, Manon's direct supervisor, returns to third-person perspective. This shift in narration hints at the biases and conflicting viewpoints that affect the progression of the case and also helps keeps readers guessing at what will happen next. Steiner skillfully develops her characterization whether readers are hearing about actions and thoughts firsthand or through an outside narrator's lens. Though the story unfolds primarily in chronological order, a few flashbacks provide background information that clarifies issues in the investigation.

The structure of the novel enhances Steiner's characterization, as readers are allowed into some characters' minds to reveal further depth beyond their actions. And while the book succeeds in its mystery plot, it is the characterizations and other rich details of Manon's world that are the most captivating part of the work. The reason the characters are so compelling is that they are highly realistic as flawed humans. Manon is the most developed character, and she is easy to identify with despite being more than a little rough around the edges. For instance, as she thinks to herself, "she was never a generous colleague or friend, never one to remember someone's hospital appointment or stressful meeting and call to say 'good luck.' Not the sort to offer childcare (Christ—she'd recoil) or help in a crisis." Her relationship flaws enhance

Susie Steiner trained as a journalist and worked for various newspapers, including the Guardian, *for twenty years before publishing her first novel in 2013. Her first Manon Bradshaw novel,* Missing, Presumed *(2016), earned much critical acclaim and became a best seller.*

the conflicts she deals with throughout the novel.

Other characters are flawed in some way as well. Ellie and Birdie long for fellowship but selfishly doubt the connections they make. Davy and others on the force resent Manon's investigative abilities. Ross and his colleagues are greedy and unethical. Steiner skillfully makes most of these characters plausibly relatable despite—or because of—the flaws. The personal quirks also contribute to the humorous element of the book, which ranges from light-hearted to dark. Details like Birdie's obsession with her weight and Davy's lack of confidence in his own abilities bring both laughs and acknowledgment of issues real people face every day.

Throughout the course of the novel, Steiner introduces several challenging themes. Perhaps most notable is her treatment of race and prejudice, which centers on the experience of Fly. Manon knows that his race will cause problems for him, and the move from London was precipitated with that in mind. Yet life in a smaller community comes with its own challenges for minorities, something Ellie predicts early on, calling Cambridgeshire "the bigotry heartlands." Sure enough, Fly, already world-weary beyond his years, feels uncomfortable in the new environment and becomes the target of prejudice. Ironically, Manon's effort to protect him from urban crime and the biased justice system backfires when he is arrested, placed in juvenile detention, and separated even further from Manon.

Fly's arrest makes Manon feel first helpless as a mother and then willing to fight against all odds to help her family, and motherhood emerges as another central theme of the novel. As the novel progresses, Manon is forced to face the fact that doing what she felt was right for Fly, rather than what was comfortable for him, may not have been the best option for their family. She also begins to struggle with the decision she had previously made to become pregnant, which originally had elated her. She is confronted with the selfishness her pregnancy suggests to Fly, and for a time even wonders if she wants the baby. By the end of the novel, she has come to terms with the reality that parenting is never easy. Parenting as a theme also relates to Ellie, whose personal choices are not always in her son's best interests despite her best intentions.

The focus on motherhood also opens up to a general examination of family and romantic relationships, especially those outside of the traditional nuclear family. Manon and Ellie grapple living together as sisters and single women, with their own parenting styles and perspectives on life. Birdie's attraction to Saskia borders on a parent-child relationship, while issues of infidelity and divorce are brought up in relation to several characters. Steiner even sneaks a hint of romance into the novel as Manon's attraction to Fly's attorney blossoms into something she cannot understand but is afraid to lose, and Davy realizes that some romance in his life might give him a deeper reason to get up in the morning.

Other elements of the story are more standard crime-novel fare and, while important to the plot, are less vividly wrought. Saskia's revelation to Birdie about her involvement in prostitution and the dangers of the escort service she worked for reveal an underlying layer of corruption in the London business world. Police procedure is also necessarily explored, and while this description can be a bit dry, Steiner inserts a sense of reality that reinforces the importance of careful police work. More interesting is the way Steiner illustrates Manon's realization that the justice system does not always work perfectly. As a police officer, Manon has investigated crimes, but when Fly is accused of Ross's murder, she is forced to more closely consider the impact of criminal investigations on the accused and their families. Despite knowing investigators Harriet and Davy personally, she comes to question their competence and dedication to her son's case, especially as evidence that they have not considered comes to light.

Critical reaction to *Persons Unknown* has been primarily positive. Many reviewers especially commented on Steiner's flair for skillfully mixing social justice themes into a compelling mystery framework, with a dose of dark humor for good measure. The *Kirkus* review noted her "complex and believable characters," particularly "a delightful protagonist who deserves a place alongside other beloved literary detectives." It was widely agreed that Steiner provided a strong continuation of the Manon Bradshaw series and left a solid platform for further installments. Several critics compared the book to the works of mystery author Kate Atkinson and noted its potential to be developed for film or television.

Near the end of *Person's Unknown*, everything is tied together in a complicated twist that brings the past and present together in unexpected ways that will keep readers on the edge of their seats. The conclusion provides just enough closure for satisfaction while leaving some open threads to make readers want to see what will happen next with Manon. Fans of the novel will be happy to know that Steiner is working on a third novel featuring the plucky detective.

Theresa L. Stowell, PhD

Review Sources

Murphy, Jane. Review of *Persons Unknown*, by Susie Steiner. *Booklist*, 1 May 2017, pp. 28. *EBSCOhost*, search.ebscohost.com/login.aspx?direct=true&db=f5h&AN=122991854&site=eds-live. Accessed 6 January 2017.

Review of *Persons Unknown*, by Susie Steiner. *Kirkus Reviews*, 21 Mar. 2017, www.kirkusreviews.com/book-reviews/susie-steiner/persons-unknown-steiner/. Accessed 6 January 2017.

Review of *Persons Unknown*, by Susie Steiner. *Publishers Weekly*, 2017, www.publishersweekly.com/978-0-8129-9834-4. Accessed 6 January 2017.

Stasio, Marilyn. "In the Best New Crime, Lethal Lasagna, Honor Killings and Nanny Cams." Review of *Persons Unknown*, by Susie Steiner, et al. *The New York Times*, 7 July 2017, www.nytimes.com/2017/07/07/books/review/in-the-best-new-crime-love-like-blood-mark-billingham.html. Accessed 6 January 2017.

Theis, Ann. Review of *Persons Unknown*, by Susie Steiner. *Library Journal*, 1 July 2017, pp. 57–58. *EBSCOhost*, search.ebscohost.com/login.aspx?direct=true&db=a9h&AN=123953358&site=eds-live. Accessed 6 January 2017.

The Possessions

Author: Sara Flannery Murphy (b. 1984)
Publisher: Harper (New York). 368 pp.
Type of work: Novel
Time: Fantastical present
Locale: An unnamed US city

Sara Flannery Murphy's debut novel, The Possessions, *imagines a world in which it is possible to contact dead loved ones through mediums who ingest a special pill.*

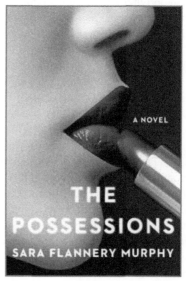

Courtesy of HarperCollins Publishers

Principal characters
EDIE, the narrator, a medium, or "body,"
    working for the Elysian Society
PATRICK BRADDOCK, her client who is con-
    tacting his dead wife
MRS. RENARD, her boss, the owner of the
    Elysian Society
SYLVIA, Patrick's dead wife

Sara Flannery Murphy's debut novel, *The Possessions*, is a literary science-fiction thriller and mystery set in a fantastical present. It centers on the idea that the dead can be channeled by mediums, known as "bodies," who take a pill known as "lotus" to allow spirits temporary possession of their physical bodies. From that concept, Murphy builds a convincing world, drawing on influences ranging from psychology to Greek mythology. The author has written about how her interest in faith and the trappings of Catholicism originally led her to the premise for *The Possessions*, which began as a book about the nature of belief. As the story developed, however, and Murphy fully embraced the supernatural element rather than keep it ambiguous, the theme of obsession emerged as a driving force. Inspired in part by classic novels such as Emily Brontë's *Wuthering Heights* (1847), Vladimir Nabokov's *Lolita* (1955), and Stephen King's *Misery* (1987), Murphy is interested in the consuming quality of desire.

The narrator and protagonist of *The Possessions* is Edie, short for Eurydice, who works as a body for an apparently reputable organization known as the Elysian Society. Murphy quickly draws the reader in through her description of the work routine of the bodies. On any given day, Edie dons a paper-thin white dress and enters a sterile room that evokes a cross between a generic hotel room and a funeral parlor. She sits in a stiff-backed chair facing her client, and after a bit of small talk—not Edie's forte—and the ceremonial handling of an object belonging to the deceased, she ingests a tiny white lotus pill. Were one to ask her, Edie would not be able to say with total accuracy what happens after that. She is essentially unconscious as the client interacts with the spirit of the dead person they have contacted as it possesses her body. The Elysian

Society maintains strict rules around these thirty-minute sessions, including no sexual contact, providing a measure of protection to the mostly female bodies compared to illicit unregulated lotus use on the streets.

It might not sound like much, but the job, if one is not careful, can take a serious physical and emotional toll. Most bodies, unaccustomed to the role of vessel, leave after a few days or weeks. A few hang on for a year or more. But Edie is committed to her job in a way that other bodies are not. When the book begins, she has been with the Elysian Society for five years. Murphy lays down many hints that her own past—Eurydice is not her real name, merely her "body" name—has driven her to the job as a form of escape. But this mystery soon becomes just one of a tangle of threads that make up the plot of this strange and intermittently beguiling novel, as Edie's very identity strains in the face of her growing obsession.

The object of Edie's obsession is a man named Patrick Braddock, a client she meets in the book's opening scene. She applies his deceased wife's lipstick—a startling and, on Edie, unfortunately, unflattering shade of plum—and their session begins. However, unlike any past client, Patrick captures Edie's imagination. As a body, she has taught herself to occupy, both in and out of the workplace, a state of total blankness. As Murphy describes her, she appears pale, washed out, and plain. Her apartment is plain, notable only for the boxes and boxes of photographs and ephemera collected from her regular clients. She is in every way a vessel, existing only to consume the grief and memory of others. But Patrick, with his undeniable good looks and polite but pointed interest in Edie herself, awakens Edie's dormant sexual desires.

Critics, such as Sarah Gilmartin in her review for the *Irish Times*, have noted that this premise is strongly reminiscent of Daphne du Maurier's gothic romance *Rebecca* (1938). In that novel, a young (and similarly unnamed) woman is wooed by an attractive and wealthy older man, but their marriage is metaphorically haunted by the ghost of her husband's first wife, Rebecca. In *The Possessions*, Murphy adds a deliciously macabre twist to this classic tale: Edie and Patrick's burgeoning romance is only possible because of the "ghost" of Sylvia, Patrick's late wife. For the protagonist of *Rebecca*, Rebecca is an obstacle to the fulfillment of desire; for Edie, Sylvia is the only route to that fulfillment.

But like Maxim, the husband in *Rebecca*, Patrick is an unusual and suspicious character. Sylvia, a beautiful woman in her thirties, reportedly drowned while the couple was on vacation at the secluded Lake Madeleine with friends, but evidence suggests that there might be more to the story. Edie, driven by her obsession with Patrick—and the strange feeling that some of her thoughts and actions are not her own—takes it upon herself to investigate Sylvia's death. This leads to some unusual measures, such as posing as a grief counselor named Lucy Woods.

Meanwhile, a secondary plot is also set into motion. At the beginning of the book, the dead body of a young girl is found in the closet of an abandoned house. Her story, or lack of one, captures the sympathy of the unnamed American city where Edie lives. The media christens the girl Hopeful Doe. Soon after the gruesome discovery, a client appears at the Elysian Society. The woman seeks vigilante justice for Hopeful Doe and begs Edie to contact the girl to reveal her identity and the name of her killer. As per Elysian Society rules, Edie must send the woman away. This is an important detail of Murphy's speculative world. Bodies like Edie are advised against reaching out to victims like Hopeful Doe because, as Mrs. Renard, the madam-like boss of the Elysian Society explains, they are often confused and angry. To ask them to revisit their deaths only causes more psychic pain. The same rule applies to people who have taken their own lives. Of course, this only raises further questions about the suspicious death of Sylvia, and what she may or may not be trying to say.

The nature of Edie's work provides for an interesting exploration of gender and the emotional labor that women are often expected to perform. There are male bodies at the Elysian Society, among them a man named Leander, who, were it not for Patrick, might make a good match for Edie. But Leander is an exceptional case. Most men do not last in the job, because as one character puts it, they "don't have the training for the work that women do." Traditionally, women are expected to bear the burdens of the world, and in line with that thinking, the bodies, playing both medium and grief counselor, become vessels for their clients' pain.

Murphy also draws, lightly, a connection between the bodies and sex workers. It is implied that the Elysian Society and its myriad rules of conduct came about as a way to protect bodies from the exploitation that they previously endured working for amateur operations. Until she meets Patrick, Edie is satisfied with the rules and the careful distance they provide, but another body, Ananke, Ana for short, is not. As the novel progresses, Edie discovers that her acquaintance is a part of a kind of larger side-hustle. Ana purchases extra pills and offers clients the chance to sleep with their former wives

The Possessions *is Sara Flannery Murphy's first novel, while her short works have appeared in publications such as the* Guardian *and* Storyglossia.

and girlfriends. At one point, she considers "going permanent," or becoming a client's former lover indefinitely. These revelations have a significant impact on the trajectory of Edie and Patrick's relationship, but they also raise interesting questions about sacrifice, desire, and female self-worth. Ana has a strong personality but has a tendency to be "spirited away" by her work. Edie loses herself on purpose—for reasons that Murphy withholds until the book's end—but her love for Patrick offers her the queasy opportunity to be herself by becoming someone else.

The Possessions received mostly positive reviews when it was published in 2017. Many critics praised Murphy as a debut talent with considerable potential and noted her skill in crafting an engaging plot that combines both classic and modern elements. In a review for the *Guardian*, Sarah Ditum commented, "Murphy shapes the supernatural element deftly, so it's as easy to swallow as a lotus pill; once you've taken it, you're delivered into an entirely compelling world with all the intoxicating imagination and white-knuckle plotting of high-Victorian sensation fiction." A critic for *Publishers Weekly* gave the book a starred review and described it as a "beautifully rendered, haunting page-turner."

Other reviewers had positive things to say about the book but critiqued particular elements. Gilmartin, for example, also praised Murphy's "convincingly otherworldly" plot, but felt that clunky and occasionally repetitive writing sometimes weighed it down. Both the reviewer for *Kirkus* and Alice V. Leaderman, writing for the *Washington Independent Review of Books*, offered a similar assessment, suggesting that issues with the characterization detract from an otherwise well-established mystery. Such issues arise in part simply due to the structure of the novel. Murphy builds her plot toward the discovery of who Edie is—or rather, the nature of her past—but that revelation may be a bit disappointing to some readers. Maintaining Edie's blankness in its service sucks some of the air out of Murphy's otherwise engrossing thriller.

Molly Hagan

Review Sources

Ditum, Sarah. "*The Possessions* by Sara Flannery Murphy Review—a Simmering Gothic Joy." Review of *The Possessions*, by Sara Flannery Murphy. *The Guardian*, 9 Mar. 2017, www.theguardian.com/books/2017/mar/09/the-possessions-sara-flannery-murphy-review. Accessed 22 Feb. 2018.

Gilmartin, Sarah. "*The Possessions* Review: Sexual Obsession from beyond the Grave." Review of *The Possessions*, by Sara Flannery Murphy. *The Irish Times*, 1 Apr. 2017, www.irishtimes.com/culture/books/the-possessions-review-sexual-obsession-from-beyond-the-grave-1.3014591. Accessed 22 Feb. 2018.

Leaderman, Alice V. Review of *The Possessions*, by Sara Flannery Murphy. *Washington Independent Review of Books*, 28 Feb. 2017, www.washingtonindependentreviewofbooks.com/index.php/bookreview/the-possessions-a-novel. Accessed 22 Feb. 2018.

Review of *The Possessions*, by Sara Flannery Murphy. *Kirkus*, 7 Nov. 2016, www.kirkusreviews.com/book-reviews/sara-flannery-murphy/the-possessions/. Accessed 22 Feb. 2018.

Review of *The Possessions*, by Sara Flannery Murphy. *Publishers Weekly*, 7 Nov. 2016, www.publishersweekly.com/978-0-06-245832-2. Accessed 22 Feb. 2018.

The Potlikker Papers
A Food History of the Modern South

Author: John T. Edge (b. 1962)
Publisher: Penguin Press (New York). 384 pp. Illustrated.
Type of work: History
Time: ca. 1950 to the present
Locale: American South

The Potlikker Papers *offers a history of food in the American South that pairs food history with social history. Civil rights, race violence, politics, and gentrification are here effectively intertwined with food consumption, distribution, and service.*

Courtesy of Penguin Press

Principal personages

BOOKER WRIGHT, a Greenwood, Mississippi, waiter whose televised commentary on NBC drew attention to segregation in food service

CRAIG CLAIBORNE, a native of the Mississippi Delta and long-time food editor of the New York Times

EDNA LEWIS, an acclaimed Virginia-born chef

GEORGIA THERESA GILMORE, a cook who supported the bus boycotts in Montgomery, Alabama

GLEN ROBERTS, the founder of Anson Mills and influential figure in heritage foods of the South

HARLAND SANDERS, the founder of Kentucky Fried Chicken

MARIAN WRIGHT, a civil rights lawyer who turned the spotlight on hunger in the Mississippi Delta

NATHALIE DUPREE, a chef and influential teacher at Rich's Cooking School in Atlanta, Georgia

SEAN BROCK, a chef and heritage foods advocate

STEPHEN GASKIN, the founder of an agricultural commune called the Farm, located near Summertown, Tennessee

The Potlikker Papers offers a history of the modern South through the lens of food. In it, John T. Edge conjoins the radical transformations of the American South from 1950 to today with the service, preparation, distribution, and consumption of food. Across five chronological sections that are divided into sixteen chapters, Edge attempts to balance interests in race relations, social justice, shifting multiculturalism, and heritage foods, all of which he sees as contributing to the unique alchemy of Southern food. Potlikker—the nutrient-rich broth leftover from the preparation of collard greens—provides the driving metaphor of this hybrid vision, as a rich-tasting and nutritional substance with deep roots across the ethnic and racial groups of the South.

Importantly, it is food culture *writ large*, rather than food itself, that seems to be at the heart of Edge's research. The book contains no recipes and few discussions of individual dishes. Instead, the cultivation and production of individual dishes, the politics of agriculture and local food supply, and the corporate proliferation of foods that lack nutrition, among other themes, are the foci rather than the actual ingredients, their preparation, and their consumption. Edge asserts that his book is a project of "remembering through food" in order to identify "sometimes lost narratives to tell old stories in new ways." Indeed, the decades under consideration in the book are rich with struggles in the American South in which race, not food, has rightly been the headline consideration. Edge argues that through the pursuit of the "unsung players" associated with the food industry, he can draw attention to their unrecognized "roles in the definition, reinvention, and redemption of the region." It is the insistence on that last word—redemption—that draws the reader's attention to the celebratory quality of Edge's vision for the New South. The book suggests that multiculturalism nourished by heritage, hybrid, and radical foodways might pave the road to a future of a region finally able to move beyond its history of slavery.

The most powerful material in *The Potlikker Papers* can be found in its first section, "Freedom Struggles," which is concerned with the decades from the 1950s through the 1970s. Across the four chapters of this section, Edge offers a consideration of the civil rights and Black Power movements seen through the lens of food history. The section also contains a powerful chapter on advocacy surrounding hunger and malnutrition in impoverished households of the Mississippi Delta. Here, Edge's asserted goal of drawing attention to unsung heroes can be clearly identified. The book leads with a study of Gloria Theresa Gilmore's role in the Montgomery bus boycotts and the subsequent years of the civil rights movement. Through catering and a home-kitchen restaurant, Gilmore provided nourishment, financial resources, and a sense of camaraderie to the movement.

Similarly, the chapter "Restaurant Theaters" presents a powerful assessment of the role that restaurant spaces played in the racial confrontations of the period. Access to food counters and service was one of the many battlefronts of segregation, a reality made even harsher through the racist conditions under which African Americans served tables and cooked food in countless restaurants where they could not eat. Here too, Edge's extensive research introduces names and stories that will be unfamiliar to most readers. Moving outside the urban loci of the civil rights movement, the balance of the section considers rural food—and its lack—in these same years. Addressing both socioeconomics and race, these two chapters consider the plight of the disenfranchised members of Southern society during these decades, and the role that food advocacy—especially pioneering efforts at community agriculture—played in mitigating some of these circumstances.

Race takes a back-burner in subsequent sections of the book, which seek to paint a more integrated or multicultural vision of the South. After such focus on race in the first chapters, the transition is somewhat awkward, as the reader becomes aware that the hippies and fast-food moguls that gain the focus of the second section largely shift the lens from the black to the white populations of the South. This trajectory toward a whiter, more prosperous, South continues in subsequent sections that "gentrify" the heritage ingredients of the region, uplift the reliance on local food, and trace the influence of high-flying and cosmopolitan celebrity chefs. In reality, minority chefs and food advocates maintain a strong voice throughout the book, but the relative force of their efforts is less prominent in these later sections of the text. One prominent exception is located in the final chapter, in which Edge turns his attention to the influx and influence of Latino chefs on Southern cuisine, projecting a future dominated by the fusion of Mexican and Southern cuisines.

If objectively less important outside the realm of food writing, these subsequent sections of the book remain interesting. They maintain a deep level of research and also cover a wide swath of knowledge gained via personal acquaintances—reflecting the successes of Edge's career, as well as the resources of the Southern Foodways Alliance, of which he is director. Across these chapters, Southern food becomes more fully integrated within the corporate and national food industry. Food writers and chefs begin to distribute the influence of Southern cuisine throughout the country, even if unintentionally. Traditional Southern ingredients are rediscovered and given new life in haute cuisine. Celebrity chefs begin to foreground the distinctive foods of the region and, eventually, even relatively humble dishes like barbeque can command the attention of nationally known chefs. In the rise of the heroic pitmaster, Edge sees the food industry's ultimate embrace of the region.

John T. Edge is the founding director of the Southern Foodways Alliance at the University of Mississippi. A contributing editor for Garden & Gun *magazine and a columnist for the* Oxford American, *he has received the James Beard Foundation's M. F. K. Fisher Distinguished Writing Award.*

Perhaps the most valuable characteristic of the book lies in Edge's ability to build a metanarrative about big-picture influences on Southern foodways, while also making the stories personal and specific. In considering the corporate marketing of Southern foods (like fried chicken), Edge exhibits the depth of his research expertise while telling compelling stories about the individuals involved with these companies and parsing the impact of their work. In contrast to these corporate narratives, Edge offers multiple accounts of community farming, radical communal agriculture endeavors, and the social justice efforts of the locavore movement. In each of these areas, Edge surprises by revealing the significance of the agrarian South. In these little-known innovations of the 1970s and 1980s, the reader can rediscover the origins of the successful farm-to-table and heritage foods movements, in which the contemporary South is a recognized leader.

Despite receiving starred reviews in such prominent publications as *Kirkus* and *Publishers Weekly, The Potlikker Papers* has also met with contentious criticism. Much of this builds on Edge's status as an industry flashpoint in arguments over race, gender, and power in Southern studies and food history. Kim Severson, writing for the *New York Times*, contextualizes these criticisms usefully, providing a larger view on the concerns inherent in the redemptive and celebratory tone that Edge strikes. In *The*

Potlikker Papers, Edge clearly attempts to circumvent some of this criticism. Especially in its early chapters, the book foregrounds race, uplifting the legacy of African American cooks and placing some focus on women's roles in these narratives. But the spotty nature of such perspectives in later sections of the book continues to make the relevance of the concerns apparent.

Assessing the lasting value of *The Potlikker Papers* may involve gauging the balance of "reckoning" and "redemption." Edge has produced a wide-ranging study of food in the history of the modern South and offered compelling reasons to (re)consider significant moments in the history of the region through the lens of food. He has also written in depth and with sincerity about race, social justice, and the compelling public health reasons to build on the local and heritage food traditions of the region. At the same time, in his haste to celebrate these successes, he sometimes loses sight of the underlying inequities—seeing, as English professor and Edge critic Scott Romine has observed, the bounty of Carolina Gold rice but not the suffering slaves whose efforts advanced the crop. By stating from the outset an interest in both "reckoning" and "redemption," Edge attempts to strike a balance between two visions of Southern culture past and present that may be mutually exclusive. The region's reckoning with the history of enslavement and racial violence is a task that remains incomplete—and *The Potlikker Papers* reminds the reader with graphic force just how recent and pervasive these crimes were in the South. For this reason, it can seem premature to strike a tone of quite such celebration in redemption. While surely most readers will long toward an integrated and multicultural vision for the future of the South, one that also maintains the region's long ties to radical and local foodways, such an idyll does not yet exist.

Indeed, if Edge's account is representative in this regard, the successes—financial and otherwise—of the New Southern cuisine rarely foreground the ugly, difficult, and painful reckoning with the sins of the region's past embedded in its foodways. Instead, they celebrate the rising future of the region and cherry pick the celebration of its past. By highlighting, if unintentionally, the unresolved debts of the region's success to the racially motivated violence of its past, Edge clarifies what is needed in order to write the celebratory, redemptive food history of the South that he so desires. Without some systematic form of atonement, there can be no redemption. As Edge notes, culinary historian Michael Twitty is mapping a model for more fully accounting the influence of African slaves on the foodways of the American South. It remains to be seen whether the lessons of these stories can move from the historic sites and plantations at which Twitty cooks into the culinary and monetary realities of the high-flying food scenes of the New South with which Edge is concerned.

Julia A. Sienkewicz

Review Sources

Cep, Casey N. "Southern History, Deep Fried." Review of *The Potlikker Papers: A Food History of the Modern South*, by John Edge. *New Republic*, 26 May 2017, newrepublic.com/article/142729/southern-history-deep-fried. Accessed 15 Feb. 2018.

"Dinner in Black and White: Cooking in the American South; Two New Books Tackle Race and American History Around the Table." Review of *The Cooking Gene: A Journey through African American Culinary History in the Old South*, by Michael Twitty, and *The Potlikker Papers: A Food History of the Modern South*, by John Edge. *The Economist*, 27 July 2017, www.economist.com/news/books-and-arts/21725549-two-new-books-tackle-race-and-american-history-around-table-cooking-american. Accessed 11 Feb. 2018.

Powell, Padgett. "Southern-Fried Baloney." Review of *The Potlikker Papers: A Food History of the Modern South*, by John Edge. *The Wall Street Journal*, 9 June 2017, www.wsj.com/articles/southern-fried-baloney-1497043707. Accessed 15 Feb. 2017.

Severson, Kim. "A Powerful, and Provocative, Voice for Southern Food." *The New York Times*, 9 May 2017, www.nytimes.com/2017/05/09/dining/southern-food-john-t-edge-profile.html. Accessed 15 Feb. 2018.

The Power

Author: Naomi Alderman (b. 1974)
First published: 2016, in the United Kingdom
Publisher: Little, Brown (New York). 400 pp.
Type of work: Novel
Time: Fantastical near future
Locales: Earth

Naomi Alderman's novel The Power *imagines a world in which women develop the ability to generate powerful electric shocks through a muscle in their bodies. This electric power alters the power balance of the world.*

Courtesy of Little, Brown Company

Principal characters

ROXY MONKE, the teenage daughter of a notorious British mob boss
TUNDE, a young Nigerian journalist
MARGOT CLEARY, an American politician
ALLIE, a.k.a. Mother Eve, an American runaway turned religious cult figure

Naomi Alderman's thought-provoking thriller *The Power* imagines a near future in which young women across the world discover that they have the ability to generate powerful, even deadly, electric shocks through a muscle in their body. This muscle—located near the collarbone, and eventually dubbed the "skein"—is present in all females, and the girls who learn to use it on their own can teach older women to do the same. The power is a strange quirk at first. Segments on the morning news laughingly dismiss it as some kind of genetic prank. Doctors speculate that it may be attributed to a virus. One prominent theory holds that skeins developed in women after World War II, when a special chemical was added to the water to protect people from a gas attack. The origin of the power, however, is not important. The book is about the effects and implications of power itself, especially as it intersects with gender, religion, and other aspects of society. With the power comes a kind of hard power historically reserved for men, and within a few years, the face of the world has been utterly changed.

The Power is Alderman's fourth novel, and her diverse creative background positioned her well to take on the sort of high-concept thought experiment she develops here. Her first novel, *Disobedience* (2006), explores the Orthodox Jewish faith and earned a slew of awards, including the Orange Award for New Writers, the Sunday Times Young Writer of the Year Award, and a Waterstones Writer for the Future Award. Alderman's second novel, *The Lessons* (2010), is about a lonely Oxford student who becomes intoxicated by a new, wealthy group of friends, while her third, *The*

Liar's Gospel (2012), is a deeply researched alternate history of the life of Jesus. Each of these works, while very different from each other, hint at the author's willingness to examine highly charged themes from interesting—and often controversial—perspectives. In 2013, Alderman was recognized as one of *Granta*'s twenty best young British novelists. That year she also concluded a period of direct mentorship by acclaimed writer Margaret Atwood, author of *The Handmaid's Tale* (1985), a classic of feminist speculative literature. The experience contributed directly to Alderman's development of *The Power*, which was released in Great Britain in 2016 and in the US the next year.

Another element of Alderman's background that informed *The Power* was her experience as a writer for video games. Between 2004 and 2007, she wrote for an alternate reality game called *Perplex City*, and in 2012 she helped launch the hugely successful fitness adventure game *Zombies, Run!* As she has told interviewers, these projects taught her valuable lessons about storytelling, particularly the need to draw the audience in with engaging, interactive elements. Echoes of this style can be seen in the construction of *The Power*. Alderman's elegant, clipped prose offers just enough detail to situate readers before the story carries them away. Take, for instance, the introduction of the character Roxy: "The men lock Roxy in the cupboard when they do it. What they don't know is: she's been locked in that cupboard before." Alderman drops the reader into the scene after it has already begun, and in doing so raises a number of questions that create forward momentum. While not an active participant in the same sense as a video game, the reader is engaged in the story, tasked with putting together pieces from the outset.

Roxy, it soon becomes clear, is the daughter of a notorious British crime boss, and one of four main characters whose perspectives make up most of *The Power*. When the reader meets her, she is fourteen and becomes one of the first girls to discover her power when men from a rival gang come to brutally assault and kill her mother. The other focal points characters are introduced with their own short sections, and the point of view alternates throughout the book. Allie, a biracial foster child in the American South, suffers the abuses of her rapist foster father. In her first scene, she uses her new power to kill him and run away. Margot Cleary is the mayor of an unnamed American city; her world is changed when her teenage daughter, Jocelyn, awakens the power in her. Finally, there is a young Nigerian man named Tunde. Studying to be a journalist, he captures one of the first videos of a teenage girl using her power and then exploits this exposure to become one of the primary chroniclers of a global revolution that follows.

The plot that eventually ties Roxy, Allie, Margot, and Tunde together travels light, but other aspects of the novel are more cerebral. Alderman creates an unusual framing device for the novel. The reader is made to understand that *The Power* is a historical document. It begins with a letter from an author named Neil (his full name is Neil Adam Armon, an anagram of Naomi Alderman) to another writer named Naomi. Neil, self-deprecating and dithering, desperately seeks Naomi's opinion on his "not quite history, not quite novel" manuscript documenting the origins of their contemporary female-dominated society, the text of which makes up the bulk of the book. There is also an accompanying collection of historical fragments—drawings of ancient objects, including a device bearing what Neil has termed the "Bitten Fruit motif" that readers will recognize as an iPad and assorted government documents.

Naomi Alderman is an award-winning British novelist and short story writer. Her other books include Disobedience *(2006),* The Lessons *(2010), and* The Liar's Gospel *(2012). She has also written for video games and co-created the best-selling fitness game* Zombies, Run!

This framing device suggests that the events of the novel happen in a distant—over five thousand years—past, and also helps set up the chronological structure of the main narrative. Sections of the book countdown the years between the discovery of the power (the Day of the Girls) and a global Cataclysm, after which, it is further suggested, the human race was forced to rebuild civilization from scratch. Neil and Naomi's brief exchange gives an inkling of the kind of future world Alderman imagines and the long-term implications of the events depicted in the main plot. It also provides a satirical twist to the overarching theme, and the conclusion of their conversation at the end of the book offers a nice kicker in terms of the book's authorship. Naomi is condescending to Neil. She writes that she looks forward to reading his manuscript because the idea of a world run by men seems like a "sexy" fantasy.

This additional narrative layer is intriguing but also problematic at times. As Amal el-Mohtar pointed out in her review for the *New York Times*, how can Alderman expect the reader to believe that future historians do not know what an iPad is, when the historic narrative they have laid out describes people using similar technology? This is a small point overall, but it and other structural paradoxes detract from Alderman's larger and more ambitious vision. Still, her central premise is powerful. She radically envisions the world in a woman's image, only to insist that power corrupts regardless of the gender of the people that wield it.

Each character in *The Power*, even the opportunistic Tunde (at least until things become untenable for his gender), seeks a specific kind of power. Margot, a mayor forced to endure the showboating of the male governor of her state, seeks political power, and leverages the military potential of the skein to get it. Roxy seeks power in the only world she has ever known, organized crime. She synthesizes a cocaine-like powder drug that enhances the power and supplies it to the army in Bessapara, formerly Moldova. The new country, led by the ex-gymnast trophy wife of its former dictator, is populated by women who were once trafficked as sex slaves. Finally, Allie seeks a spiritual power. Guided by a godlike internal voice, Allie seeks refuge in a convent after running away from her foster family. There, she adopts the name Mother Eve and, after a series of miracles (aided by the specific nature of her power), becomes the leader of a global cult of the mother. The paths of all four characters intertwine as the world changes rapidly; resistance to the newly empowered women is crushed as the once oppressed become oppressors.

Critical reception to *The Power* was mostly positive, though a few notable issues often came up. Some reviewers, including el-Mohtar, have suggested that two philosophical strands that emerge throughout the book are in contention with one another. On one hand, there is an exhilaration about a world in which women are no longer afraid. Offenses by men against women that are very real in our world, from direct physical and sexual abuse to subtler patriarchal discrimination, are eradicated as women gain power. On the other, the book is bleakly pessimistic that women would so quickly sell the possibility of a better world down the river by abusing power just as men did before them. Just exactly what Alderman means to say here—about gender, the performance of gender, or the human capacity for violence—is not always clear.

Nevertheless, even critics with reservations about the book found it to be well-written, thought provoking, and entertaining. As el-Mohtar wrote, echoing a number of other reviewers: "I was riveted by every page." Niall Alexander, in his review for the science-fiction magazine *Tor*, was similarly impressed, suggesting that Alderman surpassed much of her mentor Atwood's later work. A reviewer for *Kirkus* gave the book a starred review, while *Publishers Weekly* concluded: "Readers should not expect easy answers in this dystopian novel, but Alderman succeeds in crafting a stirring and mind-bending vision." Justine Jordan, a critic for the *Guardian*, called the book "an instant classic of speculative fiction." Outlets including the *New York Times*, the *Los Angeles Times*, the *Washington Post*, the *San Francisco Chronicle*, and NPR all named *The Power* one of the best books of 2017, and it won the prestigious Baileys Women's Prize for Fiction.

Molly Hagan

Review Sources
Alexander, Niall. "Enemies of Man: *The Power* by Naomi Alderman." Review of *The Power*, by Naomi Alderman. *Tor*, 10 Oct. 2017, www.tor.com/2017/10/10/book-reviews-the-power-by-naomi-alderman. Accessed 22 Feb. 2018.
El-Mohtar, Amal. "A Novelist Asks, What If Women's Bodies Became Deadly Weapons?" Review of *The Power*, by Naomi Alderman. *The New York Times*, 25 Oct. 2017, www.nytimes.com/2017/10/25/books/review/naomi-alderman-power.html. Accessed 22 Feb. 2018.
Jordan, Justine. "The Power by Naomi Alderman Review—If Girls Ruled the World." Review of *The Power*, by Naomi Alderman. *The Guardian*, 2 Nov. 2016, www.theguardian.com/books/2016/nov/02/the-power-naomi-alderman-review. Accessed 22 Feb. 2018.
Review of *The Power*, by Naomi Alderman. *Kirkus*, 17 July 2017, www.kirkusreviews.com/book-reviews/naomi-alderman/the-power. Accessed 22 Feb. 2018.
Review of *The Power*, by Naomi Alderman. *Publishers Weekly*, 28 Aug. 2017, www.publishersweekly.com/978-0-316-54761-1. Accessed 22 Feb. 2018.

Priestdaddy

Author: Patricia Lockwood (b. 1982)
Publisher: Riverhead Books (New York).
352 pp.
Type of work: Memoir
Time: 1982–present
Locales: Indiana, Ohio, Missouri, Georgia

Priestdaddy *is a memoir by poet Patricia Lockwood in which she chronicles her atypical life as the daughter of a married Catholic priest. Lockwood examines tradition and belief from the viewpoint of a nonbeliever while questioning whether a person can ever escape the world they have been raised in.*

Principal personages
PATRICIA, a.k.a. Bit or Trisha, the author and narrator
JASON, her husband
GREG, her father, a Catholic priest
KAREN, her mother

The first chapter of *Priest daddy*, entitled "Introductory Rites," opens with a scene in Patricia Lockwood's parents' home years after she has moved out but returned due to financial circumstances. Because she and her husband, Jason, faced high bills for treating Jason's eye condition, the couple were forced to move back with her family. The transition was a rocky and enlightening one and builds the framework for the narrative. In the introductory scene, which sets the both comic and dark tone for the memoir, Lockwood's mother, Karen, serves tea as she describes a "psychopath test" she had to pass before her husband, Greg, was allowed to become a Catholic priest. The reader later learns it took Lockwood's father a couple of times to pass.

While it is extremely uncommon for a married man with children to become a priest, the narrator's father, Greg Lockwood, did just that after watching the horror movie *The Exorcist* (1973) while on the bottom of the ocean in a submarine during his service in the United States Navy. The reader learns that he first became a Lutheran minister, but that religion did not suit him. He subsequently embraced Catholicism, took the "psychopath test" along with his family, and was ordained—setting his family on a strange path in the process.

Lockwood's memoir follows three story lines: the narrator growing up in a closed, religious household, her relationship with Jason from the time they met through their marriage, and the period when she and Jason returned to her parents' house to live. Each section is explored with honesty and humor. Through careful descriptions of her parents, and life inside the church, Lockwood creates a world that is accessible to the audience and emotionally resonant.

The heart of the book is found near the end in a brief paragraph. Lockwood writes:

> Art goes outside, even if we don't; it fills the whole air, though we cannot raise our voices. . . . On the page I am everything that I am not, because that is where I put myself. I am no longer whispering through the small skirted shape of a keyhole: the door is knocked down and the roof is blown off and I am aimed once more at the entire wide night.

Courtesy of Grep Hoax

Patricia Lockwood is the author of three books, including the poetry collections Motherland, Fatherland, Homelandsexuals *(2014) and* Balloon Pop Outlaw Black *(2012). Her memoir,* Priestdaddy *(2017), was named one of the ten best books of 2017 by the* New York Times. *Her poems have appeared in the* New Yorker, Poetry, *and the* London Review of Books.

The paragraph follows a section about entering puberty and no longer having the freedom she once did. She writes, "Many of us were actually affected, by male systems and male anger, in ways we cannot always articulate or overcome." She talks of coming from a place of diminishment that she never made it out of.

It is at this point in the book that her father's eccentricities begin to seem harmful to the family's life. She writes, speaking to her father, that she can only write what is given to her. What he gives her is a trove of stories and situations that bring into fine detail the ways in which religious belief can both reward the selfish and create a hierarchy of pain for anyone who is not male. The bishop calls her mother a different name each time he sees her; considering it funny, he pretends not to be bothered to remember her name. Her mother cooks huge dinners for the priests in training each year, and no one ever says thank you. As Lockwood prepares to leave for college, her father calls her into his study where he sits in his threadbare underwear all day watching action movies. "We can't do it, Bit," he tells her flatly. Lockwood dives into a lyrical reading of her reaction to the news. "I didn't ask a single question. When I remember this, the urge to fly back and shake my young self by the shoulders shakes my present self to the point of pain . . . I accepted the statement as a mountain, a fact on the face of the earth—as final as if he had told me I would not be going to heaven." The reader then learns her father soon after spends a great deal of money on a new guitar, once supposedly owned by Paul McCartney.

The warmth and humor of Lockwood's writing allow *Priestdaddy* to tight-walk the fine line between hilarity and darkness. In an interview with the *Los Angeles Times*, Lockwood speaks about this paradox, stating that she and her siblings developed a sense of humor "as a sort of armor . . . a front line of defense against what was basically an unreasonable atmosphere." Of her father, she describes how he "sucked up all the oxygen—he was a big screamer too, and very impulsive." She comments that she doubts her father will ever read it but that he seems like the kind of man who would want a book written about him.

Lockwood became well known in the literary world when her poem "Rape Joke" appeared on the website *The Awl*. The poem went viral and cemented her name among the best-known independent writers of the early twenty-first century. Following "Rape Joke," Lockwood published the poetry collection *Motherland, Fatherland, Home-landsexuals* (2014), which was acclaimed for the strangeness and musicality of its language. She has also been called the Poet Laureate of Twitter, where she has one of the most popular accounts on the social media platform.

These pieces of information about the writer become relevant as *Priestdaddy* progresses. Someone who follows Lockwood on Twitter would know much about her husband, Jason, who plays an important role in her memoir. The story of the beginning of their relationship is one of the most exciting and tender parts of the book.

When Lockwood was told by her father that there is no money for her to attend college and that he does not believe in higher education anyway, she decided to move to the abandoned convent next to the church where her family lived. While living in the convent, she began to take part in message boards on the internet. The late 1990s to the early 2000s was a time when the internet was still a much less structured place where people could connect over obscure topics without the help of dedicated social media sites. It was on one of these message boards that Lockwood met Jason. The two felt an instant connection and soon began spending entire nights talking on the telephone. They decided that Lockwood would go to live with him in Colorado. After a tense visit with Lockwood's family, Lockwood and Jason left together for their new home. Her father did not say goodbye.

Lockwood uses *Priestdaddy* to discuss some of the most controversial aspects of the Catholic Church as well. Midway through the book, she describes some of the older priests her family was acquainted with and who were frequently moved to new parishes. She is, of course, referring obliquely to the child abuse scandals.

In one section of the memoir, Lockwood recalls one particularly creepy bishop, who would come to their house to visit, drink wine, and continually dismiss her mother. But what she really remembers is that the bishop would regularly pull her younger brother onto his lap, caressing his head. Lockwood is vehement about the disgust she feels when recalling the power given to these men and the lengths the church went to cover up their crimes. Though her brother was not molested, Lockwood recalls that the bishop seemed to have more control over the situation than the boy's own mother on those occasions.

By structuring her story around a year spent living with her parents as an adult, Lockwood unpacks all those memories from her childhood and young adult years in a way that feels authentic and heartfelt. Often the prose reads like a catharsis for both herself and her family, as she unravels past oddities from their lives. The warmth she feels towards her mother is a particularly strong point in the book, and she tells the reader as the story closes that when Lockwood's father dies, her mother will be left with nothing: no house, no money, no security. She is simply a supporting character in the larger world of her husband.

The book ends as Lockwood has become a successful writer. She has received an advance for her memoir, she and Jason are moving into their own house, her poems have been published in *The New Yorker*, and she finally has some extra money. She takes her mother and Jason to Key West, Florida—her father refuses to go—to thank her for her support. And through her poetic language and searing descriptions, the reader has come to know, and perhaps understand, the lives of each of these people and to appreciate the challenges of understanding personal eccentricities families face. There are no villains in Lockwood's story, but there are no heroes either. Everyone is ultimately left to unravel how he or she has arrived at his or her destination.

Melynda Fuller

Review Sources

Garner, Dwight. "Patricia Lockwood Is a Priest's Child (Really), but 'From the Devil.'" Review of *Priestdaddy*, by Patricia Lockwood. *The New York Times*, 3 May 2017, www.nytimes.com/2017/05/03/books/review-priestdaddy-patricia-lockwood.html. Accessed 12 Feb. 2018.

Quinn, Annalisa. "'Priestdaddy' Shimmers with Wonderful, Obscene Life." Review of *Priestdaddy*, by Patricia Lockwood. *NPR Books*, NPR, 10 May 2017, www.npr.org/2017/05/10/527629781/priestdaddy-shimmers-with-wonderful-obscene-life. Accessed 14 Feb. 2018.

Tuttle, Kate. "Patricia Lockwood Likes to Write in Bed. *Priestdaddy* Is Her Memoir." *Los Angeles Times*, 28 Apr. 2017, www.latimes.com/books/jacketcopy/la-ca-jc-patricia-lockwood-20170413-story.html. Accessed 12 Feb. 2018.

Protestants
The Faith That Made the Modern World

Author: Alec Ryrie (b. 1971)
Publisher: Viking (New York). 528 pp.
Type of work: History
Time: 1517 to the present

In Protestants: The Faith That Made the
Modern World, *Alec Ryrie provides a survey
of the first five hundred years of Protestantism, focusing on central themes and individual leaders rather than a strict chronological history, with considerable attention to
Protestant movements outside of Europe and
North America.*

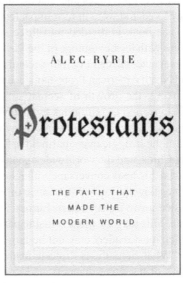

Courtesy of Viking

Principal personages

MARTIN LUTHER, a German monk and pro-
fessor of theology
JOHN CALVIN, a French reformer and theologian
HULDRICH ZWINGLI, a Swiss theologian and reformer
COUNT NICHOLAS VON ZINZENDORF, a German noble who supported Pietism
PHILIP JAKOB SPENER, a German Lutheran pastor and an early leader of the Pietist
movement
OLIVER CROMWELL, a Puritan leader of the Parliamentarians in the English Civil War,
later Lord Protector of the Commonwealth
JAKOB ARMINIUS, a Dutch theologian
HENRY VIII, the English king who broke away from Roman Catholicism and estab-
lished the Anglican Church
MARTIN LUTHER KING JR., an American Baptist preacher and a leading figure of the
American civil rights movement
CHARLES PARHAM, an American preacher and an early leader of American Pentecos-
talism
K. H. TING, a.k.a. Ding Guanqxun, an Anglican bishop in twentieth-century China
BILLY GRAHAM, a prominent American evangelical preacher and mass evangelist
WOODROW WILSON, president of the United States, 1913–21

To cover the history of a five-hundred-year old religious tradition that today comprises several hundred million adherents around the world is a daunting task. While
Protestants: The Faith That Made the Modern World is a solid, well-researched, and
engagingly written book, author Alec Ryrie does not attempt to tell the whole story of
the history of Protestantism. Instead, he gives the reader a series of detailed vignettes
covering groups and individuals that illustrate some of the major themes in the history

of Protestantism. Not many individual leaders get more than brief coverage. Ryrie's accounts reveal what Protestants historically believed, how they differed from one another in certain times and places, and how they both influenced the cultures in which they lived and were in turn impacted by those cultures.

The book is divided into three sections. The first part, "The Reformation Age," opens with the beginnings of the Reformation in the early 1500s and continues through the seventeenth century. The second part, "The Modern Age," examines how European and North American Protestants dealt with the challenges presented by Enlightenment thinking; the growth of secularism; modernizing trends in science, philosophy and theology; and the struggles over slavery. The last part of the book, titled "The Global Age," deals with the explosive growth of Protestantism in the twentieth century, looking at the struggle over apartheid in South Africa, the growth of Protestantism in Korea and China, and the worldwide expansion of Pentecostalism. In this third section, Ryrie shows that he is conversant with recent scholarship on global Christianity and demonstrates how the center of balance of Protestantism, and of Christianity as a whole, has shifted away from western Europe and North America to Africa, Latin America, and Asia. This may the most valuable part of the book simply because it covers topics with which most readers may not be familiar.

"What, actually, is Protestantism?" Ryrie asks in his epilogue. He admits that because of the great diversity of Protestant groups, it is difficult, if not impossible, to formulate a definition of the term. Protestantism, he writes, "is not a doctrine or a theology." Due to the vast diversity of Protestant groups, there would be numerous theologies involved in such a definition. Still, one might argue that Protestantism is more about these various theologies than Ryrie suggests. He focuses more on what it means to be a Protestant and how the activism of Protestants has changed the world than on what Protestants actually believe. Ryrie argues that three "key ingredients" of the modern world are rooted in Protestantism: free inquiry, a tendency toward democracy, and apoliticism. With regard to the first, although Ryrie argues that *sola scriptura*—"scripture alone"—was made a key idea of Luther's theology by later followers rather than by Luther himself, Luther's insistence that people must come to their own understanding of scripture did contribute to the toleration of free inquiry.

Secondly, Ryrie believes that Protestantism has contributed to the development and spread of democracy. When early Protestants came to believe that they had not only a right but a religious duty to stand up against rulers who "had an intolerable tendency to act in defiance of God's will," this contributed to the idea of an individual's right to challenge their government. Ryrie's argument for his third "key ingredient"— which may appear to some to contradict this premise about democracy, and may be the most controversial of these "ingredients"—is that Protestantism has historically been largely apolitical. "Protestants might have sometimes confronted or overthrown their rulers," he writes, "but their most constant political demand is simply to be left alone." Much of Protestant history in western Europe and the United States, some of which Ryrie recounts in this book, does not fit with this theme, but he does make a convincing argument that in other parts of the world, especially when dealing with oppressive governments, Protestants have tended to withdraw from political activism if it will buy them some measure of peace and freedom to pursue their own religious practices.

Protestants is a book written for an audience of engaged nonspecialists. Those with little background in church history or theology will not find themselves lost; specialists will find little to quibble about concerning what is said, and may even find some illustrative material to flesh out lectures or research projects. There may be more disputes among specialists about what is left out, and how Ryrie decided which topics merited coverage and which did not. Because only major figures are given extended treatment, some Protestant leaders covered here appear to exist in a vacuum. One of the strengths of his work is that Ryrie pulls no punches in describing how Protestants have often been found on both sides of some messy conflicts—Protestants were heavily involved in the slave trade and in owning slaves in the New World, but they were also prominent in the leadership of the movement to end the slave trade and ultimately to abolish slavery. But the enslaved people themselves are virtually absent from the book, even though they contributed significantly to the growth of two major Protestant groups—the Methodists and a wide variety of Baptists—in the American South. Neither do the black Protestant churches founded by free African Americans in the period before emancipation appear in the book, nor the special role that black clergymen had in their communities after emancipation. When the narrative reaches the role of Martin Luther King Jr. in the civil rights struggle, he appears to come out of nowhere; readers are not told about the special role that black preachers often played in their communities, or how involvement in politics and social action was virtually expected of black ministers, while such actions by a preacher in a white church would in many cases have been met with criticism. Little attention is paid to King's use of scripture in his political speeches, or how his background as a black preacher is evident in virtually every aspect

Alec Ryrie is a coeditor of the Journal of Ecclesiastical History *and is considered one of the leading authorities on the Reformation in England and Scotland. His previous books include* The Age of Reformation: The Tudor and Stewart Realms, 1485–1603 *(2009) and* Being Protestant in Reformation Britain *(2013). He teaches at Durham University and is a Church of England lay preacher.*

of his leadership in the civil rights movement. In a similar vein, the twentieth-century evangelist Billy Graham is given due attention, but there is very little about the resurgence of evangelicalism in the United States that undergirded Graham's ministry and of which he was one of the principal leaders. In general, evangelical Protestants in the United States are not covered in any detail. While the First and Second Great Awakenings were fairly significant developments in the growth of Protestantism in early America, they are barely mentioned here.

Ryrie sees "a love affair with God" as a major part of what defines Protestantism. Certainly, many of the men and women he describes in the various vignettes in the book appear to have been passionate about their relationship with God, but non-Protestant Christians might find this somewhat simplistic and perhaps offensive. Like all religious groups, Protestants have their fair share of nominal members who do not exhibit much love of anything, while Roman Catholics and Orthodox Christians through the ages have often demonstrated a deep love of God, although expressed in types of spirituality that Protestants might find difficult to understand.

Some reviewers have expressed skepticism about Ryrie's argument that Protestantism "made the modern world." It is true that in many important ways, Protestantism changed the world, but changes in the world also set the stage for Protestantism. For example, the Renaissance rediscovery of the learning and culture of the ancient Greeks and Romans made Christian scholars of the time more interested in the early Christian church and led to renewed interest in learning the original languages of the Bible. Protestantism helped along some political changes, but it also succeeded in the early days because of the protection the reformers received from certain political leaders. It is worth noting that the British edition of the book, published at the same time as the American edition, is subtitled *The Radicals Who Made the Modern World*; given that any kind of universal definition of Protestantism may be impossible, that is perhaps a better subtitle than the American version, *The Faith That Made the Modern World*. The British subtitle highlights individual actors, while the American subtitle credits the faith itself.

Protestants was generally met with high praise from reviewers. While some quibbled with what is and what is not included, most agreed that covering as much as Ryrie has in one volume is a remarkable achievement. Some noted that the Bible and the use of it by Protestants is not dealt with as much as one might expect. As to whether or not Protestants have "made" the modern world, David Walton, in a review for the *Dallas News*, concluded, "The faith that made the modern world? Please. Protestantism may have its historical sins of complicity and neglect, but, please. Let's not blame it for all this." Martin Luther, and generations of his spiritual descendants, might well agree.

Mark S. Joy, PhD

Review Sources

Castaldo, Chris. "How Protestants Changed the World." Review of *Protestants: The Faith That Made the Modern World*, by Alec Ryrie. *The Gospel Coalition*, 2 Aug. 2017, www.thegospelcoalition.org/reviews/protestants-faith-made-modern-world/. Accessed 6 Dec. 2017.

Maltby, Judith. Review of *Protestants: The Radicals Who Made the Modern World*, by Alec Ryrie. *Church Times*, 28 July 2017, www.churchtimes.co.uk/articles/2017/28-july/books-arts/book-reviews/subtitles-sects-and-slaves. Accessed 6 Dec. 2017.

Moore, Russell. "The Reformation at 500." Review of *Martin Luther: Renegade and Prophet*, by Lyndal Roper, and *Protestants: The Faith That Made the Modern World*, by Alec Ryrie. *National Review*, 26 June 2017, www.nationalreview.com/magazine/2017-06-25-2050/lyndal-roper-martin-luther-alec-ryrie-protestants. Accessed 6 Dec. 2017.

Walton, David. "A Faithful History: *Protestants* Looks at Beliefs That Reshaped the World." Review of *Protestants: The Faith That Made the Modern World*, by Alec Ryrie. *Dallas News*, Dallas Morning News, 5 Apr. 2017, www.dallasnews.com/arts/books/2017/04/05/faithful-history-protestants-looks-beliefs-reshaped-world. Accessed 6 Dec. 2017.

Prussian Blue
A Bernie Gunther Novel

Author: Philip Kerr (b. 1956)
Publisher: Marian Wood Books (New York). 544 pp.
Type of work: Novel
Time: 1939 and 1956
Locales: France and Germany

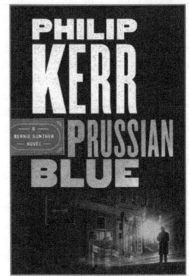

Part historical fiction, part Cold War thriller, and part police procedural mystery, Philip Kerr's twelfth entry in his popular Bernie Gunther series, Prussian Blue, *follows two separate but closely related plotlines set seventeen years apart to reach equally exciting conclusions.*

Courtesy of Marian Wood Books/Putnam

Principal characters

BERNHARD "BERNIE" GUNTHER, a fifty-something former police detective in Nazi Germany who goes by a variety of aliases, including Walter Wolf, Bertolt Gründgens, and Christof Ganz

GENERAL ERICH MIELKE, the deputy head of the Stasi, the state security service for the German Democratic Republic; based on the historical figure of the same name

FRIEDRICH KORSCH, Bernie's assistant with the Kripo, Nazi Germany's police unit, who later works for the Stasi

GENERAL REINHARD HEYDRICH, the head of the Nazi secret service and Bernie's employer; based on the historical figure of the same name

MARTIN BORMANN, the powerful deputy chief of staff to Adolf Hitler; based on the historical figure of the same name

ALBERT BORMANN, a Nazi Motor Corps general and Martin's brother; based on the historical figure of the same name

HERMANN KASPEL, an acquaintance of Bernie's and an SS captain

GERHARDINE "GERDY" TROOST, an architect

Prussian Blue picks up shortly after the previous novel in Philip Kerr's Bernie Gunther series, *The Other Side of Silence* (2016), ended. It is October 1956. Former German homicide commissar and private detective Bernie Gunther is working as a concierge at a French Riviera hotel. He holds a passport in the name of Walter Wolf. Gunther is forced to live under an assumed identity because during World War II he engaged in certain activities that might be construed as criminal. As the tourist season winds down and Bernie wonders what he will do next to earn money, he receives a letter written in the distinctive hand of his estranged wife, Elisabeth, inviting him to dinner at a posh restaurant. However, when he arrives at the restaurant, it is not Elisabeth—who was strong-armed into writing the letter—awaiting him. His dinner companion is a former acquaintance, General Erich Mielke, now the deputy head of the Stasi, the East German secret police. Mielke, combining threats with blandishments (money and a clean, new West German passport under any name), wants Bernie to carry out an assassination. Mielke tasks Bernie with traveling under guard to England to kill Anne French, a British spy who seduced and betrayed Bernie in *The Other Side of Silence*. Bernie is to employ an exotic method of murder that allows sufficient time for the killer to escape before the victim drops dead. The highly toxic element to be used is the heavy metal thallium, and its only known antidote is Prussian blue, a synthetic pigment. Prussian blue reappears throughout the novel and is used to great effect to highlight the tension between denizens of two former states that comprise modern Germany: Prussia, with its capital Berlin (where Bernie is from), and Bavaria, with its capital Munich (Adolf Hitler's adopted home).

Knowing he has no real choice, Bernie agrees to the assignment. Although he does not hate Anne enough to kill her, he figures he can slip away from his guards and escape at the appropriate time. Mielke, however, anticipates Bernie's resistance. His henchmen, including Friedrich Korsch, Bernie's former police colleague, have been given orders to hang the ex-detective from a lamppost. They let Bernie almost strangle to death, to impress upon him how serious they are.

An apparently cowed Bernie boards a train for Paris with Korsch and other guards. He is given money and a passport in the name Bertolt Gründgens. Suspecting the Stasi will kill him once the assassination has been carried out, Bernie plans to flee. Feigning a trip to the bathroom, he knocks out the guard accompanying him with a hidden leather blackjack, steals his gun, and hides the unconscious man's body. When the train makes a scheduled stop, Bernie disembarks and races to the spot where he has hidden his battered Citroën. He speeds away, knowing he has little time before his absence is discovered. The Stasi will begin their pursuit at the train's next scheduled stop, Marseilles, an hour away. As he drives toward Germany to seek refuge, he reminisces about an important case he worked on with his former colleague Korsch, less than six months before the outbreak of World War II. From this point, the main narrative of *Prussian Blue* flashes back to April 1939, with periodic returns to 1956 to show Bernie's tension-fraught progress toward his objective and his foe's terrifying efforts to intercept him.

In 1939, with war obvious on the horizon, Bernie's superior, General Reinhard Heydrich, gives him a sensitive assignment. He is to investigate a murder and, in the process, collect damaging information about Heydrich's enemies. The case concerns a civil engineer, Dr. Karl Flex, who has been killed, apparently by a sniper, on the balcony of Adolf Hitler's private home, the Berghof, in Berchtesgaden, Bavaria. Bernie has only a short time to solve the crime, because Hitler will be arriving soon at the luxurious home to celebrate his fiftieth birthday. Bernie and his assistant at the time, Korsch, travel across Germany to carry out the investigation. At the Berghof, Bernie meets Martin Bormann and other powerful Nazis. The detective also meets a Heydrich plant, Captain Hermann Kaspel, a former colleague whom Bernie does not like. The two men, both from Berlin, form an alliance for the duration of the investigation.

Together and individually Bernie, Kaspel, and Korsch frenetically pursue every lead, aided by methamphetamine, common in the area due to numerous round-the-clock construction projects being carried out prior to Hitler's arrival. The investigators are hindered by their tight deadline and by the secretive nature of the case—they can tell no one what they are doing in order to prevent unwanted publicity. If word leaks to Hitler, it might spoil birthday festivities for the tetchy dictator.

Despite such restrictions, Bernie and assistants gather clues. During an autopsy, they learn that Dr. Flex was shot from a different direction than assumed, thus the area where the bullet originated has not been thoroughly searched. The dead man was also suffering from a venereal disease, a potential motive for murder. They discover that the high-security area surrounding the Berghof is actually honeycombed with tunnels and mines that make clandestine entry and exit possible. They uncover evidence of widespread corruption: Bormann and associates (including

Courtesy of Nina Subin

In addition to the twelve books in the Bernie Gunther series of novels, author Philip Kerr has written a series of thrillers featuring soccer coach Scott Manson, as well as works of nonfiction, children's fiction, and a dozen stand-alone novels. In 2009, he won the RBA International Prize for Crime Writing and the Ellis Peters Historical Crime Award for his novel If the Dead Rise Not *(2009).*

Dr. Flex) have been receiving kickbacks from the multitude of construction projects and from the proceeds of a secret brothel that services the many workers in the area. Fortunes made from skimmed money are stashed in numbered Swiss bank accounts. Eventually, Bernie develops a theory of how the Flex murder was committed. The theory is confirmed when he locates the sniper's rifle used in the crime, and he sets about tracing the weapon to its source.

During the course of the investigators' work, unknown adversaries place obstacles in their way. Tampered car brakes cause a sudden death on treacherous mountain roads. Two Gestapo agents come for Bernie after he is accused of insulting Hitler, and he is forced to defend himself against their murderous intentions. The punishment Bernie dishes out and absorbs is brutal but not excessive in an era when Nazis used fear, torture, and executions to intimidate citizens into obedience.

Meanwhile, in 1956, the chase continues apace. Bernie travels by a variety of means—car, train, bicycle, foot—in an effort to shake his pursuers as he tracks westward toward Germany. The pressure mounts when his opponents up the ante: they kill the man he slapped on the train and also murder a police officer to frame Bernie. To foil increased scrutiny, Bernie adopts different disguises, trying to blend in with locals as mile by mile he makes his way across rural France. He hides when necessary, shelters in shadowy doorways, crawls into a drainpipe, seeks sanctuary in a church, or breaks into an empty house to rest for a few precious hours before taking flight again. In one village, where the enemy arrived first and is waiting for Bernie, he kills a Stasi man, partially to eliminate lethal danger and partially because the man shot a harmless stray cat for his own amusement. Step by weary step, Bernie approaches the German border, beyond which safety may lie.

Ultimately, both storylines converge in Saarbrücken, Germany. In 1939, Bernie chases his quarry through the Schlossberg Caves, a multilevel maze of dimly lit passageways in an old quartz mine beneath the ruins of Karlsberg Castle. In 1956, it is Bernie who takes shelter there from his pursuers.

Like its predecessors, *Prussian Blue* offers all the outstanding qualities that fans of the series have come to appreciate. Character delineation is a particular strength of Kerr. Foremost among his creations is fully rounded protagonist Bernhard "Bernie" Gunther. A relatively good man working under an evil regime between the early 1930s and the end of World War II, Bernie despises the Nazis. Circumstances, however, have dictated he must toil among them while performing the detective work at which he excels in order to stay alive. To keep his sanity and to protect his humanity, he has grown a tough shell and perfected a cynical nature. Bernie is quick with quip or insult—witty, realistic-sounding dialogue is another of Kerr's specialties—often directed in subtle fashion at the totalitarian government and its goons. Bernie is not shy about using his fists or a deadly weapon when necessary, because he is above all a survivor. Ironically, even the Nazis grudgingly admire Bernie's rebellious spirit and independence, so different from the sycophantic behavior of low-level functionaries aspiring to higher positions of power.

The plot of *Prussian Blue*, as in other entries, unfolds against the genuine, well-researched historical period the author has staked out in the early 1930s to the mid-1950s. Actual events and characters based on historical figures provide a familiar warp to contrast with the creative, skillfully twisted yarn of the author's imagination. Kerr presents a well-woven, virtually seamless story tapestry in *Prussian Blue*. All installments in the Gunther series use a blend of well-drawn fictional and historic personages. At the end of each novel, Kerr typically includes an author's note and acknowledgments pages that offer brief biographies of the real, sometimes obscure people who figured in the story. The section often brings a satisfying coda to the novel by revealing that some of the most outrageous characters depicted actually existed in real life.

Jack Ewing

Review Sources

Kramer, Jane. "The Third Reich's Good Cop." Review of *Prussian Blue*, by Philip Kerr. *The New Yorker*, 10 July 2017, www.newyorker.com/magazine/2017/07/10/the-third-reichs-good-cop. Accessed 27 Aug. 2017.

Lipez, Richard. "*Prussian Blue*: Philip Kerr's Crime Fiction at Its Best." Review of *Prussian Blue*, by Philip Kerr. *The Washington Post*, 26 Mar. 2017, www.washingtonpost.com/entertainment/books/prussian-blue-philip-kerrs-spy-fiction-at-its-best/2017/03/24/4d56f1c4-1011-11e7-9d5a-a83e627dc120_story.html. Accessed 27 Aug. 2017.

Pierce, Peter. "Crime Novels from Philip Kerr and Jo Nesbo Bring Brilliant Cops Back." Review of *Prussian Blue*, by Philip Kerr, and *The Thirst*, by Jo Nesbo. *The Australian*, 13 May 2017, www.theaustralian.com.au/arts/review/crime-nov-els-from-philip-kerr-and-jo-nesbo-bring-brilliant-cops-back/news-story/211255ff6 a34f0c2f7756a6488a3f700. Accessed 27 Aug. 2017.
Roberts, Chris. Review of *Prussian Blue*, by Philip Kerr. *Crime Review*, 27 May 2017, crimereview.co.uk/page.php/review/4820. Accessed 27 Aug. 2017.

The Radium Girls
The Dark Story of America's Shining Women

Author: Kate Moore
First published: *The Radium Girls: They Paid with Their Lives. Their Final Fight Was for Justice*, 2016, United Kingdom
Publisher: Sourcebooks (Naperville, IL). Illustrated. 480 pp.
Type of work: History
Time: 1917–38
Locales: Newark and Orange, New Jersey; Ottawa, Illinois

The Radium Girls: The Dark Story of America's Shining Women is Kate Moore's historical account of the lives of the young women who painted watch faces with glowing radium paint and succumbed to radium poisoning; they fought a fierce legal battle with their former employers to get some measure of justice.

Principal personages

AMELIA "MOLLIE" MAGGIA, dial-painter in Orange, New Jersey
CATHERINE WOLFE DONOHUE, dial-painter in Ottawa, Illinois
FREDERICK FLINN, doctor for the United States Radium Corporation
RAYMOND BERRY, lawyer who championed the dial-painters from Orange, New Jersey
LEONARD GROSSMAN, lawyer who championed the dial-painters from Ottawa, Illinois
ARTHUR ROEDER, treasurer (later president) of the United States Radium Corporation

The Radium Girls: The Dark Story of America's Shining Women, by Kate Moore, tells the tragic story of two groups of women who suffered terribly from radium poisoning, which they were exposed to during their employment painting dial-faces onto timepieces using radium paint for two US companies in the early twentieth century. The book chronicles their suffering due to capitalist greed, patriarchal neglect, and outright malfeasance on the part of their employers, and the eventual legal outcomes of their struggles.

Radium was only discovered in 1898, and the science of radiation was in its infancy. Marie Curie and her husband, Pierre Curie, were still conducting their Nobel Prize–winning research, and the world was decades away from the nuclear horror of the atomic bomb. Scientific optimism and industry reigned supreme. Radium, which emitted a soft glow even in small amounts, was quickly marketed as a wonder material—for obvious purposes like luminous paint—but its pseudo-magical appeal also saw it marketed as an ingredient in health tonics. "As radium was such a rare and mysterious element," Moore explains, "its commercial exploiters in fact controlled, to an almost monopolizing extent, its image and most of the knowledge about it."

We now know that radium is a dangerous substance. The radiation it gives off can damage tissue and increase cancer rates. Worse, if ingested it bonds with human bones in place of calcium, weakening them, and destroying the body from within for decades thereafter. The bones of someone heavily exposed to radium, exhumed years later, will still glow. This knowledge makes the early chapters of Moore's book—otherwise a cheerful story about young women out to make their fortunes and aid the war effort during World War I as demand for watches painted with luminous radium paint soared—heavy with portent.

Kate Moore is an accomplished writer with more than fifteen books published across a variety of genres. She is also the director of the critically acclaimed play about the Radium Girls, These Shining Lives *(2015).*

Moore's account focuses on two groups. The women in Orange, New Jersey, employed by the United States Radium Corporation and those in Ottawa, Illinois, employed by the Radium Dial Company. The girls are all dial-painters, working in communal spaces to paint as many watch faces as possible. Efficiency was their mandate, and the most efficient way of getting the fine control necessary for their task was to twist the tips of their brushes between their lips, drawing them to a point. "Lip . . . dip . . . paint." These three simple words when imbued by hindsight are loaded with terrible menace: because every time these women pointed their brushes, they were putting radium into their mouths.

Moore builds tension deftly in the early pages, with radium lurking in the background like the monster in a horror film. The reader knows it will strike, but the suspense and dark irony of watching these cheerful women frolic in their newfound financial success and sense of sisterhood in their jobs only makes the inevitable turn worse. One particularly chilling scene involves the girls from Orange all cramming into a dark room so that they can better enjoy the fact that they glow with a fine sheen of radium dust. They laugh about their "radium mustaches." Moore later quotes one the girls' husbands: "I remember when we were married and she hung her smock in the bedroom: it would shine like the northern lights. The first time I saw it, it gave me an eerie feeling—like a ghost was bouncing around on the wall."

Unfortunately, the radium would lead to effects much worse than an ethereal glow. Moore does not hold back on the horror of what the women experienced once the radium in their bodies began to make its presence felt. Mollie Maggia is one of the

first young women to succumb. Her fate is as terrible as anything horror film director David Cronenberg with his penchant for gruesome physical horror could conjure.
It all starts with a simple toothache, but in less than a year Mollie is dead. Wounds
opened in her mouth, never healing, and her jaw disintegrated to the point that it broke
in her doctor's hands during an exam. Doctors could do nothing for her, and she died
in agony.

Later, Mollie's colleague Marguerite Carlough suffers a similar fate. Moore's description is graphic and heartbreaking:

> Marguerite's hearing was greatly impaired in both ears because of her infected facial
> bones. . . . The pain was awful: her lower jaw was fractured on the right side of her face
> and most of her teeth were missing. Her head, essentially, was 'extremely rotten'—with
> all the putrefaction that implies. But she was alive, still. Her whole head was rotting, but
> she was still alive.

It is important to note that this is not cheap exploitation or voyeurism that Moore is
attempting in her account. Moore's unflinching look at what these women suffered reflects her commitment to conveying their experiences and the magnitude of the crimes
against them.

One by one, the women fall ill. The women are betrayed by their bodies: hips
locking in place, faces swelling with pus, legs shrinking as bone is eaten away. By the
mid-1920s, with the help of some enterprising doctors, they have identified radium as
the probable cause of their suffering. The women of Orange sue their former employer.
It is the start of a legal battle that will span decades.

In every instance, the companies in Orange and Ottawa and the men associated
with them ignore the women's concerns. They scheme to obscure evidence, attempt
every form of legal trickery possible, and lie repeatedly to protect their interests.
Moore confronts the reader with their brutal disregard for human life. Moore quotes
one industrial physicist saying "Are we in industry to help carry out some soft, silly,
social plan? . . . No. We are in industry because it is good business." In what is perhaps
the most galling moment in the entire book, Charlotte Purcell—who had an arm ampu-
tated at the shoulder in an effort to save her from her radium poisoning—confronts her
old supervisor directly. His response is glibly dismissive as he states that he does not
think there is anything wrong with her. This is when *The Radium Girls* is at its most
potent—when Moore leverages her thorough research to demonstrate, with devastating understatement, the damnable conduct of these men and the bravery of the women
who fought them.

But her editorializing occasionally becomes overwrought. For instance, when describing Mollie Maggia's posthumous vindication, years after she was said to have
died of syphilis: "The pictures of her skull, meanwhile, with her jawbone missing,
made her mouth stretch unnaturally wide, as though she was screaming—screaming
for justice through all these years. There was a smudge of dark where her eye had once
been, as though she was looking out, staring accusingly, setting straight a lie that had
blackened her name." As Genevieve Valentine puts it in her review for NPR, it is an

"odd hard sell."

Moore clearly states that her intention in writing *The Radium Girls* is to tell these overlooked women's stories, to restore their humanity. She notes, in the afterword, that all of the available accounts she found in her research were written with academic remove; the women were homogenized. It is understandable, then, that Moore takes pains to identify many of the girls (and their relations) by name and with varying levels of biographic detail. The book begins with a four-page list of the principal personages.

Unfortunately, this noble impulse leads to the book's most significant weakness. The sheer number of individuals and biographical detail quickly becomes unwieldy. It is difficult, even for an attentive reader, to keep track of who is who and the relative importance of the key characters. The structure of the book, which alternates chapter-by-chapter between the two groups of women in New Jersey and Illinois, occasionally exacerbates the problem.

The large amount of overlap between the individual women's stories might also hurt the book's pacing. The reviewer for *Publishers Weekly* notes that "in giving voice to so many victims, Moore overburdens the story line." Although every individual story is told with skill and obvious care, at the macro level the narrative sometimes drags. Other reviewers, however, had no such qualms. Catherine Hollis at *BookPage* praises the "taut pacing." Indeed, the final chapters of the book are nothing if not compelling, as the Ottawa girls find a champion in the grandiloquent lawyer Leonard Grossman. If the first part of the book feels like a horror novel, the final third is a legal thriller, with all the page-turning compulsion that implies.

In the end, Moore's book is a welcome corrective to a history of neglect. It achieves its primary goal of giving a platform to these women, who fought through their final days to achieve major legal reform and improve workplace conditions for countless people who followed in their footsteps. It is also disturbingly relevant. Women still struggle to get their concerns taken seriously in healthcare and in the workplace, and the monstrous company men that Moore writes about may be entirely too familiar to modern readers. Hopefully, the light these women have shed with Moore's help will give all foes of justice fewer places to hide.

Kenrick Vezina, MS

Review Sources

Fergusson, Maggie. "The Radium Girls—Still Glowing in Their Coffins." Review of *The Radium Girls: The Dark Story of America's Shining Women*, by Kate Moore. *The Spectator*, 11 June 2016, www.spectator.co.uk/2016/06/the-radium-girls-still-glowing-in-their-coffins/. Accessed 23 Feb. 2017.

Hollis, Catherine. "*The Radium Girls*: Darkness in Light." Review of *The Radium Girls: The Dark Story of America's Shining Women*, by Kate Moore. *BookPage*, 18 Apr. 2017, bookpage.com/reviews/21284-kate-moore-radium-girls#.Wo8MD-K6nFyw. Accessed 23 Feb. 2017.

Review of *The Radium Girls: The Dark Story of America's Shining Women*, by Kate Moore. *Publishers Weekly*, 20 Mar. 2017, www.publishersweekly.

com/978-1-4926-4935-9. Accessed 23 Feb. 2017

Valentine, Genevieve. "'The Radium Girls' Is Haunted by Glowing Ghosts." Review of *The Radium Girls: The Dark Story of America's Shining Women*, by Kate Moore. *National Public Radio*, 27 Apr. 2017, www.npr.org/2017/04/27/525765323/the-radium-girls-is-haunted-by-glowing-ghosts. Accessed 23 Feb. 2017.

Witman, Sarah. "When Undark Was Lethal: A New Look at the 'Radium Girls.'" Review of *The Radium Girls: The Dark Story of America's Shining Women*, by Kate Moore. *UnDark*, 20 July 2017, undark.org/article/radium-girls-book-review/. Accessed 23 Feb. 2017.

The Refugees

Author: Việt Thanh Nguyễn (b. 1971)
Publisher: Grove Press (New York). 209 pp.
Type of work: Short fiction
Time: Late twentieth century
Locales: Vietnam, California

This collection of eight stories, published in periodicals before Nguyễn's novel The Sympathizer *won the 2016 Pulitzer Prize in Fiction, focuses on Vietnamese refugees navigating the differences between their homeland and their new home in the United States.*

Courtesy of Grove Atlantic

Việt Thanh Nguyễn introduces the theme of the short stories in *The Refugees* in two opening epigraphs: a quote from Roberto Bolaño, who said he wrote his novel *Antwerp* for "the ghosts" for they are "outside of time," and a passage from James Fenton's poem, "A German Requiem," lamenting that it is not memories that haunt one, but rather what one must forget and go on forgetting throughout one's life.

This recurrent theme of inescapable ghosts of the past is emphasized both metaphorically and literally in the opening story, "Black-Eyed Women." In it, a refugee's brother sacrificed his life trying to save her from pirates while fleeing Vietnam to come to a country—where she says they had no belongings "except our stories." Twenty-five years later, the central character lives with her mother, with whom she shares a "passion for words." While the daughter is a ghostwriter, the mother tells horror stories, mainly about life in Vietnam during the war. The black-eyed women of the title are crones who relate many of the horrifying tales. The dead brother first appears to the mother, whom the daughter thinks is suffering from dementia, until she sees the young man herself, looking just as he did at the age of fifteen, except that he is bloated and pale, dripping sea water.

Nguyễn knows the haunted world of Vietnam from stories that he has heard and books he has read, for he was young when his parents brought him to the United States in 1975. His connection to Vietnam is thus the world of words. The female narrator of "Black-Eyed Women" says writing was like entering a fog, "feeling my way for a route from this world to the unearthly world of words." The story ends with the narrator writing down the stories her mother tells her—calling the practice hunting for ghosts, as she searches for the revenants of her haunted country.

The ghost theme is echoed in the story "War Years," in which a passionate anti-Communist whose husband and two sons died in the war and who now lives in

California tries to get money from her fellow refugees to fund a hopeless overthrow of the government in South Vietnam. The narrator-protagonist is a thirteen-year-old whose parents own a Vietnamese market in San Jose. The boy has no memories of the war or of being driven out of Vietnam after the Communists marched into Saigon in 1975. However, he knows that the still-grieving woman, Mrs. Hoa, is haunted by both the dead and the living. His mother says she hates the Communists as much as Mrs. Hoa, but that she is not throwing her money away on a lost cause. Only when Mrs. Hoa threatens to turn the community against the boy's mother and ruin her business does the mother give Mrs. Hoa some money. The story ends with a sense of helplessness that runs throughout the collection—in this case, the boy feels helpless to do anything about what happened to Mrs. Hoa and his mother and the others who were killed or driven out of their country.

In "I'd Love You to Want Me," a retired Vietnamese community college professor slowly becomes a ghost to his wife, as he succumbs to dementia. The professor and his wife escaped from Vietnam on an old fishing trawler three years after the end of the war. The wife works in the Garden Grove, California, library, managing the collection of Vietnamese books and movies for the residents of Little Saigon. The professor has begun making mistakes typical of those who experience the onset of dementia—such as putting salt in his coffee and sugar in his soup. But the wife is most upset with him calling her by an unknown woman's name. She counterfeits her husband's handwriting and writes in his notebook: "Today I called my wife by the name of Yen . . . This mistake must not be repeated." Ironically, the professor keeps another notebook detailing what he thinks is the mental deterioration of his wife. The professor's loss of memory serves as a metaphor for the loss of the past in Vietnam, for when the couple return to visit their old house in Saigon, they find the street has been renamed, just as Saigon is now Ho Chi Minh City.

"The Americans" focuses on James Carver, a sixty-eight-year-old Vietnam War veteran originally from a small town in Alabama, who dropped bombs on the North Vietnamese. His Japanese wife talks him into visiting Vietnam after the war, where their daughter Claire is teaching. Carver scorns his daughter's desire to identify with the Vietnamese in her thinking and has no time for her boyfriend, who has helped to design crude robots that can safely locate minefields. When Claire says she has a Vietnamese soul, he shouts at her that her idea is stupid, a judgment he has often made in the past. Carver likes to distance himself from everything and everyone, which is why he always liked flying, for he feels that everything looks more beautiful from a distance. Caught in a monsoon, Carver apparently must learn a lesson about strength and weakness.

"Someone Else Besides You" is narrated by a thirty-three-year-old man whose father, a high school guidance counselor and Vietnamese veteran, lives with him. The narrator was born in a refugee camp in Guam, where his father was in military service, and when the protagonist was a child, his father forced him and his brothers to do push-ups and sit-ups and practice marksmanship with a BB gun. The narrator, now grown, is divorced from his wife, and his father wants them to get back together. At the father's insistence, they visit the ex-wife and find her pregnant, much to the infuriation of the narrator's father. The narrator responds far differently, and unexpectedly, to both his ex-wife's predicament and his father's reaction. The story ends with all three of them waiting for what is to come.

The title of "Fatherland" has a double meaning, for while it recounts the visit of a daughter to Vietnam, the focus is on the father, who has a second family. The central character, the eldest child of the second family, shares the name Phuong with the eldest of the first family, who now live in America. But the American daughter has adopted the name of Vivien, after Vivien Leigh, the actress who played Scarlett in *Gone with the Wind*. It is their father's favorite film, and Phuong thinks it is not farfetched that the ruined Confederacy of the American South is like South Vietnam and her father's resentment of the country's loss of identity. Phuong envies Vivien, a successful unmarried pediatrician who has traveled widely. Yet, when Phuong tells her half sister that she wants to come to America and be a doctor and help people, too, she discovers that

Việt Thanh Nguyễn is the Aerol Arnold Chair of English at the University of Southern California. His novel The Sympathizer *won the 2016 Pulitzer Prize for Fiction, and he received a MacArthur Fellowship in 2017.*

Vivien is not a doctor but a receptionist who lost her job and that Vivien's mother does not own a beauty salon, but rather works for a beautician. As a result, Phuong becomes disillusioned with her half sister, with their family, and with the idea of America.

"The Transplant" focuses on Arthur Arellano, a fifty-year-old Californian who has a garage filled with counterfeit Chanel, Versace, and Givenchy products. The items belong to Louis Vu, whose father saved Arthur's life by donating his liver to Arthur, and Arthur allows the items to be stored in his garage as repayment. The story is complicated by Arthur being a compulsive gambler who has lost all his money and by Arthur's discovery that Louis is not all that he claimed.

In "The Other Man," a refugee named Liem goes to San Francisco to live with his sponsor, Parrish, and Parrish's lover, Marcus. Liem works hard to make a place for himself in the United States, and he realizes that he too is gay in an encounter with Marcus. In this story, Liem being a refugee seems more incidental, making the story less compelling than the others in the collection.

In her *New Yorker* review of *The Refugees*, Joyce Carol Oates calls Nguyễn, one of our "great chroniclers of displacement." Although reviewers have made much of Nguyễn being a Vietnamese refugee, he was young when he came to America and he grew up in California. Moreover, he is far from the struggling displaced Vietnamese who live in Orange County or San Jose, California. He has a PhD from the University of California, Berkeley, holds an endowed chair of English at the University of Southern California, and has authored academic works of scholarship. Several reviewers and commentators have suggested an alternative contemporary relevance of these stories, citing the plight of Syrian refugees, and the debate over travel bans and racism in America. Megan Mayhew Bergman calls the collection "as impeccably written as it is timed," reminding us of the current international human-rights drama.

Charles E. May

Review Sources

Alvar, Mia. "Ghost Stories: Vietnamese Refugees Wrestle with Memory in a New Book by the Author of *The Sympathizer*." Review of *The Refugees*, by Việt Thanh Nguyễn. *The New York Times*, 13 Feb. 2017, www.nytimes.com/2017/02/13/books/review/refugees-viet-thanh-nguyen.html. Accessed 24 Oct 2017.

Bergman, Megan Mayhew. "Viet Thanh Nguyen's *The Refugees* Couldn't Come at a Better Time." Review of *The Refugees*, by Việt Thanh Nguyễn. *The Washington Post*, 1 Feb. 2017, www.washingtonpost.com/entertainment/books/viet-thanh-nguyens-the-refugees-couldnt-come-at-a-better-time/2017/01/31/675e0e92-e7fb-11e6-b82f-687d6e6a3e7c_story.html. Accessed 24 Oct. 2017.

Li, Yiyun. "*The Refugees* by Viet Thanh Nguyen Review–Stories of Anger, Humour, and Hope." Review of *The Refugees*, by Việt Thanh Nguyễn. *The Guardian*, 27 Jan. 2017, www.theguardian.com/books/2017/jan/27/the-refugees-viet-thanh-nguyen-review. Accessed 24 Oct. 2017.

Long, Karen. "In Viet Thanh Nguyen's *The Refugees*, Wistfulness Is an Anthem of Displacement." Review of *The Refugees*, by Việt Thanh Nguyễn. *Los Angeles Times*, 9 March 2017, beta.latimes.com/books/jacketcopy/la-ca-jc-refugees-viet-thanh-nguyen-20170223-story.html. Accessed 24 Oct. 2017.

Oates, Joyce Carol. "Refugees in America." Review of *The Refugees*, by Việt Thanh Nguyễn. *The New Yorker*, 13 and 20 Feb. 2017, www.newyorker.com/magazine/2017/02/13/refugees-in-america. Accessed 24 Oct. 2017.

Reincarnation Blues

Author: Michael Poore (b. 1967)
Publisher: Del Rey (New York). 384 pp.
Type of work: Novel
Time: 2600 BCE–3400 CE
Locales: United States; India; Austria; Bridger's Planet; a prison asteroid in deep space; Germany; Scotland; Morocco; Ganymede and Europa

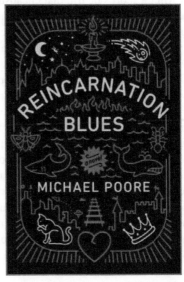

Courtesy of Del Rey

Reincarnation Blues follows a hapless human named Milo on a journey across thousands of years and millions of miles as he burns through ten thousand lives in a quest for perfection entwined with the pursuit of a love affair with Death, in the form of a beautiful, dark-haired woman called Suzie.

Principal characters

MILO, a flawed human who has died and been reincarnated nearly ten thousand times
SUZIE, a.k.a. Death, the woman he loves and meets in the afterlife after each death
MAMA, a large, motherly woman who helps guide him through his reincarnations
NAN, her companion, a cranky, cigarette-smoking woman with cats
THE BUDDHA, an elderly man whom Milo meets during one of his lives

One of the great mysteries of the ages is what happens when a person dies. Do humans have souls that wing away to some form of afterlife at the moment of death, or is there nothingness forever after once someone has taken that final breath? Michael Poore attempts to deliver tongue-in-cheek answers to these questions in *Reincarnation Blues*, a sometimes semiserious, sometimes cosmically hilarious speculative fiction romp. The novel starts, as the title suggests, with the ancient religious belief of reincarnation—that whenever a living being dies, its soul is reborn in a different form—then twists the idea out of shape like soft taffy and turns it on its head.

The concept of reincarnation is embodied in the protagonist, most commonly known as Milo. When first encountered in 2017, Milo is a middle-aged man living in the Florida Keys who works as the skipper of a charter fishing boat and is locally known as a wise man. His wisdom, readers learn within a few pages, derives from the fact that he has endured almost ten thousand lives in various forms, usually as a human but sometimes in other shapes, such as an insect or a furry animal or a tree. As he tells an elderly female friend, his is the oldest soul on the planet. Despite such a wealth of experience, Milo does not always do what is smart or right or prudent. This flaw becomes immediately apparent when Milo goes surfing at night and is promptly eaten by a cruising shark that has been, in its previous lives, several different fish, a clam, a dog, a cat, and the 1985 Strawberry Festival Queen of Troy, Ohio.

After a short side trip that encapsulates the multitude of creative ways in which he has died 9,995 times (his favorite method was being captured by the Ottoman Empire and hurled via catapult over the walls of the Habsburg city of Vienna, because it was like flying weightless), Milo awakens again in the afterlife. Here, the afterlife is a sort of way station where the newly deceased wait to be reborn. The appearance of the afterlife is different for every person, reflecting the quality of the life they just lived; in Milo's case, it is low rent and shabby, because he did not accomplish much as a twenty-first-century Florida fisherman, the latest stop on what is supposed to be a long, winding path to perfection. He is greeted by his lover Suzie, a beautiful woman with long black hair, who is always present when Milo returns to the afterlife. Suzie is Death—a Death, but not the only one—and although she could simply take Milo's life and move on, she waits for him to wake up every time. They wait together until they are joined by Mama and Nan, two women who are not quite angels and not quite gods ("Think of us as slices of the universe," Mama says), who are responsible for guiding Milo through his various reincarnations. After Mama and Nan leave Milo to rest, Suzie returns, and she and Milo make love. Suzie gives Milo a gift, an antique copper armband shaped like a snake biting its own tail—the ouroboros, a symbol of the cycle of life and death.

The gift serves as a catalyst to propel the story back to its origin in the Indus River Valley of 2600 BCE, where a precocious child called Milovasu Pradesh experienced his first life and endured his first colorful death (the result of an error in judgment while carrying out a well-intentioned plan to help fellow villagers escape the depredations of a horde of murderous barbarians). In his initial visit to the afterlife, Milo meets the three women—Suzie, Mama, and Nan—with whom he will spend considerable between-lives downtime in the future. They explain how the universe works and talk about reincarnation. They emphasize that pain is an illusion, that perfection frees a person from illusion, and that perfect people become part of everything. Milo will be given up to ten thousand lives—ten thousand chances—to learn to achieve complete enlightenment or perfection. If he is successful, he will "go through the Sun Door in a flash of golden light and become part of the Great Reality," also known as the Oversoul; if he fails, his soul will cross into Nowhere, becoming Nothingness and "vanish[ing] forever from time and space." Mama and Nan show him what Nowhere looks like: a sidewalk leading into empty space.

The novel subsequently rockets back and forth in time and place. While Milo falls in love often (68,504 times by actual count), marries (9,649 times), and produces myriad children over the course of nearly ten thousand lives, it is Suzie that he has truly loved since early in his existence. Suzie likewise loves him, on occasion contemplating giving up her occupation as Death and trading in her immortality to live as an ordinary human. Milo, who in some lives has special talents or superpowers (here he is an unbeatable racehorse, there he is a swami immune to poison; here he lives in the future as a girl genius, there he is a jazz saxophonist in the present), worries that if he does achieve perfection, he will be removed from the cycle of life and death and will be separated from Suzie forever. Similarly, he also worries that if he fails to achieve perfection, he will be permanently deleted from the universe and will still lose Suzie.

Reincarnation Blues illustrates, in sometimes brief, occasionally extended passages, Milo's dilemma in alternately reaching for and purposely sabotaging his journey toward perfection. In one chapter, for example, an arrogant Milo is the fabulously rich heir to a water cartel in the twenty-second century who attempts to seduce a similarly wealthy woman by inviting her to attend a charity ball at a fantastic heat-resistant palace he has built on the surface of the sun. When his plan fails and the sun melts his creation, Milo dies and is reborn as a humble cricket kept in a cage by a young Chinese girl in 1903.

Another chapter, set in Iowa in 2025, updates the premise of Philip Wylie and Edwin Balmer's science-fiction novel *When Worlds Collide* (1933), adapted for film in 1951. In Poore's version, one of several homages to classic speculative fiction, it is a planet-killing comet rather than a rogue planet that has taken lethal aim at Earth. Earthlings, including Milo, have just five years to build four gigantic arkships to transport a handful of humans, chosen by lottery, into Earth orbit, to Venus, to Mars, or to a moon of Jupiter. Some of these destinations figure in later installments of the story, which as a whole is a series of incidents connected by the common thread of death and rebirth and by the appearance of yet another fresh Milo, who in his mind can hear voices from previous lives.

While the Earthbound sequences in *Reincarnation Blues* are entertaining, the novel particularly soars in imagined futuristic, off-planet scenes that, with little editing, could serve as stand-alone novellas. One of these exciting miniature space epics, titled "The Hasty Pudding Affair," sees a young Milo as a scholar on Bridger's Planet in the thirty-fifty century, being falsely accused of rape. After being convicted of the crime, he is sent to Unferth, an isolated prison colony located on an asteroid in deep space—a setting reminiscent of otherworldly lockups seen in films such as *Star Trek VI: The Undiscovered Country* (1991) or *Alien 3* (1992). Brutalized by other convicts, Milo is forced to participate in a betting sport called "diving," in which contestants are expelled from an airlock, sans protection or a breathing apparatus, and must make it through the cold vacuum of space to the next airlock hatch before they die. Milo, who in this lifetime has telepathic and telekinetic powers, learns to control his mind and body and thrives in the harsh environment. Ironically, when he is later rescued and returned home, his life turns mundane and unfulfilling.

Michael Poore is the author of the critically acclaimed comic fantasy novel Up Jumps the Devil *(2012) and has published short fiction in numerous periodicals, including* Southern Review, Glimmer Train, *and* Asimov's. Reincarnation Blues *is his second novel.*

Another mini-saga is "The Family Stone," set on Jupiter's moon Ganymede in the mid-twenty-second century, where cruel Monitors of the water cartel are in control. When ordinary citizens—including Milo, his parents, and his siblings—revolt against their treatment by the cartel, they are scooped up and dumped into the ocean on neighboring moon Europa, where they join a naked tribe of islanders previously expelled from Ganymede. Those on Europa, ever vigilant of the extreme tsunamis caused by the pull of Jupiter's massive gravity, are forced under penalty of torture or death to maintain a deep-well pump that produces detoxified water for their overlords. When the islanders, reeling from an especially vicious attack by the Monitors, begin killing themselves in droves, Milo steps forward to lead them. Following the voices he hears from his previous lives, he devises a plan to foil their oppressors.

Although *Reincarnation Blues* is long and occasionally dense, particularly in places where philosophical explication is necessary, it seldom drags. The narration is stylistically straightforward, underscored with subtle satirical touches and punctuated by laugh-out-loud passages. Poore's skill at blending futuristic concepts with sympathetic characters and realistic dialogue makes him a force to be reckoned with in speculative fiction.

Jack Ewing

Review Sources
Moran, Alexander. Review of *Reincarnation Blues*, by Michael Poore. *Booklist*, July 2017, p. 24. *Academic Search Complete*, search.ebscohost.com/login.aspx?direct =true&db=a9h&AN=124094444&site=ehost-live. Accessed 22 Jan. 2018.

Review of *Reincarnation Blues*, by Michael Poore. *Kirkus Reviews*, 6 June 2017, www.kirkusreviews.com/book-reviews/michael-poore/reincarnation-blues. Accessed 22 Jan. 2018.

Review of *Reincarnation Blues*, by Michael Poore. *Publishers Weekly*, 3 July 2017, p. 57. *Academic Search Complete*, search.ebscohost.com/login.aspx?direct=true& db=a9h&AN=123879948&site=ehost-live. Accessed 22 Jan. 2018.

Sheehan, Jason. "Take a Walk on the Wilder Side of Death with *Reincarnation Blues*." Review of *Reincarnation Blues*, by Michael Poore. *NPR*, 26 Aug. 2017, www.npr.org/2017/08/26/543933403/take-a-walk-on-the-wilder-side-of-death-with-reincarnation-blues. Accessed 22 Jan. 2018.

Turner, Portia. "*Reincarnation Blues* Proves Death Can Be Funny." Review of *Reincarnation Blues*, by Michael Poore. *Chicago Review of Books*, 5 Oct. 2017, chireviewofbooks.com/2017/10/05/reincarnation-blues-michael-poore-review/. Accessed 22 Jan. 2018.

Rest in Power
The Enduring Life of Trayvon Martin

Authors: Sybrina Fulton and Tracy Martin
Publisher: Spiegel & Grau (New York). 352 pp.
Type of work: Memoir
Time: Primarily 2012–13
Locales: Florida; East St. Louis, Illinois

Rest in Power: The Enduring Life of Trayvon Martin *chronicles the life and death of Trayvon Martin, an unarmed African American teenager who was shot and killed in Sanford, Florida, by a neighborhood watch volunteer. His parents, Tracy Martin and Sybrina Fulton, recall the terrible days following their son's death but also the civil rights movement that sprang from it.*

Courtesy of Spiegel & Grau

Principal personages

Trayvon Martin, an African American teenager who was shot and killed by a volunteer neighborhood watch captain in Florida in 2012

Sybrina Fulton, his mother and coauthor of the book

Tracy Martin, his father and coauthor of the book

George Zimmerman, the volunteer neighborhood watchman who shot and killed him and was subsequently tried for and acquitted of second-degree murder

On February 26, 2012, seventeen-year-old Trayvon Martin walked from his father's girlfriend's home in a gated community in Sanford, Florida, to a nearby convenience store to buy a can of fruit juice and a package of Skittles candy. Walking back to the house, he flipped up the hood of his sweatshirt as it began to rain. He was uneasy; a man was following him, he told his friend on his cell phone. George Zimmerman, a volunteer neighborhood watchman, approached him, and within minutes—between the time his phone went dead and the time the police arrived on the scene—Trayvon Martin was dead, shot through the heart at point blank range. Elements of this story will likely be familiar to readers. Trayvon Martin's killing, and the lengthy battle for justice that followed, became international news. After the case went to trial, and Zimmerman was acquitted of second-degree murder and manslaughter, the phrase "black lives matter" gained serious traction on social media and later became applied to the civil rights movement that Trayvon's death helped galvanize. *Rest in Power: The Enduring Life of Trayvon Martin* chronicles this story from the perspective of Trayvon Martin's parents, Sybrina Fulton and Tracy Martin. In alternating chapters, Fulton and Martin, who divorced when their son was a child, write with heartbreaking candor about their grief, their anger, and their hopes for the future.

Several reviews of *Rest in Power* refer to the 2003 book *Death of Innocence: The Story of the Hate Crime that Changed America*, by Mamie Till-Mobley, whose fourteen-year-old son Emmett Till was brutally tortured

Sybrina Fulton and Tracy Martin are the parents of Trayvon Martin, an unarmed black teen who was killed by a neighborhood watchman in 2012. Fulton and Martin launched the Trayvon Martin Foundation in his memory.

and lynched in 1955. Till-Mobley made the painful decision to publish photos of her son's mutilated body, including from his open-casket funeral. She explained that decision in her memoir, published almost fifty years later: "People had to face my son and realize just how twisted, how distorted, how terrifying race hatred could be," she writes. "The whole nation had to bear witness to this." Till-Mobley helped galvanize the civil rights movement of the 1960s, but at an unfathomable personal cost. Her story provides an important lens through which to view *Rest in Power*. Like Till-Mobley, Fulton and Martin are forced to display their grief publicly to try to attain justice for their son. Days after Trayvon's death, Fulton writes, all she wanted to do was hide under the covers of her bed. But as Trayvon's killer walked free, she was compelled to advocate for her son on national television. As author Mychal Denzel Smith explained in an article for *New Republic*, "Relatives of white victims can choose to become activists—they might take up, say, the cause of gun control—but they aren't required to, and they never have to, prove that their very lives have value." For forty-five excruciating days, Fulton and Martin made this public bid for their son's humanity; only then was Zimmerman even arrested.

Rest in Power begins before the shooting, offering a glimpse into first Fulton's young life and then Trayvon's childhood. Fulton grew up in Opa-Locka, a suburb of Miami, and attended college in Louisiana. She recalls the moment her mother and older brother drove away after settling her into her freshman dorm. The anguish of the moment, she recalls, revealed "how much family really meant to me." She moved back to Miami, attending college near her home, a year and a half later. She began working for Miami-Dade County and met Martin, a truck driver from East St. Louis, Illinois, at an office Christmas party in 1993; they married in the summer of 1994. Trayvon was born in 1995 and enjoyed a happy childhood with his older half brother, Jahvaris. Fulton, who returned to school when Trayvon was two, recalls dressing the boys up in identical clothes and watching them play at her feet as she studied in the university library. As Trayvon got older, he took to calling his mother "Cupcake" because, he told her, she was so sweet. As for his ambitions, he fell in love with aviation when he was fifteen, telling his mother he hoped to become a mechanic or a pilot.

Fulton and Martin spend some time parsing the week or so leading up to Trayvon's death. He received an out-of-school suspension for having women's jewelry in his backpack. (Because he refused to say where it came from, the school punished him for burglary.) Fulton was disappointed in her son and kept him busy during his suspension performing odd jobs around the house. She and Martin arranged for Trayvon to spend the rest of his suspension in Sanford, Florida, with Martin, his girlfriend, and his girlfriend's son Chad. The night he was killed, Trayvon was preparing to watch the National Basketball Association All-Star Game with Chad. Just before the game began, at around 7 p.m., he slipped out of the house to go to the convenience store. The altercation with Zimmerman is described later, in the section of the book that relives the trial, explored from every angle, including several of the neighbors who either witnessed the shooting or heard the single gunshot and screams. However, the real heart of the book lies in the handling of Trayvon's death and its aftermath. Martin came home later that night and was surprised to discover Trayvon gone. He assumed his son was with a cousin, but the next morning, he grew worried. He called the police, who arrived at his house to file a missing person report. Sitting at the kitchen table, they unceremoniously showed Martin a picture of a body to determine whether it might be his son. "I looked at the picture, and today, four years and an eternity later, I still find it hard to describe how I felt," Martin writes.

Martin was told that the killer had claimed that he acted in self-defense and that he had been released from police custody. One officer told Martin that Zimmerman was "squeaky clean," meaning that he had a clean record, but that turned out not to be true. (Zimmerman had assaulted a law-enforcement agent several years prior.) The truth also eventually came out that the department had never run a background check on Zimmerman—though they did run a background check on Trayvon, who was a minor and, more significantly, dead when they arrived on the scene. The police also ran a drug and alcohol test on Trayvon but failed to do the same for Zimmerman. In the following days, as Fulton and Martin's attorney pushed them to publicize their grief to force first the release of the 911 calls made before and during the shooting, and then to force an arrest, much attention was paid to the trace amount of marijuana found in Trayvon's system when he died. The detail was indicative of what was to come; as Fulton writes, in sadness and disbelief, there was an overwhelming sense from the start that Trayvon was the one on trial, not his killer. She was numb after her son's death but writes with gratitude of the thousands of people—celebrities, civil rights leaders, and ordinary citizens—who offered sustained support through protest. Reverend Al Sharpton, who appeared at a rally for justice for Trayvon the day his mother died, was particularly devoted to the cause.

This solidarity, particularly after another unarmed African American teenager named Michael Brown was fatally shot by a white police officer in 2014, would coalesce into the Black Lives Matter movement. After the disappointment of the trial—outlined in even more detail in a book, which Fulton and Martin reference, titled *Suspicion Nation: The Inside Story of the Trayvon Martin Injustice and Why We Continue to Repeat It* (2014), by attorney Lisa Bloom—this movement nourishes Fulton and Martin in other ways, connecting them to others who have lost a loved one, often to state violence. At the end of the book, Fulton recalls a dream she had in which she is in an "endless field of purple"—her favorite color—and she sees "ladies crying in agony and sorrow." The women, she realized, were mothers. "And I knew that, just like me, they were mothers who had lost their children to senseless gun violence," she writes. "And while they once felt alone, they now had each other."

Fulton was inspired to make her dream a reality and soon after launched the Circle of Mothers event, in which mothers whose children have been killed come together to heal. Martin heads a partner event, the Circle of Fathers. Fulton and Martin continue to fight for justice for their son, raising awareness about racial profiling and racial discrimination in the justice system and advocating changing laws such as Florida's Stand Your Ground law, which effectively let Zimmerman claim that he shot Trayvon in self-defense. Their advocacy is important, but a poor substitute for the life of their son. Fulton's hope now, she writes, is to work to make sure that "the killing of Trayvon Martin would stand for something, so that someday the killing will stop and the healing will begin."

Despite Trayvon's killing having occurred more than four years ago, his parents' attempt to bring a sense of concrete humanity and hope to issues such as race, violence, and the criminal justice system by candidly sharing their story remains timely and significant. Reviewers generally agreed that the memoir offers further perspective into the highly covered but still ambiguous incident of Trayvon's death. The reviewer for *Kirkus Reviews* praised the authors' sincere writing this way: "Fulton and Martin are not heavy-handed on the dramatics; they speak honestly and boldly and win empathy and understanding through their expression of their bleak reality."

Molly Hagan

Review Sources

Lowery, Wesley. "Reliving the Trauma Experienced by Trayvon Martin's Parents." Review of *Rest in Power: The Enduring Life of Trayvon Martin*, by Sybrina Fulton and Tracy Martin. *The Washington Post*, 16 Feb. 2017, www.washingtonpost.com/opinions/reliving-the-trauma-experienced-by-trayvon-martins-parents/2017/02/16/940ffef0-f20a-11e6-a9b0-ecee7ce475fc_story.html. Accessed 8 Nov. 2017.

Makalani, Minkah. "What They Did to My Baby." Review of *Rest in Power: The Enduring Life of Trayvon Martin*, by Sybrina Fulton and Tracy Martin. *Slate*, 23 May 2017, www.slate.com/articles/arts/books/2017/05/rest_in_power_the_enduring_life_of_trayvon_martin_reviewed_by_minkah_makalani.html. Accessed 8 Nov. 2017.

Review of *Rest in Power: The Enduring Life of Trayvon Martin*, by Sybrina Fulton and Tracy Martin. *Kirkus Reviews*, vol. 85, no. 1, Jan. 2017, p. 1. *EBSCOhost*, search.ebscohost.com/login.aspx?direct=true&db=lkh&AN=120456456&site=lrc-plus. Accessed 8 Nov. 2017.

Ritter, Jane. Review of *Rest in Power: The Enduring Life of Trayvon Martin*, by Sybrina Fulton and Tracy Martin. *School Library Journal*, 19 Apr. 2017, www.slj.com/2017/04/reviews/rest-in-power-the-enduring-life-of-trayvon-martin-by-sybrina-fulton-and-tracy-martin-slj-review/. Accessed 8 Nov. 2017.

Richard Nixon
The Life

Author: John A. Farrell (b. 1953)
Publisher: Doubleday (New York). 752 pp.
Type of work: Biography
Time: 1913–94
Locale: United States

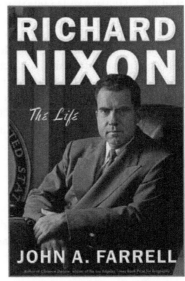

This latest biography of Richard M. Nixon, thirty-seventh president of the United States, offers a wealth of valuable detail about the life and career of this controversial leader.

Principal personages

RICHARD M. NIXON, thirty-seventh president of the United States
H. R. HALDEMAN, his White House chief of staff
JOHN EHRLICHMAN, his White House chief domestic advisor
PAT NIXON, his wife
DWIGHT D. EISENHOWER, thirty-fourth president of the United States
JOHN F. KENNEDY, thirty-fifth president of the United States
HUBERT H. HUMPHREY, vice president under Lyndon Johnson; Democratic candidate for president in 1968
LYNDON BAINES JOHNSON, thirty-fifth president of the United States; vice president under Kennedy
ALGER HISS, State Department official and accused Soviet spy
HELEN GAHAGAN DOUGLAS, 1950 Democratic candidate for Senate in California
JERRY VOORHIS, Democratic congressman from California

Why another Nixon biography? Any reasonably good university library has scores of biographies or specialized studies on some aspect of Nixon's career. Forty-four years after Nixon's resignation in August 1974 and twenty-four years after his death in April 1994, Nixon still evokes strong feelings from the public, the press, and American historians. Between 1987 and 1991, the late historian Stephen Ambrose published a three-volume biography of Nixon, often considered the standard work on the thirty-seventh president. But much new material has become available since the time Ambrose wrote, including many thousands of hours of the Oval Office tapes from the Nixon White House, and dozens of oral histories collected at the Nixon Presidential Library, Whittier College (Nixon's alma mater), and other institutions. There also was a need for a standard one-volume biography, which is what Farrell set out to write. Farrell's book is fast-paced, well-researched, and even at more than five hundred pages of text, is a relatively brief work for such a complex and controversial subject whose career spanned nearly four decades. Solidly based on primary sources plus the best of the secondary works on Nixon, it is likely to become the go-to single-volume biography. Farrell's writing style is engaging, and one reason is the little details and anecdotes—almost "throw away" lines—he sometimes includes within his descriptions of more significant issues and developments.

Those who have studied Nixon's career, or simply lived through much of it, will be familiar with many of the incidents Farrell records, and even with what has become the standard interpretation of this incidents. Virtually every scholar who has written on Nixon has noted the complexities and internal contradictions in his life, and Farrell has made these a major interpretive theme. Perhaps because many of us can see some of our own faults in Nixon's makeup, we often have some vestige of sympathy for the man, even if we are convinced of his wrongdoing. Many people who voted for Nixon every time he ran for president still had some reservations about his character—to resurrect the old cliché, they probably would not have bought a used car from him. A reviewer on the National Public Radio website describes Farrell's approach in this way: "With a mix of morbid fascination and deep empathy, Farrell humanizes Nixon, but he doesn't let him off the hook." This is an accurate assessment of Farrell's approach—he puts the blame squarely on Nixon when he deserves it, but at the same time he is not hesitant to acknowledge some of the achievements of Nixon's administration.

Nixon viewed Dwight D. Eisenhower as a model president despite the rocky relationship between the two men, and like Ike, Nixon was a political pragmatist more than an ideological conservative. Many things that might be characterized as liberal or progressive reforms were achieved during Nixon's presidency. When Nixon and his aides sensed a shift in public opinion toward more concern for the environment, administration policies also shifted in that direction. In 1970, Nixon signed the National Environmental Policy Act, established the Council on Environmental Quality and the Environmental Protection Agency, and signed the Clean Air Act. Farrell suggests that "Nixon was not averse to a Teddy Roosevelt sort of environmentalism, preserving natural resources for future generations," and notes that in a national poll of the leaders of major environmental organization leaders in 2012, Nixon trailed behind only Roosevelt as the president who had done the most for the environment. But Farrell also notes that when public opinion began to shift away from these issues, so did Nixon's attention. In a similar vein, Farrell pictures Nixon as being fairly progressive on race relations in his time in Congress and as vice president. However, in the 1960 presidential race, his failure to respond to Martin Luther King Jr. being jailed on trumped-up charges in Atlanta hurt Nixon in an election that was so close, the black vote in northern states might have made a difference. As president, Nixon took a measured approach on school desegregation. Not wanting to alienate southern white voters, his Justice Department workers took the approach of telling them, "You may not like this, we may not like it—but it is the law and it has to be done." In many localities, they brought black and white leaders together to work out approaches that could be viable. Thus, Farrell suggests, quoting historian Dan Kotlowski, "Nixon was the greatest school desegregator in American history." Farrell also cites Hugh Graham, who wrote in 1987, "The standard indictment [of Nixon as uncaring or worse on race issues] cannot account for the counterfactuals." Attempting to deal with the life of one of the twentieth century's major political figures in a one-volume biography, Farrell has to focus primarily on the most significant issues. But sometimes perhaps his pace is a little too hurried. There is very little background on how the United States got involved in Vietnam. He cites the incident in the 1960 campaign when a reporter asked Eisenhower if Nixon had contributed significantly to any major policy decisions, and Ike replied offhandedly, "If you give me a week, I might think of one." But he skips over Eisenhower's later apology for that remark and his awareness of the damage it caused. In discussing Nixon's 1962 campaign for the governor's office in California, Farrell never mentions Nixon's own explanation of why he made the run, as described in his memoirs. As Farrell correctly notes, one of the major reasons Nixon lost that election is

© Kathy Kupka

John A. Farrell has had a long career in journalism, including stints at the Denver Post, the National Journal, *and service as a White House correspondent for the* Boston Globe. *His biographies of Speaker of the House Thomas P. "Tip" O'Neill and the famed defense attorney Clarence Darrow have received high praise from historians and reviewers.*

that California voters simply did not believe he was really interested in the job—they believed he only wanted to keep his name before the public as he prepared to run for president again in 1964. But Nixon says he wanted to become governor of California, and promised to serve a full term, so he could tell the Republicans he would not be available to run against Kennedy in 1964. He believed no one would be able to defeat Kennedy, and after Kennedy died, he believed there would be such a sympathy vote for Johnson that he would likewise be undefeatable. When confronted with the direct testimony of the subject, a biographer should at least discuss why he or she has considered and then dismissed such evidence.

As he gets into the final days of Nixon's administration, and its immediate aftermath, Farrell seems to quicken his pace, and it appears that he thinks he is just reminding the reader of things that are already generally known—sometimes writing in what resembles an outline format. It may be the case today that many readers will already have the background to put these events into context, but the Nixon era is rapidly receding into what many college and high school students today would consider the distant past. One can get a sense of this by looking at Farrell's acknowledgements, where he mentions the people he had good fortune to interview before they passed away (some long before he began working on this book) and includes twenty-five names, including major figures such as Senator Edward Kennedy and President Gerald R. Ford.

Reviewers have been very positive in their assessment of Farrell's book. One incident Farrell details, based on newly released documents, has caused much comment both in reviews and in news articles about the book. This was the "Chennault affair" in the fall of 1968. Lyndon Johnson was trying to get the Paris peace talks moving forward more purposefully to end the Vietnam War, and Nixon sought to forestall this Democratic win ahead of the 1968 presidential election. Friends of Nixon therefore prevailed upon Republican activist Anna Chennault, who had been born in China and was the widow of General Claire Chennault, who had led the American Flying Tigers aiding the Chinese in World War II, to intervene. She was to convince South Vietnamese president Nguyen Van Thieu that he should disregard this new push from Johnson, and tell him that if Nixon were elected, he would negotiate better terms for South Vietnam. It has long been known that Chennault did pass this along to Thieu (who may not have needed much convincing, since foot-dragging had been the South Vietnamese position at the peace talks from the very beginning), but what Farrell has uncovered are notes from Bob Halderman showing that Nixon was involved in making this request, even ordering Halderman at one point, "Keep Anna Chennault working on SVN." Farrell sees this effort as giving "aid and comfort" to an enemy, and thus making it an act of treason. This revelation caused quite a stir even before the book was released, when Farrell published a story in the *New York Times* laying out his findings. While this illustrates the value of the recently opened files that Farrell has had access to, this bombshell revelation is not the chief value of the book, and later scholars may find it only confirms what was long suspected.

Many reviewers have felt the need to suggest dire parallels between the dark days of the Nixon administration and the presidency of Donald Trump. There is one clear parallel: both Nixon and Trump found ways to tap into the discontent of what Nixon called the "Silent Majority." But when you look at the men's backgrounds, the parallels break down. If Nixon had lived to see the rise of Donald Trump as a politician, rather than simply a wealthy businessman and celebrity, he may well have identified him as one of the privileged, "East Coast establishment" types that he had been fighting ever since the Hiss case in 1948.

Mark S. Joy, PhD

Review Sources
Bew, John. "*Richard Nixon: The Life* Sheds Light on All the President's Demons." Review of *Richard Nixon: The Life* by John A. Farrell. *New Statesman*, 2 Dec. 2017, www.newstatesman.com/culture/books/2017/12/richard-nixon-life-sheds-light-all-president-s-demons. Accessed February 13, 2018.
Goudsouzian, Aram. "Deepening the Complexity of Richard Nixon from Newly Released Material." Review of *Richard Nixon: The Life* by John A. Farrell. *The Washington Post*, 24 Mar. 2017, www.washingtonpost.com/opinions/deepening-the-complexity-of-richard-nixon-from-newly-released-material/2017/03/24/382614c8-05a4-11e7-b9fa-ed727b644a0b_story.html. Accessed February 13, 2018.

Harnisch, Larry. "Traumatized Nixon." Review of *Richard Nixon: The Life* by John
  A. Farrell. *LA Review of Books*, 29 Mar. 2017, lareviewofbooks.org/article/trau-
  matized-nixon/. Accessed February 13, 2018.
Heller, Jason. "'Nixon: The Life' Humanizes—But Doesn't Rehabilitate." Review
  of *Richard Nixon: The Life* by John A. Farrell. *National Public Radio*, 12 Apr.
  2017, www.npr.org/2017/04/12/522926517/nixon-the-life-humanizes-but-doesnt-
  rehabilitate. Accessed February 13, 2018.
Senior, Jennifer. "'Richard Nixon,' Portrait of a Thin-Skinned, Media-Hating
  President." Review of *Richard Nixon: The Life* by John A. Farrell. *The New York
  Times*, 29 Mar. 2017, www.nytimes.com/2017/03/29/books/richard-nixon-biogra-
  phy-john-a-farrell.html. Accessed February 13, 2018.

The Road to Camelot
Inside JFK's Five-Year Campaign

Authors: Thomas Oliphant (b. 1945) and Curtis Wilkie (b. 1940)
Publisher: Simon & Schuster (New York). Illustrated. 448 pp.
Type of work: History
Time: Primarily 1956–60
Locale: The United States

In The Road to Camelot, *the authors argue that John F. Kennedy's campaign for the Democratic presidential nomination began in the fall of 1956; they trace the history of this five-year effort through research in primary sources and personal interviews with some of those involved.*

Principal personages

JOHN F. KENNEDY, senator from Massachusetts who was elected president of the United States in 1960

ROBERT F. KENNEDY, his younger brother and campaign manager of the 1960 presidential campaign

JOSEPH KENNEDY SR., his father, a wealthy Massachusetts businessman and former ambassador to Great Britain

LYNDON B. JOHNSON, his running mate in 1960, a senator from Texas

TED SORENSEN, his adviser and speechwriter during his time in the Senate; a major adviser during the 1960 presidential campaign and in the Kennedy administration

HUBERT H. HUMPHREY, senator from Minnesota who was a candidate for the Democratic nomination in 1960

ADLAI STEVENSON, former governor of Illinois and the Democratic candidate for president who lost the 1952 and 1956 elections to Dwight D. Eisenhower

LOUIS HARRIS, an early pioneer in the business of public opinion polling who became a consultant to the Kennedy campaign

LAWRENCE O'BRIEN, manager of Kennedy's successful 1952 campaign for the Senate and a major aide to Kennedy in the 1960 presidential campaign

RICHARD M. NIXON, vice president of the United States under President Eisenhower, 1953–61; Kennedy's opponent in the 1960 presidential race; president of the United States, 1969–74

Today it is generally assumed that a contender for the nomination of one of the major parties for the presidency will spend years positioning themselves for the final and most visible portion of their campaign. This has not always been the case, but authors Thomas Oliphant and Curtis Wilkie argue in *The Road to Camelot: Inside JFK's Five-Year Campaign* that John F. Kennedy's run for the 1960 Democratic nomination actually began in the fall of 1956, and the book chronicles this five-year campaign for the presidency. They claim that one reason Kennedy decided to pursue the presidential nomination was that at that point in his career, he had nowhere to go but forward.

He had served in the US House of Representatives between 1947 and 1953 and, since
1952, in the US Senate. However, he had not
built a solid reputation as a leader in the Senate, having sponsored no major legislation
and having not been closely identified with
a cause or issue.

*Thomas Oliphant was a political report-
er for the* Boston Globe *from 1968 until
2005. His help in managing the reporting on school desegregation in Boston
contributed to the* Boston Globe *winning
a Pulitzer Prize in 1975. He has written
and cowritten several books.*

When President Dwight D. Eisenhower
had a heart attack in the fall of 1955, Kennedy's father, Joseph P. Kennedy Sr., believed that the health issue would make Eisenhower vulnerable as a candidate for reelection in 1956. He approached Texas senator Lyndon B. Johnson, who had recently
become the majority leader of the Senate, and suggested that he run for president in
1956, with his son, John F. Kennedy, as his vice-presidential candidate. The elder
Kennedy promised plenty of financial support if Johnson became a candidate. Oliphant and Wilkie point out that no evidence exists that Johnson showed any interest
in Joseph Kennedy's proposal. However, John F. Kennedy began to think about the
possibility of becoming a vice-presidential candidate to whoever might emerge as the
Democratic presidential nominee that year. Adlai Stevenson, a former governor of
Illinois and the Democratic candidate defeated by Eisenhower in 1952, succeeded in
getting the Democratic nomination again in 1956, but he decided to have an "open
convention" and allow the delegates to choose his running mate. Kennedy, Minnesota
senator Hubert H. Humphrey, and Tennessee senator Estes Kefauver all maneuvered
behind the scenes to become the nominee, with Kefauver ultimately selected. As it
seemingly became clear that Stevenson was headed for another defeat, Joseph Kennedy saw it best that John was not tarnished by being a part of that losing ticket. The
authors note that by Thanksgiving of that year, Kennedy had committed to running for
the presidency in the 1960 election, and they proceed to illustrate how he and his team
conducted a revolutionary grassroots campaign over the subsequent years.

Given the mythic stature that the Kennedy clan has in the eyes of many people in
Massachusetts, one might question whether two former reporters for the *Boston Globe*
could be objective in writing about John F. Kennedy. The sympathy of the authors for
the subject is evident, but not blatantly so. They do not shy from some of the more
negative aspects of the Kennedy story—his womanizing, his lackluster record in the
House and Senate, and his reluctance, at first, to make any strong commitments on the
civil rights movement, for fear of alienating white southern voters. They also note the
criticism raised when Kennedy took no part in condemning the tactics of Senator Joseph McCarthy's anti-Communist witch hunts. Perhaps where their pro-Kennedy slant
comes through most clearly—and most questionably—is in their defense of Kennedy
against the charge that his 1955 book *Profiles in Courage* was largely ghostwritten.
Ted Sorensen, a significant aide and speechwriter for Kennedy, is the one most commonly mentioned as the writer behind the book, and in his 2008 autobiography, Sorensen claimed that he did write most of the book and received payment for his work
from the Kennedy family. Scholars have generally concluded that the book was ghostwritten, but Oliphant and Wilkie suggest that the book was a "genuine collaboration"

Curtis Wilkie was a national and foreign correspondent for the Boston Globe *from 1975 until after the 2000 presidential election. He teaches journalism at the University of Mississippi and has written and cowritten several books.*

between Kennedy and Sorensen and that the basic conception of the book was all Kennedy's. However, Sorensen's contribution, if any, is never acknowledged in the text of *Profiles in Courage.*

The Kennedy campaign is often pictured as a well-oiled machine that functioned virtually without fault, but Oliphant and Wilkie describe some serious missteps. For example, they conclude that after winning the presidential nomination, "Kennedy basically bungled the process of choosing his running mate." They devote an entire chapter to "Choosing LBJ." Early on, Kennedy recognized that Johnson might be a good running mate—he could help secure the twenty-four Electoral College votes from Texas and, as a southerner, might allay the fear that many southern whites had about Kennedy's liberal views on civil rights. However, Kennedy was convinced that Johnson would never accept the vice presidency; he may have been reflecting his own views in this matter, as from early on in his campaign, he had insisted that he was running for president and had no interest in taking second-billing.

Kennedy went to the convention believing that the most likely vice-presidential prospect was Missouri senator Stuart Symington. Like Johnson, Symington had not actively campaigned for the presidential nomination in 1960, but held to some hope that a deadlocked convention might have to turn to him as a compromise candidate. Oliphant and Wilkie argue that Kennedy either did not understand or simply ignored several clear hints that Johnson would accept the vice-presidential nomination. Kennedy wanted to avoid the embarrassment of making an offer of the vice-presidential slot to anyone and then being refused. Even after deciding to offer the spot to Johnson, the Kennedy team did not handle the situation well and at one point even discussed trying to convince Johnson to withdraw his name from consideration. Oliphant and Wilkie admit that the primary sources left by those who participated in these decisions are contradictory (and possibly self-serving) and that since most of those involved have long since died, the actual details may never be known. Despite the campaign stumbling at times, it is interesting to note that Sorensen, after Kennedy had been nominated, recalled that they had won by doing exactly what Kennedy had outlined five years earlier: they needed to secure "New England, plus the primaries, plus the big Northern states, plus half the west and scattered other votes to make up for a near shutout in the south."

There are points in the book that some readers will find surprising. Some might be argued or mentioned in scattered places among the voluminous secondary literature on Kennedy, but Oliphant and Wilkie have made wide use of archival materials from actual participants in the campaign, including numerous oral interviews collected at the Kennedy Presidential Library. Given the passage of time, most the people who were interviewed have since died. One of the authors' points that goes against the grain of much of the literature on Kennedy is that neither John F. Kennedy nor his brothers were driven or dominated by their father's wishes as much as is generally believed. They listened respectfully to his advice and took his financial support gratefully, but they felt free to make their own choices. Little attention is given to the standard story that Joseph Kennedy Sr. had plans for his firstborn son, Joseph Kennedy Jr., to become president and turned to John only because Joseph Jr. was killed in action in World War II.

Likewise, it may surprise some readers how little Jacqueline Kennedy appears in this book. The widespread photo layouts and television images from the time, with the beautiful young wife at Kennedy's side, seem to suggest she had an integral part in the campaign, but her role is mentioned only briefly at scattered points in the book. Kennedy's Republican opponent in the 1960 campaign, incumbent vice president Richard M. Nixon, is also not discussed as prominently as one might expect. According to Christopher Matthews's *Kennedy and Nixon: The Rivalry That Shaped Postwar America*, published in 1996, the two US Navy veterans and congressmen who entered the House of Representatives at the same time were somewhat friendly toward one another in the early days, but little of that is shown in this book, although Kennedy did at times express some respect for Nixon's political skill. The authors also defy the conventional wisdom about the 1960 campaign by arguing that the televised debates were not as influential as generally believed; they contend that viewers saw the debates as "events" and even if their favored candidate lost the "event," it usually did not change their voting plans.

The Road to Camelot has been received well by journalists, professional historians, and political scientists as a welcome and insightful addition to the literature surrounding Kennedy's 1960 campaign. Reviewers praised its comprehensive coverage, accomplished by the depth of research the authors conducted, which includes personal interviews as well. This book's strengths lie in the detail devoted to the history of the long campaign and the authors' extensive work in the primary sources of the people who worked with Kennedy in his long quest for the presidency.

Mark S. Joy, PhD

Review Sources

Donoghue, Steve. "*The Road to Camelot* Takes a Fresh Look at JFK's 1960 Campaign." Review of *The Road to Camelot: Inside JFK's Five-Year Campaign*, by Thomas Oliphant and Curtis Wilkie. *The Christian Science Monitor*, 11 May 2017, www.csmonitor.com/Books/Book-Reviews/2017/0511/The-Road-to-Camelot-takes-a-fresh-look-at-JFK-s-1960-campaign. Accessed 19 Jan. 2018.

Logevall, Fredrik. "Making of the President, the Reboot." Review of *The Road to Camelot: Inside JFK's Five-Year Campaign*, by Thomas Oliphant and Curtis Wilkie. *The Boston Globe*, 12 May 2017, www.bostonglobe.com/arts/books/2017/05/11/making-president-reboot/yskLJPDbH9Pb9wPq8w6NKJ/story.html. Accessed 19 Jan. 2018.

Review of *The Road to Camelot: Inside JFK's Five-Year Campaign*, by Thomas Oliphant and Curtis Wilkie. *Kirkus*, 2 Mar. 2017, www.kirkusreviews.com/book-reviews/thomas-oliphant/the-road-to-camelot. Accessed 19 Jan. 2018.

Say Nothing

Author: Brad Parks (b. 1974)
Publisher: Dutton (New York). 464 pp.
Type of work: Novel
Time: Present day
Locale: Virginia

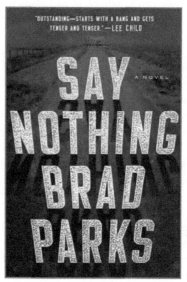

Brad Parks's thriller Say Nothing *presents a plot that could be ripped from the newspaper headlines. A public official is caught on the horns of a dilemma: if he does not exactly follow the orders of a sinister group, he will lose those most precious to him.*

Principal characters
SCOTT A. SAMPSON, the protagonist, a federal judge in Norfolk, Virginia
ALISON POWELL SAMPSON, his wife
SAM AND EMMA SAMPSON, their six-year-old twins
BLAKE FRANKLIN, his former boss, a senator running for reelection
JEREMY FREELAND, his law clerk

Modern life can be particularly perilous for those in positions of power. Public figures are visible targets and are vulnerable to scandals, coups, schemes, and not everyone can be properly protected from human predators. Such is the premise of Brad Parks's domestic suspense novel *Say Nothing*, in which the threat of violence is used to cow and manipulate for evil motives and provide a backdrop for a family's drama when their children are abducted. Parks has covered courtroom cases as a professional journalist writing for the *Washington Post* and has written prize-winning crime mysteries including his series featuring investigative reporter Carter Ross. He brings both his professional journalistic background and experiences of being a father to young children to bear in his first standalone novel.

The novel opens with Scott Sampson, a federal judge in the fifth year of his lifetime appointment, enjoying an enviable lifestyle in rural Virginia with his beautiful wife, Alison, and their bright, energetic six-year-old twins, Sam and Emma. Everything seems normal until Scott receives a text message ostensibly from his wife: she will pick up the kids from first grade at their exclusive Montessori school. But Alison arrives home alone, and denies sending her husband the message. As the couple wonders what happened, Scott receives a call that informs him that his children have been kidnapped. His twins will be held to ensure he follows instructions in deciding a case in court the next day. Scott is informed that he is being watched and if he alerts the law or anyone else, his children will be harmed. "Say nothing," the mysterious caller warns in closing.

The call sets off a fast-paced, tension-filled story punctuated with reactions any father and mother faced with a similar situation might experience: fear of loss, emotional outbursts, unusual physical reactions, moments of panic, bitter recriminations, as well as blame assessment. The story unfolds from the first-person, past-tense viewpoint of protagonist Scott, with occasional glimpses of the captive children, held in a house in an unknown location by two young men with "beards and foreign accents" that may be Turkish, presented in sections written in the third-person. During these sections the reader learns that the kidnappers are merely thuggish agents acting on behalf of at least two other people, one of whom is a woman.

The night before the court case is to be tried, a package arrives at the Samson house that holds clippings of hair from the twins. A note reminds Scott to follow orders, or more than hair will be cut. Although they've been explicitly warned to follow instructions, Scott and Alison begin to surreptitiously investigate how Sam and Emma were taken. Simultaneously, they scramble to cover the fact their children are missing to avoid attracting unwanted attention from law enforcement, thus jeopardizing their children's safety. Scott and Alison learn that witnesses swear—and video footage seems to confirm—that Alison or a lookalike, driving a car identical to the Samson's, took Sam and Emma from school. The children's absence from classes is explained as the result of illness.

At the appointed time, Scott arrives at the courthouse to hear arguments regarding the sentencing of Rayshaun Skavron, a drug dealer with a long record. Skavron sold tainted heroin to a young man, Dylan Byrd, who died of an overdose. During the proceedings, Dylan's father, Thomas Byrd, makes an impassioned plea for justice, asking for a harsh sentence to be handed down on Skavron; guidelines suggest a term of at least twelve years in prison. During testimony, Scott receives a message from the kidnappers: he is to set Skavron free. Scott does as he has been ordered.

The verdict causes pandemonium in the court. But Scott does not care, because as soon as his pronouncement is made, a security guard brings in his son, Sam. The little boy carries a note for his father: the safe return of Sam is Scott's reward for following the directives from the kidnappers. If he wants to see his daughter again, he will continue cooperating. It becomes apparent that Skavron was merely a test case, and the real reason for the kidnapping concerns another case on Scott's busy docket.

Scott rushes Sam home, where he and Alison question their son. They elicit little information, other than a vague description of the kidnappers. Alison's sister, Karen, who lives nearby, shows up for a routine visit. When she asks Sam where Emma is, he blurts out that his sister is with some men. This unintentional revelation forces Scott and Alison to tell Karen what is transpiring and leads to an emergency meeting of Alison's family members at the Samson house. In attendance are Alison's widowed mother Gina, sister Jenny Powell and her husband Jason, and Karen and her husband Mark. The arrival of the families is recorded via miniature cameras the kidnappers have planted around the house and the footage is transmitted to their computer.

Fallout from Scott's decision in the Skavron case begins with contact from Jeb Byers, chief judge of the court of appeals. His appearance indicates a possible first step in the process of Scott's impeachment since, on the surface, it looks like Scott was bribed to release the defendant. Judge Byers informs Scott that Thomas Byrd, the father of Skavron's victim, is a friend of a congressmen Jacobs and his colleague Neil Keesee, who intend to review the reason for Scott's unexpected decision in the drug-dealer's case. To temporarily defuse and delay the situation, Scott tells Byers the Skavron decision was a "matter of conscience," and makes up a story involving an imaginary defendant, Keith Bloom, who was shown mercy and afterward accomplished great things.

Meanwhile, an email from an unknown source alerts Scott to a newspaper article about an upcoming patent infringement case, *Palgraff vs. ApotheGen*, which is on his docket. The case, involving plaintiff Denny Palgraff, alleged inventor of a cholesterol inhibitor drug who is suing a large pharmaceutical company over a trademarked inhibitor maintenance drug, is potentially worth billions of dollars. Scott figures this is probably the cause of the blackmail and extortion being conducted against him and his family. This is confirmed when Palgraff's attorney, Roland Hemans, files an emergency motion for an injunction. Immediately, the kidnappers text Scott, demanding he grant the motion at a specific time, or Emma will suffer. Despite the pleas of trusted clerk Jeremy Freeland to recuse himself from the controversial case, Scott again does as he has been instructed. Soon afterward, news of the filing appears on a financial blog, making Scott wonder who on his staff is leaking information.

A professional newspaper journalist since the mid-1990s, Brad Parks debuted as a novelist with Faces of the Gone *(2009), the first of six books in his award-winning series featuring investigative reporter Carter Ross. Say Nothing (2017) is Parks's first stand-alone novel.*

To find the source of the leak, Scott secretly follows Hemans, but loses the lawyer at a gated community. He then hires a private detective, ex-lawman Herbert Thrift, paying him in cash for four days of around-the-clock surveillance of Hemans. Yet when Hemans files a motion to recuse, based on apparent conflict of interest stemming from ApotheGen's financial support of Scott's former employer, Senator Franklin, Scott realizes Hemans and the plaintiff are likely not involved in the kidnapping. Scott refuses to withdraw from the case. He tells Thrift to stop following Hemans. The detective sends Scott an email of his report, containing photos: in one, Hemans is kissing Jeremy Freeland at the door to the clerk's apartment. Now Scott understands why Jeremy wanted the judge to recuse him; now he knows the source of the information leak.

In this atmosphere of mistrust and emotional upheaval, Scott's paranoia extends to his wife. As their communication breaks down during the abduction, Scott orders Thrift to follow Alison, who he suspects may be having an affair with an old boyfriend. Scott suspects the perpetrator of the kidnapping is someone connected to the defendant in the Palgraff case, but discovering the individual will lead to further deceit, betrayal, violence, and several sudden deaths as the story continues to unfold.

Say Nothing presents a complex plot, in which complications follow organically from the actions of characters and result in logical, if sometimes unforeseen, consequences. The story touches upon the capabilities of surveillance techniques, computers, iPads, cell phones, and other technical devices, and involves detailed discussions of hedge funds, legal documents, laws, and jurisdictional issues that all demand the reader's close attention. Central issues of the novel—the exposure of the culprits, the rescue of young Emma, the strained relationships that arise among various family members during the crisis, and fallout from judicial actions Scott was forced to take that may adversely affect his career—prevail throughout. Parks is skilled at effectively managing multiple subplots. As tension ratchets up, hidden facets of the characters are revealed, making them more flawed, more human, and more engaging. As Scott and Alison's relationship unravels, they become increasingly irrational and paranoid. They accuse one another of terrible things, creating a wedge between them that may be too large to overlook when the crisis is resolved.

Reviews of the novel have been generally positive and note that the book presents not only a powerful plot, but is also emotionally gripping in the realistic depiction of how the parents react to their children's kidnapping. The *Kirkus* reviewer writes that the book has "a climax so harrowing that you'll be shaking with gratitude that it's finally over." The novel does contain some potentially off-putting scenes in which the Samson children are physically abused or graphically threatened by the kidnappers. The depictions are not gratuitous, but serve as discomforting commentary about how far true villains are prepared to go to achieve nefarious ends.

Jack Ewing

Review Sources

Anderson, Patrick. "*Say Nothing* by Brad Parks: A Thriller That Plays on Our Worst Parental Fears." Review of *Say Nothing*, by Brad Parks. *The Washington Post*, 9 Mar. 2017, www.washingtonpost.com/entertainment/books/say-nothing-by-brad-parks-a-thriller-that-plays-on-our-worst-parental-fears/2017/03/09/03136a0c-0283-11e7-ad5b-d22680e18d10_story.html. Accessed 25 Oct. 2017.

Frazier, G. Robert. "*Say Nothing*: Pure Adrenaline in Search for Kidnapped Kids." Review of *Say Nothing*, by Brad Parks. *BookPage*, 7 Mar. 2017, bookpage.com/reviews/21101-brad-parks-say-nothing#. Accessed 25 Oct. 2017.

Hubbard, Frances. "Thriller Set on Middle Peninsula Plays Out Parents' Worst Nightmare." *Daily Press*, 23 July 2017, www.dailypress.com/news/gloucester-county/dp-nws-evg-mid-say-nothing-book-20170630-story.html. Accessed 25 Oct. 2017.

Mira, Nicola. "*Say Nothing*—Brad Parks." Review of *Say Nothing*, by Brad Parks. *Thriller Books Journal*, 3 Mar. 2017, www.thrillerbooksjournal.com/say-nothing-brad-parks/. Accessed 25 Oct. 2017.

Review of *Say Nothing*, by Brad Parks. *Kirkus*, 19 Dec. 2016, www.kirkusreviews.com/book-reviews/brad-parks/say-nothing/. Accessed 25 Oct. 2017.

See What I Have Done

Author: Sarah Schmidt (b. 1979)
Publisher: Atlantic Monthly Press (New York). 336 pp.
Type of work: Novel
Time: August 1892
Locale: Fall River, Massachusetts

Courtesy of Grove Atlantic

Sarah Schmidt's debut novel, See What I Have Done, *delves into the interior lives of the Borden family in August 1892, the month in which the notorious axe murders of patriarch Andrew Borden and his second wife, Abby, were committed. Andrew's daughter Lizzie was charged with and eventually acquitted of these real-life murders. Schmidt's fictional story creates compelling psychological portraits of the family members while exploring their daily lives, which were filled with small hurts and petty jealousies that may have inspired one of them to commit murder.*

Principal characters

LIZZIE BORDEN, a Sunday school teacher
ANDREW BORDEN, her father, a prominent businessman
ABBY BORDEN, her stepmother
EMMA BORDEN, her sister
JOHN MORSE, her maternal uncle
BRIDGET SULLIVAN, a maid in the Borden household
BENJAMIN, a transient prone to violence

Since Lizzie Borden was accused, put on trial, and then acquitted of the murders of her father and stepmother, Andrew and Abby Borden, in 1892, scores of books have been written about Lizzie and the murders. Some are nonfiction accounts of the family and the trial, such as Arnold R. Brown's *Lizzie Borden: The Legend, the Truth, the Final Chapter* (1991), while others, such as Evan Hunter's *Lizzie* (1984), are fictionalized accounts that draw from the history of the trial and of Fall River, Massachusetts, where the murders took place. Did Lizzie Borden get away with murdering her own father and stepmother because a jury of her peers did not think a woman could commit such a crime, or was she rightly acquitted and the real culprit neither convicted nor found? Though the truth will most likely never be known, the speculation continues in Sarah Schmidt's debut novel, *See What I Have Done*. Schmidt is less interested in the identity of the murderer than she is in the motive, and her scrutiny of the Borden household, through a handful of narrators and a visceral writing style, results in a vivid and unsettling portrait of a troubled home and a family consumed with jealousies and resentments.

Schmidt's decisions to focus intensely on two particular days surrounding the murders and to include four different narrators elevate this novel and offer a fresh perspective on a well-known case. Schmidt's narration is divided between two family insiders, sisters Emma and Lizzie Borden, and two family outsiders, Bridget Sullivan and Benjamin. Bridget is employed as the Borden's maid, while Benjamin is a transient who has just arrived in Fall River and has a violent past. Since Schmidt alternates narrators with every chapter, readers piece together the puzzle-like events leading up to the murders while gaining insight into family relationships. Lizzie, for example, who at thirty-two is almost ten years younger than Emma, reminds Emma often of the promise she made to their dying mother to always watch out for Lizzie; she uses that promise to her advantage whenever possible, especially when Emma wants to leave and pursue a life of her own. With the exception of chapter 15, which is dated May 6, 1905, Schmidt also dates every chapter as either August 3, 1892 (the day before the murders), or August 4, 1892 (the day of the murders), choosing to highlight the events leading up to the murders rather than the later trial. In addition to providing the novel with a tight focus and emphasizing the claustrophobia within the household, this strategy also requires the characters to reminisce about past events so that they may be included in the narrative, further allowing Schmidt to build her complex portraits of the family members and their dysfunctional relationships.

While all four narrators contribute significantly to the story, Schmidt's portrayal of Lizzie shows the author's skill at characterization. Lizzie is by turns loving, childlike, and willful, a masterful liar and manipulator one minute and showering affection and kindness on her beloved pigeons the next. Schmidt also captures the deep-seated determination that fuels much of Lizzie's behavior, such as when she blackmails Emma into letting her have Emma's bigger bedroom, which she has long coveted. Lizzie is a fascinating combination of guile and childishness. In the days leading up to the murder, she demonstrates several of these qualities when, after having nightmares, she insists on crawling into her father and stepmother's bed because Emma is away visiting a friend:

> Mrs. Borden let out a little moan, pulled herself onto her elbows and sat up. She stared at me, the longest time, and I looked at her, the way the corners of her lips drooped and flattened. Then I looked at the space in the bed next to her, the space where Father had been, *it's probably still warm*, and Mrs. Borden followed my gaze, shook her head and shook her head. "No," she whispered. It made me feel like I was thirteen, like the day Father and Mrs. Borden hadn't wanted me in their bed anymore. "You can't keep coming in here after you have a nightmare, Lizzie." Father and his mean words. It took me time to get over it.

The fact that a thirty-two-year-old woman would want to climb into the bed of her stepmother, a woman she has grown to despise, because of a bad dream is childlike

Courtesy of Nicholas Purcell Studio

Sarah Schmidt coordinates the reading and literacy program for a regional public library in Australia. See What I Have Done *is her first novel.*

at best. That childishness is reinforced when Lizzie remembers her father's "mean words" for denying her entrance to their bed at age thirteen. Her father and stepmother agree that it is inappropriate to continue to allow Lizzie in their bed, but here she refuses to accept her role as an adult. While Lizzie is clearly upset by her dream and in need of comfort, it is also clear that she is determined to have her own way, and she stares at Abby, who has already said no, until she changes her mind and relents. Again, this is childish stubbornness, but it is also Lizzie asserting her dominance in the only way she can. She is controlled and often infantilized by her father and stepmother, and Schmidt's compelling characterization shows how that treatment has turned her into a crafty manipulator who is adept at controlling others.

The other standout feature of the novel is Schmidt's writing style, which incorporates repetition and visceral description, sometimes resulting in dreamlike passages. Schmidt especially focuses on the senses of smell and taste. In the opening passage of the novel, Schmidt introduces Lizzie, who finds her father, dead, in the parlor:

> He was still bleeding. I yelled, "Someone's killed Father." I breathed in kerosene air, licked the thickness from my teeth. The clock on the mantel ticked ticked. I looked at Father, the way hands clutched to thighs, the way the little gold ring on his pinkie finger sat like a sun. I gave him that ring for his birthday when I no longer wanted it. "Daddy," I had said, "I'm giving this to you because I love you." He had smiled and kissed my forehead.

The "kerosene air" implies a kind of incipient combustibility, representing either the murders, the metaphorical flames of which will consume the whole household and then the city, or Lizzie's own emotions, which she has difficulty containing. Schmidt uses the repetitive phrase "ticked ticked" in this passage and at other points in the novel, not only to show the passage of time, but also to invoke noise in the overwhelmingly silent household, the inhabitants of which seethe over perceived wrongs.

Lizzie's childlike wonder is in evidence in next paragraphs of the opening scene as well. She touches her father's bleeding hand, not to check for a pulse to see if he might still be alive, but to contemplate if even in death he might recognize her. She then wipes her bloody hand across her mouth, tasting her father's blood. This action does not appear to upset her, and she repeats it at the end of the passage, prompting speculation as to whether this is a conscious or unconscious act. These visceral details and repeated actions result in dreamlike passages that make it unclear whether Lizzie can separate fiction from reality. Schmidt uses these strategies and others to great effect throughout the novel to create contradictory, layered characters and to keep readers guessing about the identity of the murderer.

While critics have pointed out a few of the novel's flaws, the reviews were overall overwhelmingly positive. Patrick McGrath, writing for the *New York Times*, found the character of Benjamin so far removed from the story line that his narration was a distraction, though his chapters, like the others, are well-written, engrossing, and vivid. Some reviewers, such as McGrath and Mariko Hewer for the *Washington Independent Review of Books*, found the timeline confusing, since the constant bouncing back and forth between August 3 and August 4 makes it somewhat difficult to pinpoint the order of events. In general, however, critics agreed that Schmidt's portrayal of Lizzie and her visceral writing style make for a strong and compelling novel. Schmidt creates a stomach-churning feeling of claustrophobia within the household, with characters listening in on private conversations from the back staircase or bumping into one another in the too-small kitchen. The members of this troubled family cannot escape one another, resulting in a gripping page-turner of a novel.

Marybeth Rua-Larsen

Review Sources

Bradley, James. "*See What I Have Done*: Sarah Schmidt's Take on Some Murderous Minds." Review of *See What I Have Done*, by Sarah Schmidt. *The Australian*, 22 Apr. 2017, www.theaustralian.com.au/arts/review/see-what-i-have-done-sarah-schmidts-take-on-some-murderous-minds/news-story/551672d11f34ff1d49496f03c1a7a11d. Accessed 27 Dec. 2017.

Cha, Steph. "New Novel about Lizzie Borden Is a Bloody Good Read." Review of *See What I Have Done*, by Sarah Schmidt. *USA Today*, 31 July 2017, www.usatoday.com/story/life/books/2017/07/31/new-novel-lizzie-borden-bloody-good-read/513001001/. Accessed 27 Dec. 2018.

Hewer, Mariko. Review of *See What I Have Done*, by Sarah Schmidt. *Washington Independent Review of Books*, 29 July 2017, www.washingtonindependentreviewofbooks.com/index.php/bookreview/see-what-i-have-done-a-novel. Accessed 27 Dec. 2017.

Jordan, Justine. "*See What I Have Done* by Sarah Schmidt Review: Inside the Mind of Lizzie Borden." Review of *See What I Have Done*, by Sarah Schmidt. *The Guardian*, 27 Apr. 2017, www.theguardian.com/books/2017/apr/27/see-what-i-have-done-sarah-schmidt-lizzie-borden-book-review. Accessed 27 Dec. 2017.

McGrath, Patrick. "Inside Lizzie Borden's House of Horror." Review of *See What I Have Done*, by Sarah Schmidt. *The New York Times*, 22 Aug. 2017, www.nytimes.com/2017/08/22/books/review/see-what-i-have-done-sarah-schmidt.html. Accessed 27 Dec. 2017.

Scholes, Lucy. "Book Review: *See What I Have Done* Is a Sensory Take on a Sensational Murder Case." Review of *See What I Have Done*, by Sarah Schmidt. *The National*, 11 May 2017, www.thenational.ae/arts-culture/book-review-see-what-i-have-done-is-a-sensory-take-on-a-sensational-murder-case-1.14726. Accessed 27 Dec. 2017.

She Rides Shotgun

Author: Jordan Harper
Publisher: Ecco (New York). 272 pp.
Type of work: Novel
Time: Present day
Locales: Various locations in California

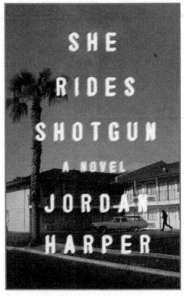

When eleven-year-old Polly McClusky's mother is murdered by gang members under orders from their leader, an imprisoned man who is an enemy of her recently released and long-estranged father, she embarks on a crime spree and life on the run with him in an effort to avoid either of them meeting a similar fate and, ultimately, to avenge the death.

Courtesy of Ecco

Principal characters

POLLY MCCLUSKY, a shy eleven-year-old
    girl
NATE MCCLUSKY, her father, an ex-convict
JOHN PARK, a police detective
CHARLOTTE, a woman connected to the Aryan Steel gang
HOUSER, a crooked sheriff
CRAZY CRAIG HOLLINGTON, leader of the Aryan Steel gang
BOXER, member of La Eme, a Mexican crime group

She Rides Shotgun is the debut novel from author Jordan Harper, who worked for several years as a screenwriter for the network television crime drama *The Mentalist* (2010–15) and previously published a collection of short stories titled *Love and Other Wounds* (2015). Similar to the stories in his earlier collection, *She Rides Shotgun* has a dark tone, a theme of flawed humanity, and a crime-centered plotline. This novel challenges ideas of who can be a hero or villain, as well as what kinds of actions are acceptable when a life is on the line.

    One of the strongest aspects of the novel, established from her introduction in its first pages, is the well-developed characterization of eleven-year-old protagonist Polly. Harper has explained in interviews that he rewrote his first draft of the novel to devote more time to Polly's perspective than he had originally. Both childishly naïve and deeply insightful, this paradoxical personality is revealed cleverly through her interactions with her beloved stuffed bear, which she carries with her at all times. Like a puppeteer, she makes the bear act out her reactions to the situations around her, essentially serving as a conduit for her emotions. In fact, early on, she remembers her mother saying, "Some days I feel like I know what that stuffed bear is thinking a hell of a lot more than I know what *you're* thinking." Polly's inability to confidently display her deep-seated intelligence also comes out in her repeated assertions that she must be from Venus. The child chooses Venus while reading a book after her mother shares the school counselor's opinion that her intelligence is at a genius level: "The book said that while Venus looked tranquil, that was just how it looked from the outside. . . . That was the way Polly felt, that outside she was quiet and calm but inside her acid winds roared." These two more abstract mechanisms of guarding herself serve successfully as sharp contrasts to the literal and more mature methods of defense she must learn and engage in later in the story.

The major plotline of the novel is, in many ways, a coming-of-age story for this eleven-year-old child. After all, she is an insecure and awkward child at the beginning, unable to act on her own despite a great level of intelligence. The story begins when Nate, Polly's father, turns up outside of her school in Fontana, California, after a five-year incarceration. At this point, Polly is torn and frightened. All she really knows of her father came from her mother: "Her dad was a bad guy and a robber and he was supposed to be in jail. He liked being a bad guy more than he'd liked being a husband or a father, that's what her mom said." She knows that his presence foretells of something dangerous, even though he explains that he was released legally; she goes along with him regardless, only rebelling briefly and quietly.

Although She Rides Shotgun *is Jordan Harper's first novel, he had previously published a short-story collection titled* Love and Other Wounds *(2015). In addition to writing these fictional pieces, he has worked in music journalism, as a film critic, and as a screenwriter.*

Within hours, Polly's father has equipped her with a baseball bat and left her alone in a motel room with only instructions to swing at anyone who tries to break in. Then, only moments after the pair's first run-in with one of the members of the gang Aryan Steel who has an order to kill Nate and his family as retribution for a life he took while in prison (that of imprisoned gang leader Crazy Craig Hollington's brother), sparks of a stronger personality show through when Polly gives in to her emotions and tries to throw herself from the car upon learning that her mother has already died. Later, overwhelmed by feelings of loneliness and clutching her bear, she calls John Park, the detective working the case of the double murder and missing persons, and informs him of their location. When her father is hurt in his confrontation with the man who directly killed her mother, and he asks her for help for the first time in order to get first aid materials, she automatically thinks to herself, "Didn't he know she was just a kid? Couldn't he see she was from Venus?"

Polly slowly but surely begins to change, however. Her father's determined quest to remove the price from her head at any cost serves as both a strangely heartwarming bonding experience with a man she barely knows and a psychologically disturbing illustration of the vengeance she craves against those who killed her mother, and of the lengths a man will go to in order to save his daughter's life. Though Nate eventually gives her the choice to be turned over to the police, she decides to stay, and as she becomes involved in his plot to ruin the Aryan Steel's business ventures and force a truce, she becomes stronger and more active in transforming herself. For instance, she and Nate resolve that she must be disguised for her safety, so she chooses red hair dye and both colors and cuts her own hair. Emerging from the process, she recognizes when looking in the mirror, "Her face looked different now, something there now that hadn't been there before, or maybe something that used to be there was gone." This physical transformation allows her an emotional growth as well, as she fully joins her father's crusade against the man who wants them dead, becoming a different person both inside and out. Training with her father, she learns to fight, taking the steps and participating in the crimes necessary to ensure freedom from their death sentences.

The story of these two conflicted characters follows several intertwined subplots told through alternating character viewpoints. Though the majority of the chapters, written from the third-person point of view, are devoted to Polly and Nate, with Harper successfully transitioning between the two drastically different characters, others focus on more minor characters. Tied together with Nate and Polly's quest to gain freedom by ruining the Aryan Steel's financial empire are three other brief stories centering on minor characters: Charlotte, a woman who has been coerced into service by Aryan Steel but wants out; Park, the detective who has been assigned to Polly's case; and Houser, a corrupt sheriff who runs an underground drug ring. Overall, the novel is broken down into four major parts chronicling Nate and Polly's mission to outsmart and defeat their enemies. Between the second and third parts, there is a short, unnumbered chapter titled "Interlude: Whale Ship Cannibals; The High Desert." This seven-page chapter sets up an ever more dangerous situation for Nate while serving as a unifying element to foreshadow a situation that might be Nate and Polly's salvation from the Aryan Steel.

Due to Harper's instinctual commitment to make the story more about Polly, Nate's characterization is less developed throughout the novel than that of his daughter, and the changes he experiences are subsequently subtler but still poignant. He is violent and ostensibly self-centered from the beginning, yet he is both villain and hero. Through his villainy, he killed a man in prison. The death was, ironically, a reaction that should have saved his life once he left, but it turned into the bounty on his head as well as the heads of his ex-wife and child. He is a hard man, both physically and emotionally, but as the days pass, he develops a strange and, under the circumstances by which it is molded, often disturbing friendship with his daughter. He teaches her to hide, to steal, and to fight. His life becomes a crusade to save his daughter's life. By the end of the novel, readers will likely sympathize with a man whose seemingly unrepentant violence should make him unsympathetic.

The critical reception of Harper's debut novel has been primarily positive. Keir Graff, for instance, wrote of it for *Booklist*, "From its bravura prologue to its immensely satisfying ending, this first novel . . . comes out with guns blazing and shoots the chambers dry. It's both a dark, original take on the chase novel and a strangely touching portrait of a father-daughter relationship framed in barbed wire." *Booklist* also included the book in its list of best crime novels for 2017. The reviewer for *Publishers Weekly* called *She Rides Shotgun* "visceral" and lauded Harper's "expert pacing and well-developed characters," and the reviewer for *Kirkus Reviews* described it as a "grim yet moving tale," also praising its "striking images" and underlying "moral core." Less positive commentary was limited, noting the overuse of vernacular language and a climax that came across as a bit too outrageous. As a caveat, however, critics also noted that such issues did not take away from the overall impact of the work.

Though Harper has expressed in interviews that he was initially concerned about trying to get into the mindset of an eleven-year-old girl, his efforts paid off in his ability to create a complex character in a compelling story. Fans of dark crime drama will be drawn into the novel, and Harper's style can be compared to that of James Ellroy, while the story line is similar to popular television programming such as *Breaking Bad* (2008–13). Harper provides a book that is gritty and rough but also affecting, offering appealing aspects for a wide readership.

Theresa L. Stowell, PhD

Review Sources

Frazier, G. Robert. "Heart-Pounding Suspense for Summer." Review of *She Rides Shotgun*, by Jordan Harper, et al. *BookPage*, July 2017, bookpage.com/features/21499-heart-pounding-suspense-summer. Accessed 26 Sept. 2017.

Graff, Keir. Review of *She Rides Shotgun*, by Jordan Harper. *Booklist*, 1 Apr. 2017, p. 26. *Academic Search Complete*, search.ebscohost.com/login.aspx?direct=true&db=a9h&AN=122226686&site=ehost-live. Accessed 26 Sept. 2017.

Review of *She Rides Shotgun*, by Jordan Harper. *Kirkus Reviews*, 1 Apr. 2017, p. 302. *Academic Search Complete*, search.ebscohost.com/login.aspx?direct=true&db=a9h&AN=122253203&site=ehost-live. Accessed 26 Sept. 2017.

Review of *She Rides Shotgun*, by Jordan Harper. *Publishers Weekly*, 24 Apr. 2017, p. 68. *Academic Search Complete*, search.ebscohost.com/login.aspx?direct=true&db=a9h&AN=122683144&site=ehost-live. Accessed 26 Sept. 2017.

The Signal Flame

Author: Andrew Krivák
Publisher: Scribner (New York). 272 pp.
Type of work: Novel
Time: 1972
Locale: Fictional town of Dardan, Pennsylvania

The Signal Flame *is a novel that explores the nature of loss. It is the sequel to American author Andrew Krivák's award-winning book* The Sojourn *(2011).*

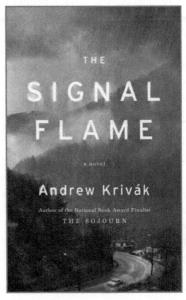

Courtesy of Scribner

Principal characters

JOZEF VINICH, an immigrant from the former Austro-Hungarian Empire who leaves his Pennsylvania property to his daughter and grandson before dying

HANNAH KONAR, his daughter, a distraught mother whose youngest son, Sam, has gone missing during the Vietnam War

BO KONAR, Hannah's eldest son, a former academic who dropped out of college

SAM KONAR, Hannah's youngest son, who enlisted in the US Marine Corps and has been declared missing in action during the Vietnam War

RUTH YOUNGER, Sam's pregnant fiancée; the daughter of the man who accidentally killed Bo and Sam's father

Andrew Krivák's first novel, *The Sojourn* (2011), was a deeply personal work of fiction. In interviews, Krivák has said that the inspiration for the protagonist, Jozef Vinich, a young American-born boy who is brought back to the "old country" (in part of the Austro-Hungarian Empire of the late nineteenth and early twentieth centuries) by his Slovak father, was his own grandfather. Like Jozef, Krivák's grandfather fought in World War I for the Austro-Hungarian army. Krivák often wondered how his grandfather survived, especially after being detained in a POW camp. He decided to explore war and survival in *The Sojourn*, a novel about the bonds of family as well as the tenuous nature of ethnic identity. Infused with a sense of familial authenticity, *The Sojourn* would go on to become a National Book Award finalist for fiction.

Krivák's second novel, *The Signal Flame* (2017), continues the story of Jozef Vinich's family. Set over the course of several months during 1972 in rural Pennsylvania, the narrative begins with the immediate aftermath of Jozef's death. It focuses primarily on the experiences of his daughter Hannah and her eldest son, Bo, who inherit Jozef's property. Although Jozef died unexpectedly, his family's capacity to mourn is somewhat diluted by the fact that Hannah's youngest son, Sam, has been declared missing in action by the US Marine Corps. Sam had been shipped to Vietnam just a few months earlier, leaving behind his pregnant fiancée, Ruth. While the family tries to stay hopeful that Sam will eventually surface, they cannot seem to escape a feeling of inevitable doom.

There are many themes throughout *The Signal Flame*, but none are quite as prominent as that of loss. Krivák makes it clear from early in the novel that the Vinich-Konar family is one that has experienced more than its share of grief. Through flashbacks, the author reveals how Hannah's husband, Bexhet, was accidentally shot and killed by their neighbor, Paul Younger, while he was hunting deer on their property one morning. As a result, Bo and Sam were raised with Jozef, whom they refer to as "Pop," as the primary paternal force in their lives. In another tragic event, Bo leaves his hometown to study classics at a college in Maryland and falls in love with one of his classmates, a Slovak American named Ann, who dies during Christmas break after being hit by a car. Devastated, Bo decides he will not return to school. He reveals this decision to Jozef, who tells his grandson that loss causes people to become "lessened and left behind." Combined with the deaths of his father and Ann, the death of Jozef and the uncertain fate of Sam paint Bo as an especially tragic character—one who is at the mercy of the world and its capriciousness.

Krivák's use of death is not senseless, however, but helps bring a larger topic into focus: the impact of twentieth-century global politics on everyday people's lives. Each of the three generations of the Vinich-Konar family have been devastated by a major world war. Jozef fought in World War I, losing many of the people closest to him in the process. His son-in-law, Bexhet, served in the American army during World War II before being imprisoned for desertion and losing precious years of what would prove to be a short life in the process. The shipment of the family's youngest member, Sam, to Vietnam destroys what little faith his family has left in serving one's nation. Through the stories of these men, Krivák demonstrates just how high the cost of war can be.

Although *The Signal Flame* is a work of historical fiction, it does not have an overly complex plot. More than anything, it can be described as a slice-of-life novel, one that provides insight into the day-to-day existence of rural Pennsylvanians and Slovak immigrants during the 1970s. Krivák spends a sizeable part of the narrative describing Bo's work at the roughing mill he took over from his grandfather as well as Hannah's work tending to the family property. As they engage in physical labor, they reflect on major and minor events of their lives. Overall, the prose feels lived in and authentic, from the joy of sitting next to a warm hearth during the Pennsylvania winters to Hannah's preparation of sour mushroom soup and prune pirohy. And while the plot may seem simple at first glance, it in fact aligns to what the story is about: waiting. This is evident in the novel's title, which is a reference to the quote—included in the book as an epigraph—from Aeschylus's play *Agamemnon* (458 BCE): "So now I am still awatch for the signal-flame, the gleaming fire that is to harbinger news from Troy." Through the Vinich-Konar family, Krivák examines the nebulous, purgatorial experience of waiting for news that will change the trajectory of one's life, and the oppositional forces of hope and dread are omnipresent throughout the narrative.

Krivák establishes the solemn tone of *The Signal Flame* in several different ways.

This is primarily evident in the novel's setting of the fictional town of Dardan, Pennsylvania. Krivák describes it as a rural town set amidst the Allegheny mountains, where most of the men work at a lumber roughing mill. He evokes quiet, natural imagery—expansive forests and herds of deer surround country homes. This depiction of Pennsylvania wilderness effectively amplifies the feeling of isolation that the characters are experiencing while navigating their grief. The way in which Krivák writes dialogue also bolsters the tone. Throughout the novel, the characters speak in simple, succinct language; most characters say what they mean without subtext. Combined with the stylistic choice to exclude quotation marks, the dialogue feels organically wrought and serious at the same time.

Andrew Krivák was a National Book Award finalist and received the 2012 Dayton Literary Peace Prize for his first novel, The Sojourn *(2011). The Signal Flame is his second novel.*

The Signal Flame is also evenhanded in its handling of gender despite the fact that the narrative's perspective seems male. Much of the story focuses on Bo, the eldest son, as he navigates the recent death of his grandfather as well as the impact of Sam's status as missing in action. As the last man of the family left, Bo's responsibilities are to take care of the women in his life, which include his mother, Hannah, and Sam's fiancée, Ruth. Still, the female characters are intelligent, multidimensional, and far from helpless. Bo and the other male characters also go against gendered stereotypes by being strong, physical laborers who define themselves as men by family and love rather than their combat experience.

As a writer, Krivák often employs the literary tool of irony. This tendency is primarily evident in the character of Ruth Younger. Although Sam could have fallen in love with any of the young women in the town of Dardan, he is drawn to Ruth, the daughter of the man who killed his father. She does not find out that she is pregnant until it is too late and Sam has already left for Vietnam. Krivák uses irony to bolster the drama of the narrative and the significance of these events in the characters' lives. Once Sam has been declared missing, Hannah and Bo are forced to develop a relationship with Ruth and try to learn to forgive her family. Krivák thus demonstrates that tragedy can be an opportunity for connection and absolution.

The reviews of *The Signal Flame* have been overwhelmingly positive, with many critics extolling the beauty of Krivák's writing and storytelling. In her review for the *New York Times*, Roxana Robinson wrote, "Krivák is an extraordinarily elegant writer, with a deep awareness of the natural world. In spare and beautiful prose, he evokes an austere landscape, a struggling family and a deep source of pain." It is true that Krivák's literary prowess is a large part of what makes *The Signal Flame* such an engaging read. He has a deft ability to capture grief in a subtle, yet powerful way through the strong development of his characters. Furthermore, the language he uses for descriptions of even the smallest, most insignificant moments is highly poetic. As such, the novel's seemingly simple story line is elevated and resonant.

One of the criticisms that can be made of *The Signal Flame* is that, at times, it can feel dark, heavy, and pessimistic. The reviewer for *Kirkus Reviews* described the novel as "a dark commemoration of a dark time but offering the slim hope that things will get better." The Konar-Vinich family is subjected to what seems like endless tragedies, which continue to unfold until the very end of the narrative. For readers, it can be difficult to accept that one family should have to endure so much loss in such a short amount of time. However, Krivák manages to use these events to demonstrate how capable humans are of compassion and love in life's worst moments, giving the story even greater nuance. As Jim Carmin wrote for the *Star Tribune*, "As more calamities unfold, the novel threatens to become one of despair and woe, yet the opposite occurs." Even though members of the Vinich-Konar family have experienced excessive loss, they find unexpected ways to rebuild their family in the rubble of their losses. In this way, the novel proves to be one of hope.

Ultimately, *The Signal Flame* is a beautifully written, compelling story. Krivák successfully mines from his own Slovak American childhood to ensure that the members of the Vinich-Konar family feel like authentic, relatable characters. It is through these characters that the author provides a unique perspective on the twentieth century and the way in which its continuous warfare devastated generations of men and their families places *The Signal Flame* alongside works such as Kurt Vonnegut's *Slaughterhouse-Five* (1969) and Tim O'Brien's *The Things They Carried* (1990). Beyond its sociopolitical commentary, however, *The Signal Flame* succeeds as a novel about the powerful experiences of loss, waiting, and hope.

Emily Turner

Review Sources

Carmin, Jim. Review of *The Signal Flame*, by Andrew Krivák. *The Star Tribune*, 30 Jan. 2017, www.startribune.com/review-the-signal-flame-by-andrew-krivak/411924636/. Accessed 26 Feb. 2018.

Robinson, Roxana. "For Two Small-Town Families, War Is the Tie That Binds." Review of *The Signal Flame*, by Andrew Krivák. *The New York Times*, 27 Jan. 2017, www.nytimes.com/2017/01/27/books/review/signal-flame-andrew-krivak.html. Accessed 26 Feb. 2018.

Review of *The Signal Flame*, by Andrew Krivák. *Kirkus Reviews*, 19 Oct. 2016, www.kirkusreviews.com/book-reviews/andrew-krivak-2/the-signal-flame/. Accessed 26 Feb. 2018.

Review of *The Signal Flame*, by Andrew Krivák. *Publishers Weekly*, 7 Nov. 2016, www.publishersweekly.com/978-1-5011-2637-6. Accessed 26 Feb. 2018.

Sing, Unburied, Sing

Author: Jesmyn Ward (b. 1977)
Publisher: Scribner (New York). 304 pp.
Type of work: Novel
Time: Largely after 2005
Locale: Mississippi

Courtesy of Scribner

Sing, Unburied, Sing *is a novel that follows an African American family living on the Gulf Coast in Mississippi that is haunted by the past. It is American writer Jesmyn Ward's third novel.*

Principal characters

JOJO, a thirteen-year-old boy who lives with his mother, sister, and grandparents on a farm

LEONIE, his mother, an African American woman

MICHAEL, his father, a white man who has been in prison for three years

POP, his grandfather, who runs a farm with livestock

MAM, his grandmother

KAYLA, his little sister

RICHIE, a dead boy whom Pop was incarcerated with decades earlier and one of the novel's narrators

The American South has long proved to be a rich tapestry for writers—a fact that has been well illustrated by authors such as Mark Twain (1835–1910), William Faulkner (1897–1962), and Harper Lee (1926–2016). And while it is considered inspirational for a number of different reasons, perhaps the most significant is the contradictions that run deep within the region's culture. On the surface, the South is composed of communities where wholesome Christian values reign supreme and everyone knows one another's names. However, it is also a place where such community members inflict terror and project prejudice on their neighbors, as evidenced by the history of harassment and violence imposed on African Americans who live there that has continued into the twenty-first century.

Mississippi native Jesmyn Ward is a writer who continues this tradition of using the South as a microcosm within which to examine America as a whole and its dark history. This first became evident in her breakthrough, National Book Award–winning novel *Salvage the Bones* (2011), which follows a working-class African American family over the course of twelve days leading up to and during Hurricane Katrina, the 2005 natural disaster that devastated the Gulf Coast and the lives of many people who lived there. Inspired by Ward's own experience surviving the hurricane, *Salvage the Bones* takes an unapologetic look at the second-class citizen treatment of African Americans and how such treatment instills fragile fault lines in families that easily break into irreparable fractures in times of crisis.

In many ways, Ward's brilliant third novel, *Sing, Unburied, Sing* (2017), feels like a continuation of *Salvage the Bones*. Like its predecessor, *Sing, Unburied, Sing* is about an African American family living in the fictional town of Bois Sauvage, Mississippi. Although it is set several years after Hurricane Katrina, the book is also about marginalized characters facing forces of impending doom. Furthermore, *Sing, Unburied, Sing* is a narrative that focuses especially on the experiences of young people of color living in the South. Just as *Salvage the Bones* was predominantly about teenaged brother and sister Skeetah and Esch, the two major story lines of *Sing, Unburied, Sing* are those of thirteen-year-old Jojo and his mother, Leonie.

The novel follows these two characters, shifting back and forth between their first-person, present-tense narrations. Jojo is the more likeable narrator of the two. Ward depicts Jojo as a sensitive, observant individual. These are qualities that allow him to take care of his younger sister, Kayla, as well as the animals on the farm on which they live. The only person Jojo does not understand is his mother; it is this lack of understanding that creates a conflicted, albeit compelling, dynamic between the two characters. Meanwhile, Jojo idolizes his grandfather, Pop, and frequently asks him to tell stories about the time he was unjustly sent to a prison called Parchman decades earlier. Pop's stories about his time at Parchman act as a vessel to introduce readers to the character of Richie. Richie was an African American boy sent to Parchman prison at the age of twelve, where, like the other inmates, he was beaten and made to work the fields like a slave. He died at Parchman and eventually becomes the third *Sing, Unburied, Sing* narrator.

Although Leonie is a less sympathetic character, she is still presented as deeply human. This is thanks to Ward's decision to write all of her characters with the same level of honest vulnerability. A young mother with two children, Leonie works as a cocktail waitress and struggles with drug abuse. She is a directionless individual until the night of Jojo's thirteenth birthday, when she receives a phone call that his father, Michael, is being released from prison. It is a seemingly innocuous moment that proves to be the novel's inciting incident, as Leonie decides that it is an opportunity for her family to be whole again. She takes Jojo and Kayla on a road trip to pick Michael up, bringing her friend Misty along. Before they leave, Misty convinces Leonie to use the trip as a chance to transport meth for a drug dealer; she agrees and thereby instigates a tragic series of events that unfold throughout the rest of the novel.

Ward's choice to alternate between different perspectives and use a first-person, stream-of-consciousness style of writing is a powerful literary tool. From chapter to chapter, readers are exposed to completely different perspectives on the exact same events. It is especially emotionally wrenching to learn how an alienated mother and son view one another. For example, Leonie thinks she is taking the actions necessary to bring her family together and subsequently is being a good mother. Contrarily, Jojo thinks she is a selfish, incompetent caretaker and does not even call her "Mom" but instead refers to her by her first name. He resents her for the way she treats his baby

Courtesy of Beowulf Sheehan

Jesmyn Ward is an American novelist best known for her best-selling and National Book Award–winning novel Salvage the Bones *(2011). An associate professor at Tulane University, in 2017 she was awarded her second National Book Award for fiction.*

sister, a character who symbolically embodies the different ways that Jojo and Leonie view the world. This is apparent even in the names they use for her; where Jojo affectionately calls his sister "Kayla," Leonie refers to her only as "Michaela." Ultimately, it is Ward's masterful use of multiple character perspectives combined with the setting of the American South that makes *Sing, Unburied, Sing* feel as though it belongs in the same canon as the Faulkner novel *As I Lay Dying* (1930).

As a work of literature, *Sing, Unburied, Sing* can be categorized as magical realism. Although the characters operate in a contemporary world, they endure supernatural experiences. This is primarily evident in the way that Ward shows how the dead continue to exist among the living. Whenever Leonie uses drugs, she sees her dead brother, Given. A high school football star, Given was killed years earlier by his white teammates on a hunting trip. The character of Richie is another ghost that follows Jojo around and provides a third-person perspective about the boy and his family's experiences. Beyond the presence of the dead, there are other aspects of the narrative that qualify it as magical realism. For instance, many of the characters have special abilities. Most notably, Jojo can understand what animals are saying. It is a power that he shares with his relative, River, whom he looks like. Between the presence of ghosts and characters with special powers, *Sing, Unburied, Sing* ostensibly should be designated as fantasy. However, Ward employs these elements in such a way that the story feels like a slightly heightened reality.

One of the most powerful themes of *Sing, Unburied, Sing* is that of generational racism. Through the story of Pop and Richie's time at Parchman, readers learn how African American men were treated as slaves long into the twentieth century. After Pop is sent to Parchman prison for upsetting some white men, he is forced to work the fields. Anyone who disobeyed the prison guards would be whipped so badly that their backs would be flayed. It is particularly disturbing knowing that Richie was only twelve years old but was still sent to prison for stealing food for his family and spared no mercy because of his age. Pop's son, Given, was also the victim of racism, dying at the hands of his white teammates simply because he won a bet. The fact that it was so easy for his teammate to pull the trigger in a moment of anger and not face any legal consequences is a testament to how African American lives are valued in American society. In a disturbing scene with a policeman, Jojo also becomes a victim of racism at the age of thirteen. While his narration is that of an innocent child, the police and the rest of the world treat him as if he were a dangerous criminal because of the way he looks. Ward is subtle when depicting these events, and yet it is still highly effective in capturing the sense of ugliness and injustice.

The reception of *Sing, Unburied, Sing* has been overwhelmingly positive. A common point of praise among literary critics has been Ward's ability to leverage a unique literary style in order to make powerful commentary. In her review for the *Atlantic*, Adrienne Green wrote, "Throughout, there's no escaping Ward's political rendering of American history. She uses a haunting, magical-realist style to masterfully warp two of life's most inflexible realities: time and death. Her book seems to ask whether a family or nation can atone for inequities that remain well and alive." Many other critics similarly marveled at Ward's ambitiousness; the scope of her story is enormous both in the number of characters that comprise the narrative as well as the significant issues that it explores. In addition to time and death, the author examines the dynamics of family, race, and life in the American South. It is a lot to balance and could easily feel overwhelming, but Ward's literary prowess prevents this from happening.

Most reviews extolled the prose of *Sing, Unburied, Sing*, describing it as "lyrical," which can be attributed to Ward's background as a poet. However, some critics have argued that, at times, this poetic tendency can feel tedious. For example, Annalisa Quinn wrote for NPR that "Ward's lyricism tips occasionally into floweriness. Lush phrases smother each other, certain metaphors begin to drag after enough uses." While some readers may become exhausted with this stylistic element of the novel, it feels fitting for the story. In his *New Yorker* review, Vinson Cunningham argued that the book's occasionally overwrought tone is "appropriate to its purposes, and its origins," and that the author's lyricism feels inextricable from the Gulf Coast politics that emerged after Hurricane Katrina. Ultimately, it can be argued that the style and tone are reflective of the tradition of southern writing and enhance the narrative's supernatural elements as well as its setting.

Sing, Unburied, Sing is demonstrative of a fiction writer at the height of her mastery. While Ward's earlier works have earned significant acclaim, the success of her third novel has been unprecedented. *Sing, Unburied, Sing* earned Ward her second National Book Award for fiction, making her the first woman to ever win the honor twice. Additionally, the novel led to Ward receiving a MacArthur Fellowship grant, and it was noted by former president Barack Obama as one of his favorite books of 2017. With such accolades, it is clear that the publication of *Sing, Unburied, Sing* has brought Ward further into the forefront of contemporary American literature as one of its most important contributors.

Emily Turner

Review Sources

Charles, Ron. "Jesmyn Ward's Powerful New Novel, *Sing, Unburied, Sing*." Review of *Sing, Unburied, Sing*, by Jesmyn Ward. *The Washington Post*, 29 Aug. 2017, www.washingtonpost.com/entertainment/books/a-powerful-new-entry-in-the-literature-of-race-in-america/2017/08/29/45cb2008-8b89-11e7-9

1d5-ab4e4bb76a3a_story.html?utm_term=.af0df667870d. Accessed 22 Jan. 2018.

Cunningham, Vinson. "Jesmyn Ward's Haunted Novel of the Gulf Coast." Review of *Sing, Unburied, Sing*, by Jesmyn Ward. *The New Yorker*, 11 Sept. 2017, www.newyorker.com/magazine/2017/09/11/jesmyn-wards-haunted-novel-of-the-gulf-coast. Accessed 22 Jan. 2018.

Green, Adrienne. "Jesmyn Ward's Eerie, Powerful Unearthing of History." Review of *Sing, Unburied, Sing*, by Jesmyn Ward. *The Atlantic*, 28 Sept. 2017, www.theatlantic.com/entertainment/archive/2017/09/jesmyn-wards-eerie-powerful-unearthing-of-history/541230/. Accessed 22 Jan. 2018.

Quinn, Annalisa. "*Sing* Mourns the Dead, Both Buried and Unburied." Review of *Sing, Unburied, Sing*, by Jesmyn Ward. *NPR*, 6 Sept. 2017, www.npr.org/2017/09/06/547560046/sing-mourns-the-dead-both-buried-and-unburied. Accessed 22 Jan. 2018.

Sandhu, Sukhdev. "*Sing, Unburied, Sing* by Jesmyn Ward Review—Slow Apocalypse of Black America." Review of *Sing, Unburied, Sing*, by Jesmyn Ward. *The Guardian*, 24 Nov. 2017, www.theguardian.com/books/2017/nov/24/sing-unburied-sing-jesmyn-ward-review. Accessed 22 Jan. 2018.

Smile

Author: Roddy Doyle (b. 1958)
Publisher: Viking (New York). 224 pp.
Type of work: Novel
Time: Early 1970s to the present
Locale: Dublin, Ireland

Roddy Doyle's novel Smile, *though darker and more downbeat in tone than much of his previous work, contains familiar elements: blunt and folksy dialogue, well-drawn characters, and forgotten memories of events from the past that, once remembered, resonate in unexpected ways in the lives of those trapped in the present.*

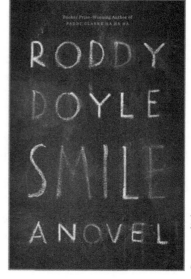

Courtesy of Viking

Principal characters
VICTOR FORDE, a failed writer
RACHEL CAREY, his ex-partner, a popular
    television personality
ED FITZPATRICK, an ex-builder who claims to be his former school classmate
BROTHER MCINTYRE, the head brother at St. Martin's Christian Brothers School
BROTHER MURPHY, a French teacher at St. Martin's
BRENDA, a married pub patron
CHARLES JACOB, Victor's boss

When first glimpsed, Victor Forde, the middle-aged protagonist of *Smile*, is sitting moodily in Donnelly's, his chosen local pub. On a downward trajectory in his life and career, Victor has recently returned to the Dublin neighborhood where he grew up. He lives in a no-frills rented flat near Donnelly's and spends his days reading, drinking, and brooding. While at the pub, Victor is approached by an aggressive man named Ed Fitzpatrick, who says he knows Victor from secondary school. Fitzpatrick seems to know a lot about Victor and recites details about the other man's public persona as a former minor celebrity. When questioned, Fitzpatrick talks vaguely about himself, hinting that he was once wealthy after making a fortune working in construction. Victor, who takes a dislike to Fitzpatrick, does not remember him from his youth. A nonreader, Fitzpatrick seems envious of Victor's supposedly cushy life as a writer, though Victor is suffering through an extended period of writer's block and has fallen on hard times.

Meeting Fitzpatrick causes Victor to reminisce about his days at St. Martin's Christian Brothers School (CBS). This establishes the novel's loose structure and movement. The narration swings back and forth between the present and various key moments in the past. Backward glances often touch upon Victor's formative years as an intelligent, sensitive child who was especially impressionable and vulnerable.

In mentally revisiting St. Martin's, Victor recalls former friends and classmates with colorful handles such as Moonshine Kelly and Willo Gaffney, as well as particular teachers. One person he vividly remembers for all the wrong reasons is Brother Murphy, a middle-aged French teacher who took a liking—perhaps innocent, perhaps not—to Victor that would forever after affect the young man's life. One day in class, Murphy carelessly remarked, "Victor Forde, I can never resist your smile." The other boys immediately interpreted Brother Murphy's interest as more than academic. They called Victor "the Queer," then thrashed and spit on him because they thought he purposely solicited attention to win favor. He accepted the punishment without complaint, a lack of resistance that suggests that Victor, who soon learned to tamp down his natural cheerfulness, may have had doubts about his own motivations. The ritual torture lasted for months, until a female teacher abruptly replaced Brother Murphy. Victor felt guilty about Murphy's dismissal, reinforcing his doubts about the possibility he was complicit in the incident.

In the present, Victor continues to run into Fitzpatrick at Donnelly's pub. They chat casually about their families, their occupations, women, and other far-ranging topics, which often involve their supposedly shared experiences at school. Though Victor is put off by Fitzpatrick's crude manner, he looks forward to their time together over drinks, since there is little else happening in his life.

Their conversations make Victor daydream about his former romantic partner, Rachel Carey, and he relives the circumstances that led to their meeting and subsequent relationship. At the time his path crossed Rachel's, Victor was widely known for his hard-hitting newspaper reviews of records and rock concerts, and he had aspirations of completing a novel, tentatively titled *Ireland: A Horror Story*. Based on his growing reputation, Victor was given a different type of assignment: to interview an up-and-coming female Irish politician. Under his skillful interrogation, the woman admitted on the record to having had an abortion. Victor's influence suddenly expanded. Though he is by nature a quiet, shy loner more comfortable behind the scenes than behind a microphone, he became identified as a supporter of Ireland's abortion referendum. He was in demand on broadcast programs as a guest who could spark spirited debates by making suggestions controversial in heavily Catholic Ireland, such as that schools should issue condoms to students as they leave on Friday afternoons. He met Rachel— who first captured public attention in her early twenties as an attractive, ambitious entrepreneur—while appearing with her on a radio station panel. Though Victor and Rachel have very different personalities, they instantly hit it off. At the beginning of their relationship, she taught him how to laugh, something he had forgotten how to do. As they drew closer, Rachel moved into his cramped apartment, rose to the challenge of relieving him of his virginity, and managed to overcome Victor's many frustrating episodes of erectile dysfunction. She enthusiastically demonstrated that sex is not just for procreation, as Victor was taught in church and school, but also for recreation.

In the present, the days crawl past. Victor and Fitzpatrick meet semiregularly, and further memories from their youth emerge. Victor remembers being recruited into the school choir and learning a mass composed in Irish to sing at the funeral of ancient mathematics teacher Brother Patch Connolly. He flashes back to another forgotten incident at school, perhaps the origin of his occasional impotence: several times, he wrestled with Brother McIntyre, the school's head brother or headmaster, ostensibly learning self-defense; as they grappled, McIntyre fondled him. Traumatized by the experience, Victor wonders if his molester engaged in other illicit activities that he has since wiped from his memory.

When revisiting earlier days, Victor would sooner dwell on happier times. He fondly recalls the moment he told her Rachel he loved her. He remembers bringing her home to his widowed mother, who was thrilled her son was involved with such a beautiful, charming woman. One particularly memorable, and humorous, recollection concerns a visit to Rachel's home for dinner. Doyle skillfully recreates a burlesque scene with a series of memorable images. Rachel's older sister Esther, who "carried a book like it was a hammer," looked like she wanted to

© Mark Nixon

Author Roddy Doyle has written novels for adults and children, novellas, plays, short stories and screenplays. His first full-length work, The Commitments, *was published in 1987. Among other honors, he won the 1993 Man Booker Prize for* Paddy Clarke Ha Ha Ha *(1993). Several of his novels have been adapted for film.* Smile *is his eleventh novel for adults.*

start a fight with Victor; her tipsy mother, losing her balance from a drink too many, almost smothered Victor with her breasts as she leaned in to set a gravy boat on the dinner table; her father, built like an over-the-hill rugby player, gruffly demanded Victor's opinion of abortion just as Victor was rendered noisily incoherent by having put a whole scalding pearl onion, concealed by the gravy, into his mouth.

Victor remembers living with Rachel in a spacious loft over the kitchen where she ran a successful catering business. When the business expanded, she became the host of *Hit the Ground Running*, a popular television series focusing on entrepreneurs. While Rachel worked downstairs, Victor toiled upstairs, trying to write a book but running out of steam by the second chapter. Rachel and Victor became known as "Ireland's first celebrity couple," though at the time Rachel's star was still rising, while Victor's was beginning to fall. They maintained cozy apartments in Paris and Barcelona (which Rachel paid for) that were seldom used. While they spent more than ten years together as man and wife, they never formally married. One day, not long after Victor appeared on a radio show and gave a detailed account of having been molested by a schoolteacher, Rachel asked him to leave. Victor knew by then that she had several other lovers. They parted amicably and kept in contact via mobile phone.

In the present, Victor falls in with a group of older pub regulars. When he does not drink enough to forget, Victor drinks enough to flirt, like the other men do, or at least to make eye contact with Brenda, a friendly, mature woman who comes to the pub on occasion to interact companionably with the male patrons. Fitzpatrick, running out of current information to impart about local, if faded, celebrity Victor and his famous ex, is by stages reduced to the status of a hanger-on. As the men drone on about mundane, everyday topics, Victor's thoughts drift, as they often do, to the past. He contemplates the fate of old friends. Some have died, a few have committed suicide, many have moved elsewhere. This guy won the lottery, that guy was involved in a car crash; this person suffers from depression, that one is an alcoholic, and the other one is recovering from a stroke. When the talk turns to children, Victor wonders about the son he and Rachel had together, whom he has not seen in three years.

The ironically titled *Smile* relates a simple, well-told tale fraught with tension. Doyle's natural use of language is as smooth, polished, and comforting as a windless ocean—and, as in the ocean, things with sharp, jagged teeth and voracious appetites lurk just out of sight beneath the surface. Issues of significance to society—homosexuality, the church as an enabler of child sexual abuse, abortion, the role of women—rise temporarily out of the murk to become part of a media feeding frenzy that sometimes leaves a permanent mark on individuals.

Victor's unique first-person narration carries most of the story. His voice is realistic and believable, if unreliable due to a haze of selective psychological amnesia, tinged by the bitterness brought on by multiple failures, and overshadowed by a gloom of self-doubt. Doyle's prose is frequently punctuated with snatches of dialogue that could identify their speakers by cadence and word use alone. All of the characters, whether major or walk-on, seem to live and breathe. They are people who might be bumped into at a supermarket, on the sidewalk, at a pub: ordinary, but with hidden depths.

After Victor, the most interesting character is antagonist Fitzpatrick, the catalyst for Victor's visits to yesteryear, who injects conflict into the plot. Fitzpatrick's unknown agenda—Who is he really? What does he want? What is his true connection to Victor?—provides an undercurrent of uncertainty throughout the novel. Doyle's skillfully rationed revelations pull the reader willingly along to the shattering conclusion.

Jack Ewing

Review Sources

Boyne, John. "*Smile* by Roddy Doyle Review: Few Laughs, but a Fine Novel." Review of *Smile*, by Roddy Doyle. *The Guardian*, 1 Sept. 2017, www.theguardian. com/books/2017/sep/01/smile-roddy-doyle-review. Accessed 16 Jan. 2018.

Charles, Ron. "Roddy Doyle Was Determined to Write a Novel That Shocked— and Succeeded." Review of *Smile*, by Roddy Doyle. *The Washington Post*, 17 Oct. 2017, www.washingtonpost.com/entertainment/books/roddy-doyle-was-determined-to-write-a-novel-that-shocked--and-succeeded/2017/10/17/f6dcb17e-b2a6-11e7-be94-fabb0f1e9ffb_story.html. Accessed 16 Jan. 2018.

Dillon, Brian. "Roddy Doyle's *Smile*: Ha Ha Ha but Ultimately a Failure." Review of *Smile*, by Roddy Doyle. *Irish Times*, 2 Sept. 2017, www.irishtimes.com/culture/ books/roddy-doyle-s-smile-ha-ha-ha-but-ultimately-a-failure-1.3200907. Accessed 16 Jan. 2018.

Lennon, J. Robert. "A Stranger from the Past Confronts Roddy Doyle's Latest Hero." Review of *Smile*, by Roddy Doyle. *The New York Times*, 31 Oct. 2017, www.nytimes.com/2017/10/31/books/review/roddy-doyle-smile.html. Accessed 16 Jan. 2018.

McAloon, Jonathan. "Midlife Anxiety: Roddy Doyle's *Smile* Reviewed." Review of *Smile*, by Roddy Doyle. *The Spectator*, 16 Sept. 2017, www.spectator.co.uk/2017/09/midlife-anxiety-roddy-doyles-smile-reviewed/. Accessed 16 Jan. 2018.

Solar Bones

Author: Mike McCormack (b. 1965)
First published: *Solar Bones*, 2016, in Ireland
Publisher: Soho Press (New York). 224 pp.
Type of work: Novel
Time: Late twentieth to early twenty-first century
Locale: County Mayo, Ireland

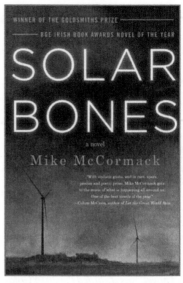

Courtesy of Soho Press

A critically acclaimed experimental novel,
Solar Bones *creatively presents the thoughts, memories, and philosophical musings of a small-town civil engineer in western Ireland. Marcus Conway draws strength from the bonds of family and takes comfort in the mathematical certainty of science in the process of navigating an increasingly complicated and chaotic world.*

Principal characters

MARCUS CONWAY, a civil engineer in his late forties
MAIREAD CONWAY, his wife, a teacher
AGNES CONWAY, his daughter, an experimental artist in her twenties
DARRAGH CONWAY, his son, a young man trying to find himself in Australia
EITHNE, his sister
ONNIE, a.k.a. Mam, his now-deceased mother
DAD, his now-deceased father
DEPUTY JOHN FRANCIS MOYLETTE, a self-important county politician
COUNCILLOR CHARLIE HALLORAN, a local politician
SHAMIE CURRAN, an irascible building contractor

Solar Bones (2016) is constructed around a gimmick. Though some reviewers of the 2016 Goldsmiths Prize winner and long-listed entry for the 2017 Man Booker Prize have noted that the well-received story is told in a single sentence, that assessment is neither accurate nor fair. A novel of more than two hundred pages written in a single, unbroken sentence would be a challenge to the comprehension abilities of even the most dedicated booklover. It is true there is not a solitary full-stop period to be found in the book, yet despite this quirk, *Solar Bones* quickly draws readers into the story and holds them to the end. This feat of uninterrupted narration is accomplished not through a single sentence, but a succession of run-on sentences, often with enjambed endings, which herald fresh fragments or extended paragraphs, all indented and uncapitalized, each break signifying a new direction. This typographical technique—a variation on

Courtesy of Maeve Curtis

Mike McCormack won the Rooney Prize for Irish Literature for his first collection of short stories, Getting It in the Head *(1996).* Solar Bones, *his fifth book and third novel, was awarded the 2016 Goldsmiths Prize and named the Bord Gáis Energy Book of the Year 2016.*

the stream-of-consciousness fiction of such authors as Henry James (*Portrait of a Lady,* 1881), Marcel Proust (*In Search of Lost Time,* 1913–27), or James Joyce (*Finnegans Wake,* 1939) that combines thoughts, feelings, and memories in a constant flow—does not hinder understanding. Rather, it adds breathing space, lending a poetic look and feel to the prose, and encourages reading passages aloud. More importantly, the gimmick has a real organic purpose, as careful readers will realize from the author's carefully planted clues.

The first and most significant of these clues is contained in the opening section. An unnamed narrator describes hearing the Angelus bell ringing from the village church in the middle of the day and gives impressions of what the sound means. The date is November 2, All Souls' Day, an annual Christian commemoration of the departed. Subsequent passages sketch in the setting: the town of Louisburgh on the coast of County Mayo, Republic of Ireland. Soon, the narrator is introduced, as the viewpoint subtly changes from third to first person. He is Marcus Conway, a middle-aged engineer, and he is sitting in the kitchen of the farmhouse where his family has lived for generations. Marcus is alone because his wife, Mairead, has gone for the day and will not return until late afternoon. His children, Agnes and Darragh, are absent.

To fill the empty hours, Marcus begins reading the local and national newspapers. Various articles help set the period: there is news about ongoing wars in Afghanistan and Iraq, and peace talks between Israel and Palestine. Ireland has suffered a recent economic collapse. Thus the wide-ranging narrative, more thought-driven than plot-driven, starts its meander.

An item about an abandoned industrial facility stirs Marcus's memories of his father, who, some forty years before, helped build the original site, a factory that manufactured acrylic yarn and fiber. Marcus remembers how good his father was at taking apart and putting together farm implements. He pictures in his mind dismantled harrows, ploughs, and cultivators, invented during medieval times and still in use in modern farming.

The machinery reminds him of a winter when he was in Prague, Czech Republic, attending a conference on bridge construction. During his free time, he roved the city. Marcus ended up at a museum featuring implements of torture, where he reflected on the ignoble use of engineering principles to make bone-breaking, flesh-tearing, blood-drawing objects like the iron maiden, the rack, and the wheel. The only other patron in the museum was an auburn-haired woman, with whom he symbolically dances around and among the exhibits. Marcus and the woman end up side by side, staring at a bladed and spiked Catherine wheel. The woman comments, "It's all about sex, isn't it." Marcus remembers how the frank remark led to a brief affair. Even more memorable is Mairead's angry reaction when she later finds out about his infidelity.

His thoughts wander farther afield. Marcus recalls meeting Mairead, who landed a post as substitute vice principal at a local secondary school after teaching in Spain, Germany, Czech Republic, and Romania. He remembers the time his wife announced she was pregnant and pictures his daughter, Agnes, as a baby. In his mind, the face of Agnes morphs into her appearance at twenty-two years of age, hosting her first solo art exhibition in Galway. The show, called *The O Negative Diaries*, consisted of a series of excerpts from newspaper crime stories, drawn in her own blood. Initially upset by the nature of her artwork, Marcus mentally cudgels himself for being a failure as a father because Agnes seems obsessed by crime and gore. However, during a celebratory dinner at a restaurant, Marcus realizes the well-attended gallery event means his daughter is a success and that her bloody artwork is merely an experiment, something different from the oils she normally produces. Marcus compares Agnes with her younger brother, Darragh, who is in Australia working with a group of friends as fruit pickers and, Marcus knows from their Skype sessions, is sporting long hair and a scraggy beard.

In thinking of the future of his children, Marcus is reminded of his own occupation: he works for the county government as a mid-level employee, responsible for making decisions about procuring materials and approving construction projects. He contemplates how engineering often overlaps with politics. He remembers complaints received by officeholders like Councillor Charlie Halloran and Deputy John Francis Moylette who exert pressure to get constituent-mollifying bridge or road repairs effected and from contractors like Shamie Curran who cut corners in the completion of construction projects that will produce adverse consequences in the future.

Periodically, Marcus is suffused with a sense of loneliness, because his family is not present. His emotions are intensified by the weather, bleak on All Souls' Day, just after Samhain, the Gaelic festival borrowed from pagan Celts to commemorate the end of the harvest and the start of winter, "when the souls of the dead are bailed from purgatory for a while by the prayers of the faithful." A former altar boy who appreciates the way religion is built upon firm principles like structural engineering, Marcus recalls the two years he spent in a seminary before studying civil engineering.

As he looks out across the bay beside the village, Marcus envisions a fishing trip he took with his father, when his dad talked about winning a race in a currach, a small wood-framed boat, and about navigating by landmarks. Thinking of his late father causes Marcus to experience a tightness in his chest and he has trouble breathing. The feeling recalls to mind a time when Mairead fell deathly ill. One of hundreds affected, she unwittingly drank water tainted by human waste, served at the restaurant where they celebrated Agnes's exhibition. The health crisis spawns a massive protest featuring bizarrely dressed demonstrators and a carnival atmosphere featuring clowns, jugglers, buskers, and more. The protest culminates in a piece of performance art: Agnes, now a celebrity because of her debut exhibition, dives naked into a huge air cushion from the top of a building.

Marcus had to take an emergency leave of absence to care for his wife—who is wracked by fever, vomiting, and diarrhea—and clean up after her. The experience makes him feel closer to his wife. He flashes back to the time she found out about his affair in Prague and then to the painful final days of Marcus's mentally failing father, who, after the death of his wife, Onnie, withdraws, locking himself inside the house and brooding without bathing, shaving, or eating properly until he is felled by cancer.

Solar Bones is a rich, multilayered novel full of memorable, well-turned phrases (such as this impression of country music issuing from a car radio: "like a steady tide from a world of manageable heartache"); snatches of meaningful dialogue; and skillfully sketched images that linger in the mind like stark black-and-white snapshots. The title refers to one of McCormack's major themes, the comparison of the structure of religion with the framework involved in engineering, two elements among several with an autobiographical basis: the author grew up on a farm in Louisburgh, became fascinated with engineering and technology, and was a gardener at a pharmaceutical company. The latter occupation he assigns to young Marcus, who muses about the "daily rites, rhythms and rituals upholding the world like solar bones."

A closely related thread throughout is that of building up and falling down. A collapsed bridge causes problems for the local community. A boom-and-bust economy hangs over the entire state of Ireland. The construction of a new national school is doomed because the concrete poured into the foundation comes from three separate sources, each of different consistency, which will fail when it expands and contracts with the weather. Marcus's father, who, in his heyday, enjoys deconstructing and assembling machinery to learn how it works, himself falls apart at the end of his life. The tale seems to explore the concept of what, ultimately, gives cohesion to human life.

Solar Bones illustrates by example that every individual has a story to tell and that every story is unique. As related by Mike McCormack, the circle of life for Marcus Conway—and by extension, the life cycle of any human—is shaped not by a smoothly drawn line, but by an almost infinite series of linked tangents given order by the inspiration of private thoughts and universal emotions and personal memories.

Jack Ewing

Review Sources

Boland, Stephanie. "Bedad He Revives: Why *Solar Bones* Is a Resurrection for Irish Modernism." Review of *Solar Bones*, by Mike McCormack. *New Statesman*, 4 July 2016, www.newstatesman.com/culture/books/2016/07/bedad-he-revives-why-solar-bones-resurrection-irish-modernism. Accessed 12 Jan. 2018.

Cremins, Robert. Review of *Solar Bones*, by Mike McCormack. *Star Tribune*, 22 Sept. 2017, www.startribune.com/review-solar-bones-by-mike-mccor-mack/446581303. Accessed 12 Jan. 2018.

Doyle, Rob. "*Solar Bones* by Mike McCormack Review: Portrait of a Universe in Dereliction." Review of *Solar Bones*, by Mike McCormack. *The Irish Times*, 7

May 2016, www.irishtimes.com/culture/books/solar-bones-by-mike-mccormack-review-portrait-of-a-universe-in-dereliction-1.2637871. Accessed 12 Jan. 2018.

Palmqvist, Lara. "*Solar Bones* Is a Single, Novel-Length Sentence That Works." Review of *Solar Bones*, by Mike McCormack. *Chicago Review of Books*, 31 Aug. 2016, chireviewofbooks.com/2016/08/31/solar-bones-is-a-single-novel-length-sentence-that-works. Accessed 12 Jan. 2018.

Sansom, Ian. "*Solar Bones* by Mike McCormack Review—An Extraordinary Hymn to Small-Town Ireland." Review of *Solar Bones*, by Mike McCormack. *The Guardian*, 4 June 2016, www.theguardian.com/books/2016/jun/04/solar-bones-by-mike-mccormack-review. Accessed 12 Jan. 2018.

Sour Heart

Author: Jenny Zhang (b. 1983)
Publisher: Lenny (New York). 320 pp.
Type of work: Short stories
Time: 1960s to 1990s
Locales: New York, New York; Shanghai,
China

Courtesy of Lenny

Jenny Zhang's debut short-story collection,
Sour Heart, *explores young womanhood and
the Chinese immigrant experience through
the eyes of various narrators.*

Sour Heart, the debut short-story collection
from poet and essayist Jenny Zhang, presents seven loosely linked stories about young
women dealing with the Chinese immigrant
experience. The teenage girls in these stories
struggle to assimilate, grow up, and assert themselves as individuals, separate from
their parents. They travel the globe and the streets of New York City; they go hungry
and gorge themselves on junk food; they care for their siblings and commit horrifying
transgressions against their friends. They are selfish, spiteful, all too giving, and full of
regret. The protagonist of the first story, "We Love You Crispina," returns as a young
woman to narrate the last story, "You Fell into the River and I Saved You!," but otherwise each story features a different viewpoint character. The common thread that binds
the stories together is one of setting: a cramped New York City apartment shared, at
one time or another, by newly arrived Chinese immigrants in the 1980s.

In "We Love You Crispina," Christina, who compulsively scratches her skin raw,
sleeps between her mother and father. On another mattress lie two failed artists: a
painter who sells umbrellas and an avant-garde filmmaker. Their daughter Annie is
the narrator of the collection's longest and most ambitious story, "Our Mothers before
Them," which takes place in the United States in the 1990s and in China during the
Cultural Revolution of the 1960s. Zhang's stories ripple outward from this point of
arrival, where immigrants have come on their journey to somewhere else.

Zhang began her writing career as a poet—her first book, a collection of poetry
titled *Dear Jenny, We Are All Find*, was published in 2012—and she has been a prolific
essayist for such outlets as BuzzFeed and the online magazine *Rookie*. The poems in
Dear Jenny demonstrate some of Zhang's enduring qualities as a writer, particularly
her ability to find poetry in colloquial language and in obscene words and images,
and these qualities are evident throughout *Sour Heart* as well. Zhang's writing has the
energy of spoken language—or, perhaps more accurately, the rush of a whispered confession; her work is intimate, sometimes shamefacedly so, as in the story "The Empty

the Empty the Empty," in which two preteen girls spend afternoons exploring each other's bodies in wonder and repulsion.

Jenny Zhang is a poet and writer living in Brooklyn, New York. Sour Heart *is her first short-story collection.*

Zhang, who has a bachelor's degree from Stanford University, also attended the Iowa Writers' Workshop, where she wrote *Dear Jenny*. It was a chance encounter on Twitter that launched her career as a fiction writer: the writer and actor Lena Dunham, creator of the HBO television show *Girls* (2012–17), reached out to Zhang on the social media platform to tell her that she loved her poems and asked to read Zhang's other work. A few years later, *Sour Heart* became the first book published by Lenny, Dunham's imprint at Random House. Some of the stories in the book were written or begun when Zhang was an undergraduate at Stanford, making *Sour Heart* a true culmination of her early work and evolving voice.

"We Love You Crispina" begins with an extended riff on bowel movements, as protagonist Christina looks back on her life as a nine-year-old girl living with her Chinese immigrant parents in various crumbling apartments across New York City. The toilet in the family's apartment in the Bushwick neighborhood of Brooklyn was perpetually clogged, she recalls, so whenever she or her parents had to relieve themselves, they would quickly bundle up to run across the street and use the bathroom at the gas station. Zhang describes this sorry ritual in detail, in one long, labyrinthine sentence that communicates both the indignity and the absurdity of living in poverty. The family did not have a toilet plunger because, according to Christina, they "were too poor and too irresponsible back then" to save the money for such unglamorous essentials. "Secretly I blamed myself for instigating all our downward spirals," Christina recalls, "like the time I asked my father if he would buy me an ice-cream cone with sprinkles, which made him realize I had been waiting all month to ask and he felt so sorry for me that he decided to buy me not only an ice cream with sprinkles but a real rhinestone anklet that sure as hell was not on the list of 'things we need to buy immediately or else we've just lost all human dignity,' and that was the sort of rhythm my family fell into—disastrous and depressing in our inability to get ahead." This lengthy passage, itself part of a much longer sentence, echoes the self-perpetuating cycle of poverty. For Christina and her parents, being immigrants meant surviving one indignity after another as they struggled to gain a foothold in the United States.

Zhang explores various aspects of the immigrant experience, but her stories do not follow the familiar template for such tales. While readers learn later in the book that Christina and her family worked their way up to a middle-class existence on Long Island, there are no clichéd "rags-to-riches" moments for Zhang's characters; each new rung on the ladder to success comes with sacrifice, often at terrible personal cost. Zhang instead focuses on the confusion of childhood, and sometimes the familial guilt of having parents who have suffered through far worse.

In "Our Mothers before Them," Zhang combines two story threads set thirty years apart, in 1966 and 1996. The 1966 section, set during the anarchic first days of China's Cultural Revolution, is kaleidoscopic, following many characters at once and capturing the mass brutality of the era; hungry children, loosed from school and routine, roam the streets, sniffing out adults they can accuse of being regime traitors and torturing them, sometimes to death. In 1996, the young narrator, Annie, and her older brother, Sammy, listen to their mother's bitter memories. A former avant-garde filmmaker and a failed singer, their mother weaponizes her trauma and regret. Annie is driven to tears because, she says, "I didn't want to hear any more stories about her youth, the way she had suffered, how she married a man who would only continue to make her suffer." Annie, in turn, is terrified to suffer the consequences of offering the wrong reaction to her parents. Needy and cruel in equal measure, Annie's mother expects total devotion from her children but does not want to see them usurp any attention from her. Annie does her best to please her mother, unable to realize that there are some wounds she cannot heal, and thus Zhang, in her characteristically sweet and vulgar way, demonstrates how pain can become an inheritance.

One of the best stories in the collection is "Why Were They Throwing Bricks?," another intergenerational tale. In it, a grandmother travels to New York from China to visit her daughter's family. Elements of the story showcase the humor of Zhang's writing, but here, as in her poems, even humor is fraught with pathos. The protagonist's grandmother is utterly devoted to her grandchildren, concocting elaborate stories about their need for her. Talking about how other people have observed this need, she humbly boasts, "They said there was no need for me to be modest. 'This child prefers her grandmother to even her own mother and father! Why sugarcoat the truth?' I had to stop myself from stopping other people from saying it after a while. Was I supposed to keep insulting everyone's intelligence? Protesting endlessly? Your nainai isn't that type of person." In fact, early in the story, the granddaughter (and later a grandson) are quite devoted to their grandmother, but as the story progresses, this devotion sours as her need for them continues to grow. It is a predictable scenario, but the story closes with an inspired, almost surreal final image that suggests all the things one cannot know about another person.

Christian Lorentzen, writing for *Vulture*, called *Sour Heart* "a forceful performance and one of the knockout fiction debuts of the year." Other reviewers likewise applauded the collection, deeming Zhang's narrative voice to be of particular note. Jia Tolentino, in a review for the *New Yorker*, called the book "astounding" and aptly observed that *Sour Heart* "combines ingenious and tightly controlled technical artistry with an unfettered emotional directness that frequently moves, within single sentences, from overwhelming beauty to abject pain." The reviewer for *Kirkus Reviews*, however, felt that Zhang's vulgarity overshadowed her skill.

Tolentino also described the book as a "feminist bildungsroman," in that "the narrators act upon their world just as much as the world acts upon them." This aspect of the stories was important to Zhang; as she said in an interview with Olivia Aylmer for *Vanity Fair*, published online in July 2017, she did not want her characters to passively participate in their lives. There are a lot of stories "about women having things done *to* them," she explained, while her personal experience suggested to her that people act on the world just as often as they are victimized by it, with outcomes both good and bad. The protagonists in *Sour Heart* make choices and, inevitably, terrible mistakes. They hurt the people around them, but they also valiantly try to make amends.

Molly Hagan

Review Sources

Lorentzen, Christian. "Jenny Zhang's *Sour Heart* Is a Knockout." Review of *Sour Heart*, by Jenny Zhang. *Vulture*, New York Media, 8 Aug. 2017, www.vulture. com/2017/08/jenny-zhangs-sour-heart-is-a-knockout.html. Accessed 20 Dec. 2017.

Stephen, Bijan. "The Grotesque Loveliness of *Sour Heart*." Review of *Sour Heart*, by Jenny Zhang. *New Republic*, 2 Aug. 2017, www.newrepublic.com/article/144163/grotesque-loveliness-sour-heart. Accessed 20 Dec. 2017.

Review of *Sour Heart*, by Jenny Zhang. *Kirkus Reviews*, 15 May 2017, www.kirkusreviews.com/book-reviews/jenny-zhang/sour-heart/. Accessed 20 Dec. 2017.

Tolentino, Jia. "Jenny Zhang's Obscene, Beautiful, Moving Story Collection, *Sour Heart*." Review of *Sour Heart*, by Jenny Zhang. *The New Yorker*, 14 Aug. 2017, www.newyorker.com/books/page-turner/jenny-zhangs-obscene-beautiful-moving-story-collection-sour-heart. Accessed 20 Dec. 2017.

Waldman, Katy. "*Sour Heart* Sets the 'Model Minority' Myth on Fire." Review of *Sour Heart*, by Jenny Zhang. *Slate*, 24 Aug. 2017, www.slate.com/articles/arts/books/2017/08/jenny_zhang_s_sour_heart_reviewed.html. Accessed 20 Dec. 2017.

Stay with Me

Author: Ayobami Adebayo (b. 1988)
Publisher: Alfred A. Knopf (New York). 260 pp.
Type of work: Novel
Time: 1985–2008
Locale: Ilesa, Nigeria

Ayobami Adebayo's debut novel, Stay with Me, *tells the story of a Nigerian marriage.*

Courtesy of Knopf

Principal characters
YEJIDE, a hairdresser
AKIN, her husband
MOOMI, her mother-in-law
FUNMI, Akin's second wife

Ayobami Adebayo's debut novel, *Stay with Me*, (2017), follows the story of a Nigerian marriage. The tale is set against the political upheaval in the country in the late twentieth century. The novel begins in the year 2008, and quickly backtracks to 1985, when the narrator Yejide and her husband Akin are having trouble conceiving a child. Yejide has consulted infertility experts, herbalists, and healers, but no one can seem to help her. Akin comes from a traditional Yoruba family, and a few years into their marriage, his family is growing increasingly frustrated with the couple's childlessness. Yejide, whose own mother died in childbirth, is similarly desperate, and after a visit from relatives, she is nearly emotionally destroyed. Akin's mother, Moomi, has arranged for Akin to take a second wife, a young woman named Funmi. (Polygamous marriages are legal in Nigeria, though less fashionable in 2017 than they once were.) Yejide and Akin—both of whom grew up in polygamous households—find the practice odious, but the pressure from Moomi and others is too much to bear. Akin gives in; he marries Funmi and Yejide must accept it. The sudden appearance of Funmi launches Yejide on a tragic odyssey, first to become pregnant, but then to protect herself, her marriage, and her children from hardship and misfortune. Her story becomes a kind of parable about love, desire, and betrayal.

Adebayo was born in 1988 and raised in Lagos, Nigeria. She studied with authors Chimamanda Ngozi Adichie and Margaret Atwood, and published several short stories in literary magazines. *Stay with Me*, her first novel, grew out of a short story begun nearly a decade ago, when Adebayo was enduring a lengthy daily commute to work at a Lagos bank. She had no time for writing at home, but began to type out notes for the story while she was sitting on the bus going to and from work. Adebayo eventually went on to earn her master's degree in creative writing from the University of East Anglia in Norwich, England. The novel underwent a number of structural transformations, and was short-listed for the Kwani? Manuscript Project, a literary prize for works-in-progress, in 2013. It was published in the United Kingdom in early 2017 and was short-listed for the prestigious Baileys Women's Prize for Fiction, but did not ultimately win it. *Stay with Me* was published in the United States several months later and was named one of the best books of the year by the *New York Times*, the *Guardian*, the *Wall Street Journal*, National Public Radio (NPR), the *Economist*, and the *Chicago Tribune*. Elements of the novel were inspired by people in Adebayo's life—most notably particular characters and their struggles with sickle cell anemia—but Adebayo has said that she wrote the book to explore traditional Nigerian ideas about women, mothers, and children.

    Stay with Me alternates chapters told from the perspectives of both Yejide and Akin, though Yejide is the book's primary subject and protagonist. As Adebayo depicts her, Yejide was a lonely child raised in a large, polygamous family. As the only daughter of a wife who died in childbirth, Yejide is shunned by her father's other wives and their children. To demonstrate her unimportance in the family structure, Yejide describes how she would get in trouble at school for fighting. Her stepmothers always threatened to beat or punish her, but never did. Her development was ultimately not their—or anybody's—concern. Yejide soon realized that she alone controlled her destiny. She recalls sitting outside the other mothers' doors each night, listening as they told their children—Yejide's stepbrothers and stepsisters—fairy tales. It is a small act of resistance; eavesdropping on other family factions is a punishable offense in a house where each wife is constantly vying to curry favor with the patriarch. The image of young Yejide listening behind doors and mentally rewriting the lore she hears foreshadows her later life and the motives that drive the choices she makes as an adult. Young Yejide vows to have her own children so that one day she will be the one telling the stories. But Yejide internalizes her stepmothers' cruelty even as she decides to forge her own path. Family secrets, jealousy, and betrayal will one day tear her own family apart.

    Adebayo also subtly makes the point that Yejide conflates her personhood with motherhood. In an interview with her publisher, Penguin Random House, Adebayo quotes a line from Taiye Selasi's 2011 short story, "The Sex Lives of African Girls." Selasi writes, "In the peculiar hierarchy of African households, the only rung lower than motherless child is childless mother." Yejide has the unfortunate distinction, for a time, of being both. Her marriage, born in love at university, begins happily enough. Akin is a successful banker. Yejide is a talented hair stylist, who runs her own salon. Both are unhappy with their childlessness, but have suffered their private heartache together, ignoring the meddlesome suggestions of Akin's family. Their lives are forever changed by the introduction of Funmi, the young woman who Moomi and Akin have chosen to be Akin's second wife. Yejide, understandably, feels deeply betrayed that her husband and mother-in-law would scheme against her in this way. Moomi, of course, sees the situation differently. Yejide's inability to bear children, in Moomi's eyes, robs her of her position as Akin's wife, but also of her gender. "Women manufacture children and if you can't you are just a man. Nobody should call you a woman," she says, adding, of Funmi, "We are not asking you to stand up from your place in his life, we are just saying you should shift so that someone else can sit down." But Yejide does

© Pixels Digital

Ayobami Adebayo is a Lagos-born novelist and short story writer. Her debut novel, Stay with Me, *was a finalist for the Baileys Women's Prize for Fiction in 2017.*

not shift quietly.

Yejide increases her efforts to become pregnant, convinced that if she is successful, Funmi will somehow disappear. Normally, the nonconforming Yejide would have no time for superstitions, but on the advice of a pregnant customer at her salon, she embarks on a journey to the Mountain of Jaw-Dropping Miracles to visit a man named Prophet Josiah. Led by a guide, Yejide climbs the mountain with a white goat. During the delirious ceremony at the summit, Yejide feeds the goat from her breast. She leaves convinced that she is pregnant. The following passages of the novel are heartbreaking, but also some of Adebayo's best. Yejide tells Akin, Moomi, and Funmi that she is pregnant, and decorates a nursery in her house. She becomes indignant when multiple doctors tell her that there is no child in her womb. Months and months pass, but Yejide still does not yield to reality. Akin encourages her to see a therapist, but the episode also leads him to make an extreme and secret decision. Soon after, Yejide really does become pregnant. She gives birth to a girl, Olamide. Hundreds attend little Olamide's naming ceremony, though the event is slightly marred by the mysterious death of Funmi. The ceremony marks a turning point; soon after, Olamide dies. The novel transforms its theme, painfully illustrating what it looks like to be childless in this context.

Yejide becomes pregnant again, but to reveal more plot might spoil Adebayo's delicate construction. *Stay with Me* incorporates a surprising amount of action in a fleet two-hundred and fifty or so pages; Pulitzer Prize winner Michiko Kakutani, the former head critic at the *New York Times*, compared the book to the thriller *Gone Girl* by Gillian Flynn. Kakutani also identified elements of Lauren Groff's *Fates and Furies* in Adebayo's novel. Kakutani took issue with the believability of one major plot point in the book, but otherwise described *Stay with Me* as a "stunning debut." "It is, at once, a gothic parable about pride and betrayal; a thoroughly contemporary—and deeply moving—portrait of a marriage; and a novel, in the lineage of great works by Chinua Achebe and Chimamanda Ngozi Adichie, that explores the pull in Nigeria between tradition and modernity, old definitions of masculinity and femininity, and newer imperatives of self-definition and identity," she wrote. Other reviewers were similarly impressed, though a reviewer for *Kirkus* complained that the novel verged on melodrama. But Trine Tsouderos, writing for the *Chicago Tribune*, called it a "triumph." "Adebayo drives the reader in a thrilling, headlong rush," Tsouderos wrote. Diana Evans, writing for the *Guardian*, praised Adebayo's sensitive rendering of womanhood and gender oppression: "Despite the intense sadness of her subject matter, [Adebayo] has produced a bright, big-hearted demonstration of female spirit." Indeed, the novel's greatest strength is its intimacy with the lives of women. It is fitting that Yejide is a hairdresser; each day she holds court in a traditionally female-dominated space. The women that gather in her salon discuss sex, children, and the weight of feminine expectation. They trade tips about infertility and breastfeeding, but they also, in one scene that speaks volumes about the power and vulnerability of being a woman, discuss ways to thwart would-be rapists as the town descends into political chaos. *Stay with Me* explores female identity in all its complexity.

Molly Hagan

Review Sources

Evans, Diana. "Stay with Me by Ayobami Adebayo Review—A Big-Hearted Nigerian Debut." Review of *Stay with Me*, by Ayobami Adebayo. *The Guardian*, 9 Mar. 2017, www.theguardian.com/books/2017/mar/09/stay-with-me-by-ayobami-adebayo-review. Accessed 3 Feb. 2018.
Kakutani, Michiko. "Portrait of a Nigerian Marriage in a Heartbreaking Debut Novel." Review of *Stay with Me*, by Ayobami Adebayo. *The New York Times*, 24 July 2017, www.nytimes.com/2017/07/24/books/review-ayobami-adebayo-stay-with-me.html. Accessed 3 Feb. 2018.
Review of *Stay with Me*, by Ayobami Adebayo. *Kirkus Reviews*, 6 June 2017, www.kirkusreviews.com/book-reviews/ayobami-adebayo/stay-with-me-adebayo/. Accessed 3 Feb. 2018.
Review of *Stay with Me*, by Ayobami Adebayo. *Publishers Weekly*, 12 June 2017, www.publishersweekly.com/978-0-451-49460-3. Accessed 3 Feb. 2018.
Tsouderos, Trine. "Ayobami Adebayo's Stunning Debut Explores Love, Marriage and Family." Review of *Stay with Me*, by Ayobami Adebayo. *Chicago Tribune*, 21 Aug. 2017 www.chicagotribune.com/lifestyles/books/sc-stay-with-me-ayobami-adebayo-books-0823-20170821-story.html. Accessed 3 Feb. 2018.

The Tea Girl of Hummingbird Lane

Author: Lisa See (b. 1955)
Publisher: Scribner (New York). 384 pp.
Type of work: Novel
Time: 1988–90; 1994–2008; 2012–16
Locales: China, Thailand, California

In The Tea Girl of Hummingbird Lane, *Lisa See deploys intimate themes of destiny and chance, motherhood and custom, to explore the enigmatic albeit prevailing boundaries between the historical forces of timeworn tradition and inescapable change.*

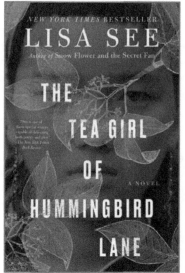

Courtesy of Scribner

Principal characters

LI-YAN, an Akha woman who becomes a
  successful tea entrepreneur
HALEY DAVIS, a.k.a. Yan-yeh, her orphaned
  daughter
CONSTANCE DAVIS, Haley's adoptive mother
DAN DAVIS, Haley's adoptive father
SAN-PA, her first husband and Haley's birth father
A-MA, her mother, village midwife and revered dream interpreter
JIN, her second husband, a wealthy Chinese business owner
CI-TEH, her best friend and business partner
TEACHER ZHANG, Spring Well Village's teacher
MR. HUANG, a tea connoisseur from Hong Kong

Before joining the global market economy in the late twentieth century, the People's Republic of China was a poor country whose centrally planned economy was in the administrative hands of Communist Party bureaucrats. Its engagement in world trade was insignificant. The Chinese central government opened its first four special economic zones (SEZs) in 1980. Intended as areas of rapid economic growth, local governments in the SEZs used tax and business incentives to attract foreign investment and technology. Over the next dozen years or so, China gradually allowed more cities to encourage internationalization and market exchanges. Since then, China's increasing economic and political prominence, as well as its blend of socialist and capitalist ideologies, has been of critical interest in both American media and various academic disciplines. In many ways, then, Lisa See's tenth novel, *The Tea Girl of Hummingbird Lane*, taps into this interest with an immersive personal story, one that adds to the ever-growing body of China's complex histories and narratives.

Told from protagonist Li-yan's first-person point of view, *The Tea Girl of Hummingbird Lane* is divided into five parts, each of which is linked not just by themes of coincidence or tropes of loss, but also by the peaks and valleys of Li-yan's life. Her story begins in 1988 in her home, the remote Akha community of Spring Well Village, on the wooded hillside of Nannuo Mountain in rural southwest China. The Akha are an egalitarian indigenous hill tribe that practices slash-and-burn agriculture to grow the crops on which they subsist, mainly soybeans, rice, and vegetables. Li-yan is taught from an early age that home is temporary, and that destiny cannot be altered. Dreams and fateful coincidences conspire in deterministic ways. Life is irrevocably caught up in the immutable Akha Law. The backdrop of Spring Well Village lays bare a profound provincialism rooted in the orthodoxy of Akha tradition, its sacred dogma and superstition. "What makes life bearable for the Akha is their belief system, which suffuses every aspect of their daily lives," wrote Helen Simonson in a review for the *Washington Post*. This pervasive belief system seems to limit Li-yan's capacity for independent thought while paradoxically also expanding it as she increasingly questions and tests its critical limitations.

Over the course of the next five to six years, Li-yan's views and impressions develop as she divides her days between performing the perfunctory labor of harvesting tea leaves with her family to exchange at the local tea collection center for money, and studying under Teacher Zhang, an exile from the capital who is "sent down to learn from the peasants." Zhang introduces Li-yan to literature, movies, new languages, and thus to new ways of being in a world she soon realizes vastly exceeds the tranquil domains of Nannuo Mountain.

For the first half or so of the novel, Li-yan experiences a series of hardships that culminate in her pregnancy as an unwed teenager while China is still under the constraints of its One Child policy. Li-yan is shamed by taboo and leaves her newborn daughter at an orphanage in a nearby city rather than kill the baby per Akha rules. Li-yan is then banished from her family and community. Despondent and rudderless, she marries the baby's father, San-pa, and together they move to Thailand. There, Li-yan learns, much to her dismay, that San-pa is embroiled in the Golden Triangle opiate trade.

After San-pa's death, Li-yan returns to Spring Well Village. Events take a propitious turn after Li-yan is placed in trade school by the concerted efforts of her mother and Teacher Zhang. Once there, she learns English and studies the craft of fermenting tea. Gradually, she develops a successful tea business that, not long after China's entry into the global economy, finds itself caught up in the vagaries of the free market economy. Meanwhile, her daughter, Haley, is raised in California by loving adoptive parents. The second half of See's novel increasingly shares its pages between Li-yan's accounts of her more auspicious moments and Haley's turbulent coming of age. Li-yan's memories of attaining financial success and true love at times seem to border on vainglorious, while Haley's teen years are filled with unsolicited adversity, rebellion, discrimination, and peer pressure.

See's novel offers an explicit discussion of Asian and Asian American stereotypes, including the myth of the model minority, and seeks to disrupt them, as seen in the transcript of Dr. Rosen's group therapy for Chinese adoptees, of which Haley is a member. As one member of the therapy group laments, Asians are prejudicially "labeled as inquisitive, persistent, and ambitious. With ingenuity fortitude, and cleverness."

See's Asian American characters notice and acknowledge that they are locked in imaginary patterns and assumptions, instituted by discriminatory expectations to perform acts of extraordinary persistence and ambition. And yet, as one might hope for, many of See's other Asian characters are nevertheless depicted—respectfully and honestly—as smart, inquisitive, persistent, and ambitious.

Many readers know See's fiction for its luminous exploration of Chinese culture. Each of her novels puts forward a different aspect, a new historical period, a different perspective. See was close to her Chinese relatives growing up and spent her youth frequenting her great-grandfather's antiques store in Los Angeles's Chinatown, where, as Diana Wagman put it for the *Los Angeles Review of Books*, she "found her literary home." See demonstrates an appreciation for Chinese culture and tradition, and in the instance of her latest novel, for Akha ritual and tradition as well.

Courtesy of Patricia Williams

Lisa See is the author of nine novels, including Snow Flower and the Secret Fan *(2005) and* Peony in Love *(2007). She has also written* On Gold Mountain *(1995), both a memoir and nonfiction biography of her family.*

Although it is far afield from historical fiction per se, it would be remiss not to mention that See has taken her time in this story to address, now and again, some of the more historical intricacies of Communist China's Cultural Revolution. Li-yan and her classmates are taught by Teacher Zhang that under leader Mao Zedong, much if not most of China's indigenous peoples were consolidated into groups of ethnic minorities. The Akha, for instance, were absorbed into the Hani—one of China's "fifty-five ethnic minorities." In the 1960s and 1970s, the Red Guards had endeavored to bring an end to the Four Olds—old customs, old culture, old habits, and old ideas. At the same time, See also introduces some balance, implying that the revolution also brought with it the rationalisms and institutions of modernization—history, materialism, and science; hospitals, factories, and better sanitation. It is in the question of history, particularly China's, that questions arise about See's lack of criticism toward the nature of today's free market economies, however. There is no mention of any of the miserable conditions of modern capitalism, nor of the rise of financialization, organized to benefit an avaricious financial system that allows for, if not directly institutes, deplorable working conditions that have merely supplanted older deplorable conditions one often associates with Communist China.

See's latest novel is neither an historical nor a political novel per se. Like many of her other novels before it, *The Tea Girl of Hummingbird Lane* is a poignant tale about the entangled vacillations endemic to personal loss and gain. All five parts present a span of narrative time that offers kaleidoscopic insight into both Li-yan's journey through life and the minutiae that ultimately shape her journey. In fact, the critical reception of *The Tea Girl of Hummingbird Lane* has been consistently positive, with critics appreciating See's continued variations on the themes of motherhood and daughterhood, love and pain. Zeynep Sen, writing for the *New York Journal of Books*, gave supportive cheer, calling it a "remarkable tale stretching three generations and two different countries," a "story of quiet rebellions, resilience and traditions." Despite lacking in both the raw de-sublimations of realism or the bold new forms of the avant-garde, See has unquestionably crafted, with the confident simplicity of her laconic prose, a novel of fantastic depths sprinkled with a verisimilitude that one can only suspect is the result of extensive research and intense personal experience. Here in the parentheses of her labor, See at once preserves and shares the obscure traditions of the Akha culture. At the same time, she tells her audience a story about the productive opacity of what frequently goes unnoticed or misunderstood in belief.

The Tea Girl of Hummingbird Lane presents a fantastic story that masterfully weaves together contingent twists of fate with the blind bargain of circumstance. Ostensibly, it is a story about one mother's dreams and determinations, and how her decisions and contemplations, her successes and mistakes, fortuitously gather together in timely coincidence to yield what will certainly seem for some nothing shy of destiny. Still, for others, it may read as middle-class fantasy with perhaps no more than commercial aims. Regardless, See's story reminds her readers that chance and fate share a common history, one defined as much by the instability of blind happenstance as by the perseverance of willful determination—and that commodities, such as tea, are symbols of worth.

Frank Joseph

Review Sources

Sen, Zeynep. Review of *The Tea Girl of Hummingbird Lane*, by Lisa See. *New York Journal of Books*, www.nyjournalofbooks.com/book-review/tea-girl. Accessed 12 Sept. 2017.

Simonson, Helen. "Lisa See's New Novel Draws Readers along a Fantastic Tea-Infused Trail." Review of *The Tea Girl of Hummingbird Lane*, by Lisa See. *The Washington Post*, 20 Mar. 2017, www.washingtonpost.com/entertainment/books/lisa-sees-new-novel-draws-readers-along-a-fantastic-tea-infused-trail/2017/03/20/11c0b9be-08fb-11e7-a15f-a58d4a988474_story.html. Accessed 12 Sept. 2017.

Review of *The Tea Girl of Hummingbird Lane*, by Lisa See. *Kirkus*, 26 Dec. 2016, www.kirkusreviews.com/book-reviews/lisa-see/the-tea-girl-of-hummingbird-lane/. Accessed 12 Sept. 2017.

Wagman, Diana. "This Is Mother Love in Lisa See's *The Tea Girl of Hummingbird Lane*." Review of *The Tea Girl of Hummingbird Lane*, by Lisa See. *Los Angeles Review of Books*, 13 May 2017, lareviewofbooks.org/article/this-is-mother-love-in-lisa-sees-the-tea-girl-of-hummingbird-lane/. Accessed 12 Sept. 2017.

Tears We Cannot Stop
A Sermon to White America

Author: Michael Eric Dyson (b. 1958)
Publisher: St. Martin's Press (New York).
    240 pp.
Type of work: Current affairs
Time: Present day
Locale: United States

Adopting the format of a sermon, academic and ordained Baptist minister Michael Eric Dyson delivers a moving polemic against American racism, urging his audience to examine their beliefs and take steps to change.

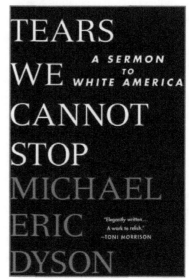

Courtesy of St. Martin's Press

In *Tears We Cannot Stop: A Sermon to White America*, Michael Eric Dyson delivers a dose of tough love to white America. Dyson, a widely respected professor, ordained Baptist minister, and public intellectual who has published nearly two dozen books and scores of articles, adopts the format of a sermon for his latest book, which proves to be a challenging yet surprisingly effective strategy. While Dyson is not always successful in defining his audience and making his ideas fit his chosen structure, his address enables a powerful personal voice to come through and includes valuable practical examples toward the book's end.

The book is divided into nine parts that correspond to the stages of the type of Christian sermons that Dyson has long preached, beginning with the "Call to Worship" and ending with a "Closing Prayer." In the opening section, Dyson explains that he tried to write a more traditional book based on analysis and scholarship, but he kept failing. He describes being called, instead, to write a sermon, arguing that "if we stick with the sermon—through its pitiless recall of our sin, its relentless indictment of our flaws—we can make it to the uplifting expression and redeeming practices that make our faith flow from the pulpit to the public, from darkness to light." Faithful to the form, he does, indeed, deliver "pitiless recall" and "relentless indictment," as he rails against the ideology and practice of whiteness as an evil that simply will not die because white people refuse to let it go.

Many readers may be shocked at his blunt statements, such as that "there is no such thing as white people" (because, as he argues, race is an invented construct) and that "you are emotionally immature about race." Equally likely to shock is his explanation that African Americans feel so terrorized in the United States that they perceive the police in the way that many white Americans perceive the terrorist group Islamic State of Iraq and Syria (ISIS). Expiation requires waking up and repenting, and Dyson knows how to get there.

Getting there, in part, requires a personal address, and this is one of the book's most notable features. That Dyson chooses to write to and for "white America" should not be taken for granted. One of the great developments in late twentieth-century African American literature was its focus on black readers. Writer Toni Morrison, who won the Nobel Prize for literature in 1993, declared that she has always written specifically about and for African Americans. This is not to say that white readers are discouraged from reading, but, rather, that she does not write primarily for their benefit. This shift proved to be revolutionary because, by claiming this freedom, Morrison vastly expanded the imaginative limits of fiction about African American life and culture. It became possible to tell the truth about race in America in new and perhaps more healing ways. The early twenty-first century brings an old set of challenges with new awareness, as racial injustice and tensions continue to plague the nation and technology and politics enable wider awareness of key issues such as police brutality. In this moment, Dyson uses a sermon to speak directly to white readers about their stubborn resistance to the ideology of whiteness. The direct address is thus a gift but also implies the existence of readers who will listen. Most importantly, it allows Dyson to speak hard truths directly to those who need to hear it.

This surprising rhetorical strategy, however, could prove to be tricky for some readers. To address "white America," Dyson must make assumptions about his audience, and the general assumption is of a reader who is largely ignorant about matters of race and about black life and culture. Thus, Dyson assumes that his audience does not know, for example, that Martin Luther King Jr. did not simply advocate peace and racial unity but also held radical views; for example, his opposition to the Vietnam War and his growing emphasis, toward the end of his life, on the scourge of poverty in America. Many of Dyson's white readers do know this, and they also know that whiteness is an invented ideology, which Dyson acknowledges, but he insists that knowing is not enough. "Yet you also know that whiteness for the most part remains invisible to many white folk," he argues. His point, therefore, is that white people must act on their knowledge to a greater extent than they have.

Yet Dyson's definition of his audience is sometimes uneven. While he sometimes assumes very little knowledge on the part of the audience, at other times he makes statements that would baffle such readers. For example, when discussing the O. J. Simpson trial, he compares Simpson's behavior to that of Clarence Thomas, saying, "Even Clarence Thomas is blacker than O. J.," before writing, "But Thomas was reviled by black culture for his dark skin." Here, he gets into the politics of skin color and victimhood within the black community. If white readers do not know some of the basics of racism, as Dyson assumes, statements like this will likely confuse such readers. This unevenness might be less problematic if readers consider that Dyson directs his rhetoric to white America as an ideology, which includes individual readers but does not necessarily rigidly define them. He addresses the collective behaviors of a group and their pernicious effects while urging individuals to take to heart his call for action.

The effect of the sermon structure is also more successful in some sections than

Courtesy of Nina Subin

Michael Eric Dyson is an ordained Baptist minister, a professor of sociology at Georgetown University, the author of several books, a contributing writer for the New York Times, *and a contributing editor for the* New Republic.

in others. In the section "Hymns of Praise," the praise is directed not toward God but toward popular singers such as KRS-One, Lauryn Hill, Tupac Shakur, Jay Z, Beyoncé, and Kendrick Lamar. Dyson describes them as "our griots" who "answer the reign of terror that consumes our days." This rhetorical twist is refreshing, as Dyson praises the artists engaging in necessary protest, but some readers may object to the linking of such music, with its at times graphic and offensive language, to a traditionally religious form. The second chapter of the fifth section, titled "Sermon," outlines the "five stages of white racial grief." These include pleading ignorance about black life and culture, denial, appropriation, revising racial history, and diluting the effects of race.

Most importantly, Dyson makes many excellent, subtle points in this chapter, such as his distinction between freedom of expression and appropriation, a difficult concept for even the most well-intentioned white readers. He also explains why the claim of "not seeing color" is actually an expression of privilege and the damage done by those who would revise racial history (such as the claim that the Civil War was not about slavery but about defending states' rights). Similarly, he argues forcefully that those who balk at affirmative action must realize that white people have enjoyed de facto affirmative action for centuries. Yet, it is not at all clear why these "stages" are ordered as such, and Dyson offers no explanation of them as a larger process. Rather, these acts seem to represent some of the most prevalent and enduring racist behaviors. Nonetheless, he ends the chapter with an exhortation ringing with clarity, telling white people to "give up myths about yourself, about your history. That you are resolutely individual, and not part of a group. That you pulled yourselves up by your bootstraps." Such powerful messages make up for the structural deficit.

Ultimately, Dyson's message is that the solution is love, not hateful vengeance. He makes this clear when he eloquently writes, "The idolatry of whiteness and the cloak of innocence that shields it can only be quenched by love . . . a public expression of love that holds us all accountable. Justice is what love sounds like when it speaks in public." Despite—or perhaps because of—the anger that infuses Dyson's frank words, he is able to see past the rage and despair to a solution. But first, he asks readers to share the pain of the racism he has endured. His sermon format and direct address to the reader allow him to share personal stories—many truly shocking—of the profound damage that racism has inflicted on him and on black communities. He tells of the first time, as a seven-year-old, that he was referred to in racist terms and denied service in a roadside restaurant; of being pulled over by the police after disciplining his child; of being refused service and publicly humiliated at his own bank; of having police brutally threaten to kill him for no reason; and of the stream of deeply disturbing, profanity-laced hate mail he receives on a regular basis (of which he includes specific and therefore especially effective examples). The stories are heartbreaking and enraging. They also inspire deep sympathy and help readers to seriously consider the practical suggestions that Dyson presents in his final chapters.

These suggestions, in the "Benediction" section of the sermon, are perhaps the most helpful part of the book for sympathetic readers, as Dyson offers concrete ideas for how to examine beliefs and take action. While his acronym for this seems somewhat forced, the suggestions are inspiring. Dyson believes that, even if the government fails to make reparations for the enduring damage caused by centuries of slavery, white individuals can do so in many ways, such as by paying black professionals a bit more for their services, donating scholarship money for students and to summer camps, sponsoring school trips for black children, and so forth. He also urges white people to educate themselves about black life and culture and provides a reading list to help people get started. At the same time, he insists that white people must also educate others, participate in rallies and events, make friends with black people, speak up about injustice, and so forth.

This practical section tempers the sense of shock and outrage that some readers may experience earlier in the book and communicates that Dyson's direct address to "white America" is not something he uses as a convenient rhetorical strategy. The title *Tears We Cannot Stop* becomes a literal exhortation to white Americans to put an end to the violence that Dyson and other African Americans have endured their entire lives. By the end of the book, he has shown that his sermon does far more than lament and pray—he is in this journey of healing for the long haul.

Ashleigh Imus, PhD

Review Sources

Fate, Tom Montgomery. Review of *Tears We Cannot Stop: A Sermon to White America*, by Michael Eric Dyson. *Chicago Tribune*, 8 Feb. 2017, www.chicago-tribune.com/lifestyles/books/ct-books-0212-tears-we-cannot-stop-michael-eric-dyson-20170208-story.html. Accessed 7 Feb. 2018.

Lozada, Carlos. "A Sermon on the Unbearable Whiteness of America." Review of *Tears We Cannot Stop: A Sermon to White America*, by Michael Eric Dyson. *The Washington Post*, 6 Jan. 2017, www.washingtonpost.com/news/book-party/wp/2017/01/06/a-sermon-on-the-unbearable-whiteness-of-america/. Accessed 7 Feb. 2018.

Phillips, Patrick. "A Cry from the Heart: Michael Eric Dyson Addresses Race Head-On." Review of *Tears We Cannot Stop: A Sermon to White America*, by Michael Eric Dyson. *The New York Times*, 12 Jan. 2017, www.nytimes.com/2017/01/12/books/review/tears-we-cannot-stop-michael-eric-dyson.html. Accessed 7 Feb. 2018.

Theft by Finding

Author: David Sedaris (b. 1956)
Publisher: Little, Brown (New York). 528 pp.
Type of work: Diary
Time: Late twentieth and early twenty-first centuries
Locales: United States, France

In the first volume of his published diaries, David Sedaris recounts his early years of wandering, the development of his writing talent, and his success as one of America's great comedy writers.

Principal personages
DAVID SEDARIS, author and narrator
DAD, his father
MOM, his mother
AMY SEDARIS, his sister
HUGH HAMRICK, his boyfriend

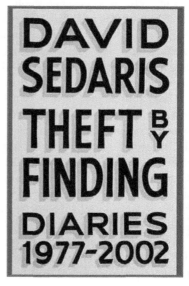

Courtesy of Little, Brown Company

The first volume of essayist David Sedaris's diary is unconventional, yet ultimately rewarding. Reflecting the quirky, hilarious musings for which Sedaris is known and loved, the book in some ways departs from the diary genre. Sedaris decided to call the diary, spanning the twenty-five years from 1977 to 2002, *Theft by Finding*, to describe his chief perspective on life. Rather than painstakingly record his thoughts and feelings, Sedaris focuses outwardly, with little attention paid to personal detail, though he sometimes omits even basic information about his own history. He shows the reader his fascination with the strange and wondrous things he finds in the world—and this innate interest forms the backbone of his narrative gift. While this approach leaves wide gaps, particularly in comparison to Sedaris's most accomplished work, it faithfully renders the author's keen powers of observation and his talent for sketching comic scenes, fueled by his longstanding fascination with the bizarre, violent, and grotesque sides of life.

Sedaris explains his approach in the book's introduction, where he says that he does not write about his feelings, partly because they "weren't that interesting (even to me) but mainly because they were so likely to change." Instead, he decided to record the moments "in which I felt truly present." For him, this often means revealing the most personal feelings and riveting drama (not to mention foibles) of the people he encounters—and the more outrageous, gross, or embarrassing, the better. Thus, in an entry from 1979, one of Sedaris's early years of wandering around the United States, semi-homeless and working odd jobs picking fruit or washing dishes, he chronicles a hotel fight between a father and daughter. Amid crass, curse-filled insults, the daughter blurts out, "Go ahead, tie me up and gag me like you did to Mom." It is this sort of lurid detail that Sedaris finds irresistible, riveting both his and his readers' attention.

Amid these vignettes, readers get a basic outline of Sedaris's life, his early years of wandering, surviving odd jobs and even odder bosses, while longing to become "educated and mature." Eventually, he enrolled in the Art Institute of Chicago, where he first studied painting and sculpture and then moved on to writing. In 1990, he moved to New York City, where he met his partner, Hugh Hamrick; wrote comic plays with his sister Amy; and began to do public readings. His big break came when radio host Ira Glass aired Sedaris's now-classic "Santaland Diaries," which hilariously chronicles his stint as a Christmas elf at Macy's department store. After this, Sedaris recounts receiving more media coverage and, eventually, the first of many book deals. Having won fame and fortune as a comedy writer, and happy in a long-term relationship, he moved with his partner to France. There Sedaris learned French and spent his time traveling the world for his book tours.

Yet a diary is meant to convey more than a skeletal trajectory, and in this case, readers familiar with Sedaris's previous work will already know this trajectory. When he announces, in the introduction, that he has included only "a small fraction" of what he actually wrote, he justifies this by suggesting that readers might prefer to skim the volume rather than read everything chronologically. Yet he also admits to having avoided certain topics that were once difficult to discuss, such as his alcoholism and homosexuality. In another genre, this type of cutting would raise no eyebrows; here, it may give readers pause to wonder what might be missing.

The diary's significant narrative gaps heighten this effect, especially in the early years. The entries relay Sedaris's ultimate success, but include virtually no details about how he became a writer. In 1982, he mentioned wanting to attend college and his anxiety over not having already done so. He began school at the Art Institute in 1984, where he focused on painting and sculpture. He managed to submit his work to art shows but, in the diary, says little about his creations. It comes as a surprise then, in 1988, when Sedaris reveals that he has published a story, divulges his wish to publish a book, and gets a job teaching writing. Readers have no idea how his interest in writing began or developed, or how he gained the credibility to secure the teaching position. The effect continues when he recounts winning a literary award in 1990 and getting booked to perform public readings. For example, readers can (and must) guess, based on the entries of 1997, that Sedaris is on a book tour.

This trait of missed details diminishes somewhat as Sedaris begins to gain recognition for his work, in the early 1990s. Here, some of his entries become longer and more developed. He documents his new relationship with the man who eventually becomes his long-term partner, and he begins to narrate comic episodes, rather than merely sketching vignettes, or recording snatches of conversation. In 1992, he tells of going on a job interview at a place called Mademoiselle, which he initially thinks is the fashion magazine, but eventually realizes is simply a temp agency for administrative jobs. In another entry, he describes his efforts to call Hugh, who is in a hotel in Boca Raton, Florida, but he keeps getting connected to various strangers. Sedaris hilariously renders his tone of mock politeness as he struggles to keep his cool.

During these years, the diary also occasionally hints at some of what has apparently been withheld in the earlier entries. Sedaris does not hide his frequent drug use early on, but the topic fades away in subsequent years until, in 1999, he suddenly admits to his long-standing alcoholism: "I'd have to double-check, but I'm pretty sure I've been drunk every night for the past eighteen years." He says this in the context of announcing that he has been sober for forty-eight hours. Later that year, he records having gone ninety days without drinking. Similarly, in 2000, he reports, with relief, that he does not have AIDS. While including almost nothing about this previously (besides mentioning the rise of the disease), he admits that this worry had always been in the back of his mind. These moments are exceptions to the diary's general silence on Sedaris's most personal struggles.

While such details and development are spotty, one thing is consistent: Sedaris's deep talent for observation—and not just for humorous, cheap, or shocking displays. One great pleasure of this volume is discovering that its author was evidently born with not just keen eyes and ears, but with a superb gift for finding wonderful moments. Yes, he is undeniably obsessed with grossness per se, particularly bodily fluids. One can imagine that he will always feel compelled to document episodes such as an entry from 1991, in which he describes, for no apparent reason, getting vomit on his hands after he picks up a paper bag contaminated with it. And when nothing of this sort has actually occurred, he sometimes goes out of his way to make it up, as in an entry from 1998. Here, Sedaris is learning French and has been instructed to write a paper on American social customs. For this, he invents a grotesque custom, according to which, on the night before a man's wedding, his parents cut off two of his fingers and bury them in a nearby parking lot. If the groom finds the fingers within eight hours, it means his marriage will last.

It would be a mistake, though, to reduce Sedaris's talent to such lurid, bizarre moments. He is, in fact, deeply interested in anything that he finds different or unusual or that makes him feel, as he writes, "truly present." And the diary reveals that this interest and his talent for rendering this quality of presence were with him from the beginning of his life. In a lovely entry from 1985, he eavesdrops on the conversation of two regulars at the International House of Pancakes, one of Sedaris's favorite haunts. The regulars are two men who happen to be blind. Sedaris delights in one man's formal speech, shown by the man's response to a Bill Withers song played on the restaurant sound system: "It may interest you to know that we can expect a new LP from this gentleman in the near future."

Despite these moments, the diary lacks the depth of much of Sedaris's other published writing, which often delivers far more than comic relief. One might even say that in Sedaris's best essays, the comic value becomes secondary as he movingly explores things like his struggles with his relationship with his father, his mother's death, or his sister Tiffany's suicide. What the diary does reveal is that sometime around 1988, its author began to interpret, not merely describe, what he saw and heard. For instance, in that year, he meets a former neighbor on the street one night, who reports that her partner has died: "'He died on me' was how she put it. She said that her brother had died on her too. Then she laughed, like they were off somewhere, hiding together." This is the sort of darkly comic perspective that many fans love about Sedaris.

Even so, the diary does not so much reveal Sedaris's development in action as point toward it. While Sedaris has said that his journaling is essential to his work, this

David Sedaris is the author of numerous nonfiction books, including Barrel Fever: Stories and Essays *(1994),* Holidays on Ice *(1997),* Me Talk Pretty One Day *(2000),* When You Are Engulfed in Flames *(2008), and* Let's Explore Diabetes with Owls *(2013).*

diary seems to offer a pale reflection of development that one senses was largely happening elsewhere, likely in drafts of his essays and other books. For this reason, and especially given that Sedaris, by his own admission, cut so much material out, the diary does not (as reviewer Rachel Manteuffel claims) reflect a precise moment at which Sedaris adopted his perspective. Nor does the diary show, as reviewer Patton Oswalt imagines, that Sedaris has overcome the "bloat" that so often plagues those whose talent wins them fame and fortune. After all, this first volume ends in 2002; so there are many years left to the story of David Sedaris.

But in the next volume, rather than reveal much about how he has personally negotiated success and its temptations, readers might anticipate what Sedaris does best. In the insightful words of critic Fiona Sturges, "his masterstroke is in acting as a bystander in his own story. It's other people's lives that Sedaris finds most fascinating and, by extension, so do we." It is this talent that ultimately makes this diary worth readers' time—and suggests that the second volume might be worth the wait.

Ashleigh Imus, PhD

Review Sources

Manteuffel, Rachel. "The Exact Date David Sedaris Found the Voice That Made Him a Star." Review of *Theft by Finding*, by David Sedaris, *The Washington Post*, 20 June 2017, www.washingtonpost.com/entertainment/books/the-exact-date-david-sedaris-found-the-voice-that-made-him-a-star/2017/06/20/59995022-503e-11e7-91eb-9611861a988f_story.html. Accessed 1 Feb. 2018.

Oswalt, Patton. "David Sedaris's Diaries Track a Path from Struggle to Success." Review of *Theft by Finding*, by David Sedaris. *The New York Times*, 29 May 2017, www.nytimes.com/2017/05/29/books/review/theft-by-finding-diaries-david-sedaris.html. Accessed 1 Feb. 2018.

Sturges, Fiona. "Theft by Finding by David Sedaris, Review—Diaries to Make You Gasp." Review of *Theft by Finding*, by David Sedaris. *The Guardian*, 14 June 2017, www.theguardian.com/books/2017/jun/14/theft-by-finding-by-david-sedaris-review. Accessed 1 Feb. 2018.

There Are More Beautiful Things Than Beyoncé

Author: Morgan Parker
Publisher: Tin House Books (Portland, OR). 96 pp.
Type of work: Poetry

Morgan Parker's second poetry collection, There Are More Beautiful Things Than Beyoncé, *explores topics including vulnerability, mental illness, and black womanhood with appropriated images and themes from popular culture.*

Courtesy of Tin House Books

Award-winning poet Morgan Parker was a graduate student in 2010, when pop star Lady Gaga teamed up with singer Beyoncé to release a song called "Telephone." At the time, Beyoncé had yet to blossom into the larger-than-life icon she has become. Parker, who was inspired to begin writing about the singer after the release of "Telephone," recalled in an interview regarding her 2017 collection that she had been concerned that the poems eventually included were not going to prove relevant for very long. Seven years later, Beyoncé provides the connective tissue for her second poetry collection, *There Are More Beautiful Things Than Beyoncé*. Parker has explained that she was drawn to juxtapositions of glamor, celebrity, and the African American female performing legacy; she wanted to apply these concepts, using largely Beyoncé as a representative, to everyday life.

Parker's poems also touch on other famous figures, such as Saartjie Baartman, referred to as the Hottentot Venus, a nineteenth-century Khoikhoi woman who was forced to perform in freak shows in London; musical performer Lady Gaga; former president Barack Obama; and former First Lady Michelle Obama. Additionally, Parker incorporates specific images from popular culture in her work, including a reference to the reality television show *Wife Swap* as well as wordplay using the lyrics of popular songs from performers and musicians such as Nelly, Jay Z, Guns N' Roses, and Lou Reed. Throughout, she intentionally cultivates a breezy, conversational tone. But, at the same time, her poems are deceptively casual. Her style encapsulates the humor, pain, and ultimate "messiness"—her own word—to describe her artistic philosophy of life.

Parker, who was raised in suburban Los Angeles and earned her MFA in New York City, published her first poetry collection, *Other People's Comfort Keeps Me Up at Night*, in 2015. The publication came after she had won the Gatewood Prize in 2013 and was hailed as a "powerful debut" by the reviewer for *Publishers Weekly*. Like *Beyoncé*, it also explores ideas of race and feminism with verve and sharp wit. In a poem called "Apology with Pearls On," Parker cheekily explores self-aggrandizing self-improvement—she is giving up "dollar Bud Thursday," she writes, "to slink / along the Chelsea circuit white-wined"—while the poem "How to P—— in Public and Maintain Femininity" is a stream-of-consciousness meditation on anxiety. Certain lines of "The Book of Exodus" cast her as a true "millennial poet," as a reviewer for the *Nation* once described her:

> I am all the plagues at once: anxiety,
> wine teeth, bad credit, general malaise.

> Sometimes at a party I escape
> to watch my lipstick fade in the bathroom mirror.

However, her candor about her depression, anxiety, and other vulnerabilities is more radical than that. Taking aim at societal ideas about how black women should behave or talk about themselves, her poems are an act of liberation.

Parker's poems and essays have appeared in the *Paris Review*, the *New York Times*, the *Nation*, and *Buzzfeed*. She is a fan of, and has been compared to, the poet Frank O'Hara, the leader of the New York School of poets in the 1950s and 1960s. O'Hara also incorporated celebrities (Lana Turner, James Dean, Billie Holiday) and pop culture (advertising slogans of the day, the ubiquity of Coca-Cola) into his work, but his influence is more apparent in Parker's conversational tone and her facility with what O'Hara called—in reference to his own work—"I do this I do that" poems, or poems that record everyday movements and thoughts. A clear example of this approach can be found in the poem "Another Another Autumn in New York":

> I will not be attending the party
> tonight, because I am
> microwaving multiple Lean Cuisines
> and watching *Wife Swap*,

It is a rule of thumb for poets, and writers in general, to avoid dating their work with such ephemera, but both Parker and O'Hara view popular culture as a kind of myth-making. Parker investigates how people currently see themselves. Her arresting voice made *There Are More Beautiful Things Than Beyoncé* one of the most popular poetry collections of 2017. Her host of fans include National Book Award–winning poet Terrence Hayes, poet Eileen Myles, novelist and essayist Roxane Gay, and television writer Lena Dunham.

Two poems in *There Are More Beautiful Things Than Beyoncé* are inspired by artists. The poem "We Don't Know When We Were Opened (Or, The Origin of the Universe)" was inspired by the artist Mickalene Thomas, whose work appears on the cover of the first edition of Parker's book. Thomas's work, like Parker's, explores the various facets of black female identity. Thomas created the cover image, a collage

Courtesy of Rachel Eliza Griffiths

Morgan Parker is an award-winning poet. Her first collection of poetry, Other People's Comfort Keeps Me Up at Night, *was published in 2015.*

that depicts a black woman, arms and legs splayed across a colorful couch, her head thrown back in laughter, relaxation, or exhaustion, after reading Parker's book. The poem and the image inform one another, with the poem including images of "bare legs" and "colors draped like / an afterthought." The collage of images culminates in a kind of thesis for the collection as a whole: "We have ideas and vaginas, / history and clothes and a mother." Later in the book, the poem "Black Woman with Chicken" is titled after a photograph by artist Carrie Mae Weems (whose work appears on the cover of the second edition of *Beyoncé*). The photograph, part of Weems's *The Kitchen Table* series (1990), depicts a young black woman sitting at a table and holding a fried drumstick. It is a commentary and a reappropriation of a racist image, as is a companion piece titled "Black Man with Watermelon." In her poem, Parker explores self-image and identity, the space between how the world sees her and how she sees herself. As a writer, she returns again and again to the idea of black women as multitudinous and contradictory. She rejects preset identities:

> Type A
> in the kitchen wanting
> more. Blurry
> princess, self-narrating.

Later, she writes the following lines:

> If you don't
> like what you
> see, remember
> I'm only
> a figment, screen
> of hunger & pining.

In addition to her struggles with depression and anxiety, Parker writes frankly about sexual desire. Her desires are fraught with the painful history of black women's rape and conquest. In two of the book's early poems, she defiantly asserts her own sexual needs. The first poem is titled "All They Want Is My Money, My P———, My Blood." In a burning one-liner, she references this inability to name and assert her own sexuality: "I know my p—— is real good because they said so." She makes references to a vagina again in "Hottentot Venus," a poem written in the voice of Sara Baartman. Baartman, who died in 1816 at the age of twenty-six, was a South African woman who spent the last five years of her life living in a cage while subjected to rape and sexual degradation. Visitors to the freak show where Baartman was "employed" admired the size of her buttocks and could pay extra to poke her with sticks. French scientist Georges Cuvier believed her to be an animal and when she died, he dissected her genitals and put them on display. Baartman's horrifying story has become an emblem of the objectification and dehumanization experienced by enslaved black women that Parker captures in the poem; this experience reverberates in contemporary society. As Parker puts it in "All They Want Is My Money, My P——, My Blood," "The present is not so different."

Beyond sex, Parker expresses her desire to be loved. Loving another person, or being able to receive love from another person, is tied to loving oneself—and the poems suggest that this is not an easy task for Parker. Her depression manifests itself in fugues of wine or Xanax (though these substances can also be celebratory), the "purgatory" of waiting in line at the grocery store Whole Foods, and the haze of a summer where everything seems right but everything is wrong, as is illustrated in the poem "Untitled While Listening to Drake." These prolonged moments of untethering, Parker writes, make her yearn for love while forgetting what it means to be loved in the first place. In another poem, titled "Delicate and Jumpy," she watches a couple wearing matching coats smoke electronic cigarettes across a subway platform. "I am a tiny robot like them," she writes, "but there is no one to love my robo-heart." Such moments of vulnerability illuminate and complicate her glib veneer. Her humor is studded with suffering. In a number of interviews, she talks about the trope of a strong black woman. Black women are strong, she says, but that internalized perception sometimes prevents them from asking for help when they need it. Part of her intention in her work, therefore, is to depict moments of weakness, and in doing so, to encourage other black women to feel okay feeling not okay too.

Molly Hagan

Review Sources

Boyd, Ryan. Review of *There Are More Beautiful Things Than Beyoncé*, by Morgan Parker. *The Los Angeles Review*, www.losangelesreview.org/book-review-things-beautiful-beyonce-morgan-parker. Accessed 11 Dec. 2017.

Lund, Elizabeth. "*There Are More Beautiful Things Than Beyoncé* and Other Best Poetry Collections." Review of *There Are More Beautiful Things Than Beyoncé*, by Morgan Parker, et al. *The Washington Post*, 21 Feb. 2017, www.washington-post.com/entertainment/books/there-are-more-beautiful-things-than-beyonce-and-other-best-poetry-collections/2017/02/21/ac4dcaaa-f20b-11e6-b9c9-e83f-ce42fb61_story.html. Accessed 11 Dec. 2017.

Rudick, Nicole. "Staff Picks: Bey, Bureaucrats, Bloody Hands." Review of *There Are More Beautiful Things Than Beyoncé*, by Morgan Parker, et al. *The Paris Review*, Feb. 2017, www.theparisreview.org/blog/2017/02/17/staff-picks-beyonce-bureaucrats-bloody-hands/17. Accessed 11 Dec. 2017.

Soto, Christopher. "Flaws and All." Review of *There Are More Beautiful Things Than Beyoncé*, by Morgan Parker. *The Nation*, 17 Mar. 2017, www.thenation.com/article/there-are-more-beautiful-things-than-beyonce-morgan-parker-poetry-review. Accessed 11 Dec. 2017.

Teicher, Craig Morgan. "Poetry to Pay Attention To: A Preview of 2017's Best Verse." Review of *There Are More Beautiful Things Than Beyoncé*, by Morgan Parker, et al. *NPR*, 8 Feb. 2017, www.npr.org/2017/02/08/513100833/poetry-to-pay-attention-to-a-preview-of-2017s-best-verse. Accessed 11 Dec. 2017.

They Can't Kill Us until They Kill Us

Author: Hanif Abdurraqib
Publisher: Two Dollar Radio (Columbus, OH). 222 pp.
Type of work: Essays

Courtesy of Two Dollar Radio

Poet and cultural critic Hanif Abdurraqib's first book of essays tackles popular culture, particularly music, through the lens of the author's unique personal experience as an African American and nonpracticing Muslim man in America, getting at the tricky intersections of race and entertainment of all kinds.

Popular music does not exist in a vacuum. It is not some sealed off product that we can look at objectively, an art that can be evaluated apart from both the specific cultural role the work assumes and the personal experience of the listener. And yet, so much of contemporary music criticism aspires to this unreachable level of objectivity. It is in many ways a dishonest approach, one that misrepresents the way that music works on the individual listener.

This sort of faux objectivity is completely foreign to Hanif Abdurraqib, a young poet and cultural critic who, during his stint as a staff writer for *MTV News*, established himself as one of the essential voices weighing in on music and culture. In his new essay collection, *They Can't Kill Us until They Kill Us*, comprised of pieces originally published by MTV and other outlets such as *Pitchfork* and *The New York Times*, the reader gets a chance to see not only Abdurraqib's impressive music pieces, but the wider range of his interests, as he weighs in on sports, politics, and the details of his own life.

But all these various threads are inseparable for Abdurraqib, who does not view different aspects of the world, either personal or political, as items to be compartmentalized, but as things that directly inform each other. As such, he might start an essay on a particular musician with a story from his own life, detailing what was happening to him when he attended a concert in question or first listened to an album, then move on to a full discussion of the musician, and then tie it back to his personal life.

In an early essay, for example, "A Night in Bruce Springsteen's America," Abdurraqib weaves together several threads with ease. After opening the essay with a mythologized vision of Springsteen on stage in New Jersey as a sort of Moses figure, he mentions that the audience at the concert reminds him of a political rally. He then shifts gears and talks about another political event he had recently attended: a visit, the day before, to Ferguson, Missouri, to see the memorial plaque of Michael Brown, a young African American man who was shot to death by a police officer despite being unarmed. This event, along with other similar incidents, led to a nationwide discussion about race and the criminal justice system.

With his personal situation at the time of the concert established, as well as his political concerns, Abdurraqib then launches into a discussion of both the concert and of Springsteen's classic 1980 album *The River*. In his analysis of the record, he concludes that it is ultimately a romantic vision of working-class life. When he looks around at the concert's workers, all people of color, and he considers his own existence as an African American man, Abdurraqib realizes that this is a fantasy that is largely based in whiteness and is not available to African Americans. As he stands among the mostly white crowd, Abdurraqib realizes that *The River* "is an album about coming to terms with the fact that you are going to eventually die, written by someone who seemed to have an understanding of the fact that he was going to live for a long time." With Ferguson in mind, Abdurraqib reflects that he is unable to "consider the future in the way that *The River* seems to consider the future. I don't fear what the future holds so much as I fear not being alive long enough to see it."

Thus, in this essay, the second in the collection, Abdurraqib establishes his method of joining the personal, the political, and the pop cultural together in a single piece, drawing larger conclusions about the state of the country. This is a method that he continues to employ throughout the book. Whether considering the punk-rock scene and its unspoken but nevertheless pronounced racism or his inability to bridge the cultural gap with the well-meaning white father of his partner, Abdurraqib shows that racial misunderstanding looms large in our nation and that different people experience things in vastly different ways based on their backgrounds. In the punk-rock piece, for example, Abdurraqib shows that although punk music is allegedly about a bunch of outsiders coming together to create their own community, they inevitably establish their own inside circle that leaves others, particularly punk fans of color such as the author, excluded from the community.

If the intersection of race and popular culture is one of the major threads in *They Can't Kill Us*, then death is the other, and specifically the question of how (or even if) to keep on living when others die and the world seems to crumble into ashes. Abdurraqib, as the reader finds out through his essays, is a man who has lost a lot of people. His mother died when he was seventeen; her throat closed up in her sleep, a side effect of a medication she was taking. In addition, he has had numerous friends die, often by suicide. Aside from the people he knew personally, those whose deaths he has seen on the news have also had an impact on him, particularly those of young African American men like Michael Brown killed by police. Add to that the despair that hit many Americans after the election of Donald Trump, and it becomes clear that Abdurraqib is writing from a place that tends toward despair. "Today, in 2016," he writes, "death is a low-hovering cloud that is always present. We know the dead and how they have died. We can sometimes watch the dead be killed."

Part of the struggle that Abdurraqib undertakes and enacts on the page is his coming to terms with a life that contains such misery. He does not offer any solutions or false hope, but he is a man capable of seeing positive aspects of life that are sustaining enough to counteract the need to give in to misery. In the book's final essay, "Surviving on Small Joys," he offers up little things, "small pockets of joy," that keep him going in the face of defeat. But even then, he realizes that this is not enough. "I want to be immensely clear about the fact that we need *more* than love and joy," he writes. "Love and joy alone will not rid America of its multilayered history of violence that has existed for longer than any of us have been alive." Nonetheless, Abdurraqib contends that in order to go on living and not admit defeat, people must hold on to whatever they can, promulgate love, and take time for themselves. In this way, Abdurraqib arrives at a sort of honest optimism, one that fully acknowledges the obstacles that it is up against, but perseveres anyway.

Hanif Abdurraqib is a poet and cultural critic. His writing has appeared in Pitchfork, *the* New York Times, *and* MTV News, *among others. He is the author of the poetry collection* The Crown Ain't Worth Much *(2016).*

    They Can't Kill Us, then, is also a celebration, a chance for the author to reflect on those good things in the world that make life worth living, whether it is the music of Chance the Rapper or the legendary basketball play in which a young Allen Iverson hit an in-his-prime Michael Jordan with a killer crossover. The former is celebrated in the book's opening piece, a prime bit of music criticism in which Abdurraqib explains exactly what it is that makes the popular Chance such a special performer. In his essay, the author identifies in Chance the same balance that the reader sees in Abdurraqib himself, that of a man who understands the misery of the world but exudes joy (or attempts to do so) nonetheless. All of this leads into a further discussion of the notion of black joy, which is a complicated thing, and one that hip-hop music is not necessarily known for expressing. Finally, Abdurraqib shows how Chance perfectly balances his music in terms of appealing to both African American and white audiences. By "mak[ing] music facing his people while also leaving the door open for everyone else to try and work their way in," he stays true to his roots while allowing white fans to find their way in, but only on Chance's terms. As such, Chance walks the balance that is necessary for succeeding, or for just surviving in this world.

    But not everyone makes it, and in the book's heartbreaking third-to-last essay, Abdurraqib once again combines music criticism with personal essay to reflect on his mother's death. Sitting in an airline terminal, listening to Future on his headphones, Abdurraqib compares that rapper's grief over breaking up with his partner to his own over his mother's death. He considers what people do with their grief and how, just as Future made an incredible run of albums after the breakup, he himself turned to writing poetry. As a result, his picture is on the front page of the local paper he is currently holding in his hands and, realizing that he cannot show this paper to his deceased mother (and also that it is her birthday), he starts crying. There are different ways to deal with grief, as Abdurraqib knows, and, as he explains, the most common way among black men to do this is to drown yourself in excess. This drowning in excess is what Future raps about on his albums, but he is able to turn it into art. For Abdurraqib, not given to excess, he lets loose with a less "manly" response, tears, but he recognizes the way in which responses to grief can be both productive and self-destructive. Abdurraqib has had more than his share of grief throughout his relatively short life.

Only by reflecting on it and turning it into his own art has he been able to keep going.

Andrew Schenker

Review Sources

Muyumba, Walton. "Hanif Abdurraqib's New Collection of Music Criticism, Essays Vibrates with Soul." Review of *They Can't Kill Us until They Kill Us*, by Hanif Abdurraqib. *Chicago Tribune*, 20 Nov. 2017, www.chicagotribune.com/lifestyles/books/sc-books-they-cant-kill-us-til-they-kill-us-hanif-abdurraquib-1122-story.html. Accessed 8 Jan. 2018.

Review of *They Can't Kill Us until They Kill Us*, by Hanif Abdurraqib. *Kirkus*, 2 Oct. 2017, www.kirkusreviews.com/book-reviews/hanif-abdurraqib/they-cant-kill-us-until-they-kill-us/. Accessed 8 Jan. 2018.

Tosiello, Pete. "Hanif Abdurraqib's Vital Meditation on Music—and Living and Dying in America." Review of *They Can't Kill Us until They Kill Us*, by Hanif Abdurraqib. *The Washington Post*, 12 Dec. 2017, www.washingtonpost.com/entertainment/books/hanif-abdurraqibs-vital-meditation-on-music--and-living-and-dying-in-america/2017/12/12/1036f616-df6b-11e7-8679-a9728984779c_story.html. Accessed 8 Jan. 2018.

The Thirst

Author: Jo Nesbø (b. 1960)
First published: *Tørst*, 2017, in Norway
Translated from the Norwegian by Neil Smith
Publisher: Alfred A. Knopf (New York). 480 pp.
Type of work: Novel
Time: Present day
Locale: Oslo, Norway, and environs

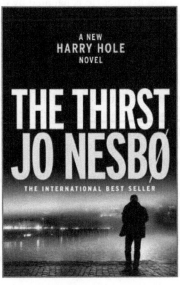

The Thirst is the eleventh entry in the best-selling mystery series featuring iconic police investigator Harry Hole, who specializes in solving serial murders. Harry, who recently retired from the force to teach at Police College, is called back onto the force to catch a serial killer who drinks the blood of victims.

Principal characters

HARRY HOLE, a former homicide detective, now a lecturer at Police College
RAKEL FAUKE, his wife of three years and a lawyer
OLEG FAUKE, his stepson and a student at Police College
KATRINE BRATT, the leader of the Oslo Police Criminal Squad
BJØRN HOLM, Katrine's former boyfriend, a forensic specialist
MIKAEL BELLMAN, the chief of police
GUNNAR HAGEN, the head of the police homicide department
ANDERS WYLLER, a handsome young detective
MONA DAA, a reporter for an Oslo tabloid
STÅLE AUNE, a psychologist and a friend and colleague of Harry's at Police College
VALENTIN GJERTSEN, a.k.a. Alexander Dreyer, an escaped psychopath and the prime suspect in a series of murders
HALLSTEIN SMITH, a psychologist and a scholar of vampirism
SVEIN FINNE, a serial rapist who has spent many years in prison

Since his introduction in *The Bat* (1997, first published in English in 2013), Harry Hole (the two-syllable surname is pronounced "HOO-leh") has captured the imagination of readers around the world. A police detective in Oslo, Norway, specializing in crimes of a serial nature, Harry is recognized both for his intuitive brilliance in interpreting clues at crime scenes—which have ranged from Scandinavia to Australia—and for his difficult personality. Headstrong, melancholy, and fearless in the pursuit of criminals who commit horrific acts for seemingly baffling reasons, Harry has been deeply wounded, both physically and emotionally, by his experiences. He chain-smokes and sometimes drinks to excess in a futile effort to quell nightmares that arise out of his troubled psyche. He is haunted by the faces of the dead, both victims of cases he has investigated and criminals he has been forced to kill in the course of his work.

In the latest installment of the series, *The Thirst*, fans are briefly treated to a different side of Harry Hole. When the novel begins, he is actually content and happy. Married for three years to his longtime love, a beautiful, dark-haired lawyer named Rakel Fauke, Harry, a longtime alcoholic, has dried out. Retired from the force in accordance with Rakel's wishes, he is now an admired, if low-paid, lecturer in investigative techniques at Police College in Oslo. He works alongside his friend Ståle Aune, a psychologist, and teaches Rakel's son, Oleg Fauke, an eager student who hopes to follow his stepfather into law enforcement. Naturally, a period of such stasis cannot endure long in Harry's world.

The catalyst for change, for Harry's return to what he does best, is a new series of horrific crimes being perpetrated in Oslo. Several women in the Norwegian capital, who went on casual dates organized through the Tinder dating app, have been stalked and assaulted in a terrifying fashion. Someone with apparent vampiric tendencies mutilated them using a medieval-style set of iron dentures and drank their blood. From evidence obtained at the crime scenes, the killer awaited victims at their residences after somehow gaining entrance. More worrying, the pace of the assaults seems to be speeding up, and citizens, abetted by the media, publicly express dismay at the inability of the police to put a stop to the violence.

Mikael Bellman, the ambitious yet corrupt chief of police, who is being considered for a prestigious governmental post as justice minister, needs a quick solution to the crimes in order to secure his promotion. Bellman approaches Harry Hole and pressures him to contribute to the investigation by threatening to expose Oleg's past as a heroin addict with a juvenile criminal record, which would disqualify the young man from joining the police force. With little choice in the matter, Harry capitulates. With the approval of his former boss Gunnar Hagen, Harry forms a special, independent unit to supplement the main investigation conducted under Criminal Squad leader Katrine Bratt. Harry's team consists of the bright rookie detective Anders Wyller, his old friend and forensic specialist Bjørn Holm, and Hallstein Smith, a psychologist working on the fringes of the profession who specializes in vampirism.

Both the Crime Squad and Harry's team intensify their investigations. The police track known sex offenders and delve into the Tinder accounts of the victims looking for clues. Harry, meanwhile, looking for insight into the mental state of the killer, questions known deviant Svein Finne, a septuagenarian imprisoned for twenty years and about to be released

Despite the best efforts of the police to prevent further attacks, additional brutal assaults occur. On one occasion, the victim survives. Under questioning, she reveals that the assailant had what appeared to be surgical scars on his face and the portrait of a demon tattooed on his chest. By the description of the tattoo and a *V* scrawled in blood on an apartment door, Harry recognizes the killer as Valentin Gjertsen, a vicious psychopath. Several years earlier, Valentin—who has engaged in aberrant sexual behavior from pedophilia to necrophilia—murdered another inmate and disfigured a prison employee while escaping from a psychiatric facility. It was suspected the killer had gone abroad and underwent plastic surgery to disguise himself. Now, after a long hiatus, Valentin, with an alias and a surgically altered face, has come back to taunt law enforcement, his bold actions daring Harry Hole in particular to try and stop him.

Complications in the investigation arise from a number of sources. Some unknown person, obviously connected to the police force, is leaking details from the crime scenes to tabloid reporter Mona Daa, who refuses to reveal the source of her stories. Evidence surfaces that the main suspect, Valentin, is not operating alone: there may be one or more other people involved in the killings. The police have to chase down a whole slew of potential leads.

Rakel, who has been suffering from headaches, suddenly becomes ill and falls into a coma. Her condition adversely affects Harry's concentration; his attention becomes divided between his wife's mysterious ailment and the investigation. Distracted, Harry

Courtesy of Thron Ullberg

Jo Nesbø has published eleven novels featuring detective Harry Hole, as well as a series of children's books and several stand-alone novels. Nesbø has won numerous honors, including the Glass Key Award (1998) and the Norwegian Booksellers' Prize for best novel (2007). His work has been translated into dozens of languages and has sold tens of millions of copies worldwide.

breaks a law-enforcement taboo by persuading the former owner of a bar, a civilian and one of few people who might be able to recognize Valentin, to keep watch at a bath house where Valentin frequented, in the hopes that he might be able to identify the killer by his distinctive tattoo. This plan fails spectacularly, causing Harry to be harshly reprimanded. In despair over what happened and unable to help Rakel, Harry falls off the wagon, making his tasks all the more difficult.

Like its predecessors, *The Thirst* offers readers a blend of the familiar and the surprising. At the center of a series of novels that are part thriller, part police procedural, and part psychological study is its driving force, Harry Hole. Alternately philosophical or foolish, cynical or romantic, sober or intoxicated, Harry is his own harshest critic. Whatever else may occur, Harry will overcome a succession of internal and external obstacles while working tirelessly toward a logical solution to the various conundrums presented. Harry's sometimes blunt, caustic manner will alienate some and attract others. He is an astute observer of clues at a crime scene and is a dedicated student of human nature, even if he is sometimes puzzled by his own inconsistent behavior.

Fans of the series, and of Nesbø's stand-alone crime novels, know that the plot will be complex, with a multitude of twists and turns leading to an unanticipated and heart-pounding climax. There will be copious amounts of blood spilled (despite the fact that, in real life, murder in Norway is a rarity). Violence, often perpetrated by individuals with severe psychological disorders, will be directed at the weak or vulnerable. Tangled, multifaceted relationships among the characters, a particular Nesbø strength marked by realistic exchanges of abrasive dialogue, will be tested in the course of the story, as Harry coaxes, deceives, or bullies others into doing his bidding for often unexplained reasons. Pace will vary, from leisurely (quiet moments spent among family members and reading reports) to breakneck (chase scenes and combat with villains). Harry and his colleagues will assemble and interpret clues in order to spiral closer to the identity and location of the perpetrator. Harry will risk his life in the ultimate capture or elimination of the culprit.

Told in the third-person point of view—usually from Harry's viewpoint but often incorporating the perspective of the killer or other major characters—*The Thirst* is structured like a three-act play, supplemented with a brief prologue that spotlights a key element of the story and an epilogue that suggests the thrust of the next entry in the series. Part I introduces the main players and sets the plot in motion. Part II presents complications that cast doubt on previous assumptions and increase the tension. Part III sweeps aside false leads and red herrings to reveal the truth, paving the way toward the memorable final confrontation between Harry and his quarry.

As the continuation of a critically and commercially well-received series, *The Thirst* fits well into the Nesbø crime canon. Its title does triple duty, describing the compulsion of the vampiric protagonist, Harry's own ill-suppressed craving for liquor, and the universal desire of humans, like the Tinder victims depicted in the novel, who are desperate to make a connection with someone, anyone, who might be compatible.

Jack Ewing

Review Sources

Elderfield, Jonathan. "Review: Latest Crime Thriller by Jo Nesbø Keeps Readers Guessing." Review of *The Thirst*, by Jo Nesbø. *The Salt Lake Tribune*, 19 May 2017, www.sltrib.com/home/5301756-155/review-latest-crime-thriller-by-jo. Accessed 5 Aug. 2017.

Sanderson, Mark. Review of *The Thirst*, by Jo Nesbø. *Evening Standard*, 4 May 2017, www.standard.co.uk/lifestyle/books/the-thirst-by-jo-nesbo-review-a3530921.html. Accessed 5 Aug. 2017.

Swedlund, Eric. "In Jo Nesbø's *The Thirst*, Detective Harry Hole Tracks a Twisted Killer." Review of *The Thirst*, by Jo Nesbø. *Paste Magazine*, 10 May 2017, www.pastemagazine.com/articles/2017/05/jo-nesbos-the-thirst-detective-harry-hole-returns.html. Accessed 5 Aug. 2017.

Turnbull, Sue. "Crime Review: A New Dark and Diverting Scandi Thriller by Jo Nesbø." Review of *The Thirst*, by Jo Nesbø. *The Sydney Morning Herald*, 14 July 2017, www.smh.com.au/entertainment/books/crime-review-a-new-dark-and-diverting-scandi-thriller-by-jo-nesbo-20170706-gx62zy.html. Accessed 5 Aug. 2017.

This Is How It Always Is

Author: Laurie Frankel
Publisher: Flatiron Books (New York). 336 pp.
Type of work: Novel
Time: Present day
Locales: Madison, Wisconsin; Seattle, Washington; Thailand

This Is How It Always Is *is about the complex desire to hide the truth in order to protect a loved one. Written by American author Laurie Frankel, the novel explores themes of family, destiny, and gender.*

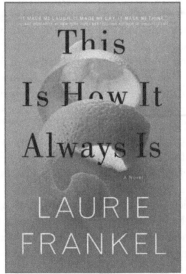

Courtesy of Macmillan

Principal characters
DR. ROSIE WALSH, the mother of the Walsh-Adams family and a physician
PENN ADAMS, a struggling novelist and the father of the Walsh-Adams family
POPPY WALSH-ADAMS, the youngest Walsh-Adams family member, a transgender girl originally named Claude
ROO WALSH-ADAMS, the oldest Walsh-Adams child
BEN WALSH-ADAMS, the second-oldest Walsh-Adams child
ORION WALSH-ADAMS, Poppy's brother and Rigel's twin
RIGEL WALSH-ADAMS, Poppy's brother and Orion's twin

It is not uncommon for writers to mine their own lives for material. John le Carré, for example, has famously used his experiences working for the UK Secret Intelligence Service during the 1950s and '60s in his best-selling spy thrillers. Meanwhile, Sylvia Plath's only novel, *The Bell Jar* (1963), is considered a thinly veiled retelling of the time she spent working at a prestigious women's magazine while grappling with depression.

American author Laurie Frankel did not build her literary reputation on semiautobiographical fiction. Her first two novels were products of her imagination; *The Atlas of Love* (2010) follows three friends who try their hands at parenting together, while *Goodbye for Now* (2012) is about a software engineer who creates a simulation program that allows people to communicate with deceased loved ones. In her third novel, however, Frankel follows in the footsteps of le Carré and Plath by using her family's experiences as a primary storytelling source.

The process of putting her life on the page began on September 16, 2016, when Frankel wrote a Modern Love column for the *New York Times* entitled "From He to She in First Grade." The essay chronicled one of the most challenging times Frankel had endured as a mother: when her six-year-old child, assigned male at birth, revealed that she identified as a girl and wanted to begin presenting as such at school. It was a frightening endeavor for Frankel and her husband as they feared for the safety of their child. And while their daughter was fortunate enough to be accepted by her peers quickly and peacefully, the event proved to be so socially complex and emotional that Frankel felt compelled to explore it further in her fiction.

The resulting novel, *This Is How It Always Is* (2017), is the story of the Walsh-Adams family, whose lives are turned upside down when their youngest member determines that she is not the gender she was originally assigned. As early as the age of three, Claude Walsh-Adams prefers to wear skirts, bikinis, and barrettes. At first, parents Rosie and Penn think it is nothing more than a phase. But as time goes on and Claude's desire to present as a girl never wavers, even when it means getting bullied at school, Rosie and Penn realize that their child is in fact experiencing gender dysphoria.

A large part of what makes *This Is How It Always Is* so engaging is its central conflict. Frankel could have easily decided to focus on the most obvious story—one in which two parents struggle to accept the truth about their child's identity. Instead, she chooses to leapfrog that narrative beat altogether. While Rosie and Penn are initially unsure of how to handle their child's transition into girlhood, their love and support throughout the process is unconditional. In an innovative twist, Frankel makes the primary source of conflict and suspense Penn and Rosie's effort to hide from others that their youngest child is transgender. This decision comes after a terrifying experience during which a six-year-old Claude is threatened by a friend's gun-slinging father in their hometown of Madison, Wisconsin. Rosie and Penn decide to move their family to the more progressive city of Seattle. By the time they move, their youngest child has adopted the name Poppy and is living openly as a girl, and the Walsh-Adams family decides that it is not necessary to tell their new Seattle friends, colleagues, and neighbors about her transition.

Poppy's secret makes for an interesting narrative, one that forces the characters to navigate many difficult scenarios. For example, when Poppy first arrives in Seattle, she becomes friends with a group of girls. For her seventh birthday party, she wants to have a sleepover with her friends, but Rosie worries about the logistics—specifically whether or not her daughter will have to change into her pajamas in front of the other girls. Years later, when Poppy is ten, she is outed to her peers as transgender. Rosie and Penn endure a whodunit type mystery in which all of their sons become suspects, while Poppy returns to presenting as male as a form of self-punishment. Ultimately, Frankel ensures that while Poppy is a typical child in many ways, she encounters numerous obstacles that her cisgender peers do not. What makes all of these events so compelling is that they feel unprecedented in fiction. Few books explore the day-to-day landscape of transgender childhood.

Frankel challenges conventional ideas of gender in a number of ways. While this is most obvious in Poppy's journey, the author also uses Rosie and Penn's relationship to demonstrate that men and women do not have to fall into traditional binary roles in order to be happy. Even before Claude is born, Frankel establishes that Rosie, who is a doctor, is the family breadwinner while Penn is the caretaker. The two split domestic duties as much as possible while supporting one another's careers. Although many outsiders question and mock their family dynamic, this is never an issue of contention between the two—Penn does not feel

Laurie Frankel is an American novelist best known for her best-selling books The Atlas of Love *(2010) and* Goodbye for Now *(2012).*

emasculated by staying home with the children and Rosie does not feel like she is a bad mother because she works full time. Instead, Frankel presents their relationship as healthy, loving, and indestructible.

Despite its complicated subject matter, Frankel ensures *This Is How It Always Is* consistently maintains a warm, light tone. She accomplishes this by constructing the majority of the narrative around Rosie and Penn's experiences as the concerned, loving parents of a transgender child. This is an interesting choice, especially considering that the book is written with a third-person omniscient narrator and subsequently has the potential to follow the story lines of any of the Walsh-Adams family members. By focusing predominantly on Rosie and Penn's inner dialogue and emotions as they do everything within their power to ensure Poppy feels safe and happy, Frankel infuses the narrative with positivity and hope.

The primary theme of *This Is How It Always Is* is destiny. Frankel leverages this theme seemingly with the intention of helping readers understand that being transgender is not a choice—people are born this way. To that end, she uses several literary devices to demonstrate the inevitability of Poppy's transition. Through flashbacks, for example, Frankel reveals that as a child, Rosie had a sister named Poppy who died of cancer. This created a desire within her to both become a doctor and to one day have a daughter whom she could name after her sister. Frankel again suggests that a divine force was in play when Penn first meets Rosie and instantly knows that they will marry and have a daughter together. The theme is furthered during Poppy's conception. Rosie, after having four sons, wants a daughter so desperately that she is willing to opt for superstition over scientific logic. She puts a spoon under the bed before turning it to face east because an old wives' tale suggests that such actions will increase the odds of having a girl. Frankel is careful to highlight the beautiful, powerful irony within these scenes. Rosie may have always known that it was her destiny to one day have a daughter named Poppy; she just did not realize the way in which that daughter would arrive.

It can be argued that one of the novel's shortcomings is the fact that it plays it safe. That is to say that the prejudice and obstacles that Poppy experiences pale in comparison to what many transgender children endure in real life. Consequently, *This Is How It Always Is* at times feels predictable. As Hanna Rosin wrote in her *New York Times* review, "What Poppy is living through is extraordinary, unimaginable, and yet one never feels she will be anything but O.K." Because the novel's happy ending appears inevitable, much of the narrative's suspense becomes deflated. However, *This Is How It Always Is* remains a page-turner due to the fact that it explores the depths of a complex, contemporary issue in an honest way. There are few characters like Poppy in fiction, which makes spending time with her throughout the novel seem like a privilege.

Reviews of *This Is How It Always Is* have been mixed, but largely positive. In addition to complaints that Frankel does not take enough storytelling risks, some critics have disliked the overly feel-good tone she employs. A reviewer for *Kirkus* wrote, "The novel is cloying at times, with arch formulations, preachy pronouncements, and a running metafictional fairy tale." Such a criticism is highly subjective—while some readers will dislike Frankel's positivity, others will find it to be a pleasure to read. After all, stories about transgender people are too often rife with bigotry and violence. With *This Is How It Always Is*, Frankel demonstrates that transgender characters are also deserving and capable of happy endings.

Ultimately, *This Is How It Always Is* explores identity and parenthood in a new, refreshing way. Through her well-crafted characters, emotional honesty, and exceptional pacing, Frankel delivers an unforgettable story about the nature of intertwined destinies and how the journey of an individual can inspire the transformation of an entire family.

Emily Turner

Review Sources

Rosin, Hanna. "In Transition: A Novel About What Happens When a Son Becomes a Daughter." Review of *This Is How It Always Is,* by Laurie Frankel. *The New York Times*, 10 Feb. 2017, www.nytimes.com/2017/02/10/books/review/this-is-how-it-always-is-laurie-frankel.html. Accessed 30 Dec. 2017.

Review of *This Is How It Always Is*, by Laurie Frankel. *Kirkus Reviews*, 24 Jan. 2017, www.kirkusreviews.com/book-reviews/laurie-frankel/this-is-how-it-always-is/. Accessed 30 Dec. 2017.

Review of *This Is How It Always Is*, by Laurie Frankel. *Publishers Weekly*, 28 Nov. 2016, www.publishersweekly.com/978-1-250-08855-0. Accessed 30 Dec. 2017.

Thunder in the Mountains
Chief Joseph, Oliver Otis Howard, and the Nez Perce War

Author: Daniel J. Sharfstein (b. 1972)
Publisher: W. W. Norton (New York). Illustrated. 640 pp.
Type of work: History
Time: Primarily 1860s to early 1900s
Locale: Pacific Northwest

Thunder in the Mountains *presents a history of the Nez Perce War of 1877 told primarily through the lives of Major General Oliver Otis Howard, commander of the Department of the Columbia in the Pacific Northwest, and Chief Joseph, a leader among the Nez Perce who refused to relinquish their claims to their original homelands and be relocated to another reservation.*

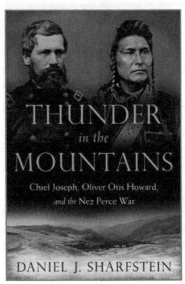

Courtesy of W.W. Norton

Principal personages

CHIEF JOSEPH, a.k.a. Heinmot Tooyalakekt or Young Joseph, chief of a non-treaty band of the Nez Perce living in the Wallowa Valley, a leader during the tribe's flight from the US Army

OLLOKOT, his brother, another leader of the Nez Perce

YELLOW WOLF (HEMENE MOXMOX), his nephew, a participant in the 1877 war

LOOKING GLASS (ALALIMYA TAKANIN), an experienced warrior, a war chief among the non-treaty Nez Perce

MAJOR GENERAL OLIVER OTIS HOWARD, a Union Army veteran of the US Civil War, head of the Freedman's Bureau, and commander of the Department of the Columbia during the Nez Perce War

CHARLES ERSKINE SCOTT WOOD, Howard's aide, later a lawyer and social activist who tried to publicize the injustices committed against the Nez Perce

COLONEL NELSON MILES, leader of the US Army forces that cut off the retreat of the Nez Perce, later made a brigadier general

GENERAL JOHN GIBBON, a US Army officer in command at the Battle of Big Hole but later an advocate for Chief Joseph's people

LUCULLUS VIRGIL MCWHORTER, a rancher near the Yakima Reservation in Washington who recorded many of Yellow Wolf's stories of Nez Perce life and the 1877 war

GENERAL WILLIAM TECUMSEH SHERMAN, Union Civil War major general and then general-in-chief of the US Army during much of Howard's later career

The conflict between the US Army and Chief Joseph's band of the Nez Perce has gained much-deserved attention in recent years, although it is not generally as well known as some of the American Indian fighting in the Great Plains or the Southwest. Chief Joseph led a small band who argued that they had not been a party to the Treaty of 1863, by which some Nez Perce leaders had signed away their rights to the traditional homeland of Chief Joseph's band in the Wallowa Valley of eastern Oregon. Chief Joseph later became a symbol of American Indian resistance to the federal government's policy of forcing tribes onto ever-diminishing reservations.

Daniel Sharfstein tells the story of the Nez Perce War of 1877, along with the background leading up to it and the aftermath of the conflict, primarily by focusing on the lives of two men: Chief Joseph and General Oliver Otis Howard, who led the early part of the army's pursuit of Chief Joseph's band. Chief Joseph was thirty-five years old in 1877 and was little known beyond the region of his homelands before the mid-1860s. The title *Thunder in the Mountain* refers to a translation of Joseph's name Heinmot Tooyalakekt from the Nez Perce language, which could be rendered in English as Thunder Rolling in the Mountains, or perhaps, Thunder Rising to Loftier Mountain Heights. Oliver Otis Howard had risen to the rank of major general during the Civil War and had ended the war with a fair reputation as an officer and fighting man. After the war, he was made head of the Freedmen's Bureau, created to help former slaves adapt to life as free people. While northerners, and especially Radical Republicans, who supported citizenship and equal rights for the freedmen appreciated Howard's work with the bureau, Southern Democrats who wanted to maintain a system of white supremacy in the postwar South fought Howard's efforts and brought charges of corruption and fiscal mismanagement against him. The Freedman's Bureau closed in 1872, and in 1874, Howard returned to active duty with the army and was given command of the Department of the Columbia, which encompassed the state of Oregon as well as the territories of Idaho, Washington, and Alaska. As Sharfstein presents it, Howard saw this command as a chance to rebuild his reputation, although he also referred to his posting to the faraway outpost in the Pacific Northwest as an "exile."

Sharfstein has written more than simply a dual biography of General Howard and Chief Joseph, although he does describe both their lives in rich detail. The book also covers the history of what has come to be known as the Flight of the Nez Perce, as Joseph's band tried to flee to Canada to escape the government's attempt to force them onto a reservation. It also attends to other figures who played a role in presenting the story of the Nez Perce to the American public and to Chief Joseph's lifelong struggle to get the government to recognize his people's claims to their lands. Sharfstein gives a detailed, engaging account of the war between the US Army and the non-treaty Nez Perce who fled with Joseph. However, the war occupies less than half the book, with much attention given to backgrounds and the earlier lives of Joseph and General Howard and to the years after the surrender of the Nez Perce. While many books picture Chief Joseph as a masterful tactician who led his people on a strategic withdrawal, he really was not a war chief, as Sharfstein shows. During the early part of their flight, the band was led by Looking Glass. After they suffered heavy losses at the Battle of the

Big Hole, the warriors lost confidence in him, and while the group moved toward the buffalo-hunting country of eastern Montana, Lean Elk became the leader. As the army closed in on them, Lean Elk reluctantly allowed Looking Glass to resume leadership, although by this time, Lean Elk was convinced that "we will be caught and killed." When the Nez Perce surrendered after the fighting in the Bear Paw Mountains of north-central Montana in October 1877, Chief Joseph emerged as the major negotiator dealing with the US Army commanders.

US Army officials and government bureaucrats generally pictured Chief Joseph as blindly seeking to preserve a way of life that had already disappeared. Many scholars since then, though often sympathetic to the struggle of the Nez Perce, have echoed this assessment. But Sharfstein presents Chief Joseph as a man who understood the ways of American society and government bureaucracy better than many people then realized. He saw, for instance, that two separate bureaucracies handled American Indian affairs in his day—the War Department and the Department of the Interior. He had a simple, albeit misplaced, faith that someone within the US government would listen to his tribe's plea for justice concerning their homeland in the Wallowa country and would restore this land to his people. In 1863, several Nez Perce bands agreed to a treaty that assigned them lands on the Lapwai Reservation in northwestern Idaho. But Joseph argued that this treaty was negotiated by chiefs that did not represent all the bands of the Nez Perce and that his band had never relinquished their claim to their lands. For the rest of his life, Joseph attempted to push his people's claim to these lands. He went back and forth between army officers and Bureau of Indian Affairs (BIA) officials and attempted at times to appeal directly to members of Congress, the president, and the American public.

There are some surprising ironies in the twists and turns of Sharfstein's account. A reader might come to the book assuming that Howard, who had struggled in the Freedman's Bureau to see that freedpeople were given a chance at full equality and secure civil rights, would surely emerge as a supporter of the claims of the Nez Perce to their homelands. In reality, however, although Howard somewhat sympathized with Chief Joseph and his people, that sympathy seemed to dissipate over time. In the late nineteenth century, Howard wrote two books—one for children and another for adults—about his life in the West. In both he

Daniel J. Sharfstein teaches law and history at Vanderbilt University, where he also codirects the George Barrett Social Justice Program. His first book, The Invisible Line: A Secret History of Race in America *(2011), received critical acclaim and the J. Anthony Lukas Book Prize.*

paid extensive attention to Chief Joseph, perhaps hoping to capitalize on the public's interest in him. But in his autobiography published in 1908, he gave minimal attention to the Nez Perce or the conflict with them. His conclusion seemed to be that the Nez Perce should just accept their lot, wherever they were, and assimilate into the dominant culture. Thus, he was neither the first nor the last American official to suggest this. On the other hand, General Nelson A. Miles, who commanded the troops that blocked the Nez Perce retreat toward Canada and who was later involved in the campaign to force the Chiricahua Apaches to accept reservation life, came to support the claims of

Chief Joseph's people to their homelands and their right to resettle there. Sharfstein's sympathy for the Nez Perce is evident, and the reader can hardly help being drawn into rooting for Chief Joseph to finally get justice. But the truth, as Sharfstein clearly shows, is that while the resistant bands of the Nez Perce were eventually allowed to settle on several existing reservations in the Northwest, the Wallowa Valley country was never restored to them.

Sharfstein's first book, *The Invisible Line: A Secret History of Race in America* (2011), was well received by scholars and reviewers alike, and there are echoes of the themes from it in this book. In his first book, Sharfstein argued that race has never been a strictly defined concept in America. Similarly, in *Thunder in the Mountains*, Sharfstein looks at what it means to be an American. According to census records, 8 percent of American Indians were citizens of the United States in 1870, although more would become citizens over the next few decades through the Dawes Act of 1887, which gave American Indian families an individual allotment of reservation land as their personal property and awarded citizenship to those who accepted these allotments. But as the freedmen's experience in the South, and the subsequent history of the Nez Perce shows, holding citizenship does not necessarily mean a group will be afforded justice. Sharfstein notes that Charles Erskine Scott Wood, an army lieutenant who served under Howard during the pursuit of the Nez Perce, later befriended Joseph and sought to publicize the foul treatment of the Nez Perce. Wood was the source of the oft-quoted observation that "Joseph cannot accuse the Government of the United States of one single act of justice." While that is not Sharfstein's thesis, it could serve as a summary of a significant story line in this book. Reviewers and historians of the American West and of American Indian policy and affairs have praised this book, and scholars working in those fields will find it a valuable addition to their libraries.

Mark S. Joy, PhD

Review Sources

Freeman, Jay. Review of *Thunder in the Mountains: Chief Joseph, Oliver Otis Howard, and the Nez Perce War*, by Daniel J. Sharfstein. *Booklist*, vol. 113, no. 13, Mar. 2017, p. 35. *Literary Reference Center Plus*, search.ebscohost.com/login.asp x?direct=true&db=lkh&AN=121554530&site=lrc-plus. Accessed 17 Jan. 2018.

Klein, Julia M. "Daniel J. Sharfstein Offers Luminescent Account of Nez Perce Tragedy in *Thunder in the Mountains*." Review of *Thunder in the Mountains: Chief Joseph, Oliver Otis Howard, and the Nez Perce War*, by Daniel J. Sharfstein. *Chicago Tribune*, 5 Apr. 2017, www.chicagotribune.com/lifestyles/books/ct-thunder-in-the-mountains-daniel-sharfenstein-books-0409-20170404-story.html. Accessed 16 Jan. 2018.

Mullis, Tony R. Review of *Thunder in the Mountains: Chief Joseph, Oliver Otis Howard, and the Nez Perce War*, by Daniel J. Sharfstein. *Military Review: The Professional Journal of the U.S. Army*, 10 Nov. 2017, www.armyupress.army.mil/ Journals/Military-Review/MR-Book-Reviews/november-2017/Book-Review-004. Accessed 16 Jan. 2018.

Romeo, Nick. "*Thunder in the Mountains* Recounts the Tragedy of the Nez Perce War." Review of *Thunder in the Mountains: Chief Joseph, Oliver Otis Howard, and the Nez Perce War*, by Daniel J. Sharfstein. *The Christian Science Monitor*, 27 Apr. 2017, www.csmonitor.com/Books/Book-Reviews/2017/0427/Thunder-in-the-Mountains-recounts-the-tragedy-of-the-Nez-Perce-War. Accessed 16 Jan. 2018.

To Siri, with Love
A Mother, Her Autistic Son, and the Kindness of Machines

Author: Judith Newman (b. 1961)
Publisher: Harper (New York). 256 pp.
Type of work: Memoir
Time: 2000–2016
Locale: New York City

In To Siri, with Love, *Judith Newman shares fifteen essays that recount how her son Gus, who has autism, uses Apple's personal assistant technology known as Siri to connect with the world.*

Principal personages
JUDITH NEWMAN, the narrator, a journalist and author
AUGUSTUS "GUS" JOHN SNOWDON, her son, who has autism
JOHN SNOWDON, her husband, a retired opera singer
HENRY SNOWDON, Gus's fraternal twin, who is neurotypical

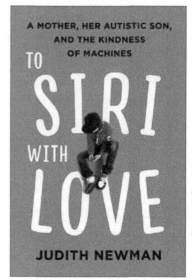

Courtesy of HarperCollins Publishers

Autism, its possible causes, and its potential treatments have been a popular topic in both fiction and nonfiction, with such books as *The Reason I Jump* (2007), by Naoki Higashida; Temple Grandin and Richard Panek's *The Autistic Brain* (2013); and *Life, Animated* (2014), by Ron Suskind helping to shed light on this mysterious condition. In 2014, Judith Newman, a writer whose works have appeared in such publications as *Vanity Fair, Harper's,* and the *Wall Street Journal,* penned a *New York Times* article about her son Gus's struggles with autism titled "To Siri, with Love." In that piece, Newman talked about how Siri, the personal assistant feature available on Apple's iOS-run products, engaged her son in ways that other people could not, listening to his queries on his various obsessions such as trains, planes, and the weather with interest and, most importantly to Newman, apparent kindness.

The column became a viral sensation, and Newman began receiving feedback from people around the world, many of whom asked her to write more about herself and her son and their experiences with Siri. This inspired Newman to collect a series of short stories and vignettes that chronicle not only her son's interactions with Siri but also her own struggles as a mother raising a child with autism. She has noted that while the book does praise technology and the difference it has made in her life, it is more of a story about family and how people can find ways to communicate with each other even under the most difficult of circumstances.

To Siri, with Love: A Mother, Her Autistic Son, and the Kindness of Machines chronicles Newman's experiences as a mother from the beginning, allowing the reader to place her struggles with Gus in context. The first essay in the book, titled "Oh No," details the challenges Newman faced in getting pregnant and how, in her words, it took seven years and $70,000 for it to finally happen. The essay goes on to explain that their twins, Gus and Henry, were born approximately seven weeks early, with Henry weighing three pounds, one ounce and Gus weighing three pounds, eleven ounces. Nevertheless, the boys managed to thrive. Still, early on, Newman noticed that something was different about Gus. She writes about how as an infant Gus did not show the same interest in toys as Henry or other children their age. She also notes that his speech was delayed and that he tended to make sounds more than using actual language. After several years of testing, Newman writes that Gus was finally diagnosed as being on the autism spectrum when he was six years old. The revelation was a devastating one for Newman, leading her to recall troubled children she knew growing up and how she treated them, not badly, but with indifference. These memories cause Newman concern for how her own child will be perceived when he goes to school.

The next essay, titled "Why?," chronicles Newman's attempts to divine an answer for why Gus has autism. Her internet research leads her to speculate on such possibilities as her husband's age at the time the boys were conceived (sixty-nine) or her own age (forty), or the fact that Newman had multiple children via in vitro fertilization. She even expresses concern that her home's proximity to the World Trade Center, and the harmful chemicals and elements released into the air when the Twin Towers collapsed during the terrorist attacks of September 11, 2001, could be a possible cause. She continues to speculate about all the possible reasons for Gus's autism. Nevertheless, she recounts that when she looks at her son, she sees the person and not his condition, and this enables her to calm down.

In "Again Again Again," Newman talks about her son's love of routine and repetition. Initially, she notes, it was not particularly troubling. She comments on how her husband is also a creature of habit and how that was part of what drew her to him. However, in her son's case, that love of sameness can border on the extreme, such as his interest in escalators or the comings and goings of subway trains. Still, she rationalizes, there are moments when she can understand what he feels. She comments on how she still has many of her parents' items in storage, and although they have been dead for years, she cannot bring herself to part with them.

The book continues along the lines established by these first three essays, with Newman, her husband, and Gus's brother, having to face and learn to overcome the challenges of raising and living with an autistic family member. Newman approaches the subject with honesty and wit throughout. In "I, Tunes," she talks about Gus's love of music and, in particular, his affection for the children's singer Laurie Berkner. Newman recalls how Gus was so enamored of Berkner, he ended up backstage at one of her concerts and found his way into her dressing room. She also notes that Gus has an aptitude for music and can play many songs on the piano by ear. But, she says, he does not play any songs by Laurie Berkner, despite knowing them all. She surmises that he believes that some things are perfect the way they are.

A columnist for the New York Times *and* People, *journalist Judith Newman has contributed to numerous national newspapers and magazines. She published the memoir* You Make Me Feel Like an Unnatural Woman *in 2004.* To Siri, with Love *is her second book.*

Toward the end of the book, which includes the original, titular essay, Newman looks ahead to the future and what life will be like for Gus now that he is older (at the time of the book's publication, he was about to turn sixteen). In the chapter "Toast," she ruminates on her and her husband's aging and believes that, when she dies, it will be Gus there holding her hand. In the final chapter, "Bye," she looks ahead to Gus growing up and slowly gaining some independence. While he will always struggle, Newman says, she also sees that he is happy and content with who he is.

In her years as a columnist and freelance journalist, Newman has earned a reputation for approaching subjects with a wry, acerbic sense of humor. Over the years, she has earned acclaim for her coverage of celebrities, among a wide range of other topics, in a voice that is honest and forthright. Her 2004 memoir, *You Make Me Feel Like an Unnatural Woman: Diary of a New (Older) Mother*, tackles her struggle to have children at forty and the ensuing drama that followed when Newman learned that she was having twins. The book balances humor and pathos in its attempt to paint an honest portrayal of the harried life of a working mother. Similarly, *To Siri, with Love* addresses a difficult and emotional situation with honesty and wit. Newman does not shy from the difficult side of dealing with a child with autism, but she always finds a silver lining, even in the most desperate of situations. Additionally, she is also honest to a fault about her own occasional reactions to her son's condition, noting, for example, that it can be exhausting listening to his recitations of bus and subway schedules.

When it was released in August 2017, *To Siri, with Love* received largely positive notices from critics, who praised the book's bittersweet tone and warts-and-all honesty. Suskind, himself the father of an autistic child, writing for the *New York Times*, deemed the book "200 pages of powerfully wrought indelicacies about life with Gus, her autistic teenage son, that will make readers squirm and laugh—yes, out loud." However, some critics warned that the book was, at times, too honest, and that Newman's willingness to bare all about her life with Gus could put some readers off. On Spectrum News, a website focused on news and opinion on autism research, Emily Willingham said, "Newman's candor can be unsettling. Her stark presentation of her own thoughts and evolution as the parent of a child on the spectrum will no doubt pain and anger some readers, feelings that certainly alloyed my reading experience."

In fact, this outspokenness has led some people in the autism community to protest the book. The passage that sparked the most vehemence was in "Doc," where Newman proposes getting her son a vasectomy to ensure that he cannot have children. Later in the book, in "Getting Some," Newman takes a much more explicit stance on the subject, confessing, "I am still deeply worried about the idea that he could get someone pregnant and yet could never be a real father—which is why I will insist on having medical power of attorney, so that I will be able to make the decision about a vasectomy for him after he turns eighteen." Outrage over these sections, as well as other parts of the book that detail the family's (and, by extension, Gus's) private life led to the hashtag #BoycottToSiri making the rounds on Twitter. Kaelan Rhywiol, a parent with autism, wrote a scathing op-ed for *Bustle*, in which she underlined Newman's invasion of Gus's privacy and her name calling. Rhywiol concluded, "I cannot judge whether or not Newman loves her son or is a good mother; that is not for me to decide. But I do think that the words she has written and allowed to be published are harmful to the autistic community." Newman has responded by stating that the book was not written for autistic readers, who tend to be literalists, but rather for neurotypical families, friends, and neighbors who may know or work with someone who is on the autism spectrum.

Despite the controversy, *To Siri, with Love* has, for the most part, received praise for its open and honest look at the trials of raising a child with autism, as well as the hope that can come from small breakthroughs, even in the most unusual of places.

Jeremy Brown

Review Sources

Fisher, Jamie. Review of *To Siri, with Love: A Mother, Her Autistic Son, and the Kindness of Machines*, by Judith Newman. *The Washington Post*, 21 Aug. 2017, www.washingtonpost.com/entertainment/books/to-siri-with-love-the-tale-of-a-mother-a-son-and-a-phone/2017/08/19/92076c72-7d26-11e7-83c7-5bd5460f0d7e_story.html. Accessed 13 Dec. 2017.

Herbaugh, Tracee M. "Book Review: Parenthood and Tech Meet in *To Siri, with Love*." Review of *To Siri, with Love: A Mother, Her Autistic Son, and the Kindness of Machines*, by Judith Newman. *Washington Times*, 29 Aug. 2017, www.washingtontimes.com/news/2017/aug/29/book-review-parenthood-and-tech-meet-in-to-siri-wi. Accessed 13 Dec. 2017.

Rhywiol, Kaelan. "Why I Believe *To Siri, with Love* by Judith Newman Is a Book That Does Incredible Damage to the Autistic Community." Review of *To Siri, with Love: A Mother, Her Autistic Son, and the Kindness of Machines*, by Judith Newman. *Bustle*, 30 Nov. 2017, www.bustle.com/p/why-i-believe-to-siri-with-love-by-judith-newman-is-a-book-that-does-incredible-damage-to-the-autistic-community-6780420. Accessed 13 Dec. 2017.

Suskind, Ron. "A Family Memoir Makes the Case That Autism Is Different, Not Less." Review of *To Siri, with Love: A Mother, Her Autistic Son, and the Kindness of Machines*, by Judith Newman. *The New York Times*, 16 Aug. 2017, www.nytimes.com/2017/08/16/books/review/to-siri-with-love-judith-newman-memoir.html. Accessed 13 Dec. 2017.

Review of *To Siri, with Love: A Mother, Her Autistic Son, and the Kindness of Machines*, by Judith Newman. *Kirkus Reviews*, vol. 85, no. 13, 1 July 2017, p. 1. *Literary Reference Center Plus*, search.ebscohost.com/login.aspx?direct=true&db=lkh&AN=123827222&site=lrc-plus. Accessed 13 Dec. 2017.

Willingham, Emily. "Book Review: *To Siri, with Love* Offers Provocative Look at Parenting." Review of *To Siri, with Love: A Mother, Her Autistic Son, and the Kindness of Machines*, by Judith Newman. *Spectrum*, 20 June 2017, spectrum-news.org/opinion/viewpoint/book-review-siri-love-offers-provocative-look-par-enting. Accessed 13 Dec. 2017.

Transit

Author: Rachel Cusk (b. 1967)
Publisher: Farrar, Straus and Giroux (New York). 260 pp.
Type of work: Novel
Time: Present day
Locales: Greater London, Paris

Transit *is the second novel in an experimental trilogy by British writer Rachel Cusk. Cusk provides the reader with scant detail, allowing for a free-flowing reading experience that explores the life of a woman on the verge of financial ruin as she reestablishes herself as a woman, intellectual, and mother.*

Principal character
FAYE, a writer and teacher

Courtesy of Macmillan

In the opening pages of *Transit*, the second book in a trilogy by British author Rachel Cusk, the reader encounters a familiar narrator, Faye. Having traveled through Greece in the trilogy's first book, *Outline*, the recently divorced Faye now attempts to settle in London with her two young sons in tow. She sits at a computer reading a spam email from an astrology service. The bot behind the email suggests that Faye has lost her way, and she finds it impossible to deny this. Adding to the flurry of confusion that plagues her, Faye tries to buy a house in the highly competitive real estate market in the city and has taken the advice of a friend: buy a bad house in a good neighborhood, rather than a good house in a bad neighborhood. By chapter's end, she has accomplished just this, with her purchase of a "virtually uninhabitable" council property in the "over-inflated" city center.

To read *Outline* or *Transit* is to find oneself inside Faye's mind rather than learning about her from any sort of outside action. Cusk—who has written three memoirs, the last of which outlines the demise of her own marriage—offers few physical details about her heroine. Instead, Cusk allows Faye to take the reader into her world, to experience her friendships, likes and dislikes, and career highs and lows. Her harrowing experience of trying to create a home out of her newly acquired flat, despite its poor condition and hostile neighbors, is one of the more vivid storylines.

One reason Cusk's narrative is so effective is that the simplicity of her sparse language allows the brutality of life to shine through. In one scene, Faye is meeting with a would-be mentee who wants to write a thesis on the work of American painter Marsden Hartley. Jane, the student, explains to Faye that she is not interested in the artist's work per se, but in the feeling she gets from looking at his work. She connects this to an intense experience she had with a married photojournalist while abroad in Paris.

Courtesy of Siemon Scammel-Katz

Rachel Cusk has written three memoirs,
A Life's Work: On Becoming a Mother
(2001), The Last Supper: A Summer in
Italy *(2009), and* Aftermath: On Mar-
riage and Separation *(2012), and ten
novels, including* Outline *and* Transit.
*Named one of Granta's Best of Young
British Novelists in 2003, Cusk is the
recipient of a Whitbread First Novel
Award and a Somerset Maugham Award.*

"He's me," Jane says, speaking of Marsden.
"I'm him, she said, then added, slightly im-
patiently: we're the same. I know it sounds
a bit strange, she went on, but there's actually no reason why people can't be repeated." By chapter's end, Faye has suggests to
Jane that she is not actually interested in the
painter; instead, her feelings about his paint-
ings have become conflated with her feelings about her experience with the married
photojournalist in Paris. The scene, which
takes an entire chapter and is set in Faye's
sitting room while her home is under construction, creates a perfect tension between
simple, understated language and the drama
of simmering emotions when two people are
discussing a difficult topic. The restrained
nature of Faye's voice conveys the tenuous-
ness women often feel in conversation.

In an earlier chapter, Faye is visiting a
stylist. She asks immediately upon sitting
down in the chair if her stylist, Dale, can "get
rid of the grey." As the two weigh the pros
and cons of dyeing her hair—Dale insists
that it is a life sentence and the sparkles look
nice as they are, while Faye is longing for change and attempting to gain some sort of
control over her chaotic present through a change to her appearance—the violence and
expectations placed on a woman's body become clearer through Cusk's expert rendering of the scene. Next to Faye sits a small child who has been brought to the salon by
his mother for a haircut. He refuses to speak, even as his stylist Sammy cajoles him
into conversation. Rather, he communicates in a fit of expressions, jolts, and twitches,
at times falling into one-word answers. Adjacent to this, Dale is telling Faye about his
friend who is a brilliant artist but also a meth addict. The tension is palpable, as the
reader is left to wonder at the small child and the meth-addicted artist. It all seems to
circle back on Faye and her unknowable present as she puts her life back together. At
the scene's end, the boy bolts from the chair, running out the front door as his mother
looks on. He slams the store's door, causing an entire shelf of products to crash down
from the wall. His silence is ultimately punctuated by violent destruction. The night
has grown dark in the interim, and Faye and Dale stare silently in shock.

The meandering way each chapter moves Faye further into the future and into the
narrative is reminiscent of the work of writers Teju Cole and W. G. Sebald, as critic
Ruth Franklin noted in her review for the *Atlantic*. In Cole's *Open City* and any of Sebald's four novels, a main character offers himself as a navigator, showing the reader a
slice of the world through curious and intelligent eyes. One quite memorable example

of this technique occurs in a chapter that features Faye's trip to a small town outside the city to attend a literary festival. The festival's speakers are captured and cataloged through Faye's extended first-person exposition, which can also be found in *Outline*.

At the conference, Faye is met by a young woman named Lauren, who helps her settle into the festival's activities. The reader only sees and hears what Faye does, before Julian, one of the speakers, enters the scene. Several other male writers then join Julian. Small details, like Faye's description of her storm-soaked clothing and participation in the panel discussion adds body to the scene:

> Water was still dripping down the back of my neck from the hair Dale had dried carefully the day before. My clothes were damp and my feet moved in water that had pooled in my shoes. The light on the stage had a blinding effect; beyond it I could just make out the oval shapes of the audience's faces. . . . I took the papers out of my bag and unfolded them. My hands shook with cold holding them. There was the sound of the audience settling into its seats. I read aloud what I had written. When I had finished I folded the papers and put them back in my bag, while the audience applauded.

Cusk offers a detailed account of Faye's discomfort but reveals nothing about the content of what she read to the audience. In such instances, *Transit* feels more like a collection of things that happen to Faye than an account of her actions; similarly passive narrators appear in the work of Cole and Sebald, as well.

Transit was widely celebrated upon its release, with reviews across major outlets, including the *Guardian*, the *New York Times*, the *Atlantic*, and others. Dwight Garner, writing for the *New York Times*, called the novel "a calm novel about chaos" and said that "Faye moves like a bee from person to person, as if from flower to flower, or like a pilgrim from station to station. Honesty is pollen here." These are apt descriptions of what makes *Transit* such a puzzling, enjoyable book. At the novel's conclusion, one feels exhilarated and exhausted after watching Faye find her path in a new landscape and lifestyle, but the language never gets ahead of the emotion within the prose. In fact, it is the restraint that Faye shows in her dealings that makes the chaos seem like it is at the door but not quite over the threshold and creates a confidence, whether real or a façade, that Faye is ultimately in control of her situation.

In a 2017 interview with Alex Zafiris for *Bomb* magazine, Cusk said, "The main difficulty of being, perhaps, is that the 'self' wants a story, wants to be explained, wants to be situated in a meaningful narrative. Because we're trapped in the self, and the self is at the center of our own experience, having that story—and being the central character in it—feels like a necessity." From beginning to end, the story in *Transit* is Faye's alone. Others share their stories and experiences with her, but it all comes to the reader through her lens and authority. This creates the idea of one's life and self being both large and small, for while it may seem that very little happens day-to-day, the most innocuous actions are a part of one's story and one's self in the world. Through Faye's narrative, Cusk conveys the sense that all aspects of a person's life matter, that no instance of experience is too small. In so doing, she challenges preconceptions of what makes one's life worth living.

Melynda Fuller

Review Sources
Franklin, Ruth. "The Uncoupling." Review of *Transit*, by Rachel Cusk. *The Atlantic*, 13 Dec. 2016, www.theatlantic.com/magazine/archive/2017/01/the-uncoupling/508742. Accessed 31 July 2017.
Garner, Dwight. "Review: Rachel Cusk's 'Transit' Offers Transcendent Reflections." Review of *Transit*, by Rachel Cusk. *The New York Times*, 17 Jan. 2017, www.nytimes.com/2017/01/17/books/review-rachel-cusk-transit.html. Accessed 31 July 2017.
Hadley, Tessa. "*Transit* by Rachel Cusk Review—A Triumphant Follow-Up to *Outline*." Review of *Transit*, by Rachel Cusk. *The Guardian*, 17 Sept. 2016, www.theguardian.com/books/2016/sep/17/transit-by-rachel-cusk-review-outline-follow-up. Accessed 31 July 2017.
Price, Adam O'Fallon. "A Tree That Is All Branches: On Rachel Cusk's 'Transit.'" Review of *Transit*, by Rachel Cusk. *The Millions*, 17 Jan. 2017, www.themillions.com/2017/01/a-tree-that-is-all-branches-on-by-rachel-cusks-transit.html. Accessed 31 July 2017.

Traveling with Ghosts

Author: Shannon Leone Fowler (b. 1974)
Publisher: Simon & Schuster (New York).
  304 pp.
Type of work: Memoir
Time: 1982–2002, present day
Locales: Ko Pha Ngan, Thailand; eastern
  Europe; London, England

*A marine biologist recalls the sudden death
of her fiancé in 2002 and her subsequent
process of coping with the loss in her first
book,* Traveling with Ghosts.

Principal personages
SHANNON LEONE FOWLER, the author
SEAN, her fiancé
ANAT AVRAHAM, an Israeli woman visiting
TALIA SHAFIR, an Israeli woman visiting
  Thailand

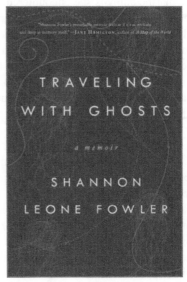

Courtesy of Simon and Schuster

Shannon Leone Fowler is a California-born marine biologist who lives in London,
England. In *Traveling with Ghosts*, her first book, she recounts the still-painful tale of
the tragically sudden death of her fiancé, Sean, in 2002. Days after their engagement,
Fowler and Sean had traveled to Ko Pha Ngan, a beautiful island in southeast Thailand. Standing in the surf one evening, Sean felt something strange brush up against
his legs. He stumbled out of the water, asking Fowler to find help. Minutes later,
he was dead. Fowler captures the disorienting moments, hours, and days following
Sean's death, as well as her long and arduous path to living with grief.

In *Traveling with Ghosts*, Fowler attempts to organize Sean's death into a coher-
ent narrative, appropriately shifting back and forth in time, including a tracing of the
hardscrabble journey through eastern Europe on which she embarked to come to terms
with her loss. While her unfortunate story is not a common one, her eloquent prose and
clear-eyed recollections make it universal, striking at the heart of the pain that comes
from having loved and lost. Fowler writes that she traveled after Sean's death to be
alone, purposefully visiting countries where English is not widely spoken, but her
book also chronicles an extraordinary tale of human connection. Along her journey,
she traveled to Israel to visit two women who helped her through those terrible days
in Ko Pha Ngan, further solidifying the meaningful friendship that had begun under
tragic circumstances.

Fowler writes that she always loved the ocean. As a young girl growing up in California, she spent summers with her grandparents in San Diego. Her grandfather was
an oceanographer, and her grandmother spent each morning bodysurfing from far out

at sea. They taught Fowler about spring tides and rip currents, and how to interact with the marine animals she encountered in the depths or on the shore. At one point, she specifically recalls shuffling her feet in the tide pools to keep the stingrays at bay. As an adult, she went on to study marine biology at the University of California, San Diego. She learned to surf and scuba dive, and for a time she taught the latter in Panama and Ireland. She studied octopus, clown fish, and sea lion pups on the remote Kangaroo Island off the coast of South Australia. In addition to an increased love of traveling, she was spiritually drawn to the ocean. She perhaps once saw the world as her grandfather, who drew maps of ocean currents for pilots during World War II, did. The maps, Fowler recalls, were different than the ones she was familiar with. "The landmasses were just featureless orange blobs," she writes. "The critical details were all in the ocean."

This intense love of the water and marine life makes Fowler's story, and her subsequent—and, at least for a time, crippling—fear of the ocean, all the more poignant. Sean had grown up in Australia, but he was not familiar with the ocean in the same way as Fowler. While he generally loathed the idea of animals brushing up against him in the water, his odd reaction in Ko Pha Ngan gave Fowler pause. She relives the minutes between initial contact and Sean's death in excruciating detail throughout the book, wondering, among other things, if she had known the seriousness of his injury then—if she had screamed for help instead of throwing on a dress—whether his life could have been saved. However, Sean, she later reveals, was stung by a rare species of box jellyfish that kills within minutes. Though the book is predominantly about Fowler and Sean's love and her grief, she also touches on the bizarre cover-up of similar deaths in Thailand in the epilogue. One woman was killed in Ko Pha Ngan a day after Sean because the resort refused to post warning signs. Thai authorities had even pressured Fowler to sign a form that ruled Sean's death a "drunken drowning."

There are two threads to Fowler's narrative that can be loosely categorized as "before" and "after." In the "before" chapters, Fowler writes about her own childhood, meeting Sean on a backpacking trip through Barcelona, and the couple's subsequent travels together. The "after" chapters chronicle the horrifying months following Sean's death, including the end of communication with his family, her friends' awkward responses to his death, and her trip through eastern Europe. Stagnating at her family's home in California, Fowler, an experienced and thrifty traveler, decided to use her life's savings—money she had been planning to use as a down payment on the house she and Sean were going to buy in Melbourne—to travel. "Seems stupid to have money & not be traveling," she wrote in her journal on the one-month anniversary of Sean's death. "Sean would." Her doctoral program allowed her to take some time off—a luxury, she concedes—and she embarked on a trip to eastern Europe. The region was cheap, unfamiliar, and, most importantly, far from the ocean, in a climate drastically different from that of the Thai beach where Sean had died.

Fowler flew to Budapest in October 2002. Her nearly three-month journey took her through Hungary, Slovenia, Slovakia, Poland, Israel (to visit Anat Avraham and Talia Shafir, the two Israeli women she met in Thailand), Bosnia and Herzegovina, Croatia, Romania, and Bulgaria. From there, she zigzagged her way through western Europe to meet her mother in Spain for Christmas. However, it is the first leg of her trip that is the focus of her story. Her journey was strange and difficult; she struggled with the various languages and, as she pushed further into the countryside, to find food and a bed. She was not renewed by the beautiful landscape. Moments of contentment and peace were hard won and often came alongside the recognition that there is profound cruelty and sadness in the world. In 2002, regions of eastern Europe were still emerging from decades of neglect by the former Soviet Union, including Poland, where Fowler visited the Auschwitz concentration camp. Her chronicle of countries in limbo is a valuable snapshot of a very specific moment in history, particularly in Sarajevo, Bosnia and Herzegovina, which had been under siege only six years before.

Fowler traveled to Sarajevo from Israel, which was then engaged in the second intifada (the second Palestinian uprising against Israeli occupation of the West Bank and Gaza Strip). She almost did not make the trip at all; Avraham and Shafir were worried that the constant bombings would make entry into Tel Aviv too dangerous. The trip was an illuminating one for Fowler, nourished by the friendship of Avraham and Shafir and their families, if curtailed by the threat of suicide bombers. Early in the trip, the women, who lived in a suburb of Tel Aviv, turned the car around two or three times before receiving the all clear to travel into the city and show Fowler the sights. When they entered a restaurant, her hosts were pleased; there were few diners present, so the likelihood of a bombing was low. Fowler's recollection of her stay with Avraham and Shafir provides a unique glimpse into life lived under the specter of death. It also illustrates a heartening relationship across countries, forged in tragedy. When Sean died, Avraham and Shafir, strangers to Fowler who were guests at the same Thai resort, changed their plane tickets and refused to leave Fowler's side as she stumbled her way first to the hospital, where Sean was officially pronounced dead, and then to the police station, where they ran interference, refusing to allow her to sign a false account of Sean's death. Their devotion to her is remarkable in itself, and a welcoming salve to the grief of the world to which Fowler bears witness on her journey.

Shannon Leone Fowler is a marine biologist who also worked for a time as a science writer for National Public Radio *(NPR).* Traveling with Ghosts *is her first book.*

Traveling with Ghosts received positive reviews from numerous sources. Critics praised Fowler's beautiful writing and her self-awareness. Elements of her story could easily seem self-serving—in the hands of a lesser writer, mention of Auschwitz, a location where untold numbers of people were brutally murdered, might seem crass in a book about personal grief—but Fowler's her skill as a storyteller (and years of painful reflection) enables her to authentically convey both her own story and the story of a world in recovery. In Sarajevo, she sidestepped landmines to view the remains of the once-spectacular National Library, decimated in 1992; the city had endured the longest siege in modern history, and six years later, visual reminders of the violence—bombed-out storefronts, walls pockmarked with sniper bullets, and makeshift graveyards for the 13,952 dead—were everywhere. "There wasn't a single structure without scars from the war," Fowler writes. Posters from 1993 yellowed on the walls, coffee shops and bars were populated by people with missing limbs, and little tourist shops sold ballpoint pens made from bullet casings. Amidst such devastation, Fowler captures a resiliency among the people that seems neither forced nor cliché. The city, she writes, "was one of the most alive places I'd ever visited. It was like a city waking up after a long nightmare."

In telling her story, Fowler admirably resists the urge to draw a neat line from Sean's death to her emergence from grief. In the book's afterword, she writes about her frustration with books and films that have "fast-forwarded" the grieving party toward recovery. Her own "triumph over grief," she writes, "took a lot longer, and was a hell of a lot harder, than I ever thought it would be." While she does use the afterword section to give readers some insight into her life in the present day, including mention of her eventual marriage, children, and divorce, she emphasizes that the book is about her relationship with Sean, his death, and the lasting emotional impact of both. Throughout the memoir, she asserts her devotion to Sean, whom she had dated for several years before becoming engaged to him days before his death. She writes about being shunted to the periphery of Sean's life in his death, and her anguish in trying to communicate the depth of their relationship. Her candor about her fears and regrets, and about her pain at not quite attaining, in the eyes of others, the status of widow, is a relief. In her writing, she embraces the messiness of the process as she lived it, and in doing so offers a reassuring hand to others who feel alone in their grief.

Molly Hagan

Review Sources

Groskop, Viv. "*Traveling with Ghosts*; *The Wild Other* Review: The Journeys That Follow Grief." Review of *Traveling with Ghosts*, by Shannon Leone Fowler, and *The Wild Other*, by Clover Stroud. *The Guardian*, 26 Feb. 2017, www.theguardian.com/books/2017/feb/26/traveling-with-ghosts-the-wild-other-clover-stroud-shannon-leone-fowler-review. Accessed 25 Sept. 2017.

Spindel, Barbara. "*Traveling with Ghosts* Tells the True Story of Great Tragedy, Remarkable Kindness." Review of *Traveling with Ghosts*, by Shannon Leone Fowler. *The Christian Science Monitor*, 22 Feb. 2017, www.csmonitor.com/Books/Book-Reviews/2017/0222/Traveling-with-Ghosts-tells-a-true-story-of-great-tragedy-remarkable-kindness. Accessed 25 Sept. 2017.

Review of *Traveling with Ghosts*, by Shannon Leone Fowler. *Kirkus Reviews*, 24 Nov. 2016, www.kirkusreviews.com/book-reviews/shannon-fowler/traveling-with-ghosts/. Accessed 25 Sept. 2017.

Review of *Traveling with Ghosts*, by Shannon Leone Fowler. *Publishers Weekly*, 28 Nov. 2016, www.publishersweekly.com/978-1-5011-0779-5. Accessed 25 Sept. 2017.

The Twelve Lives of Samuel Hawley

Author: Hannah Tinti
Publisher: Dial Press (New York). 400 pp.
Type of work: Novel
Time: Present day
Locales: Olympus, Massachusetts; other locations across the United States

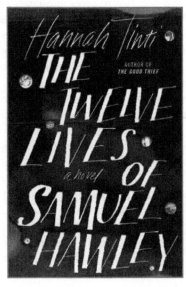

Courtesy of The Dial Press

Hannah Tinti's second novel, The Twelve Lives of Samuel Hawley, *is a coming-of-age tale about the daughter of a criminal.*

Principal characters
Loo, a young girl
SAMUEL HAWLEY, her father, a career criminal
LILY, her mother, who died soon after she was born
MABEL RIDGE, her maternal grandmother
MARSHALL HICKS, a boy in her class

Hannah Tinti's second novel, *The Twelve Lives of Samuel Hawley*, completed over the span of seven years, is a literary coming-of-age story nestled within a thriller. Loo is turning twelve years old when the book begins. It is revealed early in the story that her life up to that point had been unusual; she lived out of a suitcase, moving abruptly from town to town with her father, Samuel Hawley, a gruff, chewed-up professional criminal. Hawley may be a tough guy, but when it comes to Loo—and a handful of items that once belonged to his beloved dead wife, Lily—he is surprisingly tender. In each new motel room, he lined the bathroom with faded photographs of Lily, her toiletries, and scraps of paper bearing her handwriting. Now Hawley has decided that it is time to settle down, so he takes Loo to the tiny (fictional) fishing village of Olympus, Massachusetts, the same town in which Lily was raised. Lily's mother, a sharp and bitter old woman named Mabel Ridge, lives just outside Olympus, in rural Dogtown. Mabel is none too happy to see Hawley or her granddaughter, for reasons that reveal themselves as Tinti's novel progresses. The book follows two parallel tracks: one from the perspective of a growing Loo attempting to adjust to their new life while also uncovering information about her parents' pasts, the other tracing the history of Hawley's twelve bullet wounds, inspired by the twelve labors of Hercules. Images and histories overlap as father and daughter discover the cruelties of passing time.

Tinti cofounded the literary magazine *One Story* in 2002 and published her first book, a collection of short stories titled *Animal Crackers*, in 2004. Each story in that collection features a particular animal. She published her first novel, *The Good Thief*, in 2008, to largely positive reviews, earning herself the Center for Fiction's First

Novel Prize. As the title implies, *The Good Thief* also features a criminal protagonist; unlike *The Twelve Lives of Samuel Hawley*, it is set in the nineteenth century. In it, a boy named Ren joins a band of thieves. Elements of the tale are reminiscent of Charles Dickens, but Tinti's prose, as novelist Maile Meloy pointed out in her review of the book for the *New York Times*, is straightforward: "The effect of Tinti's steady, authoritative style is to make odd and extraordinary events seem natural." The same could be said of *The Twelve Lives of Samuel Hawley*, which also features a young protagonist. Elements of the novel may seem whimsical or exaggerated—the nerdy principal who dreams of winning a greasy pole contest; the parade of widows knocking on Loo's door, hoping to win the affections of her father; a live burial in a nest of prairie dogs; and even the strained quirkiness of Loo's young mother—and the novel's climax, which takes place in the middle of the ocean against a mustache-twirling villain, is pure melodrama in the best sense of the word. Yet Tinti creates a pleasing tension between her peculiar characters and her unadorned narrative voice. *The Twelve Lives of Samuel Hawley* is a story about the realities of love and loss, but tonally, it lands a step away from true realism.

The book was well received by critics. Pete Hamill, writing for the *New York Times*, called it "strikingly symphonic," and indeed, the complex structure of Tinti's novel resembles the intricate clocks at the heart of a subplot involving Hawley's criminal exploits. Even the novel's table of contents is creatively formatted to reflect the parallel structure of the story. At the same time, the reviewer for *Kirkus Reviews* found the proliferation of meaningful images—clocks, whales, bullets, stars—and plotlines to be "lard[ing] the narrative," sometimes "overshadow[ing] Loo's budding relationship and push and pull with Lily's mother," and described the novel as "accomplished if overstuffed." Readers will likely fall into one of these two camps. There is a copious amount of information in Tinti's book, but she doles it out with a careful hand. Particularly satisfying is the harmony between past (Hawley's thread) and present (Loo's thread). Unusual behaviors (Hawley's insistence on creating a shrine to Lily in the bathroom) and objects (a bearskin rug) are explained through backstory, but more artfully, they take on different meanings for father and daughter. The rug, for instance, one of the few mainstays in Hawley and Loo's collection of items, is a source of comfort for Loo. She fondly recalls Hawley wrapping her in its warm fur. When her boyfriend, a boy named Marshall Hicks, recoils at the sight of it on the floor of her home in Olympus, Loo is surprised; it is so familiar to her that she forgot there is a bear's head attached to it. The origin of the rug is much darker: for Hawley, it represents his first bullet wound, and his entry into a world from which he remains unable to escape.

Hannah Tinti is an award-winning novelist and short-story writer. In 2002 she cofounded the literary magazine One Story. *She is also the author of the short-story collection* Animal Crackers *(2004) and the novel* The Good Thief *(2008), her first.*

One of the most striking elements of Tinti's story is its violence. Characters are shot, battered, and bruised at nearly every plot point—and this does not even count Hawley, whose scarred body serves as a road map for the plot of the novel itself. Tinti creates self-contained vignettes for each excruciating bullet but resists the urge to make each Hawley chapter a morality tale. Life lessons for Hawley are hard won, and none of them come in the form of a physical wound. Hawley, in fact, is remarkably stubborn in his ways, clinging to his violent life even as it threatens to rob him of everything he loves. For instance, he would never forsake his beloved collection of guns. In the novel's first scene, he teaches Loo how to shoot his own father's rifle, notched with lines representing each man he killed in the war. Aside from this tender moment, Loo acquires her father's violence as if by osmosis. A good portion of the book's injuries come through her hands. One widow, Hicks's mother, wins Loo's trust, only to lose it after laughing at Lily's bathroom shrine; an enraged Loo cracks the woman's head against the bathtub. In a romantic comedy, the point at which the two characters first encounter one another is called a "meet-cute"; in *The Twelve Lives of Samuel Hawley*, the meet-cute involves Loo breaking a boy's finger and relishing the snap. Laura Collins-Hughes put it best in her review for the *Boston Globe*: "Tinti never glamorizes violence. She forces us to look at the damage wrought, to hear the crunch of bone, to see the copious blood, to take in the bystanders, now broken or dying or dead."

The realistic violence grounds the narrative, giving the book some of its most perversely satisfying moments. Tinti is at her best when she captures the messiness of life, and in that spirit her depiction of violence is appropriately gruesome and awkward. Her rendering of Mabel Ridge, Loo's maternal grandmother, is satisfying in a similar way. Mabel is both selfish and frighteningly selfless. She behaves badly for noble reasons, which makes her impossible to hate. She has her quirks—she is forever dying wool for yarn, a task that is presented as more of an affectation than an actual job—but she is more notable for her challenging emotional complexity. One of Tinti's themes is the painful repetition of living, the idea that everyone alive must suffer in some way, and how this horrible truth bonds human beings together. (She also explores the related idea of a parent's inability to protect their child from suffering.) Tinti describes this unification through pain as it occurs to Loo late in the book: "Their hearts were all cycling through the same madness—the discovery, the bliss, the loss, the despair— like planets taking turns in orbit around the sun. . . . Loo . . . felt better knowing others were traveling this same elliptical course, that they would sometimes cross paths, that they would find love and lose love and recover from love and love again." Mabel, with a reservoir of grief paved over by a brittle meanness, is an example of how repeated suffering shapes a person for good and ill. She may not have any bullet wounds, but she bears just as many scars as Hawley.

The *Twelve Lives of Samuel Hawley* is also quite cinematic, an observation reinforced by its already having been optioned for television. Tinti, a native New Englander, captures the salt-bitten landscape of small-town Massachusetts, but her story also travels through the American southwest and remote Whidbey Island off the coast of Washington State. In flashback scenes, Hawley and Lily live briefly in Alaska and then Wisconsin. Tinti paints all of these places with the same assured hand; she has explained in interviews that she wanted to depict places that she had traveled to herself. Landscapes are an important part of the narrative, perhaps because they, too, are shaped by the passage of time. Loo follows a strange collection of rocks—deposited, she finds out later, by an ancient glacier—to her first party, a bonfire in the woods. Elsewhere in the book, Hawley is nearly swallowed by landscapes, first through the displacement of water after a glacier calves and then, more literally, through burial in the sand of a prairie dog nest. The perils of nature are reflected in the rough topography of Hawley's body and, in one poignant scene, the smooth contours of outer space as drawn by Hicks across Loo's back.

Tinti's attention to detail (often supported by meticulous research), the depth of her characters, and the methodic structure of the plot and book as a whole combine to enable the novel to balance between serving as an intriguing thriller and literary fiction. Therefore, it should appeal to a wide range of readers.

Molly Hagan

Review Sources

Collins-Hughes, Laura. "Her Mother Long Dead, a Girl Traces Her Parents' Lives through Her Father's Bullet Wounds." Review of *The Twelve Lives of Samuel Hawley*, by Hannah Tinti. *The Boston Globe*, 24 Mar. 2017, www.bostonglobe.com/arts/books/2017/03/23/her-mother-long-dead-girl-traces-her-parents-lives-through-her-father-bullet-wounds/WVG36ZnjHuIta5TljOlszL/story.html. Accessed 18 Sept. 2017.

Feldman, Lucy. "Review: In *The Twelve Lives of Samuel Hawley*, Hercules Wields a Shotgun." Review of *The Twelve Lives of Samuel Hawley*, by Hannah Tinti. *Time*, 23 Mar. 2017, time.com/4710621/twelve-lives-samuel-hawley/. Accessed 18 Sept. 2017.

Hamill, Pete. "A Heroine Comes of Age with Her Pistol-Packing Father." Review of *The Twelve Lives of Samuel Hawley*, by Hannah Tinti. *The New York Times*, 11 Apr. 2017, www.nytimes.com/2017/04/11/books/review/twelve-lives-of-samuel-hawley-hannah-tinti.html. Accessed 18 Sept. 2017.

Review of *The Twelve Lives of Samuel Hawley*, by Hannah Tinti. *Kirkus Reviews*, 19 Dec. 2016, www.kirkusreviews.com/book-reviews/hannah-tinti/the-twelve-lives-of-samuel-hawley/. Accessed 18 Sept. 2017.

Review of *The Twelve Lives of Samuel Hawley*, by Hannah Tinti. *Publishers Weekly*, 9 Jan. 2017, www.publishersweekly.com/978-0-8129-8988-5. Accessed 18 Sept. 2017.

The Unbanking of America
How the New Middle Class Survives

Author: Lisa Servon
Publisher: Houghton Mifflin Harcourt (Boston). 272 pp.
Type of work: Economics, sociology, current affairs

In The Unbanking of America: How the New Middle Class Survives, *Lisa Servon examines the reasons why an increasing number of Americans do not participate in the traditional banking system and investigates the alternative options they pursue.*

How the New Middle Class Survives
LISA SERVON

Courtesy of Houghton Mifflin Harcourt

Author and professor Lisa Servon notes in the introduction to her 2017 book *The Unbanking of America: How the New Middle Class Survives*, that since her childhood in the 1960s and 1970s, the relationships between average Americans and their banking institutions have changed dramatically. A period of extensive bank consolidation led to the creation of larger and more corporate-focused banks and a corresponding decline in customer-focused local banking, which Servon recalls was once characterized by the personal relationships between the customers and bank employees. Amid that industry shift, which was influenced not only by widespread regulatory changes but also the recessions that bookended the first decade of the twenty-first century, increasing numbers of Americans stopped participating in traditional banking or never began to do so. As of the writing of her book, Servon states, more than twelve million Americans did not use bank accounts. Such individuals are commonly referred to as "unbanked," while those who do have bank accounts but also use alternative financial services are referred to as "underbanked." Servon registers her objection to such terms, as she argues that defining people who do not have bank accounts in opposition to those who do reflects an unfair value judgment. However, the terms *unbanked* and *underbanked* prove to be useful throughout her work, in which she explores not only the reasons why many people do not use traditional banking services but also the multitude of alternative services that they do use to meet their financial needs. With *The Unbanking of America*, Servon confronts misconceptions about who uses services such as check cashers and payday lenders, and concludes that the portion of Americans who are being underserved by the traditional banking industry is far larger than previously known.

Throughout *The Unbanking of America*, Servon presents a broad overview of key changes in the banking industry and the policies and historical events that allowed them to occur. According to Servon, one of the major turning points in banking in the United States came in 1999, when the US Congress passed the Gramm-Leach-Bliley Act, which enabled banks to participate not only in commercial banking activities but also in investment banking. Commercial banks had previously been prohibited from engaging in investment banking by the Glass-Steagall Act, which had been passed after the stock market crash of 1929 and restricted commercial banks from participating in certain higher-risk financial activities. The passage of the Gramm-Leach-Bliley Act, Servon explains, facilitated a dramatic increase in mergers that led to the formation of large banking conglomerates. As banks consolidated and grew larger, they began to make much of their money by collecting fees from consumers, including account-mainte-

Lisa Servon is the author of several nonfiction works, including Bootstrap Capital: Microenterprises and the American Poor *(1999) and* Bridging the Digital Divide: Technology, Community, and Public Policy *(2002). She is a professor of city planning at the University of Pennsylvania and previously served as dean of the New School's Milano School of International Affairs, Management, and Urban Policy.*

nance and ATM fees. Servon focuses particularly on the practice of overdraft protection, in which banks allow a financial transaction to go through when an account does not have enough money in it rather than declining the transaction. When such an overdraft occurs, the account holder is charged an overdraft fee, the average amount of which increased from less than twenty-two dollars to more than thirty-one dollars between 1998 and 2012. Servon also calls attention to the practice of debit resequencing, in which banks process transactions in a specific order so that a bank account is more likely to be overdrawn and incur more overdraft fees.

Although Servon focuses primarily on banking practices that remain in effect, she observes that the federal government has somewhat regulated the banking industry through efforts such as 2010's Dodd-Frank legislation, which introduced some regulations for overdraft protection and other practices. She likewise notes that banks such as Bank of America have faced legal action for their debit resequencing practices. However, she argues that despite such regulatory efforts, banks continue to deceive customers in order to bring in fee revenue. Servon cites high bank fees as one of the primary reasons why people stop using bank accounts or never sign up to begin with. She likewise devotes attention to the database known as ChexSystems, which provides information about a person's banking history and logs events such as overdrafts and bounced checks. She writes that information reported through ChexSystems has prevented more than one million Americans from getting bank accounts and has also contributed to the closure of the bank accounts of 6 percent of Americans, thus contributing to the size of the unbanked population. As she makes clear throughout the book, it is not only low-income people who do not have bank accounts or make use of alternative financial services; rather, a significant portion of unbanked or underbanked individuals are Americans who, despite their middle-class salaries, live paycheck to paycheck and have precarious financial situations.

Perhaps the most intriguing sections of *The Unbanking of America* are two chapters in which Servon documents her brief experiences working for a check-cashing shop and a payday lender, work she pursued to get a better idea of who uses such alternative financial services and why. Although, as she notes, such services are commonly perceived as predatory and geared toward individuals with little understanding of finances, she found that not all such service providers operated in a predatory fashion, and the individuals who used them typically did so due not to a lack of financial literacy but to a lack of other banking options. In the book's first chapter, "Where Everybody Knows Your Name," Servon details her experiences working as a teller at the South Bronx–based check casher RiteCheck. She explains that more than half of the residents of the Bronx region where the store is located do not have bank accounts, so many residents visit check-cashing stores such as RiteCheck to cash checks, pay bills, send money internationally, and perform other services, each for a fee. As Servon notes, the fees and available services were clearly advertised, and RiteCheck therefore offered more transparency than many major banks.

During her time working as a teller, she learned some of the many reasons that individuals, including people with bank accounts, used the store's services. Among the most significant reasons was the speedy nature of the check-cashing service, which could put money in an individual's pockets several days sooner than if that person had deposited the check in a bank and waited for it to clear. For many of RiteCheck's customers, having money for groceries, bills, or subcontractor payments immediately was worth paying a fee. The customers were well aware that using a check casher cost them money, but it was often the only option that met their particular financial needs. Servon comes to a similar conclusion in the book's fifth chapter, "Payday Loans: Making the Best of Poor Options," which covers her time at Check Center, a payday lender in Oakland, California. Although she acknowledges that payday loans are viewed by many consumer advocates as predatory and financially detrimental, she explains that payday lenders ultimately provide an essential service for people who are unable to obtain other forms of credit, such as bank loans.

In addition to widely known alternative financial services such as check cashers and payday lenders, Servon discusses some options that are more informal in nature but nevertheless play an important role for their participants. She focuses on rotating savings and credit associations (ROSCAs) and particularly a Hispanic American variant called a *tanda*, in which the participants each contribute a certain amount of money on a set schedule. The process is divided into rounds, and in each round, one of the members is selected to receive all of the money collected during that round. A ROSCA therefore enables its members to save a relatively large sum of money and prevents them from accessing the money during the saving process, as they could if the money were being deposited in a savings account. Servon goes on to profile several different innovators in the field of financial technology who are creating financial services to address existing issues within the banking industry. One company, L2C, has created a new formula for calculating credit scores that takes factors such as financial stability into account, while the Mission Asset Fund enables ROSCA participants to build their credit scores by documenting their on-time contributions. She concludes her work by addressing a variety of policy changes that could improve the financial welfare of unbanked and underbanked Americans. Among other ideas, she suggests that the federal government could subsidize banks to provide services to low-income people and that the government could begin handling banking services itself, a practice with a precedent in the postal banking services offered by the United States Postal Service prior to 1967. Such tactics, she argues, would help address the financial injustice faced by millions of Americans.

With *The Unbanking of America*, Servon has created an accessible and at times disturbing primer on the state of banking in the United States in the early twenty-first century and aptly demonstrates how contemporary banking practices are putting millions of Americans at a disadvantage. While her descriptions of banking practices and the history of banking-related legislation contain a fair amount of terminology that may not be familiar to the reader, she provides clear and accessible explanations of the concepts involved and supplies ample historical context for the hardships faced by many in the twenty-first century. While not all readers may be familiar with the workings of check-cashing shops, payday lenders, and ROSCAs, Servon succeeds in making their policies and practices clear—often far more clear than the typical bank's terms of service. Some readers may find the portions of the book dealing with Servon's in-person findings to be the most engaging and enlightening, but the remainder of the book is nevertheless peppered with findings from the many interviews the author conducted during the research process. Indeed, *The Unbanking of America* is the culmination of a long period of research, and its extensive notes, bibliography, and field-work findings demonstrate Servon's deep commitment to moving beyond stereotypes of unbanked individuals to gain a more complete understanding of their financial lives.

Reviews of *The Unbanking of America* were generally positive, with critics praising Servon's informative overview of banking history and the accessibility of her language. The anonymous reviewer for *Publishers Weekly* praised the diversity of the individuals Servon profiles, noting that the author demonstrates that the state of being unbanked or underbanked is not limited to any one demographic or income level. The *Publishers Weekly* reviewer likewise drew comparisons between the book and works by author Barbara Ehrenreich, known for the 2001 investigative book *Nickel and Dimed*. Critics particularly appreciated the portions of *The Unbanking of America* dealing with Servon's personal experiences working at RiteCheck and Check Center as well as her presentation of potential technological and policy-based solutions for existing banking issues. Although critics such as the reviewer for *Kirkus* acknowledged that much of the information Servon presents is not new, *The Unbanking of America* provides a compelling and concise overview of the financial dilemmas facing many twenty-first-century Americans.

Joy Crelin

Review Sources

Smith, David Hugh. "*The Unbanking of America* Asks Why Banks No Longer Serve the Middle Class." Review of *The Unbanking of America: How the New Middle Class Survives*, by Lisa Servon. *The Christian Science Monitor*, 12 Jan. 2017, www.csmonitor.com/Books/Book-Reviews/2017/0112/

The-Unbanking-of-America-asks-why-banks-no-longer-serve-the-middle-class. Accessed 30 Nov. 2017.

Review of *The Unbanking of America: How the New Middle Class Survives*, by Lisa Servon. *Kirkus*, 21 Nov. 2016, www.kirkusreviews.com/book-reviews/lisa-servon/the-unbanking-of-america/. Accessed 30 Nov. 2017.

Review of *The Unbanking of America: How the New Middle Class Survives*, by Lisa Servon. *Publishers Weekly*, 17 Oct. 2016, www.publishersweekly.com/978-0-544-60231-1. Accessed 30 Nov. 2017.

White, Gillian B. "Why Poor People Make Expensive Financial Decisions." Review of *The Unbanking of America: How the New Middle Class Survives*, by Lisa Servon. *The Atlantic*, 18 Jan. 2017, www.theatlantic.com/business/archive/2017/01/underbanked-servon/513542/. Accessed 30 Nov. 2017.

The Unwomanly Face of War
An Oral History of Women in World War II

Author: Svetlana Alexievich (b. 1948)
First published: *U voĭny ne zhenskoe litso*,
  1985, in the Soviet Union
**Translated from the Russian by Richard
  Pevear and Larissa Volokhonsky**
Publisher: Random House (New York). 384
  pp.
Type of work: History
Time: World War II
Locale: The Soviet Union

*Nobel Prize–winning journalist Svetlana
Alexievich's book* The Unwomanly Face of
War: An Oral History of Women in World
War II *was first published in 1985, and the
first English translation appeared in 1988.
This new translation includes fragments
once blocked by censors.*

Courtesy of Random House

Nobel Prize–winning journalist Svetlana Alexievich first published her book *U voĭny
ne zhenskoe litso* (direct translation "The war does not have a woman's face") in the
former Soviet Union, in what is now Belarus, in 1985. In the twilight of that great
power, Soviet readers were eager to critically engage with their past, and the book sold
over two million copies. It was originally translated into English in 1988, under the
title *War's Unwomanly Face*, but that version was heavily edited by Soviet censors;
this new translation from Richard Pevear and Larissa Volokhonsky, famous translators
best known for their work on classic texts such as Leo Tolstoy's *Anna Karenina* (1878)
and Fyodor Dostoevsky's *The Brothers Karamazov* (1880), introduces the full text,
with a few updates from Alexievich, to English-speaking readers for the first time.

 The Unwomanly Face of War offers a rare glimpse into the lives of the women snip-
ers, foot soldiers, and nurses who served in the Red Army during World War II. After
the war, the women faced social stigma for their service, and for years their stories
went untold and unrecorded. Inspired by the fragments she heard from the women
in her family during her youth, Alexievich set out to interview some of these women
some forty years after the end of the war. By chance, her first interviewee, a sniper in
Minsk who reportedly killed seventy-five German soldiers, introduced her to a friend,
who in turn introduced her to another friend, and so on, until Alexievich had traveled
across the country and spoken with more than five hundred women. Their stories are
about violence and war, but also about youth, hunger, menstruation, love, and countless other things.

Alexievich, a truly singular historian, makes this diversity of experience the point of her book. "I write not about war, but about human beings in war," she writes in her introduction. "I write not the history of a war, but the history of feelings. I am a historian of the soul." (She has used these same phrases to describe her larger body of work.) Alexievich makes herself a character in *The Unwomanly Face of War*, describing the women she meets and how they interact with her. She also provides a running commentary of her questions and emotions as she grapples with the women's stories and the unspeakable cruelties of which they have been both victim and perpetrator. In each interview, she writes, there are three people present: herself, the elderly woman telling the story, and the young woman being conjured in memory. Interestingly, in this new version, there are two Alexieviches as well. "I'm trying to remember the person I was when I was writing this book," Alexievich writes in her updated introduction, seventeen years after the fact. "That person is no more, just as the country in which we then lived is no more." This observation emphasizes another important theme of the book: the elusive nature of memory and, by association, the difficulty of adequately capturing the past.

Alexievich's second book, *Poslednie svideteli: Sto nedetskikh kolybel'nykh* (The last witnesses: One hundred childless lullabies), also published in 1985, collects the reminiscences of people who were young children during the war; an English translation by Pevear and Volokhonsky is scheduled for publication in 2018. *Tsinkovye mal'chiki* (1990; *Zinky Boys: Soviet Voices from the Afghanistan War*, 1992) chronicles in gruesome detail the Soviet war in Afghanistan that lasted from 1979 to 1989; the title refers to the zinc caskets in which many of the soldiers returned. In 1992, a few of the book's subjects sued Alexievich for libel, accusing her of denigrating the Soviet military. She won the case. Her most recent book, *Vremya sekond khend* (2013; *Secondhand Time: The Last of the Soviets*, 2016), explores the lives of ordinary Russians after the fall of the Soviet Union in 1991. Alexievich was awarded the Nobel Prize in Literature for her body of work in 2015. She was the first Belarusian writer to receive the award, and the first person ever to receive it for interview-based work.

Nearly one million women fought for the Soviet army in World War II. With a patriotic fervor, and occasionally a mind toward revenge for lost loved ones, most of the women interviewed enthusiastically volunteered for duty. A number even employed various cunning tactics to serve in the most dangerous positions on the front line. Divided into loosely organized sections with pull-quote titles—"Grow Up, Girls . . . You're Still Green," the title of the third section proclaims—Alexievich's first book follows her subjects from the moment the war breaks out through their initial training. Early on, the army made no uniforms in women's sizes, so women no more than five feet tall marched for miles in men's size-ten boots. Women saw their braids cut and their dresses packed away; many subjects recall a complicated relationship with traditionally feminine talismans throughout the war. One woman wore earrings while she slept in the trench. Another woman, after the war was over, literally traded in her army boots

Svetlana Alexievich is a Belarusian journalist and nonfiction writer. She won the Nobel Prize in Literature in 2015.

for a flowing dress. Trying it on in the mirror, she bursts into tears. The way she describes it, it was as if the act were a manifestation of the silence she would now be forced to endure about her experience. "I didn't recognize myself in the mirror," the woman, Valentina Pavlovna Chudaeva, tells Alexievich. "We had spent four years in trousers. There was no one I could tell that I had been wounded, that I had a concussion. Try telling it, and who will give you a job then, who will marry you? We were as silent as fish. We never acknowledged to anybody that we had been at the front." For Chudaeva, the dress was a mask over an open wound. Earlier in the interview, she recalls the moment that the war forever marked her: working as a radio operator, she received news that her father had been killed; in response, she left her post and demanded a position firing a submachine gun. She eventually became an artillery commander. "Do you understand that? Can it be understood now?" she asks, struggling to explain her decision to Alexievich. "I want you to understand my feelings. . . . You can't shoot unless you hate."

Sometimes it is difficult to follow Alexievich's larger narrative. Despite the chapter headings, fragments of monologues often skip across time and place. The effect, perhaps intentional, is of a collective and rushing stream of consciousness, a cacophony of voices, each one vying to be heard. Dwight Garner, who reviewed the book for the *New York Times*, was critical of this structure; invoking other critics of Alexievich, who have accused her of collaging her interviews at the expense of journalistic integrity, he wondered what questions Alexievich was asking her subjects and why. It is a fair point, but Alexievich, at least, is clear about what information she is looking for, and it is often the opposite of what her subjects, trained by years of propaganda and shame, want recorded. A number of women wrote to her after their interviews, begging her to strike the small and inconsequential details from their offering and to focus on the larger victory of the war. "But 'small details' are what is most important for me," Alexievich writes, "the warmth and vividness of life: a lock left on the forehead once the braid is cut; the hot kettles of kasha and soup, which no one eats, because out of a hundred persons only seven came back from the battle; or how after the war they could not go to market and look at the rows of red meat."

The details included in the book—or rather, out of which the entire book is made—are both strikingly tender and gruesome in ways that are genuinely difficult to read. Journalistic quibbles aside, Alexievich does a good job of providing emotional context for the darkest moments in her interviews. Her impressionistic arrangement, in this regard, mirrors the disorientation caused by violence committed on a scale that is impossible to logically process. In one almost surreal anecdote, a woman escaped a barge under fire at night. She was disoriented in the water, but she was determined to save at least one life. She grabbed hold of a wounded man and dragged him to the shore, only to realize that the man was really a giant fish, a white sturgeon, and it was dying. The woman wept with anger. This strange story, unimportant in the context of the larger war, poignantly illustrates the woman's feelings of futility and regret. Rebecca Reich, who also reviewed the book for the *New York Times*, described *The Unwomanly Face of War* as "less a straightforward oral history of World War II than a literary excavation of memory itself." Viv Groskop, writing for the *Guardian*, specifically praised

Alexievich's ability to convey the emotional energy of the women telling their own stories. (Alexievich has said that these women shaped her practice of tape-recording her subjects, rather than taking handwritten notes, because the silences and filler speech often proved to be just as important as the words of the stories themselves.) Groskop also praised translators Pevear and Volokhonsky for preserving these nuances in their translation.

Molly Hagan

Review Sources

Garner, Dwight. "Russian Women Speak Up about the Front Lines and the Home Front." Review of *The Unwomanly Face of War: An Oral History of Women in World War II*, by Svetlana Alexievich, translated by Richard Pevear and Larissa Volokhonsky. *The New York Times*, 25 July 2017, www.nytimes.com/2017/07/25/books/review-svetlana-alexievich-unwomanly-face-of-war.html. Accessed 26 Feb. 2018.

Groskop, Viv. "'A Monument to Courage.'" Review of *The Unwomanly Face of War: An Oral History of Women in World War II*, by Svetlana Alexievich, translated by Richard Pevear and Larissa Volokhonsky. *The Guardian*, 23 July 2017, www.theguardian.com/books/2017/jul/23/unwomanly-face-of-war-svetlana-alexievich-monument-to-courage-soviet-women-war. Accessed 26 Feb. 2018.

Reich, Rebecca. "Giving the Lie to the Notion That Warfare Is 'Unwomanly.'" Review of *The Unwomanly Face of War: An Oral History of Women in World War II*, by Svetlana Alexievich, translated by Richard Pevear and Larissa Volokhonsky. *The New York Times*, 18 Aug. 2017, www.nytimes.com/2017/08/18/books/review/svetlana-alexievich-the-unwomanly-face-of-war.html. Accessed 26 Feb. 2018.

Review of *The Unwomanly Face of War: An Oral History of Women in World War II*, by Svetlana Alexievich, translated by Richard Pevear and Larissa Volokhonsky. *Kirkus Reviews*, 1 June 2017, p. 7. *Academic Search Complete*, search.ebscohost.com/login.aspx?direct=true&db=a9h&AN=123272515&site=ehost-live. Accessed 26 Feb. 2018.

Review of *The Unwomanly Face of War: An Oral History of Women in World War II*, by Svetlana Alexievich, translated by Richard Pevear and Larissa Volokhonsky. *Publishers Weekly*, 6 Mar. 2017, p. 49. *Academic Search Complete*, search.ebscohost.com/login.aspx?direct=true&db=a9h&AN=121613582&site=ehost-live. Accessed 26 Feb. 2018.

Waking Lions

Author: Ayelet Gundar-Goshen (b. 1982)
First published: *Leha'ir Arayot*, 2014, in Israel
Translated from the Hebrew by Sondra Silverston
Publisher: Little, Brown (New York). 352 pp.
Type of work: Novel
Time: ca. 2014
Locale: Beersheba, Israel

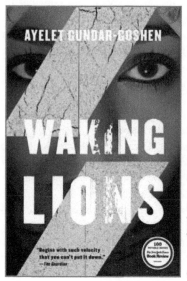

In Waking Lions, *novelist Ayelet Gundar-Goshen examines the refugee crisis in Israel and its moral implications through a tense crime thriller. After neurosurgeon Eitan Green accidentally kills a refugee and the dead man's wife blackmails him, Eitan unwittingly becomes embroiled in the criminal underworld as his family life begins to fall apart.*

Courtesy of Little, Brown Company

Principal characters

DR. EITAN GREEN, an Israeli neurosurgeon
LIAT GREEN, his wife, a police inspector
SIRKIT, an Eritrean refugee who blackmails Eitan for killing her husband in a hit-and-run
GUY DAVIDSON, employer of Sirkit and her husband at a local restaurant

Ayelet Gundar-Goshen's second novel, *Waking Lions*, is a complex and layered work that has been hailed as the author's breakthrough as an international literary star. The novel imaginatively incorporates elements of various genres, including police procedural, political thriller, and psychological morality tale. It is both an incisive examination of Israeli society, particularly regarding the country's refugee crisis, and a focused character study telling the story of a marriage in which the partners drift apart because of the secrets they keep. Gundar-Goshen, a trained psychologist, is especially adept at creating complex characters and scrutinizing their tangled actions, such as the way those of privilege look away from what they do not want to see. While the pace occasionally drags as Gundar-Goshen explores her characters' inner thoughts and demons, the last section of the novel is pure thriller, resulting in a highly dramatic and morally complicated conclusion.

The novel centers on Dr. Eitan Green, a neurosurgeon who has just been transferred from a prestigious hospital in Tel Aviv, Israel, to a less desirable one in the desert city of Beersheba for political reasons. He is unhappy about the move and loss of status, but his wife, Liat, a police investigator who is able to join the local police department, attempts to help him accept their new family situation. In an effort to release stress following the move, Green buys a new SUV to take joyrides in the surrounding desert. However, while speeding late one night and distracted

Ayelet Gundar-Goshen is an Israeli novelist, screenwriter, and psychologist. Her first novel, One Night, Markovitch *(2012), won the Sapir Prize (2013), Italy's Adei-Wizo Prize (2016), and the French Adei-Wizo Prize (2017).*

by the beauty of the moon, he inadvertently hits an Eritrean refugee, later identified as Asum. Eitan stops to assist the man but soon realizes the seriousness of his injuries and that there is nothing he can do to save him. Though he considers turning himself in to the authorities, Eitan quickly decides his life and reputation will be ruined if he accepts responsibility, so he flees the scene, believing he will not be caught.

In his panic, however, Eitan drops his wallet at the scene, and the dead man's wife, Sirkit, appears at the Green home the next day with a blackmail scheme. Eitan gives her a large sum of money as a bribe, but she wants more than money. Knowing that he is a skilled surgeon, she organizes a makeshift hospital in an abandoned kibbutz garage in the desert and forces Eitan to provide medical care to other refugees each night. Meanwhile, Liat is assigned the hit-and-run case and attempts to track down the guilty driver. Eitan must evade his wife's questions and manipulate his colleagues at the hospital in order to meet Sirkit's demands.

One of the strongest aspects of the novel is Gundar-Goshen's complex characterization, with none of the main characters as simple or easily understood as they first appear. Eitan, despite his cowardice in fleeing the scene of the car accident, is shown to initially have a strong moral compass. Importantly, it is established that he had reported his boss and trusted mentor in Tel Aviv for taking bribes. The hospital administrators, however, chose not to address the charges, and rather than taking action against the corruption, they transferred Eitan to the much more remote Beersheba hospital both as a punishment and to get him out of the way. Even after the killing, Eitan remains a sympathetic figure, especially as his eyes are opened to his own privilege and the systematic racism of his society. He develops significantly throughout the novel, becoming a classic example of the flawed protagonist who is far too realistically portrayed to be totally good or totally bad.

The two other main characters in the book, Sirkit and Liat, are equally complex. At first, Sirkit is portrayed as a heroic victim. Though illegal, her blackmail scheme appears to have noble intentions, bringing much-needed medical care to the refugee population while also giving Eitan a chance to atone for his crime and perhaps even gain a new perspective on the misfortunes of others. Although Sirkit speaks very little at first, her ability to put her community's needs before her own and her fearlessness in helping Eitan with medical procedures seem virtuous. Later in the novel, however, as more information emerges through plot twists and turns that make the book a true thriller, Sirkit is revealed to have other facets to her character. As her relationship with Eitan evolves, it becomes clear that her connection to her fellow refugees is much more complicated than is initially suggested. She comes into focus as a complex and even dangerous heroine, facing her own set of moral dilemmas pitting her self-interest against the interests of her community. Liat, too, develops into something far more than the wholly upstanding police officer, wife, and mother she seems at first. Her efforts to fit into the male-dominated police force are contrasted with her self-admitted ethnic prejudice, particularly against Arabs. Her marriage to Eitan, strong and happy at the outset, strains as both partners are shaped by their own and others' actions.

While most critics appreciated Gundar-Goshen's skill in crafting a gripping thriller, *Waking Lions* received particular praise for its layering of social themes within a plot-driven structure. For example, in her *New York Times* review, Ayelet Tsabari called the work a "commentary on privilege and otherness, challenging readers to confront their own blind spots and preconceptions." Among the many uncomfortable subjects exposed are racism, gender attitudes, economic exploitation, and bourgeois complacency and hypocrisy. While these issues are all widespread and deeply intertwined, they are arguably most clear in the depiction of the intersections between Israeli society and the refugee population.

At the outset, neither Eitan nor Liat truly understand or accept their elevated status as white. At first, Eitan can hardly tell African refugees apart, but he slowly comes to recognize, for instance, Sirkit's true beauty and his attraction to it. It is only as he spends night after night with her, working side by side in silence, observing her critically and in detail, that he comes to understand and appreciate her more fully. (And even this appreciation is problematic, based heavily on male-dominated sexuality). Ultimately, this suggests that those who are marginalized, such as refugees, remain invisible unless the people in power are forced in some way to see them as individuals. Similarly, Liat is forced to recognize her own prejudices and fight them, as part of her job, to understand and help a young Arab woman who becomes involved in a case as a corroborating witness. Gundar-Goshen effectively forces readers to see the difficulties these invisible populations face and the lengths people in power must go to remedy that invisibility.

Waking Lions was highly regarded upon release, with many reviewers calling Gundar-Goshen a literary talent to watch after only her second novel. The English translation, in particular, helped bring the author to international attention after already receiving great acclaim in Israel. Yet despite nearly universal praise for its complex characters and themes, the novel did not escape criticism. Ruth Gilligan, writing for the *Guardian*, noted Gundar-Goshen's sometimes overwrought and clichéd language, awkward similes, and misplaced humor, especially in comparison to the author's more tonally consistent debut novel, *One Night, Markovitch* (2012). Other critics took minor issue with contrived plot elements, such as Eitan leaving his wallet at the scene of his crime and an unwitting Liat being assigned to solve her husband's hit-and-run case. However, reviewers generally agreed that these small issues, common in the type of thrillers and police procedural novels that the book in some ways resembles, do not overwhelm the overall success of the book.

More troubling, perhaps, is Gundar-Goshen's inclusion of long, contemplative passages that slow the plot considerably, particularly near the middle of the novel. The novel alternates in point of view, mostly between Eitan, Sirkit, and Liat, and all three characters have these lengthy flights of introspection. They are interesting and well written, for the most part, but they slow the novel to such a degree that they detract from the main story line. Eventually, however, the pace does switch into high gear for the fast-paced, thrilling conclusion. Critics noted that the many twists are handled well, offering satisfaction for thriller fans in addition to the thought-provoking moral questions the book raises.

While there are a few issues with language, plot, and pace, there are many more riveting passages to the novel, particularly in the last third of the book as it climaxes to its gripping conclusion. Gundar-Goshen has created compelling, complex characters, characters that offer no easy answers to questions of right and wrong, and she urges readers to look straight into the eyes of the invisible and examine their own hidden prejudices.

Marybeth Rua-Larsen

Review Sources

Corrigan, Maureen. "A Fatal Hit-And-Run Leads to a Collision of Cultures in *Waking Lions*." Review of *Waking Lions*, by Ayelet Gundar-Goshen. *NPR*, 1 Mar. 2017, www.npr.org/2017/03/01/517712411/a-fatal-hit-and-run-leads-to-a-collision-of-cultures-in-waking-lions. Accessed 20 Oct. 2017.

Gilligan, Ruth. Review of *Waking Lions*, by Ayelet Gundar-Goshen. *The Guardian*, 30 Mar. 2016, www.theguardian.com/books/2016/mar/30/waking-lions-ayelet-gundar-goshen-review. Accessed 20 Oct. 2017.

Herman, David. Review of *Waking Lions*, by Ayelet Gundar-Goshen. *The JC: The Jewish Chronicle*, 11 Feb. 2016, www.thejc.com/culture/books/review-waking-lions-1.59293. Accessed 20 Oct. 2017.

Kirsch, Adam. "Israeli Immigration Thriller *Waking Lions* Becomes Global Sensation." Review of *Waking Lions*, by Ayelet Gundar-Goshen. *Tablet*, 22 Feb. 2017, www.tabletmag.com/jewish-arts-and-culture/books/225465/gundar-goshen-kirsch-waking-lions. Accessed 20 Oct. 2017.

Tsabari, Ayelet. "In This Thriller, an Israeli Doctor Can't Escape His Irresponsibility." Review of *Waking Lions*, by Ayelet Gundar-Goshen. *The New York Times*, 15 Mar. 2017, www.nytimes.com/2017/03/15/books/review/waking-lions-ayelet-gundar-goshen.html. Accessed 20 Oct. 2017.

Washington's Farewell
The Founding Father's Warning to Future Generations

Author: John Avlon (b. 1973)
Publisher: Simon and Schuster (New York).
368 pp.
Type of work: History
Time: 1790s to the present

In Washington's Farewell, *John Avlon details the creation of President George Washington's Farewell Address. Washington's public leave-taking to the American people became one of the most influential political documents in the history of the United States. Avlon argues that the precepts that Washington advocated in his farewell remain relevant and worthy of consideration for Americans in the twenty-first century.*

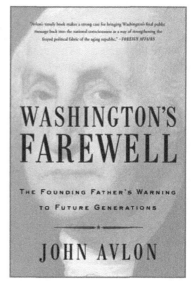

Courtesy of Simon and Schuster

Principal personages

GEORGE WASHINGTON, the first president of the United States
THOMAS JEFFERSON, his secretary of state
ALEXANDER HAMILTON, his secretary of the Treasury
JAMES MADISON, Jefferson's ally in the House of Representatives

John Avlon's *Washington's Farewell* argues passionately for the continued relevance of George Washington's Farewell Address, the first president's lengthy warning about the dangers he saw threatening the young American republic. Washington's valedictory became one of the most influential presidential statements in the history of the United States. Avlon notes that the Farewell Address was reprinted more often in the nineteenth century than the Declaration of Independence. Washington's advice became received wisdom for American leaders, especially his admonition against political entanglements with foreign countries. In time, as the United States became a great world power, such advice seemed increasingly obsolete. Washington's Farewell Address gradually came to be regarded as an important, but inevitably dated artifact, a window into the past, with little bearing on the present. School-age students exploring American history these days might be made aware of the document's existence, but few actually read it. Avlon believes such a dismissively archival approach misses the still-beating heart of Washington's message. He argues that the Farewell Address contains hard-won wisdom that speaks to the challenges facing Americans today.

As a journalist, Avlon has written about the ways that fringe activism from both the left and right distorts American politics. He helped establish the organization No Labels, dedicated to bringing together people from across the political spectrum to solve national problems. He sees in Washington's recommendations to his contemporaries a pragmatic centrism that can resonate today. In his history of the Farewell Address, Avlon does not simply recapture the past. For him, the past can shape the future. In his own words, he aimed to write "a work of popular and practical history." Avlon intends *Washington's Farewell* to contribute to ongoing discussions about what has gone wrong with public policy and discourse in America and what can be done to correct it.

Today, George Washington is the serene and incorruptible Father of his Country, whose visage graces our currency, Mount Rushmore, and countless reproductions of Gilbert Stuart's portraits. This is, in part, a result of Washington's own self-conscious understanding of his role. With discipline, Washington laboriously crafted his life into the image of his own republican ideals. Once he attained the spotlight, he conscientiously endeavored to live up to his own and others' expectations. This was the case when he commanded the Continental Army during the struggle for independence. It was also the case when, as the first president, he established precedents for the chief executive of the United States.

Washington's efforts to lay down markers for republican government were sorely tested by events during his presidency. Party strife quickly emerged. Secretary of the Treasury Alexander Hamilton promoted legislation that provided federal support for trade and manufacturing. This inspired political resistance from leaders who worried about the strength of the central government that Hamilton envisaged and who favored agrarian interests over commercial ones. Thomas Jefferson and James Madison headed the Democratic-Republican opposition to Hamilton's program. Hamilton's partisans called themselves Federalists. Foreign policy intensified these ideological divisions. The French Revolution polarized public opinion in the United States, especially once it entered its radical phase under the Jacobins. Jefferson and his followers warmly supported the French revolutionaries, even after they began using the guillotine to engineer a new republic. Hamilton and his supporters deplored the excesses of the French revolutionaries and sympathized with Great Britain when France went to war against it.

Although most historians associate George Washington with the Federalists, Avlon argues that he made a sincere effort to stay above these factions and should be designated the only president without a party affiliation. Washington tended to back Hamilton but, according to Avlon, only after carefully weighing the arguments from both sides. The president was predisposed to side with Hamilton because of fundamental agreement about the nature of the new republic. Both men possessed a national perspective born of the sacrifices that they shared while serving in the army during the Revolutionary War. Long years of campaigning across the country led Washington to reject regionalism. Although Washington was a Virginia planter, who might have been expected to toe the agrarian line laid down by Thomas Jefferson, Washington's economic thought defied easy categorization. Washington the cultivator abandoned tobacco as a financial dead end. Instead, he made wheat his primary cash crop at Mount Vernon and later launched a highly successful whiskey distillery. He encouraged other cottage industries on his plantation. He also speculated in western land. By the time Washington became president, his pecuniary ventures had made him one of the wealthiest men in America. In short, Washington was an entrepreneur. Taking the long view, the businessman-turned-president agreed with his secretary of the Treasury that encouraging commerce and carefully managing the public debt would lead to national prosperity.

Distressed by the growing party strife, Washington wanted to leave office at the end of his first term. The chiefs of both political blocs urged him to stay. He was still indispensable, a symbol of national unity. Reluctantly, Washington served another term as president. The situation did not improve for him, as debates over economic policy and foreign affairs intensified. Being the subject of partisan and highly personal attacks in the press affronted him. By 1796, he was ready to go and declared that he would not run for reelection. The president had thought long and deeply about the larger forces that had roiled his administration. Bottled up within were things that he had not yet said. As Washington prepared to retire from public life, he decided to unburden himself and share with his fellow citizens his concerns about the country's challenges.

Washington sought help in drafting his Farewell Address. Despite his political eminence, he was acutely aware that he lacked the educational attainments of many of his fellow Founders. Madison, Jefferson, and Hamilton had all attended college. Washington's formal education had ended with primary school. While many of his contemporaries were reading the classics, he was living an adventurous life as a surveyor and soldier on the western frontier. Fearful that his own prose might lack polish, Washington often turned to others to help him craft his speeches. When he contemplated retiring at the end of his first term, he sought speechwriting assistance from James Madison for a parting speech, unaware that Madison was then fomenting Democratic-Republican opposition to his administration. Washington had this manuscript in hand four years later when he called on the literary skills of his trusty colleague Hamilton, then out of office and tending a law practice in New York. Hamilton rewrote and expanded Madison's text. Then Washington painstakingly revised Hamilton's version, finishing it in September 1796. Washington did not deliver his Farewell Address before an audience. Instead, he arranged to publish it in a newspaper that was not identified with either political party. The Farewell Address was quickly reprinted by newspapers across the United States.

The harassed president achieved a monumental parting triumph. His contemporaries recognized the power of his words and the good sense of his recommendations. Politicians from both parties praised the Farewell Address, even if, as events proved, they were unprepared to follow all its policy prescriptions. They did so in the spirit that hypocrisy is the homage of vice to virtue. Washington had set a standard. He had restored himself to the place that he coveted. He was once again, in the words of his eulogist Henry Lee, "First in war, first in peace, and first in the hearts of his countrymen." The Farewell Address, effectively his last testament, entered into its remarkable career as a revered public document. Avlon provides a fascinating history of the postpublication influence of Washington's address, exploring how subsequent generations used it: both secessionists and union advocates appealed to it before the Civil War; opponents of Woodrow Wilson's League of Nations embraced it; and Nazi Bundists cited it fatuously in the 1930s. President Dwight D. Eisenhower used it as a model for his own farewell address denouncing the influence of the "military-industrial complex." In the twenty-first century, playwright Lin-Manuel Miranda adapted part of Washington's text into a hip-hop song, "One Last Time," for his award-winning musical biography *Hamilton*. For Avlon, the translation of George Washington's message into an acclaimed work of popular culture affirms that the Farewell Address is not dead. Its terms can be converted to contemporary use.

John Avlon is the editor in chief of the Daily Beast. *Prior to that role, he wrote speeches for New York City mayor Rudy Giuliani and columns for the* New York Sun. *He has also authored* Independent Nation: How the Vital Center Is Changing American Politics *(2004) and* Wingnuts: How the Lunatic Fringe Is Hijacking America *(2010).*

Washington touched on themes in his Farewell Address that Avlon believes can inform and elevate our political debates. Washington reminds Americans that more unites than divides them and that strength lies only in unity. In his day, the major division lay between North and South, whereas today it is between conservative and liberal. Whatever the particulars, Washington warned that tribalism leads to ruin. Washington famously cautions against political factionalism. By the time that he left office, he could not realistically expect parties to disappear, but he did counsel the public to temper partisan enthusiasms; only moderation of political partisanship makes for effective governance. Very familiar with debt in his personal life, Washington calls for responsible fiscal stewardship in government. This is a timely reminder of economic prudence for an era when legislatures rarely agree on budgets. Today, debate roils around so-called culture wars and the role of religion in American life. In the Farewell Address, Washington extolled the importance of religious belief for the formation of good citizens. He did not call for any denomination to be established and firmly supported religious pluralism. Rather, Avlon notes, Washington's address reminds readers that freedom of religion is not the same as freedom *from* religion and that respect for faith need not contradict a spirit of mutual tolerance in a healthy society. The haphazardly schooled first president also firmly believed in the importance of education for a thriving citizenry. His concerns remain germane in an era of intense disputes over the character and quality of public education.

Finally, Washington counseled against getting entangled in European affairs, especially the French Revolution and its attendant wars. Such advice may seem dated when the United States has been firmly committed to international alliances for decades. Avlon argues that Washington's core proposal was that Americans pursue a policy "not of isolation but independence," dealing fairly with other nations but resisting the temptation to export their ideals beyond their shores. In an interconnected world riven by ideological strife, such precepts can be challenged but are certainly worth considering.

Avlon's book is both engaging and thought-provoking. He makes a compelling case for the enduring importance of Washington's Farewell Address. Amid current contentions, Americans would do well to listen, to thoughtfully consider Washington's wisdom.

Daniel P. Murphy

Review Sources

Klang, Keith. Review of *Washington's Farewell: The Founding Father's Warning to Future Generations*, by John Avlon. *Library Journal*, 13 Jan. 2017, reviews. libraryjournal.com/2017/01/books/nonfic/soc-sci/parting-words-social-sciences-reviews-january-2017. Accessed 16 Oct. 2017.

Mead, Walter Russell. Review of *Washington's Farewell: The Founding Father's Warning to Future Generations*, by John Avlon. *Foreign Affairs*, May–June 2017, p. 161.

Saunders, Paul J. "Washington's Warnings." Review of *Washington's Farewell: The Founding Father's Warning to Future Generations*, by John Avlon. *National Interest*, July–Aug. 2017, nationalinterest.org/feature/george-washingtons-enduring-realism-21305?page=show. Accessed 16 Oct. 2017.

Review of *Washington's Farewell: The Founding Father's Warning to Future Generations*, by John Avlon. *Kirkus Reviews*, 1 Dec. 2016, p. 1.

We Were Eight Years in Power
An American Tragedy

Author: Ta-Nehisi Coates (b. 1975)
Publisher: One World (New York). 400 pp.
Type of work: Essays, current affairs
Time: 2008–16
Locale: United States

We Were Eight Years in Power *is an essay collection by journalist Ta-Nehisi Coates that explores the racial politics surrounding Barack Obama, the first African American president in US history.*

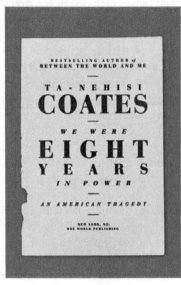

Courtesy of One World

Principal personages
TA-NEHISI COATES, the author
BARACK OBAMA, the forty-fourth president
  of the United States
MICHELLE OBAMA, his wife, the First Lady
  of the United States
HENRY GATES JR., director of African American studies at Harvard University

When it comes to race politics in America, Ta-Nehisi Coates is a reluctant thought leader. In interviews, the Baltimore native has revealed that he does not enjoy the fact that he has become white Americans' primary source on racism; ultimately, the responsibility of having people look to him as a sort of guru on systematic prejudice is one that he does not wish to bear. And yet, whether he wants to be or not, Coates is one of the most important voices in American literature on race today. His capacity for educating readers on polarizing racial issues in a compelling way is illustrated well by the overwhelming popularity of his books. His 2015 work *Between the World and Me* was a best seller that earned him the 2015 National Book Award for nonfiction and a nomination for the 2016 Pulitzer Prize for general nonfiction; his follow up, *We Were Eight Years in Power: An American Tragedy*, has enjoyed similar acclaim and sales success.

In its simplest description, *We Were Eight Years in Power* is a curated collection of eight of Coates's essays that were published in the *Atlantic* between the years 2007 and 2016. These essays explore myriad events and figures, but as a collection, they never feel disjointed or overwhelming. This is thanks to the omnipresent theme of the contemporary African American experience, which functions as another link (in addition to the effects of Barack Obama's presidency) between all of the included works. Beyond being an essay collection, the book also functions as a memoir, presenting a firsthand account of how Coates became a prominent literary voice in American culture during the time that Obama was president. It is this one-two punch of sharp cultural writing and autobiography that makes *We Were Eight Years in Power* highly engaging. The book is at once extremely informative and deeply personal.

The essays included in *We Were Eight Years in Power* explore a diverse range of subjects. The first, "'This Is How We Lost to the White Man,'" is a 2007 piece on Bill Cosby that examines the comedian's initiative to fight against racism by putting the onus on African Americans. While Coates throws no overt punches in the piece, he convincingly counters Cosby's thesis that African Americans can improve their lives simply by not engaging with hip-hop culture and by "pull[ing themselves] up by [their] own bootstraps." Subsequently, separate profiles of Michelle and Barack Obama act as bookends to the forty-fourth president's time at the White House: the second piece in the collection, titled "American Girl," captures the feeling of hope the First Lady and her husband provided African Americans in the first year of Obama's presidency; the final essay, "My President Was Black," examines the actual impact of the Obama administration as it was winding down. Coates is painstakingly honest and critical in the way that he writes about the Obamas, and this sharp, unfiltered perspective infuses the narrative with a bittersweet tone. He admits that the Obamas allowed him to feel proud about being American for the first time in his life, but he is also quick to point out the president's shortcomings. In both "My President Was Black" and "Fear of a Black President," Coates criticizes Obama for his "color-blind" policies, which he feels allowed the president to cater too much to white fears. To illustrate this fact, he cites the events surrounding the arrest of Harvard University professor Henry Gates Jr., who was apprehended by the police after trying to get into his own home because he looked suspicious to a white neighbor. Coates argues that while Obama could have used the event to speak out against racism, he instead tried to play the role of the unifier, inviting both the police officer and Mr. Gates to the White House for a beer. It is ultimately an important, convincing perspective.

In addition to exploring the significance of African American cultural and political figures, *We Were Eight Years in Power* also features a number of essays that directly address major issues in race politics. This is best demonstrated by the pieces "Why Do So Few Blacks Study the Civil War?," "The Case for Reparations," and "The Black Family in the Age of Mass Incarceration." It is in these works that Coates showcases his skills as a journalist. Each piece is overflowing with research, powerful arguments, and emotional interviews with real people who have been impacted by the very problems that he is addressing. In "The Case for Reparations," the interview with Clyde Ross, a man born into a sharecropping family whose property was stolen from them by white Mississippi authorities, is especially effective at illustrating the government's unjust housing policies toward African Americans throughout the twentieth century.

The memoir element of the book proves to be a powerful literary device, one that definitively ties the disparate essays together. Coates presents these autobiographical anecdotes in short chapter prefaces, each designed to introduce and contextualize the essay that follows. The first, entitled "Notes from the First Year," describes the low point that he was at in his life during the winter of 2007, when Barack Obama first announced his presidential bid. Coates recalls that he had just lost his third job in seven years. He wanted to give up and switch careers, but his wife, Kenyatta, would not let him. Each of the subsequent memoir chapters leaps a year into the future, thereby chronicling Coates's journey from a struggling writer on unemployment to one of the country's most famous journalists. The story of his ascension proves to be a vessel for one of the book's central arguments: that while Obama's presidency did not eradicate racism, it did facilitate the wave of African American journalists and artists that broke through to the mainstream during this time. As Coates states in the book's introduction, he was a fortunate member of this wave.

Throughout *We Were Eight Years in Power*, Coates repeatedly references writers such as Zora Neale Hurston, W. E. B. Du Bois, and James Baldwin, of whom he is a worthy successor. In "Notes from the Seventh Year," he reveals that he was saved by African American writing. For Coates as a reader, their willingness to resist sentiment and strip away illusions about black life in America made him feel as though he were not alone. These writers assured him that no matter how much white society tried to convince him otherwise, he was not crazy, and racism was indeed alive and well in the United States. In addition to providing him with feelings of solidarity and comfort, they also inspired his writing style. This is especially true of Baldwin, of whom Toni Morrison has called Coates a disciple. Coates's writing, like Baldwin's, aims to describe the world with unrelenting honesty and lyrical prose. It is his ability to deliver powerful truths through the vessel of beautiful words that makes *We Were Eight Years in Power* such an exciting addition to the canon of great African American literature.

Despite these powerful influences, Coates's literary style is very much his own. Reading through each of the eight essays in the collection makes it clear that the author is not one for employing colorful metaphors or allegories. Where the unique beauty of his voice truly shines through is in his meticulous word choice; the vocabulary Coates employs is rich and vast and somehow strikes a balance between old-fashioned and modern all at once. Furthermore, he has a tendency to use words as tools of economy: rather than describe things at length, he finds individual words that capture the essence of what he trying to express. Another quality that makes Coates's writing so engaging is the way in which he effortlessly weaves together facts, history, and cultural references. On one page alone, he segues from the political beliefs of Booker T. Washington to the lyrics of the rapper Nas with impressive dexterity. Ultimately, Coates is a scholar with a gift for imparting information to readers in a way that feels exciting and relevant to everything.

Reviews of *We Were Eight Years in Power* have been overwhelmingly positive, with many critics citing it as one of the most important books of 2017. Much of this critical acclaim has been directed at the quality of Coates's writing. Walton Muyumba wrote in his review for the *Los Angeles Times* that Coates's "prose style and literary prowess are hip-hop sharpened: he believes in the art of dexterous reference, potent, lyrical critique and political storytelling." Such praise is well deserved. The arguments and ideas posited throughout *We Were Eight Years in Power* could easily fall flat in the hands of a lesser writer. Yet Coates's primary gift is his ability to transform heavy, unapproachable topics typically reserved for academic types into urgent, exciting public conversations. His literary style seamlessly blends history and politics with autobiographical anecdotes in a way that ignites readers' attention. Perhaps the biggest

© Nina Subin

Ta-Nehisi Coates is a correspondent for the Atlantic. *He is best known for his best-selling books* Beautiful Struggle *(2008) and* Between the World and Me *(2015). He was awarded a MacArthur Fellowship in 2015.*

testament that can be made to the power of Coates's writing is that it is not only well received but celebrated by a large number of white Americans, despite the fact that it regularly criticizes them for their apathy and racism toward their black countrymen.

For some, *We Were Eight Years in Power* may feel stale or outdated. This is not because the book's content is unoriginal, but rather because some of its essays date back to 2007. Furthermore, all of these essays were first published in the *Atlantic* and have subsequently become part of the zeitgeist by way of thorough online conversation. "The Case for Reparations," for example, was a cultural phenomenon in 2014 that garnered thousands of readers' comments while also inspiring innumerable think pieces across most major publications. Therefore, the complaint that *We Were Eight Years in Power* does not feel fresh will likely come primarily from Coates fans hungry for new works. Most readers will enjoy having all of his important pieces in one compact, portable collection, as there is new value to be gleaned from reading through all of them at once in chronological order, and the introductory memoirs in each chapter provide fresh, interesting material.

We Were Eight Years in Power takes on greater urgency and importance thanks to the moment in history that it was published: with Donald J. Trump newly elected as president, 2017 proved to be a year of political polarization and heated national conversations about race. Yet timing plays only a small part in the book's success. *We Were Eight Years in Power* is an instant classic that is likely to become a regularly cited work of nonfiction in the years to come because of the power of its arguments and the beauty of its prose. Under the guise of exploring only the events that transpired during two presidential terms, it contextualizes centuries of American history with razor-sharp analysis while simultaneously providing the foundation on which a path to a better future can be built.

Emily Turner

Review Sources

Gordon-Reed, Annette. "On White Supremacy." Review of *We Were Eight Years in Power: An American Tragedy*, by Ta-Nehisi Coates. *The Guardian*, 18 Nov. 2017, www.theguardian.com/books/2017/nov/18/we-were-eight-years-in-power-ta-nehisi-coates-review. Accessed 10 Jan. 2018.

Lozada, Carlos. "Ta-Nehisi Coates and the Fear of the Black Writer." Review of
We Were Eight Years in Power: An American Tragedy, by Ta-Nehisi Coates. *The Washington Post*, 27 Sept. 2017, www.washingtonpost.com/news/book-party/ wp/2017/09/27/ta-nehisi-coates-and-the-fear-of-a-black-writer/. Accessed 10 Jan. 2018.

Muyumba, Walton. "Ta-Nehisi Coates Blazes a Singular Intellectual Path in *We Were Eight Years in Power*." Review of *We Were Eight Years in Power: An American Tragedy*, by Ta-Nehisi Coates. *Los Angeles Times*, 29 Sept. 2017, www.latimes. com/books/jacketcopy/la-ca-jc-ta-nehisi-coates-power-20170929-story.html. Accessed 10 Jan. 2018.

Review of *We Were Eight Years in Power: An American Tragedy*, by Ta-Nehisi Coates. *Kirkus Reviews*, 7 Aug. 2017, www.kirkusreviews.com/book-reviews/ta-nehisi-coates/we-were-eight-years-in-power/. Accessed 10 Jan. 2018.

Review of *We Were Eight Years in Power: An American Tragedy*, by Ta-Nehisi Coates. *Publishers Weekly*, 14 Aug. 2017, www.publishersweekly.com/978-0-399-59056-6. Accessed 10 Jan. 2018.

What It Means When a Man Falls from the Sky

Author: Lesley Nneka Arimah
Publisher: Riverhead Books (New York). 240 pp.
Type of work: Short fiction
Locales: Nigeria and the United States

This debut collection by Lesley Nneka Arimah presents twelve stories that display an impressive range of styles, from realistic stories about young Nigerian women to dystopian allegories and traditional fables.

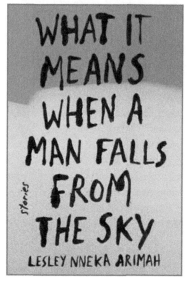

Courtesy of Riverhead Books

The twelve stories collected in Lesley Nneka Arimah's *What It Means When a Man Falls from the Sky* show the range of a writer experimenting with various modes and types of story—from domestic realism to speculative fiction to folk fables. Some of the stories are tightly structured with a self-conscious rhythmic syntax, while others wander along loosely as if they were chapters from a novel. Some stories seem to be drawn from African myth and folktale, although Arimah has said her fables are original inventions. Still others are concept-driven, postapocalyptic science-fiction tales.

A good example of Arimah's highly formalized writing can be found in the opening piece, "The Future Looks Good," which begins with an image that repeats throughout the story of a young woman who does not see what is coming up behind her as she fumbles to unlock a door. The language of the story is restrained and rhythmically paralleled by the story of a woman who has two children—one named Biafra, who has become involved with an abusive young man, and one named Ezinma, who is struggling with the key. Arimah withholds revealing who or what comes up behind Ezinma until the last, shocking line.

"War Stories" uses the formal narrative device of juxtaposition. A father tells his young daughter about his experiences as a young soldier in war, providing context for the schoolyard battles that the young girl engages in on the playground—their two "war stories" are linked together by a chess match between the father and daughter and paralleled by the central conflict between the young girl and her mother, who does not approve of her daughter's behavior.

Battles between mother and daughter are frequent in Arimah's stories, such as in "Wild," about a young woman in the United States whose mother buys her a one-way ticket to visit her aunt and cousin in Lagos, Nigeria, without her knowledge. The mother, who replaces her daughter's boyish clothes with more feminine dresses, hopes her daughter will be influenced to better behavior by her cousin. However, the aunt is also having troubles with her daughter, who has given birth to a son out of wedlock. It all comes to a head at a party when the cousin leaves the girl stranded. Unlike Arimah's formally structured stories, this piece is loose and driven by plot, reading more like a chapter in a realistic novel than a short story.

"Light" returns to Arimah's formally well-wrought technique, beginning with a tightly unified opening paragraph about a man who sends his daughter out into the world, not knowing how quickly it would "wick the dew off her" and return her to him "hollowed out, relieved of her better parts." The mother has been in the United States for three years studying for a graduate degree, while the father and daughter survive such things as the "crime scene" of her first menstrual period together. This is a lean and tightly patterned story of a father's efforts to shield his daughter while preserving her "streak of fire" that he hopes will keep the "wolves of the world" at bay.

"Second Chances" also begins with a formal introduction voiced by the young female narrator, who tells the reader to ignore the fact that her mother, who, looking like she has just stepped out of a photograph, has been dead for eight years. The story develops around the metaphor of the young woman's attempts to find the photograph of her mother and thus establish some sort of connection that she has lost.

"Buchi's Girls" is another mother-daughter story about a woman who has two daughters and must live with her sister and brother-in-law following the death of her husband. The sister's husband is a dominating force in the household who bullies Buchi and her two daughters by threatening to kill a chicken that one of the children, who has been mute since the death of her father, loves "like it was her own child." The mother has no choice but to allow the bully to succeed.

Another significant story about mother-daughter relationships, "Windfalls," focuses on a mother who uses her daughter to extort merchants to compensate her for staged childhood falls. The mother-daughter team go through life with the child sustaining several injuries, all of which, in a cruel irony, makes the mother proud of her. The story ends with a real fall when the daughter, who has become pregnant, accidently slips on some ice cream in a store and suffers a miscarriage. When the mother is awarded five hundred thousand dollars, she once again is proud at her daughter's success, oblivious to the pain the young woman has suffered by losing her child.

Arimah draws upon magical realism in the story "Who Will Greet You at Home," in which the cultural concept of the importance of motherhood is allegorized in a fable about women creating babies out of materials that then must be approved of and blessed by mothers. The story focuses on a young hairdresser named Ogechi, who tries to fulfill this cultural requirement by creating a baby out of yarn; however, it only lasts a month before it catches on a loose nail and unravels. Knowing that her own mother had formed her from mud and twigs—"pedestrian items that produced a pedestrian girl"—she is determined to create a child who will be soft and pretty and worthy of love. She tries various materials, but each time her mother laughs and rejects the fabricated infant, insisting that her daughter create a child who can tolerate hard work. The daughter leaves her mother and seeks approval from an archetypal mother named simply "Mama," who runs the hair salon where Ogechi works, for whom she creates a child made of hair swept up from the floor. According to the rules of motherhood of this hypothetical culture, the next day the hair baby will come to life and within a year will be strong and pretty. However, the child begins to suck Ogechi's hair out as she carries it. Finally, the hungry child attacks Ogechi, who, to protect herself, sets the infant on fire. In an act of rebellion against the cultural expectation of motherhood, Ogechi sets about creating a child out of dirt and the ashes of the hair child, saying, "let this child be born in sorrow," giving the child the face of her mother.

Arimah said in an interview after the publication of this book that speculative fiction has to feel real, explaining that even though the landscape is magical, the characters in the fiction do not know it is magical. In another interview, Arimah said she is drawn to magical realism not because it provides escape but because it allows a writer to insert human desires into a supernatural world and watch humanity become grotesque. The result, Arimah says, is more interesting and

Lesley Nneka Arimah won the Commonwealth Short Story Prize for Africa in 2015, the same year her story "Who Will Greet You at Home" was published in the New Yorker. *Her story "Glory" was chosen for the 2017 O. Henry Prize Stories.*

more complicated than everyday reality, and usually more sinister. Talking about her story "Who Will Greet You at Home," which originally appeared in the *New Yorker* in 2015, Arimah said she did not intend this myth to be allegorical. However, she realized as she wrote it that some of her social and cultural concerns became imbedded in the story—namely the insistence that women have to marry and have children as soon as possible in order to give their lives true purpose. "An element of surrealism in a story can put pressure on a character in ways that would be impossible in our natural world," Arimah said, thus making this story more compelling than it would have been as a strictly realistic piece.

The title story of the collection, "What It Means When a Man Falls from the Sky," is a speculative concept story that takes place in a future when global warming has caused much of the world to be flooded with water, with only Australia and Africa remaining. The central character is Nneoma, a mathematician of emotion, who makes her living by calculating and subtracting feelings from suffering humans, like sucking poison from a wound. A Chilean mathematician named Furcal has discovered a formula that explains the universe, but there is concern that the formula, which has taken the place of religion, is fundamentally flawed. Mathematicians have the ability, with the help of the formula, to take on another person's grief by eating it and bearing it themselves. The answer to the implied question of the title is that the formula, which is hoped will make it possible for humans to defy gravity, has failed.

"Glory," which was selected for inclusion in the 2017 *O. Henry Prize Stories*, is about a girl whose parents have named her Glorybetogod. However, Glory is singularly unfortunate and seems to have been born resenting the world. She meets a young man who is just the opposite—able to make friends easily and always lucky. It looks as if Glory finally has everything right and her future is assured—that the chaos of her life will "coalesce into an intricate puzzle." However, the story ends when the young man offers her a ring, and resentment and elation war within her until she makes a decision just before the end of the story. The reader is left to guess what it is.

"What Is a Volcano" is the shortest story in the collection—a fable about a feud between the god of ants and the goddess of rivers. When Ant steals River's two children, causing the death of one and hiding the other, River, with the help of other grieving women, searches the world to try to find them. The story ends in a risky image, the significance of which may be intentionally trivialized. River and the women who have traveled with her lie "catatonic with heartache, dreaming of their children." When River's surviving god-child cries from her hiding place, the bodies of River and the women hear her and their breasts weep, and that, the storyteller concludes, "since you asked, is a volcano."

"Redemption," the final story in the collection, is told from the perspective of a young girl who admires her neighbor's house girl, Mayowa, for her rebellious nature, especially after Mayowa throws excrement wrapped in newspaper against the wall of her house because her mother called Mayowa's virtue into question. When there is a possible scandal involving Mayowa and the youth minister, Mayowa and another house girl run off with the church offering. When Mayowa returns, the narrator realizes the rebel is ultimately just as powerless as she—merely another daughter in disgrace.

Lesley Nneka Arimah's debut book has been greeted with high praise. The novelist Marina Warner, in a review for the *New York Times*, called Arimah a "witty, oblique, and mischievous storyteller" and compared her magical realism to that of Nigerian poet Ben Okri and her use of science-fiction elements to the writing of Canadian author Margaret Atwood. Critic Michael Schaub, reviewing the collection for NPR Books, praised Arimah's achievement, writing, "She crafts stories that reward rereading, not because they're unclear or confusing, but because it's so tempting to revisit each exquisite sentence, each uniquely beautiful description."

Charles E. May

Review Sources

Burney, Tayla. Review of *What It Means When a Man Falls from the Sky*, by Lesley Nneka Arimah. *The Washington Post*, 14 Apr. 2017, www.washingtonpost.com/entertainment/books/lesley-nneka-arimahs-debut-story-collection-is-vibrant-and-fresh/2017/04/12/8d11fba4-1bd0-11e7-9887-1a5314b56a08_story.html. Accessed 12 Sept. 2017.

Schaub, Michael. "*What It Means When a Man Falls from the Sky* Is Defiantly, Electrically Original." Review of *What It Means When a Man Falls from the Sky*, by Lesley Nneka Arimah. *NPR Books*, 5 Apr. 2017, www.npr.

org/2017/04/05/521959681/what-it-means-when-a-man-falls-from-the-sky-is-
defiantly-electrically-original. Accessed 12 Sept. 2017.

Warner, Marina. Review of *What It Means When a Man Falls from the Sky*, by
Lesley Nneka Arimah. *The New York Times*, 5 May 2017, www.nytimes.
com/2017/05/05/books/review/what-it-means-when-a-man-falls-from-the-sky-
lesley-nneka-arimah-.html. Accessed 12 Sept. 2017.

Weiss-Meyer, Amy. Review of *What It Means When a Man Falls from the Sky*, by
Lesley Nneka Arimah. *The Atlantic*, 11 Apr. 2017, www.theatlantic.com/enter-
tainment/archive/2017/04/the-powerful-pessimism-of-what-it-means-when-a-
man-falls-from-the-sky/522687. Accessed 12 Sept. 2017.

Review of *What It Means When a Man Falls from the Sky*, by Lesley Nneka Arimah.
Kirkus, 23 Jan. 2017, www.kirkusreviews.com/book-reviews/lesley-nneka-
arimah/what-it-means-when-a-man-falls-from-the-sky. Accessed 12 Sept. 2017.

Review of *What It Means When a Man Falls from the Sky*, by Lesley Nneka Arimah.
Publishers Weekly, 27 Feb. 2017, www.publishersweekly.com/978-0-7352-1102-
5. Accessed 12 Sept. 2017.

What We Lose

Author: Zinzi Clemmons
Publisher: Viking (New York). Illustrated.
  224 pp.
Type of work: Novel
Time: ca. 1980 to the present
Locales: Philadelphia; New York City; Jo-
  hannesburg, South Africa

Courtesy of Viking

*This novel explores the devastation of los-
ing a parent to cancer. In following its protagonist, Thandi, through adolescence and
young adulthood, the novel also considers
the issues of race and immigration, moving
between the United States and Africa.*

Principal characters
THANDI, the narrator
HER MOTHER, an immigrant from South
  Africa and a nurse
HER FATHER, a college professor born in New York City
PETER, her colleague and husband
MAHPEE, their son
LYNDALL, one of her South African cousins
AMINAH, her best friend from childhood
FRANK, Aminah's longtime boyfriend

Through the voice of the novel's principal protagonist and narrator, Thandi, *What We
Lose* plunges into complex explorations of love, loss, and cultural and racial identity.
Written in a series of brief chapters and statements—with some passages consisting
only of a sentence and paired image—the novel digs deeply into the pain of Thandi's
experiences, in a technique that critics have described variously as a construction of
fragments or a collage. The novel begins with a prologue, setting Thandi and her father in the family home, as they seek to move forward after her mother's death. In
their apartment, surrounded by her mother's abandoned possessions and the Chinese
food that they have ordered in a habit formed during many months of caretaking, the
father and daughter confront their physical, palpable loss. The smells and tastes of the
Chinese food have replaced the rich flavors and aromas of her mother's African stews.
Her mother's possessions are covered in dust or buried under the objects that support a
widower's lifestyle. *What We Lose* is a coming-of-age story, as it offers glimpses into
Thandi's life from her childhood into graduate school and beyond, but it is more principally an exploration of a life unraveled by loss, and the subsequent attempt to pull its
fragments together into a new future. The book gains its title from a pamphlet, *What*

We Lose: A Support Guide, that Thandi and her father receive from the hospice after her mother's death. The pamphlet is designed to help caregivers cope with their grief. In this novel, Zinzi Clemmons offers the antithesis of such a tidy, clinical pamphlet: a novel that cuts into the pain of loss, the complexities of mother-daughter relationships, the blurred edges of race, and the failures of ideals and aspirations.

Critics have noted that *What We Lose* has elements of autobiography, but while Clemmons acknowledges the parallels between her life and Thandi's, she has eschewed any association of her novel with memoir. Like Thandi, Clemmons was raised near Philadelphia by a mixed-race South African mother and an African American father. Like Thandi, she also experienced the death of her mother from cancer when she was pursuing higher education at an elite university. These life experiences have shaped the depth and candor with which she speaks about mourning, loss, and transnational, multicultural racial identities. Nonetheless, the reader must be careful to distinguish Clemmons from Thandi. Reviewer Lucy Scholes has characterized the novel as autofiction, which shares some of the intimacies of memoir while also allowing space for greater creative freedom. Aspects of the emotions that it explores, as well as details of biography and racial identity, are commonalities that Thandi and Clemmons share, allowing the novel to have a greater sense of authenticity and raw emotion. This technique certainly contributes to the most powerful moments of the text.

Thandi is the only character in the book that the reader gets to know with any intimacy. Her mother, father, and other friends and relatives are all seen through the lens of Thandi's perceptions and priorities. This approach allows Clemmons to probe Thandi's emotions and introspections with great depth—but it also limits the reader's ability to see her through a different perspective. Thandi is not an easy figure to get close to. She often appears selfish or privileged and is open about her faults and failings. Thandi is clouded by grief through much of the novel and the fragmented form of the text evokes the imperfect vision and self-reflection of such profound emotional and psychological grief. Still, though the novel ultimately builds around the death of Thandi's mother, much of the text is concerned with other aspects of Thandi's life and upbringing. In themes dealing with race, class, and identity, Clemmons similarly exploits the fragmentary form of the text in order to offer cutting flashes of observation. The brevity of these fragments allows honesty and force. As triggers for bare emotional reaction, these passages invite the reader to engage with Thandi's subjective experiences of race, class, and identity—and her own persistent and painful sense of displacement. The greatest value of *What We Lose* may lie in its careful balancing of universal experience—the loss of a loved one—against the complex subjectivity of Thandi's identity as a "strange in-betweener." In so doing, the novel considers both the continuity of human experience and the painful realities of individual struggles.

Motherhood is a central consideration of *What We Lose*. Thandi's relationship with her mother is the most evident theme of the book, though the novel also follows Thandi's own journey into motherhood. Both her relationship with her own mother and her ultimate decision to become a mother are fraught. The reader follows the progress of Thandi's pregnancy in passages adjacent to fragments describing her mother's final illness. This narrative structure effectively strips away social ideals of femininity and motherhood—a sentiment presented in one fragment, "I do not see the mother with her child as either more morally credible or more morally capable than any other woman," which is part of an excerpt from the introduction to Adrienne Rich's 1976 *Of Woman Born: Motherhood as Experience and Institution*. These issues become larger when considered through the lens of race and nationhood. Thandi's most personal discussions of South Africa—her mother's homeland—are introduced in the passages concerning her mother's illness and commemorating her mother's death. The "motherland" seems intimately linked to the character's understanding of motherhood. Race, class, and politics become additional lenses through which motherhood and stereotypes of motherhood are raised in the text. For black families, Thandi observes, motherhood is about meaningful relationships more than biology. Another fragment, from *Common Differences: Conflicts in Black and White Feminist Perspectives* (1981), by Gloria I. Joseph and Jill Lewis, asserts that black women "are daughters all and they frequently 'mother' their sisters, nieces, nephews, or cousins as well as their own children." Much as Thandi loves her young son, the novel concludes without any sense that she has come to comfortable terms with her own motherhood. Divorced and struggling financially, she appears to be living on the edge—though the reader is aware that she is nonetheless highly privileged and with a strong, if somewhat remote, support system in her father.

Race is a second theme throughout the book. Thandi struggles with her biracial identity. She recounts experiences of being only partially accepted within the African American community. She remembers her mother's upbringing under apartheid. At an unnamed East Coast university, she studies race and privilege and believes that she is learning to fight against social injustice. But, this imperfect intellectual bubble becomes apparent after her mother's cancer treatment begins. Thandi confronts the reality of the cost and privilege of her mother's treatment—alongside the harrowing realities of the disease. Making use of a cancer treatment center in a wealthy Philadelphia neighborhood, Thandi's mother feels guilt that many of her immigrant friends could not afford such care. She suffers while watching many younger and less-privileged black patients in her clinic. Yet, the "face" of cancer treatment that Thandi encounters in pamphlets, public relations, and advertising is white, upper-class, and older—despite statistics reproduced in the novel that emphasize the prevalence of cancer in black communities. Earlier in the text, Thandi had likened her social condition as a "light-skinned black woman" to being like "a well-dressed person who is homeless." While appearing accepted, safe, and mainstream, this in-between racial position leaves an individual with "nowhere to rest, nowhere to feel safe." Her mother's experience while being treated for cancer makes this more painfully apparent, and "only reinforced how the world saw us: not black or white, not American or African, not poor or rich. We were confined to the middle, and always

Zinzi Clemmons, cofounder and former publisher of Apogee Journal, *is a contributing editor to* Literary Hub *and teaches at the Colburn Conservatory and Occidental College. She has received writing residencies at Dar al-Ma'mun in Morocco, Breadloaf, the MacDowell Colony, and the Fine Arts Work Center in Provincetown.* What We Lose *is her debut novel.*

would be." Ultimately, Thandi characterizes this outsider position as akin to the "binds of apartheid" from which her mother had been unable to truly escape.

This later comment also introduces a final key theme of the novel, which is confronting the realities and stereotypes of Africa and its peoples. In the United States, Thandi encounters many stereotypes of the continent—be it in terms of the AIDS epidemic, the plight of starving children, or the sensationalized coverage of the Oscar Pistorius trial. She absorbs these stereotypes alongside her own complicated, highly contrasting experience of South Africa. Although her mother had fled apartheid, her grandfather, aunts, uncles, and numerous cousins had remained in country. They had also thrived financially, attaining a level of extravagant wealth far surpassing Thandi's well-to-do parents. Thus, through Thandi, the reader confronts head-on any stereotypes of Africa as destitute. Indeed, to Thandi, Johannesburg is the location of her parents' lavish summer home, the place of affectionate gatherings of extended family, and even a culinary destination for fragrant curries. Thandi struggles to reconcile her African and her American pedigrees and manages to live in between the two places. Much like her perception of biracial identity, the novel seems to conclude that she is never fully at home in either place. As with the other themes of the novel, the role of Africa has both a social and a personal dynamic. Confronting larger ideas about Africa also means coming to terms with her relationship with her mother. Dearly beloved, yet at the same time somewhat distant or misunderstood, Thandi's mother is the personal embodiment of Thandi's own, complicated tie to South Africa.

What We Lose provides its readers with no tidy narrative, clear answers, or pat resolutions. Thandi offers a complicated figure, and her candid emotions, deep psychological reflection, and complicated subject position allow Clemmons to explore the themes of illness, loss, motherhood, race, and immigrant identity with depth and thoughtfulness.

Julia A Sienkewicz

Review Sources

Ganeshananthan, V. V. "Stories of Familial Unrest and Displacement." Review of *What We Lose*, by Zinzi Clemmons. *The New York Times*, 8 Sept. 2017, www.nytimes.com/2017/09/08/books/review/what-we-lose-zinzi-clemmons.html. Accessed 9 Feb. 2018.

Kola, FT. "What We Lose by Zinzi Clemmons Review—a Debut of Haunting Fragments." Review of *What We Lose*, by Zinzi Clemmons. *The Guardian*, 5 Aug. 2017, www.theguardian.com/books/2017/aug/05/what-we-lose-zinzi-clemmons-review. Accessed 9 Feb. 2018.

Scholes, Lucy. "*What We Lose* by Zinzi Clemmons, Book Review: a Story about Identity Organised around the Momentous Loss of a Parent." Review of *What We Lose*, by Zinzi Clemmons. *The Independent*, 12 July 2017, www.independent.co.uk/arts-entertainment/books/reviews/what-we-lose-by-zinzi-clemmons-book-review-a-story-about-identity-organised-around-themomentous-loss-a7836676.html. Accessed 9 Feb. 2018.

Weiss-Meyer, Amy. "*What We Lose*: A Striking Novel about Filial Grief." Review of *What We Lose*, by Zinzi Clemmons. *The Atlantic*, 1 Aug. 2017, www.theatlantic. com/entertainment/archive/2017/08/what-we-lose-confronts-the-dilemma-of-authenticity/535065/. Accessed 9 Feb. 2018.

Williams, John. "A Novelist's Meditation on Loss and Identity." Review of *What We Lose*, by Zinzi Clemmons. *The New York Times*, 25 May 2017, www.nytimes. com/2017/05/25/books/what-we-lose-zinzi-clemmons.html. Accessed 9 Feb. 2018.

When I Grow Up I Want to Be a List of Further Possibilities

Author: Chen Chen (b. 1989)
Publisher: BOA Editions (Rochester, NY). 96 pp.
Type of work: Poetry

In this debut poetry collection, Chinese-born American poet Chen Chen explores issues of family, identity, sexuality, and further possibilities with humor, pathos, and deftly lyrical turns of phrase.

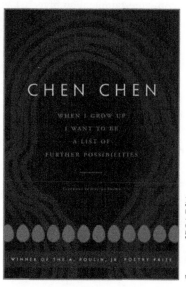

When I Grow Up I Want to Be a List of Further Possibilities, the debut collection of poet Chen Chen, is at times explicitly confessional and very personal, revealing much not only about Chen himself—whose identity as a Chinese American gay man permeates the pages, underlying even those poems that do not directly address culture or sexuality—but also about American life in the years surrounding the turn of the twenty-first century. Michelle Betters, in a review for the blog of the literary magazine *Ploughshares*, wrote that "Chen excels at uncovering the simultaneous hilarity and trauma of the everyday"; these details of daily life and popular culture that fill Chen's poems firmly place his work in its historical and cultural context. In his review of the collection for NPR, Craig Morgan Teicher asked the question, "What does Millennial poetry look like?" Future historians who may wish to know what it was like to grow up at the turn of the twenty-first century will find in Chen's poetry a fresh voice that conveys a wealth of cultural information.

Chen's poetry has sometimes been compared to that of Frank O'Hara, the mid-twentieth-century New York School poet, with whom Chen shares a lively sense of humor, vivacity, cleverness, and sass. His poems also recall those of Oscar Wilde, especially in his quickness, sense of fun, and love of self-display. In this collection, tense relations with his mother are a recurring theme, as are both his parents' disdain for their son's sexuality, which (in Chen's portrayal) they perceive as a decadent American aberration.

Much of the humor of Chen's poems—and the poems very often try to be, and frequently succeed at being, funny—might remind some readers of the ironic and self-effacing autobiographical sketches of the writer and comedian David Sedaris. In "I'm not a religious person but," for example, he writes, "My best friend said to stop / sleeping with guys with messiah complexes. My mother said she is / pretty sure she had sex with my father so I can't be some new / Asian Jesus."

Chen's language is colloquial and vernacular, his phrasing and rhythms often informal. His poems deviate from conventional poetic stanzas and are typically formatted as lines of irregular length. Often the works look and sound epistolary, as if the poem's narrator is writing a letter or sending an email to a friend. Still, although his phrasing is stripped down and lean, Chen's poems do not lack lyricism. Often they achieve rhythm and music through their use of repetition, particularly repetitions of clauses, phrases, and individual words. The poem "In the Hospital" is representative of these rhythmic devices, not only because it features an anecdotal narrative, but also because it plays with variations on a repeated phrase. "My mother was in the hospital & everyone wanted to be my friend," reads the first line. Variations in subsequent lines include "My mother was in the hospital & no one wanted to be her friend" and "My mother was in the hospital / & I didn't want to be her friend." This repetition, with a focus on the words "mother" and "I," creates a kind of music. Family, and mothers in particular, is a constantly recurring motif; in some poems, Chen is explicitly hostile toward his mother, partly because she seems to have been the parent who most objected to his sexuality. He mentions mutual violence between them, as well as an aborted effort, at age thirteen, to run away.

Chen writes from a first-person perspective, making himself, both literally and symbolically, the first person in many of the poems. In this sense, he follows in the footsteps of a long line of American confessional poets, such as Robert Lowell, Sylvia Plath, and Anne Sexton, but Chen exhibits in his poems a more pronounced sense of humor and self-ridicule than any of those figures. His speaker is often honest about his own shortcomings, as in one poem in which he would rather stay home and snuggle with his partner than attend a farewell party, or in the title poem of the collection, in which he admits to personal faults but ultimately conveys hope for positive change. Other poems directly present the speaker's fraught relationships with his parents and often lead to expressions of sarcasm to which the parents cannot respond. Many of the poems in this collection focus on the teenage years, and their tone is often overtly (and perhaps self-mockingly) adolescent.

When describing the effect of most of Chen's lyrics, words such as "witty," "clever," "amusing," "playful," and "self-conscious" are apt. Often the topics he chooses seem somewhat trivial, and his phrasing can sound slightly juvenile—Chen tends to skate, albeit with real skill and expertise, on life's surfaces—but there is a darkening and deepening of tone in some of the poems in the book's second half, such as "Kafka's Axe and Michael's Vest," in which the speaker wonders what it would be like to commit matricide. And even his shallower-seeming poems are packed with honesty and emotional intensity that defy the often-prosaic images and straightforward language he uses to construct them.

To compose his often lighthearted verse, Chen draws on a wide array of literary techniques. "Self-Portrait as So Much Potential," for instance, opens with off-kilter comparisons: "Dreaming of one day being as fearless as a mango. / As friendly as a tomato." In the same poem, Chen plays with alliteration: "I'm a rusty yawn in a rumored year. I'm an arctic attic."

Chen's phrasing is typically conversational and idiomatic, as seen in "I'm not a religious person but," which begins, "God sent an angel. One of his least qualified, though. Fluent only in / Lemme get back to you." Sometimes the jokes seem strained, as in the reference later in that poem to "football blimps that accidentally intercept prayers / on their way to heaven." Occasionally, though, Chen employs a tone that is lyrical in every sense, as in "Race to the Tree," which includes the lines "oh / moon, hungry moon, unkissed / & silent, I would kiss you."

In other poems, Chen uses all the tools at a poet's disposal, including anaphora and similes (as in "West of Schenectady"), ever-lengthening lists (as in "Self-Portrait With & Without"), comically preposterous fantasies (as in "First Light"), and bizarre, surrealistic imagery (as in "How I Became Sagacious"). Reiterated phrases help organize poems such as "To the Guanacos at the Syracuse Zoo" and "Ode to My Envy," lists of questions help a poem such as "Antarctica" cohere, internal rhyme pops up in a lyric titled "Poem,"

Courtesy of Jess Chen

Chen Chen was born in China in 1989 and grew up in Amherst, Massachusetts. He holds both BA and MFA degrees in creative writing. When I Grow Up I Want to Be a List of Further Possibilities *won the 2016 A. Poulin Jr. Poetry Prize and was long-listed for the 2017* National Book Award *for poetry.*

and clever parodies of phrasing from another (nonliterary) genre help organize a work titled "In This Economy." In general Chen reveals a command of a range of poetic devices. He even occasionally uses conventional stanzas (as in "Song of the Night's Gift"), and often he alludes to or even imitates other poets, as in "For I Will Consider My Boyfriend Jeffrey," with its explicit echoes of a famous poem by Christopher Smart. Many of the poems in this collection end with an effectively memorable final line; in "For I Will Consider," this line reads, "For he looks happy & doesn't know I'm looking & that makes his happiness free."

Chen writes poems that are easy to enjoy. They are, in general, the opposite of dark, heavy, or depressing. "Song of the Anti-Sisyphus," for instance, begins by announcing, "I want to start a snowball fight with you, late at night / in the supermarket parking lot. I want you / to do your worst. I want to put the groceries in the car first." In lines such as these, the poet's lighthearted style makes the work accessible and full of pleasure. In the foreword to the collection, poet Jericho Brown notes that Chen's poems have a "singular and sustained voice" and remarks that the collection is "beautifully necessary."

Robert C. Evans, PhD

Review Sources

Betters, Michelle. "Humor, Candor & Collision in Chen Chen's *When I Grow Up I Want to Be a List of Further Possibilities*." Review of *When I Grow Up I Want to Be a List of Further Possibilities*, by Chen Chen. *The Ploughshares Blog*, Emerson College, 17 Aug. 2017, blog.pshares.org/index.php/humor-candor-collision-in-chen-chens-when-i-grow-up-i-want-to-be-a-list-of-further-possibilities/. Accessed 1 Jan. 2018.

May, James Davis. "Earnest, Funny, and Fun: Chen Chen's *When I Grow Up I Want to Be a List of Further Possibilities*." Review of *When I Grow Up I Want to Be a List of Further Possibilities*, by Chen Chen. *The Rumpus*, 16 June 2017, www.therumpus.net/2017/06/when-i-grow-up-i-want-to-be-a-list-of-further-possibilities-by-chen-chen. Accessed 1 Jan. 2018.

Nguyen, Jeff. Review of *When I Grow Up I Want to Be a List of Further Possibilities*, by Chen Chen. *Harvard Review Online*, 16 May 2017, www.harvardreview. org/?q=features/book-review/when-i-grow-i-want-be-list-further-possibilities. Accessed 1 Jan. 2018.

Teicher, Craig Morgan. "Poetry to Pay Attention To: A Preview of 2017's Best Verse." Review of *When I Grow Up I Want to Be a List of Further Possibilities*, by Chen Chen, et al. *NPR*, 8 Feb. 2017, www.npr.org/2017/02/08/513100833/poetry-to-pay-attention-to-a-preview-of-2017s-best-verse. Accessed 1 Jan. 2018.

Review of *When I Grow Up I Want to Be a List of Further Possibilities*, by Chen Chen. *Publishers Weekly*, 27 Mar. 2017, www.publishersweekly.com/978-1-942683-33-9. Accessed 1 Jan. 2018.

Zeiser, John W. W. Review of *When I Grow Up I Want to Be a List of Further Possibilities*, by Chen Chen. *The Los Angeles Review*, 25 June 2017, losangelesreview. org/book-review-grow-want-list-possibilities-chen-chen. Accessed 1 Jan. 2018.

Where the Past Begins

Author: Amy Tan (b. 1952)
Publisher: Ecco (New York). 368 pp.
Type of work: Memoir
Time: 1950s–present
Locales: Oakland, California; San Francisco, California; Geneva, Switzerland

Courtesy of Ecco

In Where the Past Begins, *novelist Amy Tan looks back on the events that shaped her life and how these events continue to inspire and inform her writing.*

Principal personages
AMY TAN, a novelist
DAISY, her mother
JOHN, her father
PETER, her older brother
JOHN JR., her younger brother

In the nearly thirty years since the release of her debut novel, *The Joy Luck Club* (1989), Amy Tan has earned critical praise and popular acclaim for her writings on the Chinese American experience, particularly as it relates to the relationships between mothers and daughters. In her 2017 memoir, *Where the Past Begins*, Tan blends past and present, through journal entries, poems, essays, and email exchanges with her editor, to paint a picture of her life and the experiences that have led her to where she is today. The book does not simply document her life chronologically. Instead, it moves between events fluidly, allowing them to coalesce over the course of the book until a complete portrait of Tan, as a writer and a person, is revealed.

Tan notes in the introduction that *Where the Past Begins* was going to consist solely of emails between herself and Ecco Press editor and founder Dan Halpern. These emails were collected during the writing of Tan's novel *The Valley of Amazement* (2013). As Tan perused the emails, she came to feel that they did not warrant being the sole subject of a book but that they could be included as part of a larger work, a pastiche of sorts, of missives and memories from her life.

The book's chapters tend to flow into one another in a casual, elegant way. In the first chapter, "A Leaky Imagination," Tan talks about her childhood fascination with drawing and writing, and how those fascinations continue into today. Tan notes how these interests stem from an innate curiosity, which she believes was inherited from her mother. She also goes on to point out the differences between drawing and writing, noting that, when drawing, she allows herself to be imperfect, but when it comes to writing, she feels perpetually dissatisfied. Nevertheless, she wonders whether the two interests are somehow intertwined and whether the visual metaphors she often employs in her writing stem from her child-hood love of drawing.

She compares the art of writing to play-ing music, something she is also intimately familiar with. In the book, Tan describes her lifelong love affair with music that be-gan even as a child, listening to the music of Carl Stallings, who composed the back-ground music for the Looney Tunes cartoon shorts between 1936 and 1958. She believes that it was Stallings compositions, which employed classical themes while comple-menting the action onscreen (such as using a xylophone to illustrate Wile E. Coyote's tiptoeing footsteps) that first instilled in her a desire to see stories in music. Later, she re-counts how she sat in on the scoring sessions for the 1993 film adaptation of *The Joy Luck Club* and how listening to Rachel Portman's soundtrack brought her to tears. Tan also notes that for years she has harbored a desire

Courtesy of Julian Johnson

Amy Tan is the author of a half-dozen novels, the memoir The Opposite of Fate *(2004), and two children's books. A film adaptation of her debut novel,* The Joy Luck Club *(1989), was released in 1993.*

to compose music and that desire has manifested itself in dreams that she already has become a composer. She goes on to say that dreams have inspired other works of hers, such as her two children's books, *The Moon Lady* (1992) and *Sagwa, the Chinese Siamese Cat* (1994).

Where the Past Begins also talks about Tan's childhood in Oakland, California, where she lived with her parents and her two brothers during the 1950s. Tan writes about how her mother, who had been orphaned at nine after her father's death and mother's subsequent suicide, wanted her children to have every chance at success and to avoid the hardships she had had to endure. Tan recounts how her mother had mar-ried a wealthy man in Shanghai and had four children with him: three daughters and a son, who died of dysentery at the age of three. Tan's mother's first husband was cruel and mistreated her, forcing her to escape Shanghai and leave her daughters behind. In Tianjin, she met John Tan, whom she would marry, and the two moved to America to start a family.

The struggles and hardships endured by Tan's mother led her to become strict, forcing her children to succeed. Tan and her brother Peter were given piano lessons, which Tan found difficult. Her mother would chide her and tell her that she was lazy for not practicing enough. But, Tan recalled, her mother was also kind and forgiving, such as when Tan made a mistake during a recital. Tan goes on to say that music still plays a large role in her life and that she is sorry that her mother (who died in 1999) is not around to share it with her today.

The book also talks about Tan's struggles with her moods, some of which have been affected by epilepsy, an effect of having contracted Lyme disease in 1999. Other problems with mood have stemmed from episodes of depression that have struck Tan off and on throughout the years. She recounts how, when *The Joy Luck Club* was published, she cried because she was afraid of what being a published novelist could mean. These emotions, she says, can inform a writer's work, and even if they cannot get to the root of those feelings, they can be used to help give a story a deeper weight and meaning.

Additionally, Tan talks about drawing on actual memories, however painful, in the writing process. This leads her to discuss the fallout of the death of her father and her brother Peter, from brain tumors when Tan was fifteen. She recalls how, in a fit of grief, her mother threatened her with a meat cleaver, saying that she was going to kill Tan, then Tan's younger brother, John, and then herself. Tan, who was in the midst of her own grief, encouraged her mother to do it but, at the last minute, stayed her hand by pleading, "I want to live!"

While this may have been an extreme case, Tan says that her mother often nurtured such dark thoughts and threatened suicide on several occasions. But, Tan says, those dark thoughts stemmed from the difficult life she had been forced to endure in Shanghai. In the book, Tan recounts how she invited her mother over to spend the afternoon telling stories about her life and, as she talked, her mother began to recall things even more vividly until it seemed that she was almost reliving them. This prompts Tan to wonder whether there are traumatic events in her own life that she can recall and dig into to help tell a story more viscerally and vividly. With this in mind, she tries an exercise, writing down a painful memory from childhood in which her mother tried to leap from the car in an attempt to kill herself.

Although Tan's mother is the largest-looming presence in *Where the Past Begins*, the book also discusses Tan's father, John. She notes that his dying when she was so young is part of the reason why fathers are not as large a factor in her stories. Tan devotes an entire chapter to her memories of her father, recalling the photos he took with his Rollei camera, many of which she still possesses, and the letters and sermons he wrote as a Baptist minister. She also wonders, in the wake of the controversial 2016 presidential election, how he would have voted and, after examining the man that he was through what little she has of him, Tan believes he would have voted for a better world.

The last sections of the book are devoted to Tan's thoughts on reading and writing, two things that have been defining elements in her life and career. She writes about being given what she thought was an IQ test at six years old. The test led her parents to believe that she was smart enough to become a doctor, a notion that made Tan uneasy, as she did not feel that assessment was accurate. Later, she learns that the test was not an IQ test but that she was simply a part of a study on early readers. She feels blindsided by the revelation, but also strangely grateful as, even though the test was something of a deception, it gave her parents hope.

Tan also sifts through old letters that she wrote to her mother during her years in college and how, only with the benefit of the passing of the years, can she understand some of the feelings her mother was trying to express in those letters. She later ruminates that, while they wrote letters to each other during the years they were apart, it was Tan's writing of *The Joy Luck Club* that illustrated how close she and her mother actually were.

A large portion of the book is also devoted to email exchanges between Tan and Halpern. These exchanges are light and humorous, but also give insight into the editorial process of her latest novel, *The Valley of Amazement*.

Throughout the book, there are digressions, which she labels "Quirks," that consist of poems, journal entries, and random thoughts that offer further insight into Tan's views on the world.

In the epilogue, Tan describes her writing room, situated in an alcove off her San Francisco home. She talks about the view from her window and how she can see Angel Island, where Chinese immigrants were once taken before entering the port of San Francisco. She ruminates on those immigrants and how they would write poems on the walls of the immigration station to stave off their loneliness. She then notes the scrub jays, red tail hawks, and hummingbirds that fly past her window, reminders of the life that is all around her. She also reflects on the pictures on her bookshelf, pictures of loved ones who are still here and those who have died. Eventually, she says, she writes.

When *Where the Past Begins* was released on October 16, 2017, it earned positive reviews. Writing for *USA Today*, Emily Gray Tedrowe praised the book, calling it a "richly varied, thought-provoking book." Although most reviews were positive, many critics took issue with some of the Quirks, feeling that they were an unnecessary distraction. They also felt that the section devoted to the emails did little to add to the overall book. Charles Caramello, in a review for the *Washington Independent Review of Books*, said of the email chapter, "Tan offers cogent, even compelling, reasons for the types of content she has chosen, but at least one choice—a long series of emails between her editor and herself, largely shoptalk—does not make captivating reading."

Amy Tan has, for nearly thirty years, proven to be a powerful and honest voice in fiction. In *Where the Past Begins*, readers are able to trace the paths that she has taken over the course of her life that have led her to that place. The book shows the difficult, fractured, but ultimately strong relationship with her mother that has provided the framework for some of the complicated mother-daughter connections in her novels. Although this is a nonfiction book, it is very much of a piece with her fiction and can sit comfortably alongside it in her body of work.

Jeremy Brown

Review Sources

Brandeis, Gayle. Review of *Where the Past Begins*, by Amy Tan. *The San Francisco Chronicle*, 18 Oct. 2017, www.sfgate.com/books/article/Where-the-Past-Begins-A-Writer-s-Memoir-12288508.php. Accessed 7 Dec. 2017.

Caramello, Charles. Review of *Where the Past Begins*, by Amy Tan. *Washington Independent Review of Books*, 17 Nov. 2017, www.washingtonindependentreviewofbooks.com/index.php/bookreview/where-the-past-begins-a-writers-memoir. Accessed 7 Dec. 2017.

Miller, E. Ethelbert. Review of *Where the Past Begins*, by Amy Tan. *New York Journal of Books*, www.nyjournalofbooks.com/book-review/where-past. Accessed 7 Dec. 2017.

Tedrowe, Emily Gray. "Amy Tan Mines Painful 'Past' in Moving New Memoir." Review of *Where the Past Begins*, by Amy Tan. *USA Today*, 16 Oct. 2017, www.usatoday.com/story/life/books/2017/10/16/amy-tan-mines-painful-past-moving-new-memoir/731844001. Accessed 7 Dec. 2017.

Review of *Where the Past Begins*, by Amy Tan. *Kirkus*, 17 Oct. 2017, www.kirkusreviews.com/book-reviews/amy-tan/where-the-past-begins. Accessed 7 Dec. 2017.

Review of *Where the Past Begins*, by Amy Tan. *Publishers Weekly*, www.publishersweekly.com/978-0-06-231929-6. Accessed 7 Dec. 2017.

Whereas

Author: Layli Long Soldier
Publisher: Graywolf Press (Minneapolis).
120 pp.
Type of work: Poetry, autobiography, history

Courtesy of Graywolf Press

Layli Long Soldier's poetry collection
Whereas, *heavily postmodern and experimental at first, becomes increasingly accessible as it develops. It recounts the author's personal experiences while also reflecting on the experiences of Native North Americans in general, both in the past and more recently.*

Many of the poems in Layli Long Soldier's collection *Whereas* may remind readers, for better or worse, of the poetry of Gertrude Stein. These readers may feel the same sort of exasperation, when faced with various poems in *Whereas*, as that felt by London publisher Arthur C. Field, who famously wrote Stein a rejection letter reading, in part, "Being only one, having only one pair of eyes, having only one time, having only one life, I cannot read your M.S. three or four times. Not even one time." Long Soldier's poetry, like Stein's, is often heavy with repetition and stylistic conceits that some readers will find opaque to the point of being impenetrable. Consider, for instance, the following extract from "Diction," set flush right on the page:

> Plains Indi-
> til 1890, when a
>
> Wounded Knee. By
> left in the continen-
> on at the time the
> By way of contrast,
> were still coming. By
> Knee, the population of
> 0, there would be only
> reservations in the west.

One sees the game being played: readers are invited to fill in the blanks for themselves. The idea is arguably clever; one could imagine an entire essay being written to explain and justify the aesthetic implied here. But such an essay might be more interesting than the poem it justified. Some readers, faced with poems such as this one, may simply throw their hands up in despair and move on to other pursuits.

But readers who push through to the end of the volume will be in for some pleasant surprises. Along the way, the phrasing becomes more and more accessible, and Long Soldier seems less and less interested in simply recording her own random thoughts and perceptions. She also seems less and less obsessed with writing about writing; fewer and fewer poems are written about the process of composing poems (a common topic among contemporary poets), and increasingly, vivid imagery appears, as in the following lines from "Steady Summer":

> in midday open
> two horseflies love-buzz
> a simple humid meeting
> motorized sex in place
> then loose again
> infinite circle eights

More and more, as the volume proceeds, perceptions appear to which most readers can relate, as in this sentence, from the prose poem "Tókȟaȟ'aŋ": "Or the large tree shadow, the trunk of it, with finger and limb-tips across the lawn to my toe." But the real revelations in this book begin, one might argue, in the course of a poem called "Dilate," in which the speaker describes the moments immediately following the birth of a daughter. From this point forward, Long Soldier focuses less on playing word games than on communicating common human experiences—archetypal events to which many readers will instantly be able to relate. Suddenly the phrasing seems less odd, and the twists of language are put into the service of some recognizable desire to communicate with other people. Section 2 of the poem "Left," for instance, opens with the lines "The night I bled was a long loop a circle night sub-earthly black and red / hands outstretched to the dark I felt my way to the sink and toilet." These lines are truly memorable, partly because of the poetic devices used—the inventive metaphor, the striking word "sub-earthly," the internal rhyme of "bled" and "red," the alliteration of "bled" and "black," and so on—but more so because all these devices are in the service of communicating an experience that most readers will instantly be able to understand, yet that immediately catches readers

Layli Long Soldier is an Oglala Lakota poet and artist. Her second book, Whereas, *was a finalist for the 2017 National Book Award in poetry. She has received a 2015 Lannan Literary Fellowship and a 2016 Whiting Award, both for poetry.*

off-guard because of the abrupt suddenness with which it is introduced. When Long Soldier writers like this, her words serve a real purpose.

This kind of writing becomes increasingly prominent as the book progresses. The last poem in the first section, titled simply "38," is highly accessible, reading almost like prose, but still filled with enough wordplay to make it interesting both as an informative narrative and as a piece of striking writing. Here, as in many other texts in the latter part of the volume, Long Soldier succeeds in explaining her ideas clearly while also highlighting the mechanics of her writing:

> Without money, store credit, or rights to hunt beyond their ten-mile tract
> of land, Dakota people began to starve.
> The Dakota people were starving.
> The Dakota people starved.
> In the preceding sentence, the word "starved" does not need italics for
> emphasis.

This poem, like many of the more accessible poems in this book, benefits from a strong narrative thrust. The narrative itself is often at least as interesting as the techniques used to tell it, and the combination of an intriguing narrative and clever word-play contributes to the success of most of the successful poems in this volume.

This is especially true in part 2 of the book, a single long poem titled "Whereas," from which the title of the whole volume is derived. An introduction to this section explains the origins of the ensuing poem:

> On Saturday, December 19, 2009, US President Barack Obama signed the Congressional
> Resolution of Apology to Native Americans. No tribal leaders or official representatives
> were invited to witness and receive the Apology on behalf of tribal nations. President
> Obama never read the Apology aloud, publicly—although, for the record, Senator Sam
> Brownback five months later read the Apology to a gathering of five tribal leaders,
> though there are more than 560 federally recognized tribes in the US.

In this respect, Obama the Democrat fell short of Brownback the Republican, though Brownback too could have done more (more than a hundred times more, in fact). But if this opening makes it sound as if Long Soldier is about to embark on an extended series of political complaints, the lines that follow are often more personal rather than explicitly ideological. The poem is divided into three sections, titled "Whereas Statements," "Resolutions," and "Disclaimer." In the first section, the repeated opening "Whereas" is often used to deal with autobiographical matters rather than with political matters per se—although the autobiographical is, for Long Soldier, inextricably linked with the political. One of the longer of these statements begins, "WHEREAS I did not desire in childhood to be a part of this but desired most of all to be a part. A piece combined with others to make up a whole. Some but not all of something," before eventually working its way around to the sort of memorable phrasing that might almost be called lyrical: "I think of Plains winds snow drifts ice and limbs the exposure and when I slide my arms into a wool coat and put my hand to the door knob, ready to brave the sub-zero dark, someone says be careful out there always consider the snow your friend." Phrasing such as this is a long way from the often mystifying and even exasperating phrasing common at the beginning of the book. Here, Long Soldier speaks as one human being to another, and although many of her typical techniques are still present (the absence of conventional punctuation, for instance), there is no difficulty at all in following both what she is saying and the underlying implications.

Especially vivid is another "Whereas" statement, in which the speaker drives to a motel to meet an unidentified stranger:

> On time I pulled my wheels up close swung my legs from out the car door paced my steps as if this were a normal thing. I knocked that moment I did not waste. He opened the motel door a thick figure at the threshold he stood wearing sunglasses. But in that moment I didn't waste I didn't need to see his eyes or smile lines so much as I needed his presence so I didn't hesitate to invite him to get his things to come to my house and out from a dark room my father entered.

Here are many of the techniques of phrasing that Long Soldier's readers will be used to by now: the unconventional syntax; the lack of standard punctuation; the ways her phrases can look both backward and forward, modifying phrasing that both precedes and follows (as in the line "I knocked that moment I did not waste"), and so on. But there is no difficulty following the meaning here, which seems the kind of meaning to which anyone can relate. In poems such as this one, Long Soldier writes not as a sophisticated, postmodern, game-playing poet, but as one human being making solid, often moving connections to others. Thoughts of Gertrude Stein (or at least of Stein at her most Steinian) have disappeared, and readers will feel as if they are in the presence of a writer far more interested in communicating than in merely toying with words.

Robert C. Evans, PhD

Review Sources

Collis, Stephen. "Between the Grasses and the Sentence." Review of *Whereas*, by Layli Long Soldier. *Jacket2*, 26 July 2017, jacket2.org/commentary/between-grasses-and-sentence. Accessed 7 Feb. 2018.

Diaz, Natalie. "A Native American Poet Excavates the Language of Occupation." Review of *Whereas*, by Layli Long Soldier. *The New York Times*, 4 Aug. 2017, www.nytimes.com/2017/08/04/books/review/whereas-layli-long-soldier.html. Accessed 7 Feb. 2018.

Freeman, John. "Why You Should Be Reading Poet Layli Long Soldier." Review of *Whereas*, by Layli Long Soldier. *Los Angeles Times*, 5 May 2017, www.latimes.com/books/jacketcopy/la-ca-jc-layli-long-soldier-20170426-story.html. Accessed 7 Feb. 2018.

Hoover, Elizabeth. Review of *Whereas*, by Layli Long Soldier. *Star Tribune*, 25 Aug. 2017, www.startribune.com/review-whereas-by-layli-long-soldier/441675933/. Accessed 7 Feb. 2018.

Kane, Katie. Review of *Whereas*, by Layli Long Soldier. *The Georgia Review*, 23 Oct. 2017, thegeorgiareview.com/fall-2017/on-whereas-by-layli-long-soldier/. Accessed 7 Feb. 2018.

Word by Word
The Secret Life of Dictionaries

Author: Kory Stamper (b. ca. 1975)
Publisher: Pantheon Books (New York). 320 pp.
Type of work: Language, literary history, memoir

In Word by Word: The Secret Life of Dictionaries, *Merriam-Webster lexicographer Kory Stamper provides a behind-the-scenes glimpse of the making of one of the United States' most popular dictionaries.*

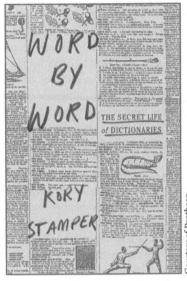

Courtesy of Pantheon

Among the countless books published around the world every year, dictionaries are perhaps some of the most mystifying. Perceived by some as an omniscient and infallible arbiter of language, the dictionary's origins are murky, and likely only the most dedicated dictionary users might wonder about the individuals and processes responsible for its creation. With her 2017 book *Word by Word: The Secret Life of Dictionaries*, Kory Stamper sheds light on the little-known process of revising and adding to a dictionary, a process that is often lengthy and entails not only the writing of definitions but also extensive research and a great deal of reading. A lexicographer and editor for Merriam-Webster since 1998, Stamper is well versed not only in the little-known duties of the company's editorial team but also in the history of dictionaries themselves and the complex, oft-frustrating workings of the English language. *Word by Word* blends entertaining anecdotes from Stamper's time at Merriam-Webster with intriguing historical and linguistic lessons. Stamper also explores the role and purpose of the dictionary, which she argues is less a gatekeeper of proper language and more a living document that reflects how people use words, rather than how some purists believe words should be used.

A brief preface provides the source of the book's title, explaining that lexicographers approach their work word by word. Stamper then begins her intriguing work with the chapter "Hrafnkell: On Falling in Love," in which she chronicles her own beginnings as a child and later young adult fascinated with language. An avid reader since early childhood, Stamper was introduced to new forms of language in college, when she took a class on Icelandic family sagas. Captivated by the unfamiliar terms and pronunciations, she moved on from Old Norse to Old English, studying the roots of the modern English language and developing an interest in etymologies and archaic meanings of words. After a string of customer-facing jobs like insurance claims adjuster, which she credits with giving her the people skills necessary to interact with the public as part of her later duties, Stamper took a position with the dictionary publisher Merriam-Webster, generally considered the oldest dictionary publisher in the United States. The publisher's name was derived from those of Noah Webster, who published his first English dictionary in 1806, and the Merriam brothers, who bought the rights to Webster's dictionary in 1844 and created a new dictionary based on that original work. The company went on to publish numerous editions of its international and collegiate dictionaries as well as other reference works.

In recounting her early days at Merriam-Webster, Stamper provides an enlightening depiction of the company's office and of her colleagues on the editorial floor, nearly silent introverts who are delighted to spend their time immersed in the written word. Her description of her colleagues and their environment—one in which, in her early years at the company, lexicographers made lunch plans by silently passing index cards back and forth—amuses and illustrates the amount of dedication and temperament one needs to engage deeply with language day in and day out. Stamper goes on to describe the process of writing or revising a dictionary definition, which has changed somewhat because of technological progress but remains largely intact. As she explains, much of the research that lexicographers perform involves reading a variety of publications and noting unusual uses of words. Sentences containing such words are collected as citations, which are then used to determine the different definitions, or senses, each word can have. Some words may be used in only one sense, while others—particularly, as Stamper later notes, short verbs such as *take*—can have many different senses and be used in different contexts. To help dictionary users gain a better understanding of particular words, lexicographers at times include example sentences or sentence fragments to demonstrate how the words are used.

Over the course of *Word by Word*, Stamper dedicates individual chapters to language-related issues and aspects of the dictionary-making process, including the mechanics of writing definitions, the procedures followed at Merriam-Webster, and her own dealings with the public. She notes that since the 1860s, Merriam-Webster has been committed to responding to correspondence from dictionary users, answering a vast assortment of questions about specific words and broader areas of language. In an amusing anecdote, Stamper catalogs some of the many questions she and her colleagues receive that have little to do with their work and are truly "outside the scope of [their] knowledge," including such memorably confusing questions as "Are babies natural?" The company's policy of accepting and responding to public inquiries also has a dark side, and Stamper notes that she and her colleagues have often received letters and emails from individuals who are angry about the inclusion of certain words in the company's dictionaries, convinced that questionable etymologies are unquestionable truths or confident that the dictionary is doing a disservice to the English language.

Of particular interest to readers intrigued by the process of creating a dictionary is Stamper's discussion of small words that, despite their brevity, prove particularly tricky to define. Stamper recalls that for the eleventh edition of *Merriam-Webster's Collegiate Dictionary* (2003), she was responsible for revising the definition of the word *take*. She documents the challenging and lengthy process from start to finish,

Kory Stamper is a lexicographer and an associate editor for Merriam-Webster. Word by Word: The Secret Life of Dictionaries *is her first book.*

noting that she began by sorting citations—sentences in which the word *take* was used in various ways—into piles based on part of speech and later the sense in which the word was used. Along the way, she suffered a major setback when the company's cleaning staff moved twenty-odd carefully organized piles, creating a jumbled mess for Stamper to re-sort. After a month of full-time work, Stamper ultimately added another sense to the definition of *take*: "to accept the burden or consequences of," as in "She took all the blame for it." In addition to providing a clear, practical illustration of the processes Merriam-Webster lexicographers undertake regularly, Stamper's description of her monumental effort calls attention to the sheer amount of work that goes into publications as ubiquitous as a dictionary. She also highlights one particularly tricky aspect of the English language, observing that some of the shortest words can be easily understood in context by native speakers but can be hard to define clearly and concisely.

One crucial point Stamper raises in *Word by Word* concerns the role of the dictionary, which some consider a linguistic gatekeeper responsible for defining the bounds of proper language. While Stamper acknowledges that in the past dictionaries were created to document only the most "correct" words and definitions and did function as gatekeepers, she notes that that "prescriptivist" style of dictionary largely fell out of fashion in the second half of the twentieth century. By the second decade of the twenty-first century, the bulk of English-language dictionaries published in the United States, including Merriam-Webster's publications, take a descriptivist approach—that is, they document not how one person or group believes English words should be used but how the words are being used in written language. In light of that approach, Merriam-Webster dictionaries include words that likely would have been rejected by earlier gatekeepers, including slang terms such as *ain't* and variants such as *irregardless* as well as swears and disparaging slurs. Stamper notes that Merriam-Webster's descriptivist approach has been a source of controversy since the publication of the third edition in 1961, and those controversies have at times involved her personally. She discusses multiple incidents, including the controversy that arose following the dictionary's 2003 decision to acknowledge committed relationships between same-sex partners in the definition of the word *marriage* in response to changes in usage. While that change was met with little fanfare or controversy when it was originally made, in 2009, an online community opposed to same-sex marriage began an email campaign harassing Merriam-Webster and Stamper specifically for the change. In the chapter "Nude: On Correspondence," Stamper documents Merriam-Webster coming under fire because its existing definition for *nude* included, as the third sense of the definition, a reference to the color of a white person's skin. Although the definition reflected how the word was sometimes used in society, as many products labeled nude in color are in fact a beige or pale tan by default, some individuals found that sense of the definition to be racially insensitive, and Stamper and her colleagues concurred. Stamper recounts that she found enough evidence of the word *nude* being used to describe other skin tones that she could revise the definition to eliminate potential racial insensitivity while still reflecting the word's usage in society.

An engaging and entertaining work, *Word by Word* sheds light both on a lesser-known corner of the publishing industry and on numerous intriguing elements of the English language. Stamper's work is often funny and—as might be expected from a dictionary editor—characterized by witty wordplay: when describing the process of editing previously published definitions, for example, she writes, "It is your *memento moron*: no matter how smart and excellent, remember that you, too, will f—— up." Although some of Merriam-Webster's processes and procedures may seem foreign to readers less versed in dictionary creation, she explains the key points of her work responsibilities clearly and strategically places illuminating anecdotes that illustrate just how challenging and rewarding the work of a lexicographer can be. Throughout the book, Stamper's devotion to words is palpable and goes beyond love to a true appreciation of the English language, with all its messiness.

Reviews of *Word by Word: The Secret Life of Dictionaries* were largely positive, and critics appreciated the work's behind-the-scenes view of both Merriam-Webster and the wider world of English-language dictionaries. Reviewers praised Stamper's often-humorous tone and overall approach to her subject, and a critic for the *New Yorker* called the book "an unlikely page-turner." In addition to appreciating the ways in which Stamper injected life into a potentially stodgy topic, critics particularly called attention to her discussions of dialect as well as the various anecdotes dealing with the occupational hazards of a lexicographer's interactions with the public. Some reviewers found that despite its generally accessible approach, *Word by Word* "bogs down occasionally in the swamps of industry jargon," as the critic for *Publishers Weekly* wrote. However, such critics nevertheless praised the book and Stamper's writing, with the *Publishers Weekly* critic saying that Stamper uses words "with such aplomb that readers might just feel like applauding."

Joy Crelin

Review Sources

Garber, Megan. "The Case against the Grammar Scolds." Review of *Word by Word*, by Kory Stamper. *The Atlantic*, 16 Mar. 2017, www.theatlantic.com/entertainment/archive/2017/03/the-case-against-the-grammar-scolds/519552. Accessed 30 Nov. 2017.

Review of *Word by Word*, by Kory Stamper. *Kirkus Reviews*, Jan. 2017, p. 1. *Literary Reference Center Plus*, search.ebscohost.com/login.aspx?direct=true&db=lkh&AN=120456268&site=lrc-plus. Accessed 30 Nov. 2017.

Review of *Word by Word*, by Kory Stamper. *The New Yorker*, 10 Apr. 2017, p. 68. *Literary Reference Center Plus*, search.ebscohost.com/login.aspx?direct=true&db =lkh&AN=123458233&site=lrc-plus. Accessed 30 Nov. 2017.
Review of *Word by Word*, by Kory Stamper. *Publishers Weekly*, 5 Dec. 2016, p. 60, *Literary Reference Center Plus*, search.ebscohost.com/login.aspx?direct=true&db =lkh&AN=120042207&site=lrc-plus. Accessed 30 Nov. 2017.

The World of Tomorrow

Author: Brendan Mathews (b. ca. 1969)
Publisher: Little, Brown (New York). 560 pp.
Type of work: Novel
Time: June 1939
Locale: New York City; Ballyrath, Ireland

Set against the backdrop of the 1939 New York World's Fair and unfolding over one whirlwind week, this sprawling and impressive debut novel from Brendan Mathews features a large cast of characters whose lives intersect due to a series of mysterious and inexplicable circumstances.

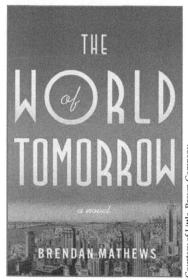

Courtesy of Little, Brown Company

Principal characters

MARTIN DEMPSEY, an Irish jazz musician, the eldest of the three Dempsey brothers
FRANCIS DEMPSEY, an escaped convict, the middle Dempsey brother
MICHAEL DEMPSEY, a former seminarian, youngest Dempsey brother
TOM CRONIN, a farmer and former Irish Republican Army (IRA) soldier
LILLY BLOCH, a Jewish Czech photographer
JOHN GAVIGAN, an aging Irish American gangster, Cronin's former boss
ROSEMARY DEMPSEY, Martin's wife
PEGGY DWYER, Rosemary's sister
ANISETTE BINGHAM, a Manhattan heiress

In the spring of 1939, the world stood on the brink of war as rising fascism threatened Europe. For many Europeans, a frightening, unknown future lay ahead. However, back in America, there was a growing sense of hope and optimism. On the rebound from the Great Depression, fewer Americans were finding themselves out of work, and scientific advancements in transportation, communications, and food production were capturing people's imaginations. This spirit of promise and progress was exhibited nowhere better than at the 1939 New York World's Fair, which serves as the backdrop of Brendan Mathews's sweeping debut novel, *The World of Tomorrow* (2017).

Taking its title from the theme of the fair, which opened in Flushing Meadows-Corona Park, Queens, on April 30, 1939, the novel tracks a wide cast of characters whose lives converge in New York over the course of one week in June of that year. At its center is the story of three Irish brothers, who, after being suddenly reunited for the first time in a decade, unwittingly get involved in a series of harebrained adventures that take them all over the city, from working-class dwellings and haunts in the Bronx and the Bowery to lavish hotels and mansions on Fifth Avenue. Gangsters, jazz musicians, nouveau riche maidens, psychics, and even ghosts make appearances in Mathews's 500-plus-page novel, which emphasizes the importance of family ties and the value of striving toward a better future.

The World of Tomorrow opens with Francis Dempsey and his younger brother Michael sailing on the MV *Britannic*, an ocean liner en route to New York City. Francis, a peddler of illicit luxury goods, has just escaped from Mountjoy prison in Dublin, while Michael has abruptly left seminary school. Days before their voyage, the two brothers are granted furloughs from their respective institutions to attend the funeral of their father in their hometown of Ballyrath, Ireland. During the funeral, the brothers are unexpectedly whisked to freedom by their father's close friends, who, unbeknownst to them, are members of the Irish Republican Army (IRA).

When the safe house Francis and Michael are sent to accidentally blows up, the two are falsely suspected of being behind the bombing, which kills three men. The bombing leaves Michael deaf, mute, and shell-shocked, but he escapes with Francis, who also steals a substantial IRA war chest that had been secretly stored at the house.

With the money, Francis and Michael board the *Britannic* posing as obscure Scottish aristocrats. On the ship, Francis dines with a group of American first-class passengers, among whom are Manhattan heiresses Delphine Bingham and her daughter Anisette. Francis tells the Binghams that his younger brother has been gravely injured in a foxhunting accident and that he is transporting him to New York for medical treatment. Anisette becomes smitten with Francis, "a handsome mix of toughness and deviltry," and her social-climbing mother is taken in by his faux regal charm.

Upon arriving in New York, Francis and Michael reunite with their older brother Martin, a moderately successful jazz musician who has lived in New York for ten years. A hot jazz purist, Martin has recently quit a well-paying gig as a clarinet player in a popular but uninspiring hotel band. This decision has vexed his wife, Rosemary, who raises their two daughters, Katherine and Evelyn, in a cramped apartment in the Bronx. Martin, though, has assembled a band of top nightclub players for his sister-in-law's upcoming wedding, and hopes they will bring him back into the limelight.

Martin's plans are disrupted, however, when Francis abruptly shows up at his apartment. Bearing news of their father's death, Francis invites Martin back to the Plaza Hotel, where he and Michael continue their aristocratic farce. There, Francis gives Martin the full story, prompting feelings of disbelief and dread in Martin, who instantly fears for his brothers' safety. Nevertheless, Martin later hosts the brothers at his apartment, where

Brendan Mathews is a professor of creative writing and literature at Bard College at Simon's Rock. He has authored many acclaimed short stories, which have been featured in The Best American Short Stories *anthology and other prominent literary publications. The* World of Tomorrow *is his debut novel.*

Francis wins the affections of Rosemary's sister, bride-to-be Peggy Dwyer, a brassy blonde who performs as an Aquagal in a water-ballet revue at the World's Fair. Further complicating matters is Michael, who, stuck in a hallucinatory haze, befriends the ghost of the recently deceased Irish poet William Butler Yeats. Though stretching the bounds of believability, Yeats's metaphysical exchanges with Michael inject notes of biting levity into the novel.

The novel adopts a more serious tone, however, with the characters of Tom Cronin and Lilly Bloch, both of whom feature prominently in the story's plot. Cronin is a former IRA assassin who has left his criminal past behind for life as a farmer in Dutchess County, New York. Unfortunately, that past catches up to him when news of the Dempsey brothers' heist in Ireland surfaces. Cronin is forced out of retirement by his former boss, John Gavigan, an octogenarian Irish American kingpin who is out for blood, revenge, and glory. Cronin reluctantly accedes to Gavigan's demands and embarks on a hunt for the Dempseys.

Lilly Bloch, meanwhile, finds herself in an even more dire predicament. A Jewish Czech photographer, Lilly has spent the previous three months in New York on an artist's fellowship but is now facing deportation back to her native Prague, which has been recently occupied by Nazi Germany. Lily's visa is due to expire in a week, and when her efforts to obtain an extension come to naught, she is forced to confront the prospect of returning to Prague. While contemplating her future, Lilly wanders the streets of New York, surreptitiously capturing strangers in intimate moments with her camera. One of those strangers is Michael, who falls into Lilly's orbit after being deserted by Francis in front of the Metropolitan Museum of Art. Struck by his "tragic" appearance, Lilly invites Michael back to her studio in the Bowery, where he becomes a willing photographic subject. In between snapshots, the two communicate their dilemmas to each other via hand-drawn sketches and charades, providing some of the novel's most touching scenes.

Michael's disappearance becomes a cause for concern, however, and sparks a citywide manhunt. By this time, Francis has already made the rounds, first wooing Peggy at the Savoy Ballroom in Harlem, then Anisette during an elaborate dinner hosted by the Binghams at their castle-like mansion on Fifth Avenue. Following a second date with Anisette, Francis is kidnapped by Cronin, who has been hot on his trail and who, readers learn, has a deep-rooted connection to the Dempsey family. Cronin subsequently takes Francis to Gavigan, who, after catching wind of his aristocrat charade, blackmails him into taking part in an outrageous assassination plot against the king and queen of England during their visit to the World's Fair.

After leading the search for Michael, Martin is charged with tracking Francis down at the fair before he goes through with the assassination. Martin hopes to make it back in time for Peggy's wedding reception, where his new band will showcase their chops before an audience that includes the legendary music producer John Hammond. Still, Martin, like so many other characters in the novel, has a backup plan in place, as well as a backup persona, in case they need to be enacted by the novel's cinematic climax.

The World of Tomorrow is an ambitious novel, vast in scope with an omniscient narrator that seamlessly weaves in and out of the thoughts, memories, and backstories of more than a dozen characters. Mathews has said that this freewheeling approach was inspired in part by the music of renowned American jazz pianist and bandleader William "Count" Basie, who was known for giving his musicians time to solo, on after another, during performances. Keeping in that spirit, Mathews, too, provides his characters with solo opportunities—not just principals, but also relatively unimportant secondary characters, including the Bingham's on-call family doctor, Dr. Theo Van Hooten, Cronin's top henchman Jamie, and a psychic named Madame Eudoxia. Though entertaining, these digressions sometimes detract from the story's plot and overall power, a sentiment held by many critics.

Still, even when the novel meanders, it feels secure in its intent and purpose, and Mathews steers it back on course when necessary. In the meantime, he holds the reader's attention with sharp, penetrating prose, which brings the sights, smells, and sounds of 1939 New York to sparkling life. In the Bowery, Lilly takes candid snapshots of a street hawker with "an extravagantly unkempt, almost Prussian mustache," stubble "like iron filings," and who resembles "a penniless officer in a nineteenth-century novel." Stumbling down Fifth Avenue, Michael smells "hot asphalt and human sweat, the exhaust of automobiles, the dank rot of rubbish bins, and the moldy stink of the storm drains." At the Bingham mansion, which looks "like it had been constructed from spun sugar and marzipan," Francis listens to Anisette launch into a violin solo whose "first note was a starter's pistol in a musical steeplechase that cleared every high note without pause."

This historical and cultural backdrop has appeared before in literature, most notably in American author E. L. Doctorow's 1985 National Book Award-winning novel *World's Fair*, which follows a nine-year-old Bronx-bred boy as he makes repeated visits to the 1939 fair. Like that novel, *The World of Tomorrow* eventually spends time at the fair that inspired its title. It gives attention to centerpiece attractions like the Trylon and Perisphere, as well as to the dozens of other futuristic structures and world pavilions that occupied more than 1,200 acres of ground. But against this "magic city of fountains, neon, spotlights, and fireworks," Mathews grounds readers with an all-encompassing portrait of New York, capturing the city in all its seedy and sophisticated glory. The resultant effect is akin to the hypnotic spell cast by a classical Hollywood film.

At one point, a character even expresses wishes for "a Hollywood ending, where all the right people get married and the music swells as the screen fades and the words THE END float on the screen." The artificiality of the novel only adds to its allure, however, and readers will likely find comfort in its assemblage of richly drawn characters. In a representative review for *NPR*, Jason Sheehan comments that the novel "finds odd little corners of time and place and character to get into and, in those corners, it finds both a balancing seriousness and a wideness of vision that makes it somehow all okay."

The World of Tomorrow will appeal to readers looking for a pleasurable escape, but also to those looking for a poignant exploration of familial bonds, friendship, and love. Mathews's characters are all striving to better themselves in hopeful anticipation of a brighter future—one that, in the months and years following the 1939 World's Fair, would be irrevocably shaped by a devastating world war.

Chris Cullen

Review Sources

Baker, Kevin. "A Debut Novel Imagines Political Intrigue at the 1939 World's Fair." Review of *The World of Tomorrow*, by Brendan Mathews. *The New York Times*, 13 Sept. 2017, www.nytimes.com/2017/09/13/books/review/world-of-tomorrow-brendan-mathews.html. Accessed 23 Jan. 2018.

Gill, John Freeman. "'The World of Tomorrow' Captures Swirling New York in 1939." Review of *The World of Tomorrow*, by Brendan Mathews. *The Washington Post*, 3 Sept. 2017, www.washingtonpost.com/entertainment/books/the-world-of-tomorrow-captures-swirling-new-york-in-1939/2017/09/03/4c7dea36-8f5b-11e7-84c0-02cc069f2c37_story.html. Accessed 23 Jan. 2018.

Sheehan, Jason. "'The World of Tomorrow' Is a Huge Story, Told Intimately." Review of *The World of Tomorrow*, by Brendan Mathews. *National Public Radio*, 6 Sept. 2017, www.npr.org/2017/09/06/547560578/the-world-of-tomorrow-is-a-huge-story-told-intimately. Accessed 23 Jan. 2018.

Vognar, Chris. "In a Madcap, Sprawling Debut Novel, Brendan Mathews Revives an American Dream." *The Dallas Morning News*, 31 Aug. 2017, www.dallasnews.com/arts/books/2017/08/31/brendan-mathews-interview. Accessed 23 Jan. 2018.

Review of *The World of Tomorrow*, by Brendan Mathews. *Publishers Weekly*, 15 May 2017, www.publishersweekly.com/978-0-316-38219-9. Accessed 23 Jan. 2018.

The World to Come

Author: Jim Shepard (b. 1956)
Publisher: Alfred A. Knopf (New York). 272 pp.
Type of work: Short fiction

This is another collection of stories, mostly based on well-researched historical events, often catastrophes, by a writer who specializes in the fictionalization of the factual.

Courtesy of Knopf

Acclaimed author Jim Shepard begins the extensive acknowledgements section of his fifth short-story collection, *The World to Come*, with the following disclaimer: "Most of the stories in this collection would have been hugely diminished without crucial contributions from the following sources." He then lists dozens of histories, diaries, journals, letters, and oral reports. The deep well of research material, most of it historical, indicates that facts are crucial to Shepard's fiction, contributing to his unique literary niche. For while historical fiction is common, historical short fiction is much rarer. Shepard has published novels, including the much-praised *The Book of Aron* (2015), but his earlier story collections built his reputation as a highly original voice drawing on the past to illuminate the present and even the future. *The World to Come* further builds that reputation.

In this collection, Shepard's realm of reality ranges from the 1600 BCE eruption of the volcano Thera on the island of Santorini, which signaled the beginning of the end of the Minoan civilization, to a train wreck in modern-day Canada that nearly destroyed an entire town. What unites most of the stories is disaster. The fact-based episodes that ground the ten stories include the starvation of the crew of the HMS *Terror* in the Arctic in the 1840s, the destruction of an Australian town by a hurricane and flood in the 1800s, and the 1961 sinking of a US radar station in the North Atlantic known as Texas Tower no. 4. It is the story of the latter that opens the collection.

"Safety Tips for Living Alone" may seem like a reductive and wry title for what Shepard terms "one of the Air Force's most lethal peacetime disasters." However, the fact that the title is taken from a booklet distributed to wives of military personnel gives the story painful poignancy. The title actually highlights the dual focus of the story—the men who are killed in the destruction of Texas Tower no. 4 and their widowed wives. The tower is an offshore platform that looks like an oil rig, but that was established to detect incoming Russian bombers in the era of the Cold War.

Shepard's meticulous research reveals that mistakes were made in the construction of the radar station: the technology of oil rigs in the Gulf of Mexico was used in the

North Atlantic, where the weather is often much more violent. Although much of the story details the weaknesses of the tower's construction, frequently the narrative shifts from the men on the tower to the wives waiting at home. The navy tries various means of bracing the tower to make it safer, but they are usually ineffective. Although evacuation is ordered when a hurricane approaches, it is delayed due to the threat of Russian spy trawlers getting their hands on classified equipment on the platform and then called off due to the weather conditions.

Shepard details preparations for the coming storm in a style that mixes elements of journalism and literary thriller. Though the first storm is weathered, the station is badly damaged and the characters' dread of the inevitable grows. The men's fear is juxtaposed against the women's anger. The tension continues to grow as the remaining skeleton crew face another, final storm. After the disaster, the government report on the situation

Courtesy of Barry Goldstein

Jim Shepard is an award-winning short-story writer, novelist, and teacher. His story collection Like You'd Understand Anyway *(2007) was a finalist for the National Book Award, and his works have been widely anthologized in best-of-short fiction collections.*

is contrasted with the grief of the victims' families. The story ends with a description of the last thing their husbands saw—a giant wave that emphasizes the frailty of human existence.

One technique Shepard uses to begin several stories is to establish a brief background about the central male character as a boy dreaming of adventure. "HMS *Terror*" begins with the narrator describing himself at eight looking forward to a career at sea. On July 4, 1845, he makes an entry in his journal identifying himself as Lieutenant Edward Little, serving on the HMS *Terror* as part of the Franklin Expedition—well known to history buffs as a doomed attempt to locate the magnetic North Pole and chart the Northwest Passage. The journal format (another technique Shepard uses multiple times throughout the collection) helps account for how the reader has received the narrative, even though there are no survivors to tell the tale. Lt. Little himself foreshadows this outcome, writing of his hope that the journal will be of "sufficient interest" in the event the expedition fails to return. Shepard realistically renders the account in the formalized language of nineteenth-century history and fiction.

The story is made up of short journal entries mainly on the weather, the food, the sights, and, eventually, the tragedies, while also describing Little's difficulty connecting with others, including a woman back home. As is typical of polar accounts, much is made of the intensity of the cold—the temperature is 72 degrees below zero Fahrenheit, so fish thrown onto the ice freeze as soon as they land and a wet shirt breaks in half, among other amazements. But the air of adventure gives way to hardship. As time passes into November 1847, Captain Franklin and other officers are dead of scurvy. By summer 1848, the supplies are depleted and the few survivors are forced to set out on foot to hunt for food, with little success. Finally, they are forced to cannibalism. The last entry in the journal, as Little lies in the embrace of his dying companion, notes that he looks at him "as if in glimpsing his humanity I might confirm my own."

"Positive Train Control"—one of the few tales in the collection set in modern times—is another story that begins with a young boy's fascination, this time with trains. When the narrator (who, like Lt. Little, is a mostly solitary figure) begins to work on the railroad as a young man, he comes to know the dangers of the job, especially with oil trains like one that exploded in Quebec three years before. He is acutely aware of the failing infrastructure of the railroads, at least in part the fault of government deregulation. He points out how the big railroad companies have cut costs, as in the case of the exploded Canadian train, which was over a mile long and had a one-man crew. Again, there is an air of journalism about Shepard's writing, as the line between his factual research and his fiction blurs.

The narrator's description of his job is interspersed with details of his troubled family life, including his parents' disappointment in him even compared to his missing, drug-addict brother. Inevitably, the story ends with a tragic wreck. Here, Shepard provides no explanation of how the reader gets a first-person description of the crash, bringing the fictional aspect to the fore more so than in the journal-based stories. The story ends with the narrator filming the landscape from the moving train and resolving to show his parents about his job before witnessing the derailment and explosion.

"Cretan Love Song" differs from the other disaster stories in significant ways. First of all, it is less an historical account than a poetic reverie or lament, beginning with the third-person narrator asking the reader to imagine they are a Minoan on the island of Crete in 1600 BCE as the volcanic island of Thera (modern Santorini) erupts. More specifically, readers are asked to imagine themselves as a man with a son, running, hopelessly, to get home to his wife. The shortest piece in the collection, it ends with the shockwave, huge beyond all precedence, bearing down on this man.

A few of the stories are not about historical disasters or catastrophes. One, "The Ocean of Air," is another first-person example of Shepard's skill in mimicking historical language, in this case the style of an eighteenth-century memoirist. It also begins with a narrator describing himself as a boy dreaming of bigger things. As a child, Joseph-Michel Montgolfier—based on the real-life pioneer of balloon flight—thinks of himself as an amphibian living in both his imagination and the real world. He makes his first balloon after a winter morning trying to warm a shirt over the hearth and noting how the fabric billows and lifts with the heat. Much of the story is then based on Montgolfier's many efforts to construct a balloon that can carry men aloft, interspersed with details of his personal life, particularly his marriage. He and his brother develop a balloon so ambitious and promising that the French Academy of Sciences appoints a committee, which includes the famous scientist Lavoisier, to investigate it. Montgolfier becomes the first man in history to engage in untethered free flight. The story concludes with him beginning his descent, marveling at the horizon, observing that so much below is still in shadow that it seems the sun has risen for him alone—a poetic image foreseeing the future of air travel.

Another story that is not about a catastrophe, though it still has elements of tragedy (as well as comedy), is "Wall-to-Wall Counseling." Set in the present, it is narrated by a woman who works for the public relations arm of America's largest health insurance company, which is facing a scandal brought on by the company's denying claims to the entire Eastern Seaboard for absurd reasons. Things only get worse when the company refuses to cover a liver transplant for a little girl who is appearing on the television show *America's Got Talent*. Meanwhile, the narrator's troubled sister comes to stay, among other issues she faces at home. No extensive historical context seems necessary for this story about corrupt big business and the mayhem of modern family life.

The title story, perhaps the most affecting and engaging in the collection, while set in the past, also has little need for extensive and exact historical detail. Although it does draw on historically accurate attitudes toward women in mid-nineteenth-century New England, its power is based on the reader's identification with individual characters. The plot centers on two isolated and lonely farmers' wives in rural nineteenth-century America, who, much to their own surprise and ultimate sorrow, fall passionately in love. This is a first-person story told through the diary of a young wife, who writes of emotions, fears, joys, or sorrows that are not found in the other written records of the family farm while also noting mundane details of daily life.

With Shepard's style again adapting to the language of the time period, "The World to Come" is among the most poetic pieces in the collection. The narrator has lost a young child and is lonely and isolated until she becomes friends with a neighbor woman named Tallie, who also seems lonely with a husband who takes her for granted. They talk and share, and one day, without warning, they kiss. Both women then must confront something for which they say there are no instruction books. The encounters and kisses continue until Tallie's husband takes her away, and the narrator's husband threatens to give her laudanum to calm her down. The journal continues to alternate poetic and prosaic entries, with colorful references such as to a "sudden wealth of fireflies blown about in the evening breeze" followed by workaday material such as "fourteen dollars from the sale of milk and butter." After Tallie's death, the narrative ends with the central character still stricken by grief, caught up in a series of imaginings about her loved one.

Critical reception to *The World to Come* was overwhelmingly positive. Lisa Zeidner, reviewing the book for the *Washington Post*, called Shepard "an outrageously versatile and gifted fiction writer who is deeply at home in a research library." She noted the rarity of historical short stories, as the medium usually does not have the room for lots of context, factual or otherwise. Many other reviewers agreed with her that Shepard is the exception to the rule. For example, the *Kirkus* review labeled him "a stylist whose fictional expansiveness underscores his singularity."

Charles E. May

Review Sources

Romeo, Nick. "*The World to Come* Blends History and Fiction in a Short Story Collection." Review of *The World to Come*, by Jim Shepard. *The Christian Science Monitor*, 27 Mar. 2017, www.csmonitor.com/Books/Book-Reviews/2017/0327/The-World-to-Come-blends-history-and-fiction-in-a-short-story-collection. Accessed 11 Jan. 2018.

Taylor, Craig. "Wind, Waves and Weather: Jim Shepard's Stories Force Men Out of Their Element." Review of *The World to Come*, by Jim Shepard. *The New York Times*, 28 Feb. 2017, www.nytimes.com/2017/02/28/books/review/world-to-come-stories-jim-shepard.html. Accessed 11 Jan. 2018.

Review of *The World to Come*, by Jim Shepard. *Booklist Online*, 1 Jan. 2017, www.booklistonline.com/The-World-to-Come/pid=8602923. Accessed 11 Jan. 2018.

Review of *The World to Come*, by Jim Shepard. *Kirkus*, 15 Dec. 2017, www.kirkusreviews.com/book-reviews/jim-shepard/the-world-to-come-shepard/. Accessed 11 Jan. 2018.

Zeidner, Lisa. Review of *The World to Come*, by Jim Shepard. *The Washington Post*, 17 Feb. 2017, www.washingtonpost.com/entertainment/books/the-world-to-come-stories-by-jim-shepard/2017/02/16/7ad6e7ce-f46b-11e6-8d72-263470bf0401_story.html?utm_term=.ae98b5d83e60. Accessed 11 Jan. 2018.

You Don't Have to Say You Love Me

Author: Sherman Alexie (b. 1966)
Publisher: Little, Brown (New York). 464 pp.
Type of work: Memoir, poetry
Time: 1970s to present day
Locales: Spokane Indian Reservation, Well-pinit, Washington; Seattle, Washington

Poet, author, and filmmaker Sherman Alexie wrote this memoir of his life as a tribute to his mother after her death. The book explores his complicated relationship with his parents, life on an American Indian reservation, and his health problems, along with a number of other personal and broader cultural issues.

Courtesy of Little, Brown Company

Principal personages
SHERMAN ALEXIE JR., poet and writer who grew up on the Spokane Indian Reservation
LILLIAN ALEXIE, his mother
SHERMAN ALEXIE SR., his father
DIANE, his wife

You Don't Have to Say You Love Me is a brutally honest memoir that takes readers in many directions but focuses on the challenges of growing up on the Spokane Indian Reservation in Washington State. Award-winning author Sherman Alexie chronicles his life, beginning in serious illness due to hydrocephalus (too much cerebral fluid in the skull) and severe poverty. Early in the work, Alexie admits to being an unreliable narrator but also insists, "I remember everything." The resulting work is in turns heart-breaking, frustrating, and funny. Alexie's skillful storytelling reveals anger, mourning, irony, pride, or amusement depending on the episode he is relating at any given moment.

The stories themselves are told in varied forms, including autobiographical prose, free verse, prose poetry, and eulogy. The organization is loosely chronological, but it is filled with flashbacks, sideline discussions of issues facing Alexie's Spokane/Coeur d'Alene people and other American Indians, and repeated passages. These seemingly disjointed elements combine to provide a hauntingly beautiful and strangely unified tribute to the author's family.

The death of the author's mother, Lillian, in 2015 was the inspiration for the book, and Alexie dedicates much of the memoir to his conflicted relationship with her. He details his childhood in a difficult home environment, punctuated by moments of love and achievement. For example, he reveals the problems resulting from his parents' alcoholism, but he also remembers the moment his mother claimed sobriety in an effort to protect her children, and he honors her dedication in never returning to alcohol. While he grumbles about her intense attention to the quilts she made and sold to support their family, even at the expense of attention to her children, he admires her workmanship and desire to work hard. Though he struggles with his mother's often cold personality—something he felt directed at himself even more than at his siblings—he examines the reasons behind her demeanor. For Alexie, the storytelling process helps him understand that his mother's actions illustrated love for him and allows him to truly mourn for her, admitting that the sorrow surrounding her has affected every nuance of his life.

As he explores his highly complicated relationship with his mother, Alexie also discusses a more simple love for his gentle father. While Lillian took responsibility for her children's well-being, Alexie Sr. was running from the difficulties of life on the reservation by turning to alcohol. Intelligent and talented at sports, music, and dancing, Alexie's father "turned into an inert man—into inertia itself," unable to take responsibility for his family. Yet his consistently kind ways made him beloved by many, not least his children. Alexie is unflinching in realizing that his undying love for his father turned him against his mother, whom he came to blame for the family's poverty and indeed all the challenges they faced. The author also reexamines his prior literary output through the lens of his relationships with his parents, acknowledging that "I have, in a spectacular show of hypocrisy, let my father off the hook for his lifetime of carelessness." In describing his parents, Alexie examines different forms of love and the way they shape lives.

One of the key thematic ideas Alexie explores is that of loss. He evocatively notes that "I was born from loss and loss and loss and loss and loss and loss and loss and loss and loss and loss and loss and loss and loss. And loss." This repetition stresses the multi-generational loss experienced on a cultural level by all American Indian peoples, a legacy seemingly so enduring it becomes rote. It also evokes Alexie's tangible personal losses: the loss of his mother (and of a consistently positive relationship with her), the loss of his father, the loss of his older half sister, and the loss of his health. Finally, it also calls to mind more universal themes of loss, such as the loss of innocence common to many coming-of-age tales and the environmental loss witnessed in the Pacific Northwest.

Alexie is highly effective at detailing loss and other challenges at both the personal level and as emblematic of reservation life. One striking problem that he stresses is sexual abuse. He not only talks about his own abuse at the hands of a pedophile on the reservation, but also points to this issue as a common occurrence in his community and, historically, among American Indians in general. Significantly, he also shows how this pattern of abuse shapes even the narratives of the victims. For example, Lillian told a teenage Alexie that she was born after her own mother was raped, but Alexie's sister was told that Lillian was the love child of an adulterous affair. Alexie also heard conflicting stories about Lillian herself being raped, resulting in the birth of his half sister, Mary.

Other challenges discussed in the memoir are similarly complex in that they permeate various aspects of Alexie's life. He ties his mother's problems, and his contentious relationship with her, to what he sees as their shared bipolar disorder. With both mother and son prone to volatile outbursts, they fought frequently and sometimes violently. As an adult, Alexie admits that he still struggles with the mental illness that plagued his mother and himself, but he stresses that he is being treated and does not allow his illness to affect his own family.

Like bipolar disorder, cancer runs in Alexie's family and is also prevalent in the wider community in his hometown of Wellpinit, Washington. Because of environmental problems, lung cancer is common on the reservation, and Alexie's mother and grandmother both died of the disease. Indeed, the writer predicts that he and his siblings will eventually develop cancer as well, victims not only of a terrible disease but also of circumstance. He rails throughout the book at the unfairness of the disease, including a poem cursing cancer with raw emotion. He blames his mother's death and his own susceptibility to cancer on his father's cigar smoke, radon in the shoddy family home, and the nearby uranium mines.

Sherman Alexie is a critically acclaimed poet, novelist, short-story writer, filmmaker, and performer. His awards include the PEN/Faulkner Award for Fiction, the PEN/Malamud Award for Excellence in the Short Story, a PEN/Hemingway Citation for best first fiction, a Pushcart Prize, and a National Book Award for young people's literature.

The uranium mines are one example of the social justice issues regarding reservation life that Alexie brings to light throughout *You Don't Have to Say You Love Me*. Two uranium mines and a uranium mill were located close to the reservation, and traffic traveling to and from the mines dropped dust and rocks, polluting the air those dwelling on the reservation had no choice but to breathe and the groundwater they used for sacred rituals. Along similar environmental lines, Alexie discusses the loss of salmon as a resource of the Salish peoples of the Pacific Northwest. A more cultural example of injustice comes in Alexie's descriptions of education on the reservation. Readers familiar with Alexie's body of work will not be surprised at the stories he divulges about his teachers. For example, he compares one of his elementary teachers, a white woman, to the soldiers who tortured prisoners at the notorious Abu Ghraib prison, and the American Indian children to the victims. It was this type of situation that taught him about racism, both explicit and systematic. Not only was Alexie treated badly by teachers, but he was endlessly bullied by students as well. In addition, as a bright and ambitious student, he was constrained by the poor quality of the schooling on the reservation. By eighth grade, he left to attend a local public school where he was one of only a few nonwhite students, a step he attributes to his will to expand beyond the limitations of his past.

Though Alexie focuses especially on his younger years, he does include discussion of his later life. In addition to depicting his reactions to his parents' deaths, he continues to narrate his own challenges and significant experiences. One revealing instance is a brain surgery he had in 2015. He shares fears over the potential loss of words and stories and an inability to function. Fortunately, he came through the surgery with his faculties intact, but he candidly points out how his struggles in the recovery process have complicated his continuing ability to work.

Despite the sadness that permeates the book, Alexie's humor often provides comic relief even in the most difficult situations. For instance, in the midst of several chapters about his mother's funeral, the author inserts a bathroom story worthy of a middle school boy. The humor is often given in the form of sarcastic comments that might inspire a snort of ironic understanding. One example is when he points out the reason for his mother's burial date of July 6, because "Yes, saying good-bye to a Native American woman would have cost us more on Independence Day." In a later chapter, he talks about a time when his mother gave food from their bare cupboards to a poor white family, and he points out that even in his fifties, he still resents that she gave away some peaches that were his favorite food.

You Don't Have to Say You Love Me immediately became a best seller upon release, boosted by a highly positive reception from critics, who noted that Alexie's first memoir fit well with his early poetry, stories, and novels. However, many reviewers did remark on elements that some readers might find problematic. One is Alexie's use of repetition. There are several chapters that repeat content almost verbatim, and some parts have been largely covered in previous works. While these parts generally stress aspects of the author's relationship with his mother, making their inclusion perhaps necessary in the illustration of his grief, they can detract from the flow of the narrative. A second element that some critics found distracting is the seeming disordered organization of the memoir. Alexie jumps around in time and topic, often without a clear purpose for doing so.

With his powerful memoir, Alexie has constructed a literary work that gives grief a personality, confronts problematic family relationships, and probes issues at both personal and universal levels.

Theresa L. Stowell, PhD

Review Sources

Graham, Nicholas. Review of *You Don't Have to Say You Love Me*, by Sherman Alexie. *Library Journal*, 15 Apr. 2017, p. 91.

Seaman, Donna. Review of *You Don't Have to Say You Love Me*, by Sherman Alexie. *Booklist*, 1 May 2017, www.booklistonline.com/You-Don-t-Have-to-Say-You-Love-Me-Alexie-Sherman/pid=8732291. Accessed 2 Oct. 2017.

Yeh, James. "Sherman Alexie and the Tricky Art of Memoir." Review of *You Don't Have to Say You Love Me*, by Sherman Alexie. *The New York Times*, 13 June 2017, www.nytimes.com/2017/06/12/books/sherman-alexie-and-the-tricky-art-of-memoir.html. Accessed 2 Oct. 2017.

Review of *You Don't Have to Say You Love Me*, by Sherman Alexie. *Kirkus*, 21 Mar. 2017, www.kirkusreviews.com/book-reviews/sherman-alexie/you-dont-have-to-say-you-love-me/. Accessed 2 Oct. 2017.

Review of *You Don't Have to Say You Love Me*, by Sherman Alexie. *Publishers Weekly*, 3 Apr. 2017, www.publishersweekly.com/978-0-316-27075-5. Accessed 2 Oct. 2017.

Category Index

CATEGORY INDEX

TITLE INDEX

Author Index